Lecture Notes in Computer Science 8823

Commenced Publication in 1973
Founding and Former Series Editors:
Gerhard Goos, Juris Hartmanis, and Jan van Leeuwen

T0236565

Marta Indulska   Sandeep Purao (Eds.)

Advances in Conceptual Modeling

ER 2014 Workshops, ENMO, MoBiD, MReBA,
QMMQ, SeCoGIS, WISM, and ER Demos
Atlanta, GA, USA, October 27-29, 2014
Proceedings

 Springer

Volume Editors

Marta Indulska
The University of Queensland
UQ Business School
St Lucia, QLD 4072, Australia
E-mail: m.indulska@business.uq.edu.au

Sandeep Purao
Penn State University
316B Information Sciences and Technology Building
University Park, PA 16802, USA
E-mail: spurao@ist.psu.edu

ISSN 0302-9743   e-ISSN 1611-3349
ISBN 978-3-319-12255-7   e-ISBN 978-3-319-12256-4
DOI 10.1007/978-3-319-12256-4
Springer Cham Heidelberg New York Dordrecht London

Library of Congress Control Number: 2014950800

LNCS Sublibrary: SL 3 – Information Systems and Application, incl. Internet/Web and HCI

Typesetting: Camera-ready by author, data conversion by Scientific Publishing Services, Chennai, India

Printed on acid-free paper

Springer is part of Springer Science+Business Media (www.springer.com)

Preface

This companion volume to the ER 2014 conference contains the proceedings of workshops associated with the 33rd International Conference on Conceptual Modeling (ER 2014), held in Atlanta, GA, USA, during October 27-29, 2014.

The ER conference is the premier international venue for research related to conceptual models and modeling for information systems, and increasingly, in several related domains. The main conference consists of regular and short papers, keynotes, panels, an educational symposium, demos, and tutorials. The conference, thus, provides a large spectrum of choices for researchers and practitioners to engage with foundational and contemporary concerns related to research and practice.

In keeping with the ER conference series tradition, the aim of the ER workshops was to provide a intensive collaborative forum at which researchers and industry professionals could gather to exchange innovative ideas related to conceptual modeling and its applications. This year the workshops featured a wide range of domains, including requirements and enterprise modeling, modeling of big data, spatial conceptual modeling, exploring the quality of models, and issues specific to the design of Web information systems.

Through a call for proposals, followed by a competitive review process, six workshops, some new and some established, were selected:

- First International Workshop on Enterprise Modeling (ENMO 2014)
- Second International Workshop on Modeling and Management of Big Data (MoBiD 2014)
- First International Workshop on Conceptual Modeling in Requirements and Business Analysis (MReBA 2014) (formerly known as RIGiM - International Workshop on Requirements, Intentions and Goals in Conceptual Modeling)
- First International Workshop on Quality of Models and Models of Quality (QMMQ 2014)
- 8th International Workshop on Semantic and Conceptual Issues in GIS (SeCoGIS)
- 11th International Workshop on Web Information Systems Modeling (WISM 2014)

The selected workshops attracted a total of 59 submissions. Following a review process carried out by each of the relevant Program Committees, a total of 24 full papers were accepted, resulting in an acceptance rate of 40%. Six papers were accepted as short papers based on high review scores and their focus on cutting-edge topics. In addition, the workshops also contained panels with experts to discuss emerging topics, and keynotes from established scholars in each community. The workshops were an integral part of the conference in Atlanta and occupied a companion track to the regular papers.

The workshops, and this resulting volume, would not be possible without the hard work of a large collection of people. I would like to thank the organizers of the six workshops for their efforts, dilligence, and timely collaboration. Thank you also to the Program Committees of these workshops, as well as their external reviewers, who ensured, through the review process, that the best papers were selected. A very special thanks also to the conference chair, Sandeep Purao, for his support and help with developing the final workshop program.

This companion volume also contains three papers describing the innovative research software that were presented at the conference. We thank Akhilesh Bajaj, the conference demo chair, for coordinating these demos.

Last but not least, thank you to all of the authors who submitted their high-quality work to the ER 2014 workshops this year. The workshop series, and its established quality, cannot exist without the continued support of such authors.

July 2014   Marta Indulska
                                                                                        Sandeep Purao

Organization

ER 2014 General Chair

Sandeep Purao   Penn State University, USA

ER 2014 Workshops Chair

Marta Indulska   The University of Queensland, Australia

First International Workshop on Enterprise Modeling – ENMO 2014

ENMO 2014 Workshop Chairs

Sergio de Cesare	Brunel Business School, UK
Guido Geerts	University of Delaware, USA

ENMO 2014 Program Committee

Balbir Barn	Middlesex University, UK
Palash Bera	Saint Louis University, USA
Frederik Gailly	Ghent University, Belgium
Giancarlo Guizzardi	Federal University of Espírito Santo, Brazil
Pavel Hruby	CSC, Denmark
Mark Lycett	Brunel University, UK
William E. McCarthy	Michigan State University, USA
Daniel E. O'Leary	University of Southern California, USA
Chris Partridge	BORO Solutions, UK
Oscar Pastor	Universitat Politècnica de València, Spain
Geerts Poels	Ghent University, Belgium
Hans Weigand	Tilburg University, The Netherlands

Second International Workshop on Modeling and Management of Big Data – MoBiD 2014

MoBiD 2014 Workshop Chairs

Il-Yeol Song	Drexel University, USA
Juan Trujillo	University of Alicante, Spain

David Gil   University of Alicante, Spain
Carlos Blanco   University of Cantabria, Spain

MoBiD 2014 was organized within the framework of the following project
GEODAS-BI (TIN2012-37493-C03-03) from the Ministry of Economy and Competitiveness (MINECO).

MoBiD 2014 Program Committee

Yuan An   Drexel University, USA
Marie-Aude Aufaure   Ecole Centrale Paris, France
Michael Blaha   Yahoo Inc., USA
Rafael Berlanga   Universitat Jaume I, Spain
Paulo Carreira   DEI/IST Taguspark, Portugal
Gennaro Cordasco   Università di Salerno, Italy
Alfredo Cuzzocrea   University of Calabria, Italy
Gill Dobbie   University of Auckland, New Zealand
Eduardo Fernández   University of Castilla-La Mancha, Spain
Pedro Furtado   Universidade de Coimbra, Portugal
Matteo Golfarelli   University of Bologna, Italy
H. V. Jagadish   University of Michigan, USA
Magnus Johnsson   University of Lund, Sweden
Nectarios Koziris   Technical University of Athens, Greece
Jiexun Li   Drexel University, USA
Stephen W. Liddle   Brigham Young University, USA
Antoni Olivé   Universitat Politécnica de Catalunya, Spain
Jeff Parsons   Memorial University of Newfoundland, Canada
Oscar Pastor   Universitat Politècnica de València, Spain
Mario Piattini   University of Castilla-La Mancha, Spain
Nicolas Prat   ESSEC Business School, France
Sudha Ram   University of Arizona, USA
Carlos Rivero   University of Sevilla, Spain
Colette Roland   Université Paris 1 Panthéon - Sorbonne, France
Pablo Sánchez   University of Cantabria, Spain
Keng Siau   University of Nebraska-Lincoln, USA
Alkis Simitsis   Hewlett-Packard Co., California, USA
Alejandro Vaisman   Université Libre de Bruxelles, Belgium
Panos Vassiliadis˘   University of Ioannina, Greece

First International Workshop on Conceptual Modeling in Requirements and Business Analysis – MReBA 2014

MReBA 2014 Workshop Chairs

Renata Guizzardi   Universidade Federal do Espírito Santo, Brazil
Jennifer Horkoff   University of Trento, Italy
Camille Salinesi   Université Paris 1 Panthéon - Sorbonne, France

MReBA 2014 Steering Committee

Colette Rolland	Université Paris 1 Panthéon - Sorbonne, France
Eric Yu	University of Toronto, Canada

MReBA 2014 Program Committee

Thomas Alspaugh	University of California, Irvine, USA
Daniel Amyot	University of Ottawa, Canada
Claudia Cappelli	NP2TEC/Universidade Federal do Estado do Rio de Janeiro, Brazil
Jaelson Castro	Universidade Federal de Pernambuco, Brazil
Fabiano Dalpiaz	Utrecht University, The Netherlands
Sergio España	Universitat Politècnica de València, Spain
Aditya Ghose	University of Wollongong, Australia
Aneesh Krishna	Curtin University, Australia
Paul Johannesson	KTH Royal Institute of Technology, Sweden
Ivan Jureta	University of Namur, Belgium
Sotirios Liaskos	York University, Canada
Lin Liu	Tsinghua University, China
Lidia Lopez	Universitat Politècnica de Catalunya, Spain
Pericles Loucopoulos	University of Manchester, UK
Luiz Olavo Bonino da Silva Santos	Bizzdesign, The Netherlands
Andreas Opdahl	University of Bergen, Norway
Anna Perini	Fondazione Bruno Kessler, Italy
Jolita Ralyté	University of Geneva, Switzerland
Bill Robinson	Georgia State University, USA
Samira Si-Said Cherfi	Conservatoire National des Arts et Métiers, France
Pnina Soffer	University of Haifa, Israel
Vitor Souza	Universidade Federal do Espírito Santo, Brazil
Sam Supakkul	Sabre Travel Network, USA
Lucineia Thom	Universidade Federal do Rio Grande do Sul, Brazil
Roel Wieringa	University of Twente, The Netherlands
Jelena Zdravkovic	KTH Royal Institute of Technology, Sweden

First International Workshop on Quality of Models and Models of Quality – QMMQ 2014

QMMQ 2014 Workshop Chairs

Samira Si-Said Cherfi	Conservatoire National des Arts et Métiers, France
Oscar Pastor	Universitat Politècnica de València, Spain
Charlotte Hug	CRI - Université Paris 1 Panthéon - Sorbonne, France

QMMQ 2014 Program Committee

Jacky Akoka	CNAM & TEM, France
Saïd Assar	Telecom Ecole de Management, France
Laure Berti-Equille	Institut de Recherche pour le Développement, France
Lotfi Bouzguenda	ISMIS, Tunisia
Cristina Cachero	University of Alicante, Spain
Isabelle Comyn-Wattiau	CNAM – ESSEC, France
Rebecca Deneckère	CRI - University of Paris 1-Panthéon Sorbonne, France
Sophie Dupuy-Chessa	UPMF-Grenoble 2, France
Mahmoud El Hamlaoui	IRIT – Université Toulouse 2 - Le Mirail, France
Virginie Goasdoue-Thion	University of Rennes 1, France
Cesar Gonzalez-Perez	Spanish National Research Council, Institute of Heritage Sciences, Spain
Roberto Lopez-Herrejon	Johannes Kepler Universität, Austria
Roman Lukyanenko	Memorial University of Newfoundland, Canada
Wolfgang Maass	Saarland University, Germany
Raimundas Matulevicius	University of Tartu, Estonia
Jeffrey Parsons	Memorial University of Newfoundland, Canada
Verónika Peralta	University of Tours, France
Erik A. Proper	CRP Henri Tudor, Luxembourg
Jolita Ralyté	University of Geneva, Switzerland
Sudha Ram	University of Arizona, USA
Farida Semmak	Université Paris-Est Créteil, France
Guttorm Sindre	Norwegian University of Science and Technology, Norway
Pnina Soffer	University of Haifa, Israel

8th International Workshop on Semantic and Conceptual Issues in GIS – SeCoGIS 2014

SeCoGIS 2014 Workshop Chairs

Mir Abolfazl Mostafavi	Université Laval, Canada
Andrea Ballatore	University of California, Santa Barbara, USA
Esteban Zimányi	Université Libre de Bruxelles, Belgium

SeCoGIS 2014 Steering Committee

Claudia Bauzer Medeiros	University of Campinas, Brazil
Michela Bertolotto	University College Dublin, Ireland
Roland Billen	Université de Liège, Belgium
Jean Brodeur	Natural Resources Canada, Canada

Christophe Claramunt	Naval Academy Research Institute, France
Eliseo Clementini	University of L'Aquila, Italy
Esteban Zimányi	Université Libre de Bruxelles, Belgium
Mir Abolfazl Mostafavi	Université Laval, Canada

SeCoGIS 2014 Program Committee

Alia I. Abdelmoty	Cardiff University, UK
Mohamed Bakillah	University of Edinburgh, UK
Phil Bartie	University of Edinburgh, UK
David Bennett	University of Iowa, USA
Michela Bertolotto	University College Dublin, Ireland
Roland Billen	Université de Liège, Belgium
Patrice Boursier	University of La Rochelle, France
Jean Brodeur	National Resources Canada, Canada
Bénédicte Bucher	Institut Géographique National, France
Adrijana Car	German University of Technology, Oman
Christophe Claramunt	Naval Academy Research Institute, France
Maria Luisa Damiani	University of Milan, Italy
Clodoveu Davis	Federal University of Minas Gerais, Brazil
Andrew Frank	Technical University of Vienna, Austria
Bo Huang	The Chinese University of Hong Kong, SAR China
Krzysztof Janowicz	University of California, Santa Barbara, USA
Marinos Kavouras	National Technical University of Athens, Greece
Margarita Kokla	National Technical University of Athens, Greece
Sergei Levashkin	CIC-IPN, Mexico
Ki-Joune Li	Pusan National University, South Korea
Thérèse Libourel	Université de Montpellier II, France
Jugurta Lisboa Filho	Universidade Federal de Viçosa, Brazil
Miguel R. Luaces	Universidade da Coruña, Spain
Jose Macedo	Federal University of Ceara, Brazil
Alberto Marquez	Universidad de Sevilla, Spain
Pedro Rafael Muro Medrano	University of Zaragoza, Spain
Dieter Pfoser	Institute for the Management of Information Systems, Greece
Andrea Rodriguez Tastets	University of Concepción, Chile
Markus Schneider	University of Florida, USA
Sylvie Servigne-Martin	INSA de Lyon, France
Shashi Shekhar	University of Minnesota, USA
Spiros Skiadopoulos	University of the Peloponnese, Greece
Emmanuel Stefanakis	Harokopio University of Athens, Greece

Kathleen Stewart Hornsby	University of Iowa, USA
Kerry Taylor	CISRO, Australia
Sabine Timpf	University of Augsburg, Germany
Peter Van Oosterom	Delft University of Technology, OTB, GIS Technology, The Netherlands
Antonio Miguel Vieira Monteiro	INPE, Brazil
Nancy Wiegand	University of Wisconsin, USA
Stephan Winter	University of Melbourne, Australia

11th International Workshop on Web Information Systems Modeling – WISM 2014

WISM 2014 Workshop Chairs

Flavius Frasincar	Erasmus University of Rotterdam, The Netherlands
Geert-Jan Houben	Delft University of Technology, The Netherlands
Philippe Thiran	Namur University, Belgium

WISM 2014 Program Committee

Syed Sibte Raza Abidi	Dalhousie University, Canada
Djamal Benslimane	University of Lyon 1, France
Maria Bielikova	STU, Slovakia
Alessandro Bozzon	Delft University of Technology, The Netherlands
Marco Brambilla	Politecnico di Milano, Italy
Sven Casteleyn	Jaume I University, Spain
Richard Chbeir	Bourgogne University, France
Jose Palazzo Moreira de Oliveira	UFRGS, Brazil
Olga De Troyer	Vrije Universiteit Brussel, Belgium
Roberto De Virgilio	Roma Tre University, Italy
Oscar Diaz	University of the Basque Country, Spain
Flavio Ferrarotti	SSCH, Austria
Martin Gaedke	Chemnitz University of the Technology, Germany
Giancarlo Guizzardi	UFES, Brazil
Hyoil Han	Marshall University, USA
Zakaria Maamar	Zayed University, UAE
Viorel Milea	Erasmus University of Rotterdam, The Netherlands
Oscar Pastor	Universitat Politècnica de València, Spain
Dimitris Plexousakis	University of Crete, Greece

Hajo Reijers   Eindhoven University of Technology,
                                        The Netherlands
Davide Rossi   University of Bologna, Italy
Riccardo Torlone   Roma Tre University, Italy
Lorna Uden   Staffordshire University, UK
Erik Wilde   UC Berkeley, USA
Guandong Xu   University of Technology Sydney, Australia

WISM Reviewers

G. Baryannis
M. Kompan

ER 2014 Demonstrations Chair

Akhilesh Bajaj   University of Tulsa, USA

Table of Contents

1st International Workshop on Enterprise Modeling (ENMO14)

Preface to ENMO 2014

2nd International Workshop on Modeling and Management of Big Data (MoBiD14)

Preface to MoBiD 2014
Extracting Value from Big Data

1st International Workshop on Conceptual Modeling in Requirements and Business Analysis (MReBA14)

Preface to MReBA 2014

1st International Workshop on Quality of Models and Models of Quality (QMMQ14)

Preface to QMMQ 2014

8th International Workshop on Semantic and Conceptual Issues in GIS (SeCoGIS14)

Preface to SeCoGIS 2014

11th International Workshop on Web Information Systems Modeling (WISM14)

Preface to WISM 2014

ER'14 Demonstrations

Preface to ENMO 2014

The objective of the Workshop on Enterprise Modeling (ENMO) is to provide an international forum for exchanging ideas on the latest developments in the area of enterprise modeling by both academics and practitioners. Enterprise modeling can be broadly defined as the use of conceptual specifications as part of business applications. It draws from diverse disciplines such as information systems, computing, business and philosophy. The main goal of the workshop is to create an environment that allows cross-fertilization between research and practice and across the different enterprise modeling sub-disciplines.

Enterprise modeling is a fundamental part of Information Systems Development (ISD) in the business domain. Within ISD enterprise modeling represents the phase in which the enterprise (or one of its parts) is conceptually modeled in order to satisfy a set of given requirements or, more in general, the business needs of the organization.

This workshop is aimed at bringing together Enterprise Modeling researchers and practitioners as a means to discuss recent developments in the field and debate open issues. ENMO 2014 will specifically focus on two important issues: (1) the role of ontology in enterprise modeling and (2) methods for managing change.

The workshop received 7 submissions, from which the Program Committee selected 3 very high quality full papers corresponding to an acceptance rate of 43%. Two keynote talks and all the accepted papers are organized in two sessions. The first session is dedicated to the two keynotes, while the research papers will be presented in the second session.

We would like to express our gratitude to the Program Committee members for their qualified work in reviewing papers, the authors for considering ENMO as a forum to publish their research, and the ER 2014 organizers for all their support.

July 2014

Sergio de Cesare
Guido Geerts
Program Chairs
ENMO 2014

Model Based Enterprise Simulation and Analysis
A Pragmatic Approach Reducing the Burden on Experts

Vinay Kulkarni, Tony Clark, Souvik Barat, and Balbir Barn

{vinay.vkulkarni,souvik.barat}@tcs.com,
{t.n.clark,b.barn}@mdx.ac.uk

Abstract. Modern enterprises are complex systems operating in highly dynamic environments. The time to respond to the various change drivers is short and the cost of incorrect decisions is prohibitively high. Modern enterprises tend to exist in silos leading to fragmented knowledge with little support available for composing the fragments. Current practice places a heavy burden on experts by requiring a quick and comprehensive solution. This paper proposes a model based approach to this problem in terms of a language to be used for enterprise simulation and analysis that is capable of integrating the 'what', 'how' and 'why' aspects of an enterprise. Possible implementation is also hinted.

1 Introduction

Modern enterprises operate in a highly dynamic environment wherein changes due to a variety of external change drivers require a rapid response within a highly constrained setting. The cost of an erroneous response is prohibitively high and may possibly reduce options for subsequent changes in direction. Two further issues compound the problem. Firstly, the large size of modern enterprises means the understanding of 'what' is the enterprise, 'how' it operates and 'why' it so exists is available for highly localized parts only. Secondly, existing tool support addresses only one aspect, for instance, i* (http://www.cs.toronto.edu/km/istar/) addresses the 'why' aspect, BPMN tools (http://www.softwareag.com/corporate/products/aris/default.asp) address the 'how' aspect, ArchiMate (http://www.visual-paradigm.com/) addresses the 'what' aspect, etc. Moreover, these tools are not only non-interoperable but also paradigmatically different.

As a result, today, experts are forced to follow a process wherein: the problem under consideration is first decomposed into its 'why', 'what' and 'how' parts; these sub-problems are solved individually and independently making use of the available tool support to the extent possible; and the part-solutions are composed into a whole. This intellectually demanding endeavour becomes even more challenging due to the fractured knowledge and non-interoperable nature of current EA tools. The former constitutes the intrinsic complexity whereas the latter can be viewed as accidental complexity.

This paper explores whether model based engineering (MBE) can take some burden off experts' shoulders by reducing the intrinsic complexity. MBE has been used

M. Indulska and S. Purao (Eds.): ER Workshops 2014, LNCS 8823, pp. 3–12, 2014.

to good effect in systems development where models of systems are analysed before they are built. In some cases, parts of systems can be generated from models or run directly from models, thereby reducing the development and maintenance times.

Our proposal is that the application of MBE techniques to organizational decision making involves providing models that reflect the perspective of the key decision makers. To achieve this we apply techniques from Domain Specific Modelling (DSM) that engineers languages (DSLs) to contain concepts that are closely aligned with a given domain. In this way the key stakeholders engage with a support system that is business-facing. We construct an extensible core language that is used as the target of translations from a range of DSLs each supporting an organization analysis and simulation use-case. We then construct a virtual machine to support executed simulation for the core language. Thus, we envisage a system whereby an organization is modelled from a given viewpoint and transform the model so that what-if (*i.e.*, what will be the consequences of such and such action) and if-what (*i.e.*, what would have led to such and such situation) simulation can take place. Results of the simulation help determine choices between organizational change alternatives.

The rest of the paper is organized as follows: section 2 provides motivation in the light of current state, section 3 outlines the proposed solution rationale as well as the set of key features of enterprise specification language, section 4 describes ongoing work towards realization of the proposed solution, and section 5 concludes stating future research necessary.

2   Motivation

Key decision makers of an enterprise need knowledge about the current state of the enterprise, a set of change drivers, and a set of possible states (each of which is an improvement in terms of a well-defined evaluation criterion) so as to be able to make informed and preferably data driven decisions. Such a precise understanding of the current state of enterprise includes the understanding of 'what', 'how' and 'why' aspects of an enterprise and their interrelationships in order to provide answers to questions such as: *What optimization levers are still untapped? Will a change in business strategy percolate through to the IT systems? Will a particular change deliver the promised ROI? Which strategy is most likely to lead to a given desirable outcome?* Moreover, this understanding is required from multiple perspectives and at varying degrees of detail.

The current state-of-the-art of enterprise specification can be broadly classified as: those focusing on the 'what' and 'how' aspects [1,2,3] and those focusing on the 'why' aspects [4,5,6]. Supporting infrastructure for the former, with the exception of (http://www.visual-paradigm.com/) to an extent, is best seen as a means to create high level descriptions that are meant for human experts to interpret in the light of synthesis of their past experience. The stock-n-flow model [7] provides an altogether different paradigm for modelling the 'what' and 'how' aspects and comes with a rich simulation machinery for quantitative analysis (http://www.iseesystems.com/). Elsewhere, several BPMN tools providing simulation capability exist but are limited to the 'how' aspect only (http://www.softwareag.com/corporate/products/aris/default.asp). Technology infrastructure for 'why' aspects (http://www.cs.toronto.edu/km/istar/) is comparatively more advanced in terms of automated support for analysis. However, correlating the 'what' and 'how' aspects of enterprise with the 'why' aspects still remains a challenge.

Given the wide variance in paradigms as well supporting infrastructure, the only recourse available is the use of a method to string together the relevant set of tools with the objective of answering the questions listed earlier. A lack of tool interoperability further exacerbates automated realization of the method in practice. As a result, enterprises continue to struggle in satisfactorily dealing with critical concerns such as business-IT alignment, IT systems rationalization, and enterprise transformation.

3 Proposed Solution

3.1 Rationale

From an external stakeholder perspective, the organization can be viewed as something that raises and responds to a set of events as it goes about achieving its stated objectives. The interface abstraction seems an appropriate fit to meet this perspective and can be extended with negotiation mechanisms such as specification of quality of service (QoS) and expectations from the environment – both of which are negotiation enablers. For instance, they allow definition of multilevel contracts, each promising to honour delivery of the stated objective at the specified QoS level iff the specified level of expectations from environment are met. An interface abstraction can only specify the 'what' and the 'why' of an organization. By providing an abstract implementation of an interface as a component the 'how' of an organization can also be specified. Such an (Interface, Component) tuple seems appropriate to abstractly capture an enterprise for the purpose of machine-based analysis.

Compared to the external stakeholders such as Customer, Regulating Authority *etc.*, internal stakeholders such as COO, CFO need views of the enterprise at a more granular level such as viewing the IT services organization as a set of interacting business units namely Sales & Marketing, Human Resources development, Software development, Quality control, Project management etc. Each of these business units have individual and independent objectives and can deploy different strategies to achieve them. Therefore, it seems the (Interface, Component) tuple can suffice to specify individual business units also. However, since these business units together constitute the organization, a [de]composition mechanism seems required. This requirement can be met if the component abstraction is first class as well as compositional.

We propose a modelling language engineering solution based on the principles of separation of concerns [8] and purposive meta-modelling. We posit a core language defined in terms of generic concepts such as *event, behaviour, property, interface, component, composition,* and *goal*. They constitute a minimal set of concepts necessary and sufficient for enterprise specification as argued below. The core language can be seen as a meta-model template where the generic concepts are placeholders. In the proposed approach a template emits the desired purposive meta-model

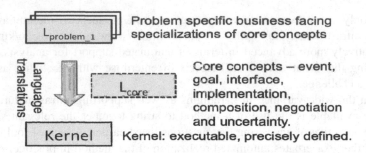

Fig. 1. Relation between Core, Kernel and DSLs

(i.e. a DSL) through a process of instantiation wherein the placeholder generic concepts are replaced by purpose-specific concepts. Our proposal is to construct an extensible kernel language that supports the same set of core concepts and supports both analysis and simulation. As purpose-specific DSLs and the kernel language share the same set of core concepts, the DSLs can be mapped onto the kernel language as shown in Figure 1. In other words, kernel language can be used as the target of translations from a range of DSLs. Each DSL supports an organization analysis and simulation use-case. We then aim to construct a virtual machine for the kernel language so that it is executable. Model execution supports organisation simulation and some analysis use-cases. Links to external packages such as model-checkers will complete the analysis use-cases.

The meta-modelling approach is suited to the open-ended problem space of enterprise modelling: any number of meta-models can be defined, relationships spanning across the various meta-models specified and the desired semantic meaning imparted etc.

Organisations consist of many autonomous components that are organized into dynamically changing hierarchical groups, operate concurrently, and manage goals that affect their behaviour. We aim for the kernel language to reflect these features by having an operational semantics based on the Actor Model of Computation (AMC) [9] and its relation to organisations, or *iOrgs* [10]. Our claim is that the AMC provides a suitable basis for execution and analysis of the core concepts and can be used to represent the features of a component. The key features that must be supported by the kernel language are detailed in [11].

4   Validation

Consider an organization that provides software development services. A client supplies a requirement for a system and expects to receive a completed system for an agreed price. It is in the interests of the service provider to deliver the system whilst minimizing costs and achieving a minimum QoS level.

The costs and QoS represent aspects of the business strategy for the organization. These can be decomposed into sub-goals that are eventually ascribed to various elements of the business such as individuals and departments. Such goals will contribute to the way in which the elements respond to events and requests that occur during the life-time of the organization.

An organization will naturally decompose into elements that correspond to physical or logical aspects of the business such as individuals, departments or IT components. Many of these elements will be autonomous, for example an individual will not wait to be instructed to perform a task, but may, at any time, decide on a course of action. Indeed, such autonomous behaviour can have important ramifications for the success of the overall business strategy. An individual who is highly motivated can proactively perform tasks that pre-empt future requirements. In addition, an individual whose goals are not aligned to those of the organization can take actions that are in their own interests and that are inconsistent with those that are imposed on them. In the case of the software services organization, an individual who is repeatedly overlooked as team-leader, may start to delay the delivery of software components.

Decision making and negotiation is an important part of implementing complex tasks within any organization. Individuals will make decisions that are based on their local knowledge and beliefs regarding the current situation. For example, without further direction, an individual may use a particular language to specify a software component because they believe it to be effective based on previous experience. Negotiation occurs whenever resources are limited, a programmer may need to negotiate regarding the availability of computing resources, and a manager may negotiate to take designers from one department to another for the duration of a project. The success of negotiation will depend upon a variety of factors, not least the local knowledge of the individuals that are participating.

In addition to long-lived groups that correspond to organizational components that might be seen on a conventional organogram, the life-time of a group may be much shorter; for example, a group of software designers that are convened and subsequently dissolved at the start of a project. Such groups need not have a physical realization, for example, operating via electronic communication mechanisms, however they have collective knowledge, may negotiate collectively and respond to events and requests as a group.

A senior decision maker may be interested in modelling the software service provider from a variety of perspectives. In all cases they are interested in minimizing costs and achieving a given minimum QoS. Perspectives include:

- Varying the number of resources available, for example changing the number of designers (who are relatively expensive) or the number of programmers.
- Imposing certain business directives such as a requirement that agile development methods should be used compared to traditional waterfall.
- Varying the abilities of individual roles within the organization with the resulting impact on the costs of development and QoS.
- Varying the roles within an organization. A specific role may be defined that is responsible for identifying opportunities for sharing good practice between different projects. Simulations can be run both with and without individuals responsible for the new role.

Given the requirements outlined above, our proposal is that the concepts can be represented using a fixed collection of concepts that include components, interfaces, events, goals and behaviour. These concepts can be implemented using features from the Actor model of computation and Multi-Agent Systems.

```
act resource_manager(time,resources,queue) {
  advance_time(t,d) =
    case (t+d) <= time {
      true -> time
      else t + d
    }
  Request(t,filter,action) ->
    case t <= time {
      true ->
        let requested = filter(resources)
        in case requested {
          Fail ->
            become re-
source_manager(time,resources,queue+[Request(t,filter,action)])
          Success(some_resources) -> {
            become resource_manager(time,resources-some_resources,queue);
            action(time,some_resources)
          }
        }
      else become resource_manager(time,resources,queue+[Request(t,filter,action)])
    }
  Release(t,some_resources,d,next) ->
    case queue {
      [] -> {
        become resource_manager(advance_time(t,d),resources+some_resources,[]);
        next(advance_time(t,d))
      }
      request:queue -> {
        become resource_manager(advance_time(t,d),resources+some_resources,queue);
        next(advance_time(t,d));
        send self request
      }
    }
}
```

Fig. 2. ESL Resource Manager

The kernel language is currently in development and is based on earlier work on the LEAP language and associated toolset [12,13,14]. The hypothesis of LEAP and the subsequent development of the ESL language is that, unlike current languages such as ArchiMate and KAOS, it is not necessary to provide a large diversity of modelling elements in order to capture the elements of interest when analysing aspects of organisations. LEAP proposes that components, ports and connectors can be used in conjunction with information models and behaviour rules in order to represent organisational features. However, this aspect alone is insufficient, and a key property of the LEAP and ESL languages is that they offer *higher-order features* including first-class components, functions and procedures.

Higher-order features provide a basis for abstraction over patterns of structure and behaviour that cannot otherwise be achieved by languages that are limited to first-order features. Abstraction is an important aspect of the EASE-Y approach because we aim to tailor the same architecture to multiple problem cases. Abstraction through higher-order features means that models can be parameterised with respect to different behaviours.

As an example of the use of higher-order features that implement a pattern of behaviour, consider the implementation of a resource manager to be used by the software service provider. In this case the resources are software engineers and the resource manager is to be used to simulate different strategies for implementing development projects.

```
act traveller(name,goals,plan,location,line) {
  Go(target) ->
    case plan {
      [] ->
        prove PlanJourney({location},{line},{target},plan) <- [],tube_planner {
          become traveller(name,goals,plan,location,line);
          send self Do
        } print('FAIL\n')
      else become traveller(name,goals+[Go(target)],plan,location,line)
    }
  Do ->
    case plan {
      [] ->
        case goals {
          g:gs -> {
            become traveller(name,gs,plan,location,line);
            send self g
          }
          else print(name + ' travels are complete.\n')
        }
      Move(_,location):plan -> {
        become traveller(name,goals,plan,location,line);
        print(name + ' moves to ' + location + '\n');
        send self Do
      }
      Change(_,_,line):plan -> {
        become traveller(name,goals,plan,location,line);
        print(name + ' changes line to ' + line + '\n');
        send self Do
      }
    }
}
```

Fig. 3. Planning

Figure 2 shows the implementation of a resource manager in the ESL kernel language. The resource manager is defined as an actor-behaviour. An actor is created with a behaviour that can be changed using the command **become**. The resource manager is parameterised with respect to the current time, the list of available resources and a queue of pending resource requests. The behaviour of an actor defines the interface of messages that the actor can process. Each message is handled in a separate thread of computation. In this case the resource manager can handle Request and Release messages. A request for resources includes the time at which the request is made, a resource filter and an action. The resource filter is a predicate that can be applied to the currently available resources to determine whether the request can be satisfied. The filter returns Fail when there are insufficient resources and returns Success otherwise. The action is supplied with the allocated resources. The higher-order features (filter and action) allow the resource manager to be used in a wide range of different resource allocation simulations. When the resources are released, the procedure next is used as a continuation.

In addition to rule-based execution, actors will be goal-driven and will need to plan. The ESL kernel language provides a deduction engine that can be used to develop plans in response to requests that are received as messages.

Figure 3 shows an outline of an underground train traveller actor that uses a collection of rules and a simple planner to construct plans when instructed to go to a target station. The ESL construct **prove** is used to construct a plan that is then enacted when the actor sends itself a Do message. Actions within the plan are either Move between stations or Change train lines. Figure 4 shows a general purpose

```
planner = rules {
  Solve(state,goal,plan,plan)   :- Subset(goal,state).
  Solve(state,goal,sofar,plan) :-
    Action(action,precons,add,delete),
    Subset(precons,state),
    \+ Member(action,sofar),
    DeleteAll(state,delete,remainder),
    Append(add,remainder,newState),
    Append(sofar,[action],sofar'),
    Solve(newState,goal,sofar',plan)
}
```

Fig. 4. A General Purpose Planner in ESL

STRIPS-like planner implemented in the ESL kernel. The language provides PROLOG-like deduction rules that are integrated with the actors and the associated information structures. The planner is used in the definition of a rule-set called tube_planner used in Figure 3. It is not envisaged that the senior decision makers will need to understand these concepts and features because the intention is to use techniques from language-engineering and model-driven development to offer a business-facing interface for each of the use-cases. For example, a decision maker in the software services example may be offered a simple interface that allows them to vary number of elements in a pre-populated model of their organization. Figure 5 shows the proposed EASE-Y architecture and the various stakeholders that take part in the process of developing a language for a particular use-case, deploying the language on the architecture and then using it to model part of an organisation, populate various concrete scenarios and perform simulation and analysis.

It remains a research question as to how much variability can be exposed in such a domain-specific way. Therefore, the proposed architecture for simulation and analysis will involve a number of stakeholders and involve a development process for each use-case. In the first instance the architecture will need to be tailored for a specific class of use-cases, for example languages may be developed that support software development companies. This will involve collaboration between a general domain expert and a language engineer and will result in a language definition that translated to a kernel using the general concepts. Secondly, the language will be tailored to the needs of a specific company involving collaboration between a company-specific domain expert and a language engineer. Thirdly, a domain specific language that is suitable for the decision maker will be produced. This will involve an expert in user-interface design. Finally the decision maker will be able to use the system unaided to configure various scenarios and run analysis and simulation. Of course, there are many opportunities within this process for reuse.

We modelled an IT services provisioning organisation in terms of i* (the 'why' aspect) and system dynamical (largely the 'what' aspect with little bit of 'how'). We used i* and system dynamic models individually and independently to answer a set of questions. However, it was very hard to answer questions that need information of all the three aspects together. This was largely due to the paradigmatic differences between the two models and non-interoperable nature of the tools. We are in the process of specifying the same example using the proposed kernel language. We are confident of being able to answer all the questions herein.

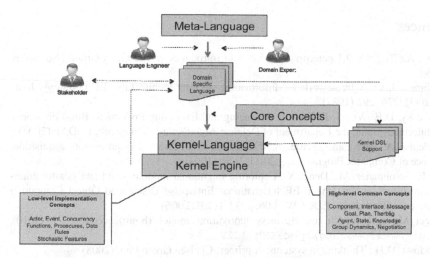

Fig. 5. EASE-Y Architecture

5   Conclusion and Future Work

Modern enterprises are complex systems operating in increasingly dynamic environment. Understanding of the 'what', 'how'' and 'why' aspects is essential for quick and comprehensive change response. We proposed a model based solution for reducing this inherent complexity and proposed technology infrastructure for automation. We believe this will take a significant burden off experts' shoulders. We hope to have an illustration of the proposed approach along with the supporting technology infrastructure ready very soon.

However, several challenges remain to be addressed pertaining to both inherent as well as accidental complexity. As regards the former, there is a need to support the inescapable realities of 'negotiation' and 'uncertainty'. Barring [15,16,17] very little work is reported. Paradigmatic differences and non-interoperable nature of existing EA modelling tools introduce accidental complexity which can only be addressed through a manual method. Automation support based on meta-model mapping and model transformation seems definitely possible. This can also help in maintaining the various models always in sync – a key unmet requirement that leads to eventual disuse of EA modelling tools. Size of modern enterprises and nature of problems they face results in very large enterprise models. Precision of analysis, speed of simulation,   and life cycle support for these models that typically exist in a distributed manner are major hurdles to be overcome for the proposed approach to be useful and usable in real life. Many of the lessons learnt from use of MBE in application generation [18,19] seem readily applicable. Success depends principally upon the quality of models and only partially on the proposed technology infrastructure which is but a solution enabler. Ensuring semantic validity of enterprise models is another important challenge that needs to be addressed for the proposed approach to be usable in real life.

References

1. Josey, A.: Togaf v 9.1 enterprise edition - an introduction. The Open Group (November 2009)
2. Zachman, J.A.: A framework for information systems architecture. IBM Systems Journal 26(3), 276–292 (1987)
3. Wisnosky, D.E., Vogel, J.: Foo. In: Managing and Executing Projects to Build Enterprise Architectures Using the Department of Defense Architecture Framework, DoDAF (2004)
4. Dardenne, A., van Lamsweerde, A., Fickas, S.: Goal-directed requirements acquisition. Science of Computer Programming 20(1), 3–50 (1993)
5. Yu, E., Strohmaier, M., Deng, X.: Exploring intentional modeling and analysis for enterprise architecture. In: 10th IEEE International Enterprise Distributed Object Computing Conference Workshops, EDOCW 2006, p. 32. IEEE (2006)
6. Object Management Group. Business motivation model (bmm), version 1.1 (2010), http://www.omg.org/spec/BMM/1.1/
7. Meadows, D.H.: Thinking in systems: A primer. Chelsea Green Pub. (2008)
8. Tarr, P., Ossher, H., Harrison, W., Sutton, S.: N degrees of separation: multi-dimensional separation of concerns. In: Proceedings of the 21st Int. Conf. on Software Engineering, pp. 107–119 (1999)
9. Hewitt, C.: Actor model of computation: scalable robust information systems. arXiv:1008.1459 (2010)
10. Hewitt, C.: Norms and commitment for iorgs (tm) information systems: Direct logic (tm) and participatory grounding checking. arXiv:0906.2756 (2009)
11. Kulkarni, V., Clark, T., Barn, B.: A Component Abstraction for Localized, Composable, Machine Manipulable Enterprise Specification. In: 4th International Symposium on Business Modeling and Software Design (2014)
12. Clark, T., Barn, B.: Goal driven architecture development using LEAP. Enterprise Modeling & Information Systems Architectures-An International Journal 8(1), 40–61 (2013)
13. Clark, T., Barn, B.S., Oussena, S.: LEAP: A precise lightweight framework for enterprise architecture. In: Proceedings of the 4th India Software Engineering Conference, pp. 85–94. ACM (2011)
14. Clark, T., Barn, B.S., Oussena, S.: A method for enterprise architecture alignment. In: Proper, E., Gaaloul, K., Harmsen, F., Wrycza, S. (eds.) PRET 2012. LNBIP, vol. 120, pp. 48–76. Springer, Heidelberg (2012)
15. Jennings, N.R., Faratin, P., Lomuscio, A.R., Parsons, S., Wooldridge, M.J., Sierra, C.: Automated negotiation: prospects, methods and challenges. Group Decision and Negotiation 10(2), 199–215 (2001)
16. Bartolini, C., Preist, C., Jennings, N.R.: A software framework for automated negotiation. In: Choren, R., Garcia, A., Lucena, C., Romanovsky, A. (eds.) SELMAS 2004. LNCS, vol. 3390, pp. 213–235. Springer, Heidelberg (2005)
17. Olfati-Saber, R., Fax, J.A., Murray, R.M.: Consensus and cooperation in networked multi-agent systems. Proceedings of the IEEE 95(1), 215–233 (2007)
18. Kulkarni, V., Reddy, S., Rajbhoj, A.: Scaling up model driven engineering – experience and lessons learnt. In: Petriu, D.C., Rouquette, N., Haugen, Ø. (eds.) MODELS 2010, Part II. LNCS, vol. 6395, pp. 331–345. Springer, Heidelberg (2010)
19. Hutchinson, J., Whittle, J., Rouncefield, M., Kristoffersen, S.: Empirical assessment of MDE in industry. In: Proceedings of the 33rd International Conference on Software Engineering, pp. 471–480. ACM (May 2011)

3D vs. 4D Ontologies in Enterprise Modeling

Michaël Verdonck, Frederik Gailly, and Geert Poels

Faculty of Economics and Business Administration, Ghent University,
Tweekerkenstraat 2, 9000 Ghent, Belgium
{michael.verdonck,frederik.gailly,geert.poels}@ugent.be

Abstract. This paper presents a comparison between a 3D and a 4D ontology, with the purpose of identifying modeling variations that arise from using these different kinds of ontologies. The modeling variations are illustrated by using two enterprise modeling enigmas to which both ontologies are applied. The goal of our comparison is to demonstrate that the choice of an ontology impacts on the representation of real world phenomena and will eventually result in different enterprise models.

1 Introduction

Enterprise Modeling can be defined as expressing enterprise knowledge, which adds value to the enterprise or needs to be shared. It consists of making models of the structure, behavior and organization of the enterprise [1]. To construct these models, enterprise modeling utilizes conceptual modeling languages. The goal of enterprise modeling is to represent or formalize the structure and behavior of enterprise components and operations in order to understand, engineer or re-engineer, evaluate, optimize, and even control the business organization and operations [2]. Over the years, various methods and modeling techniques have been introduced, which led to a plethora of various enterprise modeling approaches and tools. However, these existing approaches to enterprise modeling lack an adequate specification of the semantics of the terminology of the underlying enterprise meta-model, which leads to inconsistent interpretations and uses of knowledge [3].

In order to provide a foundation for enterprise modeling by means of a formal specification of the semantics of enterprise models and to describe precisely which modeling constructs represent which phenomena, ontologies were introduced [4]. We can define an ontology as a formal specification of a conceptualization [5]. Within the IS domain, similar problems occurred, resulting in the use of ontologies to analyze and improve existing conceptual modeling languages [6]. A great deal of research has been done in analyzing, evaluating and improving the modeling grammars and constructs of conceptual modeling languages with ontologies. This resulted in enriching existing conceptual modeling languages with modeling rules that have their origin in a formalized ontology. We can define this practice as *ontology-driven conceptual modeling* (ODCM). In this paper we have decided to focus on core ontologies in order not to concentrate on a single domain. Core ontologies (also called foundational ontologies) can be defined as ontologies that provide a broad view of the world, suitable for many different target domains [7]. We can distinguish between two kinds of core

M. Indulska and S. Purao (Eds.): ER Workshops 2014, LNCS 8823, pp. 13–22, 2014.

ontologies with respect to their view about the persistence of objects through time, i.e. 3D and 4D ontologies. *3D ontologies* hold that individual objects are three-dimensional, have only spatial parts, and wholly exist at each moment of their existence. *4D ontologies* hold that individual objects are four-dimensional, have spatial and temporal parts, and exist immutably in space-time [8].

Although OCDM leads to theoretically sound models, a recurring problem in this practice is the degree of complexity that results from this formalization. The translation of these ontological axioms results in complex formal modeling rules and consequently ontology-driven conceptual modeling languages that can be hard for a modeler to appropriately apply. As a consequence, an increasingly problematic bottleneck in IS and enterprise modeling has come about, i.e. a growing demand for constant creation of formal models in specific and dynamic operational contexts, combined with a lack of people who are capable and willing to perform the modeling required [9]. It is the author's belief that this bottleneck can be reduced by aiding the modeler in the choice of a suitable ontology, saving time and effort in comparing and evaluating various ontologies. One way to do this is to link an ontology with the 'goal' or purpose and intended use of the conceptual model. An example of such a goal could be to improve the communication by means of using a limited set of concepts and relationships. Other goals could be based upon re-engineering purposes or system analysis. Since every goal has different kinds of purposes and intended uses, they could be linked to different kinds of ontologies. Nowadays it is up to the modeler to choose the ontology he would like to integrate into the conceptual model. A clear motivation of why the chosen ontology is the better fit is difficult to find.

Having this in mind, the goal of this paper is to explore the impact of choosing a certain ontology by understanding and demonstrating that, depending on the aspect of the real world that has to be modeled, the choice of an ontology will impact the modeling of these real world phenomena and will eventually result in different enterprise models. We intended to do this by comparing the modeling variations that arise by using two rather different ontologies on similar enterprise modeling enigmas. In section 2, we will introduce the two foundational ontologies and motivate our choice for picking these two specific ontologies. Section 3 will then demonstrate the modeling variations that arise by applying the ontologies on the same modeling enigmas of real-world phenomena in the enterprise domain. Finally in section 4, we will discuss the result of the overall comparison of both the ontologies and explore the kind of modeling purposes they can be applied to.

2   The BORO and eUFO Ontology

The ontologies that will be compared are eUFO (essential Unified Foundational Ontology) [10] and BORO (Business Object Reference Ontology) [11]. Our choice for these two specific ontologies is driven by various reasons. A first argument for comparing these ontologies is that they are both used in the domain of conceptual modeling and that they are both reference ontologies. Reference ontologies can be defined as rich, axiomatic theories, whose focus is to clarify the intended meanings of terms used in specific conceptual modeling domains [12]. Even though we could say their roots are the same, their branches stretch out in different ways, which brings us to our second argument of comparison: the purpose of their existence and their intended use. eUFO was developed for analyzing modeling languages and to improve them. More specifically, the aim of eUFO is to improve the truthfulness to reality (domain appropriateness) and conceptual clarity (comprehensibility appropriateness) of a modeling language [10]. Or in other words, the stronger the match between reality and its representing model, the easier it is to communicate and reason with that model [13]. The second ontology, BORO, was developed for re-engineering purposes and to integrate systems in a transparent and straightforward manner [11]. By using business objects, its purpose is to make systems simpler and functionally richer so that in practice, they would be cheaper to build and maintain. A last but nonetheless important argument for comparing these ontologies is that eUFO was originally developed based on UFO, a 3D ontology, having a focus on endurants. BORO was developed from the very beginning as an ontology of perdurants, making it a 4D ontology. Below, we will first give a brief description of both ontologies and how they came to exist. Then we will give a quick overview of the concepts they cover.

2.1   eUFO

Since eUFO is derived from UFO, we will first give a small introduction of this ontology. UFO is a reference ontology of endurants, which is based on a number of different theories such as philosophy of language, formal ontology, linguistics, cognitive psychology and philosophical logics [14]. Since UFO is a 3D ontology, it focuses less on processes and events. In order to deal with time and changes, additions to UFO have been made whereas UFO can be grouped into three compliance sets, namely, UFO-A: an ontology of endurants; UFO-B: an ontology of perdurants, and UFO-C, which is built upon UFO-A and B to compose an Ontology of Social Concepts [13]. With the purpose of simplifying the philosophical terminology of UFO and harmonizing it with the informatics terminology, a simplified version was created based upon UFO-A and UFO-B, called the essential Unified Foundational Ontology (eUFO) [10]. Our motivation to evaluate eUFO in this paper and not UFO comes from the fact that eUFO is a simplified version and therefore is less complicated. It is also based upon an ontological view of endurants and also contains perdurants. This makes eUFO more practical for comparing it to another ontology than UFO.

2.2   BORO

BORO is a reference ontology that uses object semantics with the goal of developing models that are functionally rich and structurally simple [11]. Object semantics can be explained as objects where time is treated as another dimension, making it easier to capture change patterns. In other words, object semantics defines objects as four-dimensional extensions in space and time. The origin of BORO lies in the re-engineering of existing information systems into conceptual models with the goal to integrate and align these systems. The re-engineering of these existing systems can be described in two stages: reverse engineering and forward engineering. In the first stage, the existing system's business entities are translated into business objects. The second stage involves the process of modeling with these newly developed business objects. During the second stage or forward engineering, the inaccuracies and constraints of the existing systems are identified and corrected. The power of BORO can be found in the principle of re-use, i.e. it provides a framework that both enables and encourages high levels of reuse. These intended higher levels of re-use would lead to reducing the effort needed to re-develop a system. Another strength from BORO for re-engineering purposes can be found in the extra fourth dimension it offers. The main advantage of perdurantist approaches is simplicity as everything (e.g., individual objects including processes) is treated in a similar way [15].

2.3   Introducing eUFO and BORO

In this section we give a brief overview of the concepts in BORO and eUFO in order to provide a better understanding of the enterprise modeling enigmas in the following section. However, for a complete understanding of these concepts, we refer to [10], [11] and [14].

Both BORO and eUFO make a distinction between so called entities and entity types. In BORO these are called elements (or individuals or bodies) and classes (or types), in eUFO they are called individuals and universals. From then on, many differences arise between the two ontologies. While eUFO clearly distinguishes different kinds of individuals and has many sub-categories within these individuals, BORO does not. In BORO, all elements have a spatio-temporal extension and so are all, by definition, physical. Classes are any collections of objects; hence they may have similar features but do not necessarily have to. For example, the class person classifies all elements that are persons. An important feature of elements is that they are space-time based and thus four-dimensional. BORO is a timeless ontology in the sense that the real world is modeled with a view from nowhere; hence the model is not relative to the view of a specific person or situation. In BORO a fundamental relation between elements is whole-parts. Whole-part patterns also explain how different four-dimensional objects overlap. This overlap can be both spatial and/or temporal. For example, if a car was red last week and is green this week, we can see this as a red temporal part followed by a green temporal part, where the temporal parts are time-slices of the whole car. Classes in BORO are defined as sets and therefore are immutable, similarly to sets in mathematical set theory.

In eUFO, individuals are 'things' that have a unique identity. They exist in time and space in "the real world". Universals are feature-based classifiers that classify, at any moment in time, a set of individuals with similar features. Universals are equivalent to classes in BORO. Looking closer at individuals, there is a distinction between substance individuals, trope individuals and events. The latter can be defined as a perdurants while the former two can be seen as endurants. Substance individuals are fully present whenever they are present, i.e., they are in time. Examples are a person or an amount of seawater. *Events* are individuals composed of temporal parts. They happen in time in the sense that they extend in time accumulating temporal parts [16]. An example is today's rise of the sun. Whenever an event is present, it is not the case that all its temporal parts are present. *Trope individuals* are defined through their relations with other individuals, i.e., they are existentially dependent on other individuals. Examples are the red color of the sunrise or a certain skill of a person.

To capture relations between objects, BORO makes use of *tuples*. The extension of a tuple is given by the places that the objects occupy in the relation therefore the use of the mathematical definition to define the identity of a tuple. For example, in the tuple *<John, John's childhood>*, *John* occupies place 1 of the tuple and *John's childhood* place 2. Therefore in BORO the identity of an element is defined by its 4D spatiotemporal extension, the identity of a class by its instances (or members) and the identity of a tuple by the places in the tuple. Elements, classes and tuples are the three types of objects that exist in BORO; all objects must be an instance of one of those three types.

In eUFO, relations are expressed using relators. Relators are trope individuals with the power of connecting entities. The relationships can be either formal or material. Formal relationships are direct relationships between two or more entities. They can be based on existential dependency or on part/whole relations. Material relations however have a material structure of themselves; they have a relator, or mediating individual, with the purpose of connecting individuals. Material relationships include examples such as 'enrolled at', 'working at' or 'being connected to'. In order to represent changes, BORO introduces change objects called states and events. States and events are types of physical bodies and represent temporal parts. States are bounded by events. Change can be defined as a succession of temporal parts. States are seen as 'change objects' and thus also have a four-dimensional extension. Events are change objects, similar to states, but of a different kind. While events and states are both temporal parts, events unlike states do not persist through time. They only occupy an instant in time; they have a zero thickness along the time dimension. In eUFO, time and changes are being expressed by events, roles and phases. The creation, change and destruction of substance individuals are being executed by object participation events. Since trope individuals are existentially dependent upon substance individuals, object participation events indirectly also impact trope individuals. Phases are universals that can be used to express different time-changes in a substance individual.

3   Enterprise Modeling Enigmas

Our enterprise modeling enigmas are chosen as such so they would address rather different aspects of the ontologies, making this comparison more interesting. Also, we will not be using a modeling language with the purpose to remain 'neutral' on this aspect; we will instead use a generic and abstract form of representing some of the enigmas.

3.1   The Troy Enigma

Let us start with our first enterprise enigma, which will focus on how both ontologies view the persistence of objects through time. The enigma involves the fusion of two departments in a company Troy, specialized in IT security. The first department was responsible for the IT support of the back office while the second department was responsible for the IT support of the front office. Since both the responsibilities of front and back office have grown closer to each other and started using the same information systems, the higher management of Troy decided that both the IT support departments fulfill similar tasks and can therefore be fused into one. This new department would simply manage all IT support for both front and back office. Let us now describe this situation with both ontologies:

In eUFO, both departments and the company are substance individuals. The company and the departments are linked with each other through formal relationships since the departments are parts of the company. The departments each also assume a role, that of support for respectively the front and back office. The number of personnel of the departments, their efficiency, the total cost and other characteristics can be defined as qualities of the department. The decision taken by the higher management can be seen as an event. This event results in different object participation events. The first being two object destruction events that eliminate the two existing IT departments and further one object creation event, which creates a new IT department as a new substance individual. The destruction of the two existing departments also invokes the destruction of the roles they assumed, the qualities they embedded and the relations that were formed with these departments. For a more detailed explanation on how this 'destruction' is actually performed, we refer to [17]. The creation of the new IT department also indirectly creates a new role, new relationships and new qualities that are a combination of the roles, relationships and qualities from the two departments that ceased to exist. Figure 1 gives a graphical representation through time.

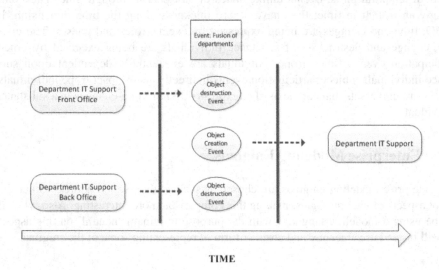

Fig. 1. eUFO and the Troy enigma

In the ontology of BORO, the fusion of the departments is viewed in a different way than that of eUFO. Both the IT support departments for respectively front and back office are individual objects. Each of them share a spatio-temporal part with respectively the role of IT support front office and the role of IT support back office. Also all the characteristics of the departments (efficiency, cost factors, etc.) involve spatial and/or temporal parts of the departments. We can also identify many tuples around these departments such as <Front office IT support department; Front office> based upon their support function towards the front office.

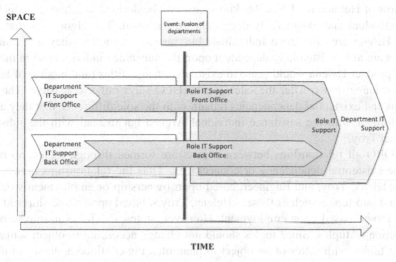

Fig. 2. BORO and the Troy enigma

The roles of IT support front office and of IT support back office are now also part of a new role: IT support. The two original departments no longer share a spatial part with the object company. After the fusion event, the spatio-temporal extensions of both the front and back office stop. Instead, the spatio-temporal extension of a new object, the IT Support department starts. Figure 2 gives a graphical representation on a space-time map.

3.2   The Helena Enigma

Our second enterprise enigma emphasizes existential dependencies within the ontologies. The enigma involves the sale of a graphical design product called Helena being owned by another IT security company called Archea and sold to the company Troy. Since the product exists out of many complex algorithms, there is a specific team of engineers working at Archea for the continuous maintenance and further development of these algorithms. Since the team's know-how is essential for the proper functioning of Helena, the team is also being transferred to Troy. Although there is an event 'Sale of Helena', we will not focus on this event since time dependency was discussed during the previous enigma.

According to eUFO, both the company Archea, Troy and the product Helena are substance individuals. Before the sale, Archea owned Helena and therefore they formed a material relationship linked through the relator ownership. The team that was linked to Helena is a part of Archea and therefore, a formal relationship exists. The engineers working in the team however do not have a formal relationship with Troy. Instead, we have a material relationship between the engineers and the company Troy connected through the relator 'employment'. Also, a material relationship exists between Helena and the team through the relator 'Maintenance and development'. Let us take a look at the details of both the team and Helena. The team has a unique know-how of Helena. In eUFO, this know-how can be defined as a 'mode', which is a trope individual and existentially dependent on the team. The algorithms that are a part of Helena are also trope individuals but instead of modes, they are qualities. Qualities are also existentially dependent upon the substance individual so in the case that the product Helena would cease to exist, also the qualities (and modes) of Helena would no longer exist. After the sales event, eUFO stays rather consistent. The relationships and existential dependencies remain with the sole difference that they are no longer formed with the substance individual Archea but instead with the substance individual Troy.

In BORO all relationships between objects are formed through tuples, no matter what the existential dependency or connector is. Thus the relationships between the objects Helena, Troy, and Engineer, based upon ownership or employment would all be formed into tuples such as these: <Helena, Troy>, based upon ownership and <Engineer, Troy>, based upon employment. However, states also have an impact on the construction of tuples. Since tuples should not change according to object semantics, we form tuples with states of an object to guarantee the continuous nature of tuples. The reason for this is that we cannot construct two tuples where both Troy and Archea own the product Helena. Instead, the product Helena has two separate states: Helena owned by Archea and Helena owned by Troy. This allows us to create the following two tuples: <Helena owned by Archea, Archea> and <Helena owned by Troy, Troy>. These tuples thus represent the relationship between the object Helena and the objects Archea and Troy, based on ownership without contradicting one another.

4   Discussion

At a first glance, the modeler can become rather overwhelmed by the many different concepts that eUFO introduces, resulting in many relationships and dependencies between these concepts. Important aspects are existential dependency and rigidity, which are used as a way to classify and distinguish the concepts from one another. As a consequence, eUFO can seem rather complex, requiring more time to fully understand all of its concepts and dependencies. Since everything in the BORO ontology can be defined as a timeless object, it has no need for ways to classify or distinguish these objects, resulting in fewer concepts and dependencies and therefore strikes as less complex than eUFO does. However, BORO's way of viewing real-world phenomena in four-dimensional extensions feels rather unnatural in human thinking. A similar ascertainment is found in [18], where object-oriented analysis and design are rather difficult to learn and practice, even though they are practiced intensively in industry and academics. So in a way, both ontologies have a more complicated aspect than the other, depending on the perspective.

If we return to the different goals of enterprise models [2] and according to the intended purpose of the ontologies, eUFO would for example be better fit to formalize, understand and explain structures and behaviors of the enterprise. BORO according to its origin would be better fit to engineer or re-engineer enterprise structures. However, the modeling enigmas above demonstrate that both ontologies expand their original purposes. eUFO's advantage of having a high semantic preciseness and richness of concepts could prove very practical in re-engineering or optimizing the business organization and its operations. BORO's integrated approach and the simplicity towards objects and processes can be used to deliver a general overview of the whole organization and all of its components.   With these first observations we intend to conduct further research on this topic, by identifying different kind of purposes and uses of enterprise models, and associating them with ontologies.

5   Conclusion

The enterprise modeling enigmas above demonstrate that there are some great differences between the ontologies eUFO and BORO. Since each has a different foundational view of the real world, the resulting enterprise model will also be different. We argue that a modeler will benefit from a better understanding and comprehension in ontologies and the modeling variations they bring about. This should also lead to a more motivated choice of an ontology. These modeling variations were demonstrated when applying both BORO and eUFO to the enterprise modeling enigmas above, resulting in rather different representations of the real world.

References

1. Vernadat, F.B.: Enterprise modeling and integration (EMI): Current status and research perspectives. Annual Reviews in Control 26, 15–25 (2002)
2. Vernadat, F.: UEML: Towards a Unified Enterprise Modelling Language. International Journal of Production Research 40, 4309–4321 (2002)
3. Grüninger, M., Atefi, K., Fox, M.: Ontologies to support process integration in enterprise engineering. Computational & Mathematical Organization, 381–394 (2000)
4. Opdahl, A.L., Berio, G., Harzallah, M., Matulevičius, R.: An ontology for enterprise and information systems modeling. Applied Ontology 7, 49–92 (2012)
5. Gruber, T.R.: A Translation Approach to Portable Ontology Specifications. Knowledge Acquisitions 5, 199–220 (1993)
6. Wand, Y.: Ontology as a foundation for meta-modeling and method engineering. Information and Software Technology 38, 281–287 (1996)
7. Guarino, N., Oberle, D., Staab, S.: What Is an Ontology? In: Handbook on Ontologies, pp. 1–17 (2009)
8. Hales, S.D.S., Johnson, T.T.A.: Endurantism, perdurantism and special relativity. The Philosophical Quarterly 53, 524–539 (2003)

9. Hoppenbrouwers, S.J.B.A., Proper, H.A., van der Weide, T.P.: A fundamental view on the process of conceptual modeling. In: Delcambre, L., Kop, C., Mayr, H.C., Mylopoulos, J., Pastor, Ó. (eds.) ER 2005. LNCS, vol. 3716, pp. 128–143. Springer, Heidelberg (2005)
10. Guizzardi, G., Wagner, G.: Can BPMN Be Used for Making Simulation Models? In: Barjis, J., Eldabi, T., Gupta, A. (eds.) EOMAS 2011. LNBIP, vol. 88, pp. 100–115. Springer, Heidelberg (2011)
11. Partridge, C.: Business Objects: Re-engineering for Reuse. Butterworth-Heinemann (2005)
12. Masolo, C., Borgo, S., Gangemi, A., Guarino, N., Oltramari, A., Schneider, L.: Wonder-Web Deliverable D17. The WonderWeb Library of Foundational Ontologies and the DOLCE ontology (2002)
13. Guizzardi, G., Wagner, G.: Using the Unified Foundational Ontology (UFO) as a Foundation for General Conceptual Modeling Languages. Theory and Applications of Ontology: Computer Applications, 175–196 (2010)
14. Guizzardi, G.: Ontological Foundations for Structural Conceptual Models. Springer, Heidelberg (2005)
15. Al Debei, M.M.: Conceptual Modeling and the Quality of Ontologies: Endurantism Vs Perdurantism. International Journal of Database Management Systems 4, 1–19 (2012)
16. Guizzardi, G., Wagner, G., de Almeida Falbo, R., Guizzardi, R.S.S., Almeida, J.P.A.: Towards Ontological Foundations for the Conceptual Modeling of Events Background: The Unified Foundational Ontology (UFO). In: Ng, W., Storey, V.C., Trujillo, J.C. (eds.) ER 2013. LNCS, vol. 8217, pp. 327–341. Springer, Heidelberg (2013)
17. Masolo, C., Guizzardi, G., Vieu, L.: Relational roles and qua-individuals. In: AAAI Fall Symposium on Roles, pp. 103–112 (2005)
18. Hadar, I.: When intuition and logic clash: The case of the object-oriented paradigm. Science of Computer Programming 78, 1407–1426 (2013)

Applications of Ontologies in Enterprise Modelling: A Systematic Mapping Study

Vitor Afonso Pinto[1], Camila Leles de Rezende Rohlfs[1],
and Fernando Silva Parreiras[1]

LAIS – Laboratory of Advanced Information Systems, FUMEC University
Av. Afonso Pena, 3880, Belo Horizonte 30130-009, Brazil
vitor.afonso.pinto@gmail.com, camilaleles@fumec.edu.br,
fernando.parreiras@fumec.br

Abstract. Ontologies have been used in several fields as an engineering artefact with the main purpose of conceptualizing a specific object of study. Therefore, it is reasonable to think about using ontologies to support enterprise modelling. In this paper, we investigate the application of ontologies in enterprise modelling. We performed a comprehensive systematic mapping study in order to understand the usage of ontologies to enterprise modeling. We group the results by business areas, business segments, languages, environments and methodologies. We conclude that ontologies are applicable to assist enterprise modelling and have been used specially in Industry, Health and Environment and Government.

Keywords: Ontology; Enterprise Modelling; Systematic Review; Enterprise Architecture.

1 Introduction

Ontologies are used to conceptualize domain knowledge. They have been used in fields like knowledge management, artificial intelligence and bioinformatics, among others. In parallel, organizations have been working on modelling their business services and processes, information systems and technical infrastructure [1], [2]. The purpose of this paper is to understand how ontologies have been used to support enterprise modelling.

In this paper, we present a comprehensive literature review on the state-of-the-art in the research field of ontologies. The main objective of this research is to understand the use of ontologies in enterprise modelling. More precisely, this paper aims to answer the following research question: What are the uses of ontologies in enterprise modelling? To answer this question, 1079 ontology related papers were analyzed.

We organize this paper as follows. Section 2 describes the theoretical foundations. Section 3 describes the research methodology underlying our survey. Section 4 presents the results obtained. Section 5 presents the threats to validity of this paper. Finally, section 6 concludes the paper.

M. Indulska and S. Purao (Eds.): ER Workshops 2014, LNCS 8823, pp. 23–32, 2014.

2   Background

2.1   Ontology

Conceptual modelling (or ontology) describes information related to an application domain and includes the vocabulary, constraints and means to obtain information inferences [3]. The term "Ontology" has been used with different meanings, depending on the community [4]. However, in the computational sense, ontology represents an engineering artefact whose purpose is to conceptualize a specific object of study [5]. In this way, ontology is defined as an explicit, formal and shared specification of a specific concept [4].

Ontologies have been used in diverse fields, such as: knowledge management, information integration, cooperative systems, information retrieval, e-commerce, semantic web, among others [6]. According to [7], ontologies are used in Knowledge Engineering, Artificial Intelligence and Computer Science. For these authors, ontologies are also used in applications related to natural language processing, intelligent integration information, integration of databases, bioinformatics, and education.

2.2   Enterprise Modelling

Building an architectural model of an enterprise is a discipline that organizes and structures components from business and IT, and their relationships that seek to increase organizational performance through better management of complexity.

A business process model is part of enterprise modelling and can be defined as the operational representation of activities, sequences and routes, aiming to reach goals [8]. For these authors, the business process can be modelled in a single segment perspective (orchestration) or in a multiple segment perspective (coreography). This approach enables enterprise modelling: while orchestration describes the organizational internal process, the coreography handles the external process integration, that is, those processes shared by different organizations.

According to [9], business process modelling is an important resource for an efficient management, since models constitute the basis for communication, redesign, implementation and processes control. These authors state that the efficiency of organizational processes can be increased depending on a consistent documentation of the process steps.

2.3   Ontologies for Enterprise Modelling

An organization, in the information age, is compounded by other organizations which share the job, all of them connected to a central organization which holds strategic brands and technologies [10]. Considering ontologies as structures capable to organize information from concepts and their relationships [11], it would be reasonable to think about using ontologies to support enterprise modelling.

3 Research Method

This research aims to analyze publications related to the use of ontologies to enterprise modelling, by executing a systematic literature review, also known as systematic mapping study. According to [12], a systematic review is a means of evaluating and interpreting available research relevant to a particular research question, topic area, or phenomenon of interest. This kind of study comprises three consecutive phases: planning, execution and results. In order to ensure the validity of our literature review, we based this research on guidelines proposed by [12].

3.1 Planning

The main purpose of this phase is to deliver a protocol which drives the research efforts. There are four stages associated with the planning phase: (1) Research Background, (2) Research Questions, (3) Research Strategy and (4) Data Extraction Strategy.

Research Background. In this stage we analyzed the existing literature and identified definitions [11, 4], classifications [7], languages [3, 6, 5], environments and methodologies [13, 14] related to ontologies, and definitions [10], classifications [15], segments [9] and business units [8] related to Enterprise Modelling.

Research Questions. In this stage we defined the research questions addressed by this study. The main research question addressed by this study is: RQ1. What are the use of ontologies to enterprise modelling? With respect to ontologies and enterprise classification, we considered a number of issues: RQ1.1. In which business segments were ontologies used for enterprise modelling? RQ1.2. In which organizational functions were ontologies used in enterprise modelling? RQ1.3. What are the preferred languages to build enterprise modelling ontologies? RQ1.4. What are the preferred tools to build enterprise modelling ontologies? RQ1.5. What are the preferred methodologies to build enterprise modelling ontologies?

Research Strategy. Following guidelines proposed by [12], in this stage, we defined the strategy used to search for primary studies, including search terms and resources to be searched. We conducted searches for primary studies in the following electronic databases: Association for Computing Machinery (ACM), Elsevier peer-reviewed full-text articles (ScienceDirect) and Institute of Electrical and Electronics Engineers (IEEE). The search string used in this procedure is composed of two parts: Enterprise Modelling AND Ontology. In order to improve this initial structure, we determined synonyms, related terms and alternative spellings. We incorporate these additional keywords using boolean operators "AND" and "OR", providing a conceptual and complete query which was used as a basis to construct the final search strings. We then used the advanced search tool to adapt the conceptual string to each electronic database syntax and searched for these terms in the title and in the abstract of the paper. The conceptual query had the following structure:

{[(ENTERPRISE AND ONTOLOGY) OR (ENTERPRISE ARCHITECTURE AND ONTOLOGY) OR (ENTERPRISE ENGINEERING AND ONTOLOGY) OR (ENTERPRISE MODELLING AND ONTOLOGY) OR (ENTERPRISE MODELING AND ONTOLOGY)] OR [(ENTERPRISE AND ONTOLO-GIES) OR (ENTERPRISE ARCHITECTURE AND ONTOLOGIES) OR (ENTERPRISE ENGINEERING AND ONTOLOGIES) OR (ENTERPRISE MODELLING AND ONTOLOGIES) OR (ENTERPRISE MODELING AND ONTOLOGIES)]}

Data Extraction Strategy. in this stage we defined the strategy to extract data from selected papers, including the selection criteria and the forms to extract the data from papers. We considered a paper as relevant based upon three selection criteria: (1) the paper presents the use of ontologies to enterprise modelling; (2) the paper answers the research question; (3) the paper is published in the last ten years. As exclusion criteria, we decided not to select those papers written in other languages than English neither those belonging to out of scope venues (e.g: BPM as "beat per minute" - health). In order to address the research questions and issues, we decided to group the selected papers in six main categories: Business Area, Organizational Function, Ontology Language, Ontology Methodology, Ontology Environment and Ontology Hierarchy

3.2   Execution

The main purpose of this phase is to perform activities which extract and synthesize data from papers. There are three stages associated with the execution phase: (1) Select Primary Studies, (2) Execute Data Extraction and (3) Synthesize Extracted Data.

Select Primary Studies. The automatic search resulted in 1079 papers potentially being relevant for our survey. IEEE delivered 82% of the results, followed by ScienceDirect (11%) and the ACM (7%). An initial manual filtering was then executed to refine the results, according to the defined data extraction strategy. We applied inclusion and exclusion criteria based on the abstract, introduction and conclusion of each paper. From the 1079 papers, 240 (about 22% of the total) were retained for further analysis. In order to retain only studies exploring the use of ontologies to enterprise modelling, we analysed the details of the 240 papers. After this detailed analysis, we obtained 105 primary studies (9.7% from total). The complete list of accepted papers is described in Appendix A.

Execute Data Extraction. In this stage, we aimed to collect the information needed to address the questions of this review. After the search and selection procedures, the primary studies were examined through the extraction forms, created in the START tool [16]. The papers were analysed considering the information required by each research question. The extraction forms were filled with text excerpts from the primary studies to answer each question.

Synthesize Extracted Data. In this stage, we collated and summarized the results of the included primary studies. The data extracted and synthesized in this stage is presented in the results section which can be read next.

4 Results

4.1 Overview of Studies

The final list of paper was limited to the past decade, with studies from 2000 to 2013. The investigation of use of ontologies to enterprise modelling was in continuous rise from 2008 to 2012, as presented in Figure 1.

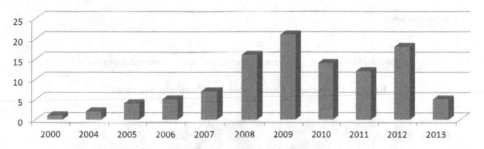

Fig. 1. Year Distribution

Most part of studies analyzed (61%) reported the use of ontologies intending to contribute to knowledge management. Second (21%), studies indicated use of ontologies to support the systems interoperability. Another portion of the studies (18%) used ontologies aiming to enable information retrieval.

The same distribution can be observed when different business segments are compared, except for services and virtual enterprises. According to studies, services enterprises used ontologies mainly for information retrieval while virtual enterprises used ontologies mainly aiming at systems interoperability, as presented in Figure 2.

Studies also indicated that knowledge management can be carried out with both formal and informal ontologies. However, studies indicated that companies prefer more formal ontologies when the concern is systems interoperability or information retrieval, as presented in Figure 3.

4.2 Evaluation of Research Questions

RQ1. What are the use of ontologies to enterprise modelling? This research question aimed to explore how ontologies could be used in enterprise modelling. As there are several types of enterprises, we consider relevant indicating the business areas (or segments) which are already using ontologies to improve their modelling. Looking inside the organizations, we consider interesting to point out

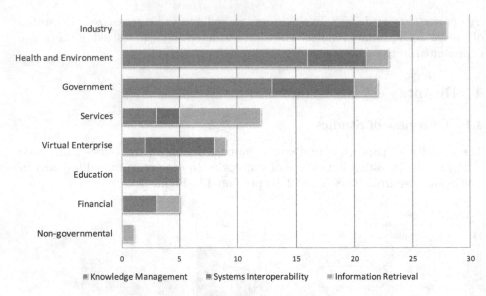

Fig. 2. Purpose of Ontologies by Business Segment

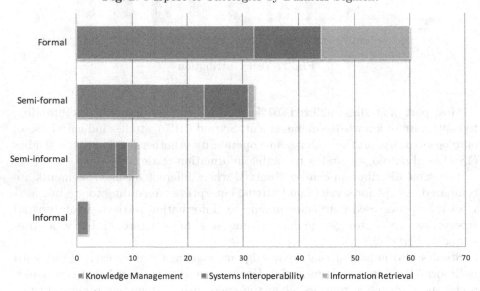

Fig. 3. Ontologies Purpose and Formalism

the organizational functions which use ontologies to support their modelling. On the other hand, we consider relevant indicating how the ontologies have been created, that is, the methodologies, languages and tools used for this purpose. Drawing on these conclusions, we may direct efforts of both ontology and enterprise modelling researchers towards a more conscious and coordinated use of conceptual knowledge.

RQ1.1. In which business segments were ontologies used to enterprise modelling? Most of the analysed studies is focused on Industry(27%), Health and Environment(22%) and Government(21%). Services(11%), virtual enterprise(8%), education(5%), financial(5%) and non-governmental organizations(1%) are the remaining business areas.

RQ1.2. In which organizational functions were ontologies used in enterprise modelling? Sixty-six percent of the analysed studies are related to Operations and to Research and Development (R&D) functions. A low percentage of analysed studies are related to Human Resources (HR) or Marketing.

RQ1.3. What are the preferred languages to build enterprise modelling ontologies? Most of analysed studies (48%) used the language OWL (Ontology Web Language) to represent ontologies. But it is important to mention that thirty-six percent of the studies did not mention the language used.

RQ1.4. What are the preferred tools to build enterprise modelling ontologies? 50 analysed studies (48%) did not mention the environment used to support ontology building. Most of the 55 remaining studies (69%) used the PROTEGE tool, which is a free and open source platform developed by Stanford Center for Biomedical Informatics Research.

RQ1.5. What are the preferred methodologies to build enterprise modelling ontologies? Less than 15% of the analysed studies mentioned the methodology used to build ontologies. There seems to exist an opportunity for researching the perception of engineers regarding the value of methodologies used to build ontologies. Figure 4 shows that most of the analyzed papers did not mention the methodology used to model organizations. Analyzing this figure, we can visualize that great part of analyzed papers used OWL with PROTEGE as a tool to enable enterprise modelling.

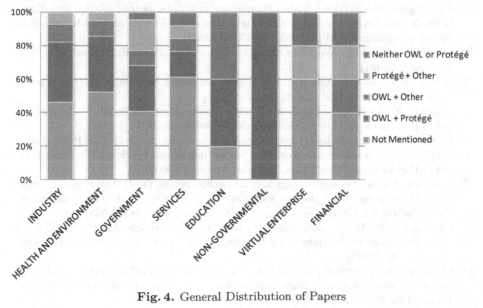

Fig. 4. General Distribution of Papers

5   Threats to Validity

In this Section, we address the limitations of this mapping study. First, only papers written in English were considered. Additionally, during data extraction, it was necessary to interpret the subjective information provided by studies. This happened because many studies did not present objective details regarding the topics investigated. Another potential threat to validity is the natural limitation of search engines, which may have caused the loss of relevant papers.

6   Conclusion

A state of the art survey on the applications of Ontologies in Enterprise Modelling has been given in this paper. The analysis presented shows that ontologies are used to assist in organizational modelling. Most of analyzed papers did not mention the methodology used to model enterprises. Thus, we believe that studies focusing on perception of relevance of methodology use for enterprise modelling is interesting in this context. OWL seems to be frequently combined with the PROTEGE environment. Therefore, studies to improve the link between language and environment must be performed. The results also highlight the need of further studies on enterprise modelling in organizations such as non-governmental, financial and educational. There seems to exist an opportunity for researching the use of ontologies to model HR and Marketing organizational functions.

References

[1] Papazoglou, M.: Service-oriented computing: concepts, characteristics and directions. In: Proceedings of the Fourth International Conference on Web Information Systems Engineering, WISE 2003, pp. 3–12 (2003)

[2] van Hee, K.M., et al.: Workflow management: models, methods, and systems. The MIT press (2004)

[3] Angele, J., Lausen, G.: Ontologies in F-logic. In: Staab, S., Studer, R. (eds.) Handbook on Ontologies, 2nd edn. Springer (2009)

[4] Guarino, N., Oberle, D., Staab, S.: What is an ontology? In: Staab, S., Studer, R. (eds.) Handbook on Ontologies, 2nd edn. Springer (2009)

[5] Guarino, N.: Formal ontology and information systems, pp. 3–15. IOS Press (1998)

[6] Baader, F., Horrocks, I., Sattler, U.: Description logics. In: Staab, S., Studer, R. (eds.) Handbook on Ontologies, 2nd edn. Springer (2009)

[7] Gomez-Perez, A., Fernandez-Lopez, M., Corcho-Garcia, O.: Ontological Engineering with examples from the areas of Knowledge Management, e-Commerce and the Semantic Web. Springer-Verlag New York, Inc., Secaucus (2003)

[8] Groner, G., Asadi, M., Mohabbati, B., Gasevic, D., Boskovic, M., Parreiras, F.S.: Validation of user intentions in process orchestration and choreography. Information Systems (2013)

[9] Overhage, S., Birkmeier, D., Schlauderer, S.: Quality marks, metrics, and measurement procedures for business process models. Business & Information Systems Engineering 4(5), 229–246 (2012)

[10] Fox, M.S., Gruninger, M.: Enterprise modeling. AI Magazine 19(3), 109 (1998)
[11] Guarino, N.: Formal ontology, conceptual analysis and knowledge representation. International Journal of Human-Computer Studies 43(5), 625–640 (1995)
[12] Kitchenham, B.A.: Procedures for undertaking systematic reviews. Technical report, Computer Science Department, Keele University (2004)
[13] Sure, Y., Staab, S., Studer, R.: Ontology engineering methodology. In: Staab, S., Studer, R. (eds.) Handbook on Ontologies, 2nd edn. Springer (2009)
[14] Mizoguchi, R., Kozaki, K.: Ontology engineering environments. In: Staab, S., Studer, R. (eds.) Handbook on Ontologies, 2nd edn. Springer (2009)
[15] Nonaka, I., et al.: The Knowledge-Creating Company: How Japanese Companies Create the Dynamics of Innovation: How Japanese Companies Create the Dynamics of Innovation. Oxford University Press (1995)
[16] Hernandes, E.M., Zamboni, A., Fabbri, S., Thommazo, A.D.: Using gqm and tam to evaluate start - a tool that supports systematic review. CLEI Electron. J. 15(1) (2012)

Appendix: List of Papers

#	Title	#	Title
1	SEMPATH Ontology: Modeling Multidisciplinary Treatment Schemes Utilizing Semantics	33	Research of Plant Domain Knowledge Model Based on Ontology
2	An Enterprise Ontology-Based Approach to Service Specification	34	Conceptual Modeling of Spatial Database Based on Geographic Ontology
3	A Negotiation Protocol to Support Agent Argumentation and Ontology Interoperability in MAS-Based Virtual Enterprises	35	An Application Model of SKOS-Based Ontology of Water Resources
4	An Ontology-Based Distributed Case-Based Reasoning for Virtual Enterprises	36	An Ontology-Based Framework to Model a GlobalPlatform Secure Element
5	Domain Modeling for Enterprise Information Systems - Formalizing and Extending Zachman Framework Using BWW Ontology	37	Emergency Response Organization Ontology Model and its Application
6	Ontology-centric, Service-Oriented Enterprise Campaign Management System	38	Towards an ontology of help to the modeling of accident scenarii: Application on railroad transport
7	WSMO-PA: Formal Specification of Public Administration Service Model on Semantic Web Service Ontology	39	Modeling and management of ontology-based credit evaluation meta-model
8	Advanced enterprise process modelling utilizing ontology semantics	40	Aligning medical ontologies by axiomatic models, corpus linguistic syntactic rules and context information
9	Enterprise Ontologies for Planning and Integration of Business: A Pragmatic Approach	41	An integrated spatial DSS design in Hydroinformatics based on ontology and domain modeling
10	Integrating Process and Ontology for Supply Chain Modelling	42	Research on emergency case ontology model based on ABC ontology
11	Ontology based knowledge modeling and reuse approach in product redesign	43	Ontology for Heart Rate Turbulence Domain From The Conceptual Model of SNOMED-CT
12	Ontology Model-Based Static Analysis on Java Programs	44	Ontology based data warehouse modelling - a methodology for managing petroleum field ecosystems
13	Ontologies and Rules for Rapid Enterprise Integration and Event Aggregation	45	Ontology and automatic code generation on modeling and simulation
14	A Multi-Dimensional Ontology Model for Product Lifecycle Knowledge Management	46	Open-Environmental Ontology Modeling
15	Research on manufacturing resource organization model based on ontology	47	A knowledge model for Mechatronic Product Development Based on ontology
16	Research and Application on OWL Ontology-Based Product Design Knowledge Model	48	Modeling the military role of computer generated force based on ontology
17	Using ontologies for representation of individual and enterprise competence models	49	Modeling and Building an Ontology for Neuropediatric Physiotherapy Domain
18	Ontology-based modeling of manufacturing information and its semantic retrieval	50	Project Approval Ontology Model and Its Application
19	The srBPA ontology: A formal representation of the Riva-based business process architecture	51	An ontology-based model for personalized financial planning product design
20	Ontology-based service-oriented architecture for emergency management in mass gatherings	52	Supporting Value Chain Integration through Ontology-Based Modeling
21	A Use Case Diagrams ontology that can be used as common reference for Software Engineering education	53	Ontology based data warehouse modeling and managing ecology of human body for disease and drug prescription model
22	An ontology-based environment for effective collaborative and concurrent process engineering	54	Wind turbines' condition monitoring: an ontology model
23	A Process-Driven and Ontology Based Software Product Line Variability Modeling Approach	55	Ontology-based technology model for the use in the early stage of product development

24	An ontology-based architecture for distributed digital museums	56	A Study on Marine Information Sharing and Integration Model Based on Ontology
25	Extensive overview of an ontology-based architecture for accessing multi-format information for disaster management	57	Ontology Modeling of Emergency Plan Systems
26	Virtual Laboratory ontology for engineering education	58	EDVO: A "One-Station" Emergency Response Service Model Based on Ontology and Virtual Organization
27	An Ontology-Based #x00026; Distributed Service Model for EG	59	Ontology meta-model for building a situational picture of catastrophic events
28	An Ontology-Based Architecture for Service Discovery	60	Modelling Energy and Transport Infrastructures as a Multi-Agent System using a Generic Ontology
29	The Smart Architect: Scalable Ontology-Based Modeling of Ancient Chinese Architectures	61	Ontology for Heart Rate Turbulence domain applying the conceptual model of SNOMED-CT
30	Using Ontologies to Aid the Teaching of Software Engineering	62	Research of Land E-Government Decision Support System Based on Ontology and Workflow Model
31	Semantic Information Integration for Electronic Patient Records Using Ontology and Web Services Model	63	SimPHO: An ontology for simulation modeling of population health
32	Home-based telemonitoring architecture to manage health information based on ontology solutions	64	POWER: programme for an ontology based working environment for modeling and use of regulations and legislation
65	An Approach of Domain Ontology Construction Based on Resource Model and Jena	88	Ontology Modeling for Goal Driven E-Government
66	An Ontology Based Architecture for eGovernment Environments	89	Enabling product traceability through data modeling and semantic web service ontologies
67	Ontology-Based Conceptual Domain Modeling for Educational Portal	90	Mapping the business model canvas to ArchiMate
68	OntoMobiLe: A Generic Ontology-Centric Service-Oriented Architecture for Mobile Learning	91	Enterprise ontology based splitting and contracting of organizations
69	Research on Architecture of Tacit Knowledge Transfer Based on Ontology	92	Enterprise ontology in enterprise engineering
70	Ontology-Based Modeling of Breast Cancer Follow-up Clinical Practice Guideline for Providing Clinical Decision Support	93	The pragmatics of event-driven business processes
71	A proposed architecture and ontology for a software system for managing patient #x2019;s health record	94	Enhancing Enterprise Resource Planning users?? understanding through ontology-based training
72	Reference Architecture for Medical Imaging Annotated in a GRID: Ontology-Based Services	95	Analysis of shipbuilding fabrication process with enterprise ontology
73	A model of intelligent distributed medical diagnosis and therapy system based on mobile agent and ontology	96	Design of product ontology architecture for collaborative enterprises
74	Service Management Model Based on Ontology	97	Knowledge sharing in virtual enterprises via an ontology-based access control approach
75	Designing a Conceptual Model for Herbal Research Domain Using Ontology Technique	98	Constructing an enterprise ontology for an automotive supplier
76	Knowledge Exploitation through Modeling, Navigation and Querying, an Ontology-Based Integrated Architecture	99	Business concepts ontology for an enterprise performance and competences monitoring
77	An architecture based SKOS ontology for scalable, efficient and fault tolerant grid resource discovery	100	The development of an ontology-based expert system for corporate financial rating
78	Geospatial semantic Web: architecture of ontologies	101	4 - An ontology for e-business models
79	Delineation and interpretation of gene networks towards their effect in cellular physiology- A reverse engineering approach for the identification of critical molecular players, through the use of ontologies	102	An ontology-based business intelligence application in a financial knowledge management system
80	Ontology-centered integration of project management, cost and resource modeling with analysis, simulation and visualization: a case study of space port operations	103	Considering environmental assessment in an ontological framework for enterprise sustainability
81	Shale-gas ontology, a robust data modeling methodology for integrating and connecting fractured reservoir petroleum ecosystems that affect production complexities	104	Rule-based ontological knowledge base for monitoring partners across supply networks
82	Re-use of an ontology for modelling urban energy systems	105	A Web-based Product Service System for aerospace maintenance, repair and overhaul services
83	Application of Emergency Case Ontology Model in Earthquake		
84	An Ontology-based Service Model for Smart Infrastructure Design		
85	Geo-ontology model based on description logic		
86	Hierarchical Ontology on Multi-scale Road Model for Cartographical Application		
87	Integration of product models by ontology development		

Preface to MoBiD 2014

Due to the enormous amount of data present and growing in the Web and other data sources such as sensors and social networks, there has been an increasing interest in incorporating this huge enormous of external and unstructured data, normally referred to "Big Data", into traditional applications. This necessity has made that traditional database systems and processing need to evolve and accommodate them to this new situation. We view that several key themes with the Big Data trend include (i) using a cloud for large-scale external and internal data; (ii) providing an easy-to-use but powerful services to access/manage/analyze the big data in the cloud; (iii) defining a problem-solving space and developing an architecture for a big data environment to conceptualize goals, tasks, and problem-solving methods to apply to domains; and (iv) managing big data and analyzing them to discover business values.

Therefore, this new era of cloud environment and Big Data requires conceptualization and methods to effectively manage big data and accomplish intended business goals. Thus, the objective of MoBiD'14 is to be an international forum for exchanging ideas on the latest and best proposals for modeling and managing big data in this new data-drive paradigm. Papers focusing on novel applications and using conceptual modeling approaches for any aspects of Big Data such as MapReduce, Hadoop and its ecosystems, Big Data Analytics, social networking, security and privacy, data science approaches, etc. are highly encouraged. The workshop will be a forum for researchers and practitioners who are interested in the different facets related to the use of the conceptual modeling approaches for the development of next generation applications based on Big Data.

The workshop has been announced in the main announcement venues in order to attract papers from 9 different countries distributed all over the world: France, Greece, India, Japan, Kenya, Korea, Spain, United Kingdom and USA. We have finally received 14 papers and the Program Committee have selected 6 papers, making an acceptance rate of 42%. We also have an invited keynote on Extracting Value from Big Data by Sudha Ram.

We would like to express our gratitude to the Program Committee members for their hard work in reviewing papers, the authors for submitting their papers, and the ER 2014 organizing committee for all their support.

July 2014

Il-Yeol Song
Juan Trujillo
David Gil
Carlos Blanco
Program Co-Chairs
MoBiD'14

Extracting Value from Big Data

Sudha Ram

Department of MIS
University of Arizona, Tucson
ram@eller.arizona.edu
www.insiteua.org

Abstract. The phenomenal growth of social media, mobile applications, sensor based technologies and the Internet of Things is generating a flood of "Big Data" and disrupting our world in many ways. This data is becoming strategically critical to enterprises of all sizes and types. Fueled by new technologies, companies are routinely generating upwards of 20 Petabytes of data each day – a petabye is one million gigabytes or approximately 6 billion digital photos or 20 million four-drawer filing cabinets filled with text.

In today's world, it is not enough for companies to track their sales, marketing, financial, and other internally generated data. They need to combine their internal data with external sources of data such as blogs and reviews about their products, Twitter and Facebook comments, as well as data from online discussion forums, to develop insights for improving performance and remaining competitive. The challenge here is to deal with a nonstop flood of data being generated at an increasing rate.

This talk will examine the paradigm shift caused by Big Data and focus on how to use "Data Science" to harness its power and create a smarter world. Much of the discussion on Big Data has centered around four "Vs" i.e. Volume, Velocity, Variety, and Veracity. This talk will delve deep into several other interesting and important characteristics to understand the nature of Big Data. These characteristics make it challenging to model and manage big data, yet, they provide the potential to unlock the value of Big Data. Using examples of research projects from the INSITE center (www.insiteua.org), we will examine how value can be extracted from Big Data by employing different analytical techniques. In particular, the focus will be on large scale network analysis and visualization techniques, to understand relationships among the various types of data and develop prediction models. Our examples will span a number of areas including, healthcare, online news propagation, and education. The talk will highlight promising directions for research using Big Data analytics.

A Semi-clustering Scheme for High Performance PageRank on Hadoop

Seungtae Hong[1], Jeonghoon Lee[2], Jaewoo Chang[1], and Dong Hoon Choi[2,*]

[1] Dept. of Computer Engineering, Chonbuk National University, Jeonju, South Korea
{dantehst,jwchang}@jbnu.ac.kr,
[2] Korea Institute of Science and Technology Information (KISTI), Daejeon, South Korea
{jhoon,choid}@kisti.re.kr

Abstract. As global Internet business has been evolving, large-scale graphs are becoming popular. PageRank computation on the large-scale graphs using Hadoop with default data partitioning method suffers from poor performance because Hadoop scatters even a set of directly connected vertices to arbitrary multiple nodes. In this paper we propose a semi-clustering scheme to address this problem and improve the performance of PageRank on Hadoop. Our scheme divides a graph into a set of semi-clusters, each of which consists of connected vertices, and assigns a semi-cluster to a single data partition in order to reduce the cost of data exchange between nodes during the computation of PageRank. The semi-clusters are merged and split before the PageRank computation, in order to evenly distribute a large-scale graph into a number of data partitions. Our semi-clustering scheme drastically improves the performance: total elapsed time including the cost of the semi-clustering computation reduced by up to 36%. Furthermore, the effectiveness of our scheme increases as the size of the graph increases.

Keywords: Large-scale graph analysis, semi-clustering, Hadoop, PageRank.

1   Introduction

PageRank [1,2] algorithm is commonly used for the link analysis of web graphs, hypertext clustering [3], social network analysis [4], among many others. In social network, for example, it is utilized based on the estimation of relative importance of people to other parties. The algorithm is also used to calculate the value of each vertex in a pathway network in bioinformatics [5].

There are a number of previous researches on PageRank computation of large-scale graph analysis on Hadoop [6, 7, 8, 9]. The performance of the PageRank relies on how the input data is partitioned and distributed on Hadoop cluster. The effectiveness of the data partitioning is solely dominated by the resulting data locality in each node of the cluster, and this would differ depending on the type of problem that the graph is used for. According to [10], partitioning data by domains is known to be effective for analyzing web graphs of global Internet service companies. However, the

---

* Corresponding author.

M. Indulska and S. Purao (Eds.): ER Workshops 2014, LNCS 8823, pp. 35–44, 2014.

domain-based partitioning is limited to specific applications such as large-scale graphs dealing with multi-languages, multi-nations, etc.

PageRank calculates each vertex's rank based on the ranks of neighboring vertices for a given graph. PageRank computation on Hadoop with default data partitioning method performs poorly because Hadoop scatters even a set of directly connected vertices to arbitrary multiple nodes. Hence, the cost of data exchange often considerably increases in different multiple nodes. An optimal data partitioning of a large-scale graph on Hadoop cluster would find all connected components of a graph and allocate each component to a node. However, the cost of finding the connected components is too expensive [11].

In this paper we propose a semi-clustering scheme to address the problem mentioned above, and a way to improve the performance of the PageRank on Hadoop. The semi-clustering scheme divides a graph into a set of groups (or semi-cluster), each of which consists of connected vertices, and assigns a semi-cluster to a single data partition in order to reduce the cost of data exchange between nodes during the computation of PageRank on Hadoop. Furthermore, semi-clusters are merged and split in order to evenly distribute a large-scale graph to nodes in Hadoop cluster. Through experiments, we show that the semi-clustering based partitioning improves the performance of PageRank computation. The total elapsed time including the time spent for semi-clustering has been drastically reduced by up to 36% as the graph size increases. Therefore, semi-clustering scheme is effective for the large-scale graph processing.

Our contributions are summarized as follows:

- We provide a new partitioning method based on semi-clustering in order to improve the performance of PageRank computation on Hadoop cluster. A graph is partitioned into a set of semi-clusters, each of which consists of reachable vertices from starting vertices. So, we can partition a graph with semi-clustering scheme at a low cost on Hadoop cluster that consists of cheap commodity servers. This also reduces the cost for exchanging data among nodes of Hadoop cluster.

- We reconstruct semi-clusters by merging/splitting semi-clusters before allocating semi-clusters to nodes of Hadoop cluster. This maintains the balance of the data distribution between nodes in the PageRank computation.

- We show that application of semi-clustering in PageRank algorithm improves the performance by up to 36%, compared with the PageRank computation without semi-clustering. Also, we show that better performance outweighs the additional cost of semi-clustering.

The rest of the paper is organized as follows. Section 2 explains the related work. Section 3 describes the details of our semi-clustering scheme. In section 4, we analyze the performance of the semi-clustering scheme using the reference data and the PageRank computation with our semi-clustering scheme. Finally, Section 5 concludes our paper with future directions.

2   Related Work

Large-scale graphs are commonly encountered in a number of industries and academic areas such as web service, social communication, and bioinformatics among others. These graphs are processed in parallel on multi-core processor based cluster computing systems using data-intensive parallel programming models such as Hadoop [12], Pregel [13], M3R [14], to name a few. These models are based on partitioned parallelism and split data in a set of partitions, each of which is allocated on a node of a cluster. Graph processing using the default data partitioning of Hadoop requires frequent access to neighboring vertices stored in other computing nodes, thus it suffers from low performance. Pregel-based on vertex-centric and bulk synchronous processing is very efficient for large-scale graph processing because it relies on in-memory processing and exchanges messages through IPC. GPS [15] and Giraph [16] are modeled from Pregel and published as open source codes. M3R, a memory based MapReduce runtime system, has been developed by utilizing a distributed memory model named APGAS (asynchronous partitioned global address space). To shuffle data, M3R uses the memory of each node, rather than the disks. M3R can execute Hadoop applications without any modification since it can use HDFS directly. However, these vertex-centric and in-memory programming models are not commonly used due to the cost of the RAM requirement for in-memory processing. Hadoop is still widely used for large-scale graph processing because of the simplicity of programming and low cost without RAM requirement.

Hadoop provides two default partitioning techniques for data parallelism; hash-based and range-based. The hash partitioning technique splits the graph data based on the fixed hash values. It is inefficient because it does not consider the connectivity of graph data. On the other hand, the range partitioning technique can maintain the connectivity of the graph data. However, it is limited to specific types of issues. Lin [10] partitioned input data based on the range partitioning technique which groups related vertices to a data partition according to the domain names. Although the scheme shows improved performance of PageRank of a large-scale graph from multiple domians, it is impossible to be applied to a large-scale web graph which comes from a single domain. Thus, we do not consider the partitioning technique proposed in Lin because we only deal with graph data sets from a single domain.

3   Semi-clustering Scheme for Improving the Performance of PageRank

Performance of PageRank computation on Hadoop heavily depends on how data is split into each node of Hadoop cluster. It would be efficient if all the vertices in a connected component are stored in a node, which is not always the case. The pattern of connections between vertices in a graph usually follows the power law described in [17], and it is often too large to assign a connected component of a large-scale graph to a single node. Therefore, it is inevitable that such a connected component needs to be split before being assigned to multiple different nodes. In this case, neighbors of a vertex are not assigned to the same node, and the cost of data exchange possibly gets expensive. The cost of finding connected components is extremely high, even if each connected component is small enough to be stored in one single node. Therefore, data partitioning scheme according to connected components is not effective for improving the performance of PageRank computation on Hadoop.

To solve these problems, we propose a semi-clustering scheme for improving the performance of PageRank on Hadoop. Outline of the scheme is as follows:

i) A group of reachable vertices from a vertex is assigned to a single data partition to reduce the cost of data exchange among nodes. To achieve this, we start traversal from a vertex (i.e. starting vertex) with the highest outdegree (i.e. the number of outgoing edges of a vertex) and create a semi-cluster that consists of groups of vertices reachable from the starting vertex, and then assign it to a single data partition. Multiple starting vertices may be selected on purpose.

ii) Semi-clusters are allowed to overlap vertices with each other to reduce the cost of access to the vertices stored in different nodes. Overlapped vertices are within ∂ hop distance from each starting vertex of two adjacent semi-clusters. ∂ is a determinant of how many hops would be traversed from starting vertices to create semi-clusters. It allows semi-clusters to be overlapped with each other. Overlapping vertices reduces the amount of excessive accesses to different nodes for PageRank computation.

iii) To evenly distribute the number of vertices as much as possible, we merge or split existing semi-clusters to reconstruct more elaborate semi-clusters that fit to each node of Hadoop cluster. A semi-cluster is split based on threshold Θ, which is calculated by the number of physical nodes and the number of overlapped vertices.

The semi-clustering scheme consists of 4 steps; sorting of vertices in a graph, creation of initial semi-cluster, reconstruction of initial semi-cluster, and allocation of reconstructed semi-clusters to partitions.

3.1   Sorting of Vertices in a Graph

In this step, each vertex is arranged in descending order based on its outdegree. To create a semi-cluster, an initial candidate set (of vertices) is generated first and then select starting points. To reduce the cost of generating the candidate set, vertices with outdegree value of 1 are filtered out. Because such vertices do not help create initial semi-clusters and are merged into a semi-cluster through the expansion of reconstruction step (described in section 3.4). The process goes as follows:

i) In Map phase, calculate outdegree for each vertex and output <outdegree, vertex ID> pairs for vertices with the outdegree greater than 1.

ii) In Shuffling phase, sort <outdegree, vertex ID> pairs by outdegree in descending order.

iii) In Reduce phase, output the sorted <outdegree, vertex ID> pairs to HDFS.

```
1:   Method Map(vertex_id V, adjacencyList [L₁,L₂, …])
2:     count <- 0
3:     for all Lᵢ ∈ [L₁,L₂, …] in V do count++
4:     if count > 1 then emit(count, V)
1:   Method Reducer(outdegree count, iterator_vertexid [V₁,V₂, …])
2:     for all Vᵢ ∈ [V₁,V₂, …] do emit(count, Vᵢ)
```

Algorithm. 1. Sorting of vertices of a graph

3.2   Creation of Initial Semi-clusters

In this step, we create initial semi-clusters by traversing a given graph from each vertex (i.e. starting vertex) in the candidate set. Multiple vertices can be selected as starting vertices by their outdegree sorted in descending order. The process goes as follows:

i) Select a candidate set from the sorted <outdegree, vertex ID> pairs for creating initial semi-clusters.

ii) From each of the vertices in the candidate set, find its neighbors within 1 hop distance and create initial semi-clusters. Since the candidate set is arranged based on outdegree, we start creating a new semi-cluster from a vertex with the largest number of outgoing edges (i.e. outdegree).

iii) Check if a new created semi-cluster is contained in another semi-cluster. If all the vertices in the new semi-cluster are contained in another semi-cluster, then the new one is neglected. Otherwise, set the new semi-cluster to an initial semi-cluster and the starting vertex to its centroid.

iv) Repeat ii) and iii) until all vertices in the candidate set are used up.

If we assume that the average outdegree of a vertex is o, then the maximum cardinality, n, of a candidate set for creating initial semi-clusters is calculated by the equation (1), where ∂ is a determinant of how many hops are to be traversed from starting vertices.

$$ n = \left\lceil \frac{\# \ of \ vertices}{o^\partial} \right\rceil \quad \cdots \quad (1) $$

```
1:  Method Map(vertex_id V, adjacencyList [L₁,L₂, …])
2:    for all Lᵢ ∈ [L₁,L₂, …] do
3:      centroid <- find_candidate_vertex(V)
4:      if centroid != null then    // if a selected vertex is a candidate
5:        cluster_id <- set_clusterId(centroid)
6:        emit(Lᵢ, cluster_id) // output the (adjacent vertex_id, cluster_id)
7:      else emit(V, [L₁,L₂, …])    // output the (key, value) pair as it is
1:  Method Reducer(vertex_id V, iterator_clusterInfo [C₁,C₂, …])
2:    adjacencyList <- 0
3:    for all Cᵢ ∈ [C₁,C₂, …] do
4:      cluster_id <- IsSuitable_clusterId(Cᵢ) // check relation of in-
clusion
5:      if cluster_id == null then adjacencyList <- Cᵢ
6:      else cluster = create_InitSemiCluster(Cᵢ, adjacencyList)
7:    emit(cluster_id, cluster)
```

Algorithm. 2. Creation of initial semi-clusters

Figure 1 shows the example of creation of initial semi-clusters. In this case, n is assumed to be 4, and ∂ is 1 for the step of creating initial semi-clusters. The initial semi-clusters, (semi-cluster$_1$, semi-cluster$_2$, semi-cluster$_3$, and semi-cluster$_4$) are created using the vertices within 1 hop distance from v_1, v_7, v_5, and v_{14}.

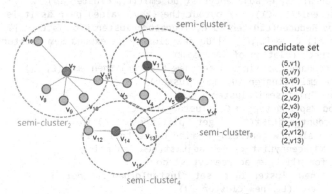

Fig. 1. Example of creation of initial semi-clusters (n = 4)

3.3 Reconstruction of Semi-clusters

Assigning initial semi-clusters to each node of Hadoop cluster still results in data exchange among different nodes. It often causes the skewed elapsed time for tasks. To moderate this, initial semi-clusters are expanded with ∂-1 hop in the similar way as creating initial semi-clusters. Then semi-clusters are reconstructed by merging and splitting operations according to the size of semi-clusters. This helps increase the cohesion within a semi-cluster and reduce the coupling between semi-clusters. The process goes as follows:

i) Expand the initial semi-clusters to the vertices within ∂-1 hop distance from its centroid. Expansion needs to be done in the identical order that the previous step was done. At this point we can save cost by reusing the result of initial semi-clusters.

ii) If all vertices in an expanded semi-cluster are also present in another expanded semi-cluster, we merge the two semi-clusters. If there are any vertices that are not included in any of the expanded semi-clusters, we add that particular vertex to the closest adjacent semi-clusters.

iii) If the number of vertices in an expanded semi-cluster is greater than the split threshold Θ, we divide the semi-cluster. If we assume the average indegree of a vertex is i, then Θ is calculated by equation (2) in the worst case, where o is the average outdegree of a vertex in the semi-cluster.

$$\Theta = \frac{\# \text{ of vertices} \times (1+(i-1) \times o^{\partial})}{\# \text{ } of \text{ } physical\_nodes} \qquad \ldots (2)$$

Split of a semi-cluster is similar to the initial semi-cluster creation process. Pick a starting vertex of the highest outdegree and traverse vertices within ∂ hop distance from it. At this time, the centroid of this expanded semi-cluster cannot be a starting point. Create a semi-cluster consisting of the starting vertex and its ∂ hop distance neighbors. Newly created semi-cluster contained in existing semi-cluster is neglected. Otherwise, it becomes a reconstructed semi-cluster whose centroid is the starting vertex.

In order to evenly assign reconstructed semi-clusters to Hadoop cluster nodes, pair-wise inter-connectivity among semi-clusters needs to be considered while the

```
// Job for Expand the initial semi-clusters and Merge expanded semi-clusters
1: Method Map(cluster_id C, cluster_info CI)
2:    vertex_id <- get_vertexID(CI), adjacencyList <- get_adjList(CI)
3:    if is_BorderPoint(vertex_id) then   // find vertex_id to expand
4:      for all Lᵢ ∈ adjacencyList do emit(Lᵢ, cluster_id)
5:    else emit(C, CI)    // output the (key, value) pair as it is
1: Method Reducer(cluster_id C, iterator_clusterInfo [C₁,C₂, …])
2:    for all Cᵢ ∈ [C₁,C₂, …] do new_cluster <- expand_SemiCluster(C, Cᵢ)
      // check relation of inclusion
3:    if compare_ExistingCluster(new_cluster) then emit(C, Cᵢ)
4:    else emit(cluster_id, new_cluster)
// Job for Split semi-clusters
1: Method Map(cluster_id C, cluster_info CI)
2:    if count_adjList(CI) > get_splitThreshold() then
3:      for all new_centroidᵢ ∈ find_newCentroid(CI)
4:        adjacencyList <- get_adjList(new_centroidᵢ)
5:        for all Lᵢ ∈ adjacencyList do
6:          new_cluster_id <- set_clusterId(new_centroidᵢ)
7:          emit(Lᵢ, new_cluster_id)
8:    else emit(C, CI)   // output the current cluster as it is
1: Method Reducer(cluster_id C, iterator_clusterInfo [C₁,C₂, …])
2:    for all Cᵢ ∈ [C₁,C₂, …] do
3:      splitted_cluster = create_splittedSemiCluster(Cᵢ, adjacencyList)
4:    emit(cluster_id, splitted_cluster)
```

Algorithm. 3. Reconstruction of Semi-Cluster

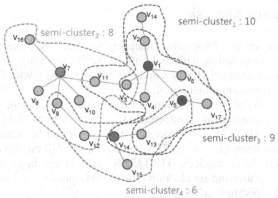

Fig. 2. Example of expand of semi-cluster ($\partial = 2$)

reconstruction of semi-cluster step is in progress. The inter-connectivity is computed by the number of directly connected vertices between two semi-clusters. Two semi-clusters that have numerous directly connected vertices can be assigned to one partition. Thus, data exchange between nodes can be reduced.

Figure 2 shows the example of Algorithm 3 where ∂ is 2. The semi-cluster$_1$ expands by 1 hop from the existing semi-clusters, so that v_5, v_{13}, and v_{14} are added to the semi-cluster. Each semi-cluster expands to neighbor vertices by 1 hop and they are reconstructed to semi-clusters with the cardinality of 10, 8, 9, and 6.

3.4   Allocation of Semi-clusters

Based on pair-wise inter-connectivity among semi-clusters, semi-clusters are assigned to each partition via round-robin method. Inter-connectivity depends on the vertices directly connected to each other between two adjacent semi-clusters. This information is calculated in the previous step of reconstruction of semi-cluster. Thus, no additional cost is required. This helps evenly distribute the semi-clusters to nodes and improve the utilization of Hadoop computing resources. The process goes as follows:

i) Starting from two reconstructed semi-clusters with the highest inter-connectivity, union vertices in the semi-cluster pairs. By doing this, we do not allow vertices to be duplicated more than once in a single partition, while allowing vertices to be duplicated in semi-clusters. Thus, we can achieve the high data locality with reduced duplicates.

ii) Union of vertices in reconstructed semi-clusters is assigned to each partition via round-robin fashion.

```
1:  Method Map(cluster_id C, cluster_info CI)
2:     adj_Clusterid <- get_nearestCluster(CI)
3:     union_clusterInfo <- union_cluster(C, adj_Clusterid)
4:     emit(C, union_clusterInfo)
1:  Method Reducer(cluster_id C, iterator_clusterInfo [C₁,C₂, …])
2:     for all Cᵢ ∈ [C₁,C₂, …] do emit(C, Cᵢ)
// for Partitioner class
1:  Method getPartition(cluster_id C, cluster_info CI)
2:     num_partition <- getPartitioner(C)
3:     return num_partition
```

Algorithm. 4. Allocation of Semi-Clusters

4   Performance Analysis

To prove the effectiveness of the semi-clustering scheme, we measure the execution time of PageRank computation with and without semi-clustering. In the experiment, PageRank algorithm is iterated 10 times and ∂ is set to 3. Joycrawler 0.2 [18] was used as a PageRank algorithm implementation.

We used four graph data sets in [19] to measure the execution time of PageRank and semi-clustering: web graph from Stanford.edu (281,903 vertices, 2,312,497 edges) and web graph from Google (875,713 vertices, 5,105,039 edges) for small data sets, Live Journal online social network (4,847,571 vertices, 68,993,773 edges) and Orkut online social network (3,072,441 vertices, 117,185,083 edges) for large datasets. We ran PageRank and semi-clustering on Hadoop cluster that consists of 7 physical machines (master: 1, slave: 6) specified in Table 1.

Table 1. Specification of physical machine

CPU	AMD Opteron Processor 4180	Main Memory	32GB
HDD	100GB	OS	Ubuntu 12.04

Figure 3 shows the performance results of PageRank algorithm for small datasets. In the case of web graph from Google, the execution time of PageRank after semi-clustering was reduced by 63.1%. However, when adding the execution time of semi-clustering to that of PageRank, the total execution time exceeds that of PageRank without semi-clustering.

Figure 4 shows the performance results of PageRank algorithm for large datasets. In the case of Live Journal online social network, the total execution time of PageRank with semi-clustering is reduced by 33.4% compared with that of PageRank without semi-clustering. In the case of Orkut online social network, the total execution time is reduced by 36.2%.

Figure 5 shows the comparison of execution time of semi-clustering and reduced execution time of PageRank after semi-clustering. The result indicates that PageRank computation with semi-clustering improves the performance as the number of vertices and edges increases, which confirms that the proposed scheme is effective for large-scale graph processing.

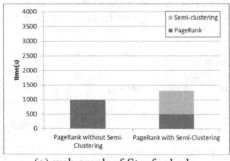
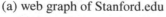

(a) web graph of Stanford.edu

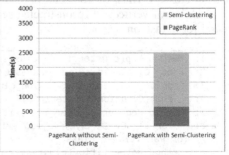

(b) web graph from Google

Fig. 3. PageRank execution time (small datasets)

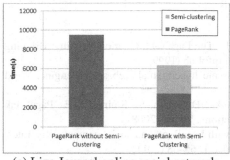
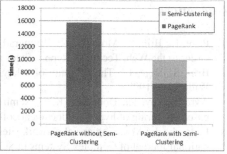

(a) Live Journal online social network   (b) Orkut online social network

Fig. 4. PageRank execution time (large datasets)

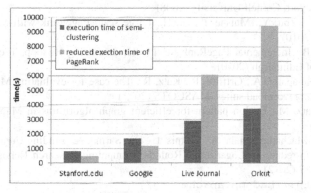

Fig. 5. Comparison of execution time

5   Conclusion and Future Work

In this paper, we proposed a semi-clustering scheme for improving the performance of PageRank on Hadoop. For each vertex which contains a lot of outgoing edges, the semi-clustering creates a group (or semi-cluster) of reachable vertices that starts traversing from it. By allocating a semi-cluster into the same data partition, the proposed scheme reduces the cost of shuffling and performs efficient computation in graph analysis on the Hadoop. Experimental results show that PageRank computation with the semi-clustering improves the performance by up to over 36% as the number of vertices and edges increases. Therefore, our scheme can be largely effective for large-scale graph analysis. As a future work, we plan to refine the semi-clustering algorithm by reducing overlap vertices among partitions and evaluate the clustering quality by using similarity measures such as Jaccard index and silhouette coefficient.

Acknowledgement. This work was supported by the KISTI R&D Program ["Building Scientific Big Data Platform"] and ETRI R&D Program [14ZS1400, "Development of Big Data Platform for Dual Mode Batch-Query Analytics"] funded by the Government of Korea.

References

1. Page, L., Brin, S., Motwani, R., Winograd, T.: The PageRank Citation Ranking: Bringing Order to the Web, Technical Report, Stanford InfoLab (1999)
2. Brin, S., Page, L.: The anatomy of a large-scale hypertextual web search engine. Word Wide Web (1998)
3. Avrachenkov, K., Dobrynin, K.V., Nemirovsky, D., Pham, S., Smirnova, E.: PageRank based clustering of hypertext document collections. SIGIR (2008)
4. Pedroche, F.: Modeling social network sites with PageRank and social competences. International Journal of Complex Systems in Science 1, 65–68 (2011)
5. Ivn, G., Grolmusz, V.: When the web meets the cell: Using personalized PageRank for analyzing protein interaction networks. Bioinformatics Advance Access (2010)
6. Busa, N., Jagtap, U., Prateek, U., Arms, W.: PageRank calculation using MapReduce. Technical Report, Cornell University (2008)
7. Chang, S.-H., Zhu, Y., Malshe, P., Li, H.: Large scale PageRank with MapReduce. In: CloudCom (2010)
8. Abdullah, I.B.: Incremental PageRank for Twitter data using Hadoop. Technical Report, University of Edinburgh (2010)
9. Chen, Y., Ganapathi, A., Griffith, R., Katz, R.: The case for evaluating MapReduce performance using workload suites, MASCOTS (2011)
10. Lin, J., Schatz, M.: Design pattern for efficient graph algorithms in MapReduce, MLG 2010 (2010)
11. Rastogi, V., Machanavajjhala, A., Chitnis, L., Das Sarma, A.: Finding Connected Components on Map-reduce in Logarithmic Rounds. Computing Research Repository (CoRR), abs/1203.5387 (2012)
12. Hadoop, http://hadoop.apache.org/
13. Malewicz, G., Austern, M., Bik, A., Dehnert, J., Horn, I.: Pregel: A system for large-scale graph processing, SIGMOD (2010)
14. Shinnar, A., Cunningham, D., Herta, B., Saraswat, V.: M3R: Increased performance for in-memory Hadoop jobs, VLDB (2012)
15. Salihoglu, S., Widom, J.: GPS: A graph processing system, SSDBM (2013)
16. Giraph, http://incubator.apache.org/giraph/
17. Chakrabarti, D., Faloutsos, C.: Graph mining: Laws, generators, and algorithms. ACM Computing Survey 38 (March 2006)
18. Joycrawler, http://code.google.com/p/joycrawler/
19. Stanford Large Network Dataset Collection, http://snap.stanford.edu/data/

Energy Consumption Prediction by Using an Integrated Multidimensional Modeling Approach and Data Mining Techniques with Big Data

Jesús Peral[1], Antonio Ferrández[1], Roberto Tardío[2], Alejandro Maté[2], and Elisa de Gregorio[2]

[1] Language Processing and Information Systems Research Group, Department of Software and Computing Systems, University of Alicante, Spain
[2] Lucentia Research Group, Department of Software and Computing Systems, University of Alicante, Spain
{jperal,antonio,rtardio,amate,edg12}@dlsi.ua.es

Abstract. During the past decades the resources have been used of an irresponsible and negligent manner. This has led to an increasing necessity of adopting more intelligent ways to manage the existing resources, specially the ones related to energy. In this regard, one of the main aims of this paper is to explore the opportunities of using ICT (Information and Communication Technologies) as an enabling technology to reduce energy use in cities. This paper presents a study in which we propose a multidimensional hybrid architecture that makes use of current energy data and external information to improve knowledge acquisition and allow managers to make better decisions. Our main goal is to make predictions about energy consumption based on energy data mining and supported by external knowledge. This external knowledge is represented by a torrent of information that, in many cases, is hidden across heterogeneous and unstructured data sources, which is recuperated by an Information Extraction system. This paper is complemented with a real case study that shows promising partial results.

Keywords: Big Data, Data Mining, Information Extraction, Energy.

1 Introduction

During the past decades the resources have been used of an irresponsible and negligent manner. Therefore guidelines of the European Union [4] [2] [14] and other international organizations [1] are promoting initiatives in order to act responsibly and efficiently to ensure the sustainability of cities.

Several initiatives have highlighted how Information and Communication Technologies (ICT) can be used to achieve cities' climate targets by lowering energy use and greenhouse gas (GHG) emissions from other sectors. Some of these initiatives include proposals such as dematerialisation and demobilisation, as well as comprehensive concepts for smart logistics and smart cities [8]. Hilty [6], describes

M. Indulska and S. Purao (Eds.): ER Workshops 2014, LNCS 8823, pp. 45–54, 2014.

how ICT can be seen as an enabling technology for improving or substituting processes in other sectors. GeSI published a report that focused on the potential for reducing GHG emissions in six different sectors: power, transportation, agriculture, building, manufacturing and consumer and services. According to the report 2020 [15] of the Climate Group and McKinsey, ICT is a key player in the battle against climate change and offers the possibility of 7.8 Gt reduction of CO_2 emission in 2020. In addition, the European Commission is stressing the importance of ICT for energy reduction and sustainability and invests in research in this area [13]. The plans have amongst others resulted in a number of research programmes combining ICT with Energy.

According to the Climate Group, a smart city is a city that uses data, information and communication technologies strategically to provide efficient services to citizens, monitors policy outcomes, manages and optimises existing infrastructure, employs cross-sector collaboration and enables new business models [15]. One of the main aims of this paper is to explore the opportunities of using ICT as an enabling technology to predict energy consumption in cities.

This paper presents a study in which we propose a multidimensional hybrid architecture that makes use of current energy data and external information to improve knowledge acquisition in order to make better decisions by managers. The aim of this paper is to make predictions about energy consumption based on energy data mining and supported by external knowledge. This external knowledge is represented by a stream of information that, in many cases, is hidden across heterogeneous and unstructured data sources, which is recovered by an Information Extraction system.

The remainder of this paper is structured as follows. In the next section, the related work is reviewed. Thereafter, our proposal of an architecture of an integrated model capable to use data mining in combination with external data is presented. We lead the explanation of this architecture in the next section with a case scenario. Finally, we include a discussion of the advantages of the model and the difficulties related to its implementation as well as the further directions of this research.

2   Related Work

In this section we explore ICT solutions for smart sustainable cities. Although, very often there is no an explicit connection between smart and sustainable cities, it is obvious that ICT plays an essential role for supporting the transition to more sustainable cities, not only regarding the management of urban systems but also offering more support for sustainable urban lifestyles. Mitchell [8] has defined five main opportunities for how ICT can contribute to the reduction of energy use in cities. Four of these have direct effects and one has indirect effects on the reduction of energy use. For this purpose he makes use of opportunities. The first one is labelled as dematerialisation. Here, physical products or services are converted to digital ones (we can imagine how the CDs are now streamed music and the bank offices are online banking services mainly). According to

Hilty [6] software represents the immaterial resources and the services provided represent the value that could become the pattern for a discontinued economy. The second opportunity is demobilisation, where everything that has been digitalised can be transported via the telecoms network instead of being physically transported. We are now aware how transport and travel are totally or partially replaced by telecommunications. The third opportunity is mass customisation where less resource use is accomplished through intelligent adaptation, personalisation and demand management. The fourth opportunity, intelligent operation, involves more resource-efficient operations of, for instance, water, energy and transport systems. The fifth and indirect opportunity is soft transformation where the existing physical infrastructure is transformed because of new opportunities presented by the information paradigm. These principles can be applied to product design, architecture, urban design and planning at regional, national and global levels [8]. The Smarter2020 report identifies ICT solutions by combining the abatement potential of ICT (called change levers) with economic end-use sectors. Somewhat similar to the opportunities put forward by Mitchell, the change levers are 1) digitalisation and de-materialisation, 2) data collection and communication, 3) systems integration and 4) process, activity and functional optimisation.

With the aim of mapping out ICT solutions which have the potential to offer beneficial environmental effects, [6] used a combination of economic sectors and environmental indicators to compile a list of ICT solutions for sustainable development: e-business, virtual mobility (teleworking, teleshopping, virtual meetings), virtual goods (services partially replacing material goods), ICT inwaste management, intelligent transportation systems, ICT in energy supply, ICT in facilities management and ICT in production process management. In addition to this, The Climate Group [15] proposes a comprehensive list of possible ICT solutions that can be implemented, as well as setting out metrics in order to understand which solutions could be implemented to reach a specific city's goals.

3   Architecture

The goals of our proposed system are i) mining techniques applied on the energy consumption information stored in a local Data Warehouse (DW), to make predictions about consumption; ii) to enrich that information with other unstructured context-sensitive Big Data information to increase the accuracy of such predictions; iii) the integration of the extracted information by using specialized ontologies. To support the above processes, we propose the architecture shown in Figure 1, which is based on our previous approach [7].

Initially, the user can apply Data Mining (DM) techniques (such as decision trees, artificial neural networks, support vector machines or others) on consumption data stored in a local DW for making predictions. However, in order to improve predictions, our system allows the user to query for other data sources, local or external, in order to obtain new information on the context. Then, the new data is integrated with consumption information to enrich our DW and

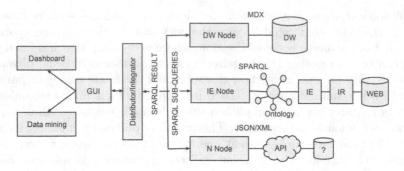

Fig. 1. Overview of the proposed architecture to access/integrate structured/ unstructured and internal/external data

carry out the process again to generate better predictions. Such queries are done through the user interface module (GUI, Graphical User Interface), which allows the user to introduce the search criteria in a parameterized and controlled way. For example, the user can select consumer information, for 2013, with information on natural disasters, political changes or financial crisis to enrich predictions.

In addition, our architecture is also based on the one presented in our previous paper [10], where i) we have added the Information Extraction Node (IE Node) . Moreover, the user's information need is previously known in order to develop the IE Node, which will extract structured-information from unstructured Big Data (e.g. the Web); ii) internal and external data have been integrated; iii) the new obtained structured-information will enrich the DM application (explained in detail in Section 4) in order to reach the final solution (to improve the prediction calculation process). It is important to mention that other specialized source nodes, such as the QA node, can be incorporated to the system (in the figure is presented as N Node indicating that there may be N nodes). These nodes contain the original internal information and the external information used to enrich the previous one.

This architecture distinguishes two phases: (i) the system setup; and (ii) the running phase (for further details, consult [10]). The first phase prepares the source nodes, where the required information will be searched, by creating the corresponding ontologies just the first time that the source node is connected in our framework. Whereas the second phase is run in real-time, when the user poses his/her information need through the GUI element. It passes the user's requirement to the Distributor/Integrator element, which selects the sources to be searched (e.g. it runs the Machine Learning -ML- process on the DW Node, and in parallel, it runs the IE Node in order to extract additional information that can enrich the DW Node results). Then, the Distributor/Integrator coordinates the running of each specialized node, gathering the output of these nodes in order to send the fused information to the GUI element. Finally, the GUI is responsible for displaying the results as a dashboard that integrates both IE and DW results.

In our architecture, we propose the use of SPARQL [11] language for the integration of different sources. Furthermore, our architecture is based on the implementation of Map Reduce paradigm [5] and the use of a universal multidimensional model. In [7] we proposed a metamodel for creating multidimensional data model that supports the definition of events, and dimension attributes, complete dimensions for both internal and external elements, in order to improve the flexibility and scalability allowing the addition of new sources data.

In Figure 2 we can see the universal multidimensional model created for our case study. In this figure it is possible to distinguish between local and external elements. The local elements are facts, dimensions and attributes of the dimensions present on DW node. The energy consumption (fact without asterisk) is analyzed in terms of the dimensions Producer, Consumer, Power Source and Time. As for external elements, they are present in the local schema from external sources such as IE node. Thus, the external facts Natural Disaster, Political Changes and Financial Crisis among others are defined in order to enrich the original DW information of consumption.

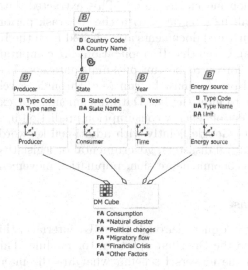

Fig. 2. Multidimensional model built to support the integration of the DW data with other sources

3.1   Setup Phase

In this phase, the specialized source nodes are prepared just the first time that they are connected to our framework, in order to integrate them in the global system.

(1) **The DW Node.** The DW ontology [12] is created, which will allow us to analyze an integrated view of data. The ontology relates the tables and attributes considered as the internal data and it is used for setting the binding points or connections between the stored internal data and the obtained

external data in order to perform the integration between both data. This ontology can be enriched (to include terms and concepts not considered in the internal repository of information) with well-known ontologies as the ontology for Socio-Technical Systems (STS) or the ontology for the ICT domain related to energy consumption proposed in [3].

(2) **The Information Extraction (IE) Node.** IE is the task of automatically extracting specific structured information from unstructured and/or semi-structured machine-readable documents. Each IE application is specifically designed for each specific extraction process, which fills the slots of a set of predefined templates that determines the information that is searched in the collection of documents. However, part of the template can be dynamically generated, for example, when the IE template is defined to extract "natural disasters", but it can be dynamically refined in order to require "natural disasters in 2012" or "in Detroit". In our case scenario, the IE Node will scan unstructured documents in order to extract previously defined data that can enrich the consumption prediction process (e.g. natural disasters, governmental or legislative decisions, wars, economic crisis, recession, population movements, etc.). This extracted data will populate a database that will be integrated with the ML task performed on the DW Node. The unstructured documents are selected from the IE Node (e.g. from specialized Webs). Given that IE applications are computationally costly, IE applications are forced to be run on small datasets. Therefore, an Information Retrieval process must be run (e.g. through search engines such as Google) in order to filter the Big Data documents. For example, the information requirement of "energy consumption prediction in Alabama State in 2012", is posed to Google, jointly with additional keywords selected by the IE Node (e.g. natural disasters, governmental or legislative decisions, wars, economic crisis, economic depression, population movements).

3.2   Running Phase

When the user makes a query through the GUI interface, this is generated in SPARQL and sent to the Distributor/Integrator module. This module verifies in conjunction with the universal schema what are the internal and external elements and with those it generates the corresponding queries for each module. Queries are distributed in SPARQL language towards each of the nodes. The node itself, if necessary, is responsible for translating the query into the local repository language. For example, in the case of DW Node query is translated to MDX language (as the work presented in [9]), however, in the case of IE Node this is not necessary since the ontology supports SPARQL queries directly. Then queries are run on each source and the results are returned to each module. Since integration is based on the intersection of RDF triples [7], each module is responsible for translating the results into this format if necessary. After that the Distributor/Integrator module performs the intersection of the RDF triples. Finally, the ranks generated using outcome data are returned to the DM application, where the process is relaunched to generate new and improved predictions.

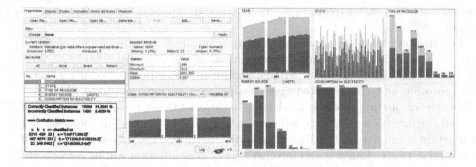

Fig. 3. Data mining procedure with the structured data

4   Case Scenario

After introducing the system architecture, we illustrate the application of our framework to the scenario in which the objective is to carry out consumption prediction by using the input data downloaded from EIA (Energy Information Administration) website (http://www.eia.gov/). These data will be used to find out what will be the consumption of energy in the next year in a particular state. The model shown in Figure 2 captures the structure of the initial information to be analyzed.

The experiments of Figure 3 makes reference to the DM node (Figure 1) in its first phase (i.e. only taking into account the internal data). In order to predict the "consumption for electricity" variable, we start with a preprocessing step to discretize that numerical variable. This is necessary to work with DM algorithms for prediction. In our case, we have experimented with several numbers of discretizations, in particular 3, 5 and 10 ranges or bins. The experience is obviously the more we discretizate the more imprecise is the accuracy, (i.e. there are more errors in the classified instances because there are more output/classes and it is easy to misclassify them). We also have made several test with different DM algorithms, such as decision trees, artificial neural networks, support vector machines among others. Figure 3 shows the results with 3 ranges (consumption levels: low, medium and high) for the output and with a decision tree as one of the techniques more precise in this context. On the right site the correlation among the output (energy consumption) and the rest of the variables (Year, State, Type of Producer, Energy Source) is shown. On the left side of the figure the load of the data is presented and the confusion matrix with the accuracy of the DM is represented.

Once the basic experiments have been done, the main challenge is to improve the accuracy of the data mining node by enriching it with the new variables obtained from the DW and IE node (right side of Figure 1 that complement the initial data mining experiments shown in Figure 3).

The idea of this dynamic improved model can be shown in the following small example. We start defining a set of keywords for searching: war, global/world stock market/exchange (Stock Exchange), Wall Street, bankrupt (bankruptcy), financial crisis, recession, political decisions (legislation, payment suspension, etc..), Natural disaster (tropical storm, hurricane, typhoon, etc..), oil/petroleum price.

Looking at the energy consumption data in the U.S. from 1990 to 2012 it can be observed 3 turns in total consumption of the country: 1990-1992, 2000-2001 and 2007-2009. In these periods, significant deviation between the actual consumption and the expected energy consumption have occurred. The main objective of our approach is to detect "a priori" these possible variations in actual consumption using external data sources and to modify the forecasts, it is important to emphasize the dynamic nature (like in real life) of our approach: the external data are changing and forecast energy consumption will be recalculated in short and/or long terms as they become different events happening.

To see how the external data affect the predictions of energy consumption, we have focused on the example of the global economic crisis that began in August 2007. Other factors (such as a natural disaster, political decisions, etc..) were omitted in order to simplify the example.

In the 2007 crisis, we can distinguish several stages in the process, but we will focus on the first two phases [1]:

"Phase one on 9 August 2007 began with the seizure in the banking system precipitated by BNP Paribas announcing that it was ceasing activity in three hedge funds that specialised in U.S. mortgage debt. ... It took a year for the financial crisis to come to a head but it did so on 15 September 2008 when the US government allowed the investment bank Lehman Brothers to go bankrupt. ..."

Our approach performs an update of the energy consumption prediction in the U.S. at the request of the user. Let suppose the user recalculates monthly energy consumption prediction. If we are in 2008, and we focused on economic issues (as explained above), the user will recover documents with the related keywords: "financial crisis", "recession" and "bankrupt". At the end of September 2008 the user will recover documents in which it can be detected many keywords associated with a major financial crisis that they will mark a period of a big economic recession. Words like: "Banking Crisis", "bankruptcy", "sub-prime crisis", "collapse", "financial shocks" will be found in the documents. From these retrieved documents the Databases would be filled with the Facts to analyse (Disaster, Crisis, Political, etc...). All this new information will be incorporated into the model to recalculate the energy consumption prediction and it will increase its accuracy being closer to real consumption.

In this scenario, external data indicate that there will be a recession in the coming years that will cause a reduction in energy consumption. This was confirmed with the real data: in 2008 there was a decrease in energy consumption in the U.S. of 1.07% (compared to 2007) and in 2009 a decrease of 1.29% (compared to 2008).

Figure 4 represents this information obtained from the IE node (on the right side) integrated with the original energy consumption data from DW Node (on

---

[1] Guardian http://www.theguardian.com/business/2011/aug/07/ global-financial-crisis-key-stages, "Global financial crisis: five key stages 2007-2011"

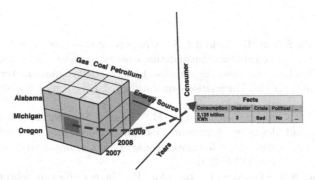

Fig. 4. Information extraction in order to provide data mining process with valuable information

the left side). The goal here is to enrich the original data mining model with a novel approach that represent an approximation of a dynamic data mining model. It collects all the information required in the cube. In addition, the nature of our architecture proposal makes very flexible to change the cube by adding new measures in its dimensions.

5   Discussion

In this paper we have presented an approach to allow data mining predictions with heterogeneous Big Data structures in an integrated way. In the original model the objective is to carry out consumption prediction by using the input data of EIA. Since this part of the work does not present a big novelty our main goal is to improve the accuracy of the original data mining model by enriching it with the new variables obtained from the IE node.

We represent a multidimensional cube where we can appreciate the information obtained from the IE node integrated with the original energy consumption data from DW Node. The objective of this cube is to enrich the original data mining model with a novel approach that represent an approximation of a dynamic data mining model.

The main future work is to carry out an efficient implementation of the model and evaluate it. Some of the difficulties are related with the own data nature as they represent very heterogeneous information.

Acknowledgments. This work has been funded by the Spanish Ministry of Economy and Competitiveness under the project Grant GEODAS-BI (TIN2012-37493-C03-03), by the Generalitat Valenciana under the project Prometeo (PROMETEOII/2014/001) and the University of Alicante, within the program of support for official master studies and research initiation (BOUA of 30/07/2013).

References

[1] Abdelaziz, E., Saidur, R., Mekhilef, S.: A review on energy saving strategies in industrial sector. Renewable and Sustainable Energy Reviews 15(1), 150–168 (2011)

[2] Benzi, F., Anglani, N., Bassi, E., Frosini, L.: Electricity smart meters interfacing the households. IEEE Transactions on Industrial Electronics 58(10), 4487–4494 (2011)

[3] Daouadji, A., Nguyen, K.-K., Lemay, M., Cheriet, M.: Ontology-based resource description and discovery framework for low carbon grid networks. In: 2010 First IEEE International Conference on Smart Grid Communications (SmartGrid-Comm), pp. 477–482. IEEE (2010)

[4] de Almeida, A.T., Fonseca, P., Bertoldi, P.: Energy-efficient motor systems in the industrial and in the services sectors in the european union: characterisation, potentials, barriers and policies. Energy 28(7), 673–690 (2003)

[5] Dean, J., Ghemawat, S.: Mapreduce: simplified data processing on large clusters. Communications of the ACM 51(1), 107–113 (2008)

[6] Hilty, L., Lohmann, W., Huang, E.: Sustainability and ICT - An overview of the field. POLITEIA 27(104), 13–28 (2011)

[7] Maté, A., Llorens, H., de Gregorio, E.: An integrated multidimensional modeling approach to access big data in business intelligence platforms. In: Castano, S., Vassiliadis, P., Lakshmanan, L.V.S., Lee, M.L. (eds.) ER 2012 Workshops 2012. LNCS, vol. 7518, pp. 111–120. Springer, Heidelberg (2012)

[8] Mitchell, W.J.: E-topia:" urban life, Jim–but not as we know it". MIT Press (2000)

[9] de Moreira, F.L., de Freitas Jorge, E.M.: Sparql2mdx: Um componente de tradução de consultas em ontologia para data warehousing. In: Workshop de Trabalhos de Iniciação científica e Graduação, WTICG-BASE (2012)

[10] Peral, J., Ferrández, A., Gregorio, E.D., Trujillo, J., Maté, A., Ferrández, L.J.: Enrichment of the phenotypic and genotypic data warehouse analysis using question answering systems to facilitate the decision making process in cereal breeding programs. Ecological Informatics (2014), http://dx.doi.org/10.1016/j.ecoinf.2014.05.003

[11] Pérez, J., Arenas, M., Gutierrez, C.: Semantics and complexity of sparql. ACM Transactions on Database Systems (TODS) 34(3), 16 (2009)

[12] Santoso, H.A., Haw, S.-C., Abdul-Mehdi, Z.T.: Ontology extraction from relational database: Concept hierarchy as background knowledge. Knowledge-Based Systems 24(3), 457–464 (2011)

[13] Smit, G.J.: Efficient ICT for efficient smart grids (2012)

[14] Vine, E.: An international survey of the energy service company (ESCO) industry. Energy Policy 33(5), 691–704 (2005)

[15] Webb, M., et al.: Smart 2020: Enabling the low carbon economy in the information age. The Climate Group. London 1(1), 1 (2008)

Benchmarking Performance for Migrating a Relational Application to a Parallel Implementation

Krishna Karthik Gadiraju, Karen C. Davis, and Paul G. Talaga

Electrical Engineering and Computing Systems
University of Cincinnati
Cincinnati, OH- 45221-0030
gadirakk@mail.uc.edu, karen.davis@uc.edu, talagapl@ucmail.uc.edu

Abstract. Many organizations rely on relational database platforms for OLAP-style querying (aggregation and filtering) for small to medium size applications. We investigate the impact of scaling up the data sizes for such queries. We intend to illustrate what kind of performance results an organization could expect should they migrate current applications to big data environments. This paper benchmarks the performance of Hive [20], a parallel data warehouse platform that is a part of the Hadoop software stack. We set up a 4-node Hadoop cluster using Hortonworks HDP 1.3.2 [10]. We use the data generator provided by the TPC-DS benchmark [3] to generate data of different scales. We use a representative query provided in the TPC-DS query set and run the SQL and Hive Query Language (HiveQL) versions of the same query on a relational database installation (MySQL) and on the Hive cluster. We measure the speedup for query execution for all dataset sizes resulting from the scale up. Hive loads the large datasets faster than MySQL, while it is marginally slower than MySQL when loading the smaller datasets.

Keywords: Hive, Hadoop, benchmarking, big data, SQL, queries.

1 Introduction

Big data refers to petabyte scale datasets that cannot be managed and analyzed using traditional database management systems and data warehouses. The last decade has seen an enormous rise in the size of data collected by different organizations. According to Baru et al. [1], studies have indicated that enterprise data is estimated to grow from 0.5 ZB in 2008 to 35 ZB in 2020. Traditional relational database systems are considered incapable of handling data of such scale. However, it is not always clear to a smaller organization what performance gains they can expect to achieve for their application with a modest investment in additional hardware. One such organization approached us with this question. After analyzing their current configuration and typical queries, we selected a hardware/software configuration and test query to enable us to provide some indication of what they could expect if they scaled up their data. Their application only runs one data intensive query at a time, and they wished to own their own hardware, so our experiments target this scenario. There are no other results in the literature that address this question.

M. Indulska and S. Purao (Eds.): ER Workshops 2014, LNCS 8823, pp. 55–64, 2014.
© Springer International Publishing Switzerland 2014

In this paper, we discuss the features of Apache Hive, and compare its performance against a relational database system. We use a query and data that are a part of the TPC-DS [19] benchmarking standard. In the following sections, we briefly describe the features of Hive. We present our experimental setup, procedures, and results obtained. We analyze the results and offer conclusions. We also suggest some future work.

2   Apache Hive

Apache Hive is a distributed data warehouse that is a part of the Hadoop software stack. Queries in Hive are written in HiveQL (Hive Query Language), which follows a syntax similar to SQL. Queries written in HiveQL are translated into a series of MapReduce [2] jobs. The HiveQL query is translated into a DAG (Directed Acyclic Graph) of MapReduce jobs. MapReduce is a parallel programming framework. The MapReduce jobs defined in the DAG are executed in parallel on the different nodes in the cluster where the data is stored to obtain the results. A typical Hive installation has a Metastore [20], which is used to store the metadata related to the tables and columns, a Thrift server [20], which provides a client API for executing the HiveQL statements, external interfaces such as command line interface (CLI), a driver [20], which is responsible for management of the life cycle of a HiveQL statement, a compiler [20] which is used to translate a HiveQL statement it receives from the driver into a DAG of MapReduce jobs. Once the DAG of MapReduce jobs is prepared by the compiler, the driver invokes the execution engine [20] (which in the case of Hive is Hadoop) to execute the MapReduce jobs. A Hive data model consists of tables, partitions and buckets [20]. A Hive table is similar to a table in a relational database and is made up of rows and columns. Each time a table is created in Hive, a new directory is created on HDFS (Hadoop Distributed File System) and data related to that table is stored in that folder. A table can have one or more partitions. Each partition is stored as a separate directory within the table directory and the data is stored in whichever partition directory it belongs to. The partitions can be further sub-divided into buckets, depending upon the hash of a column in the table [20]. The buckets are stored as individual files within their respective partition directories.

3   Experimental Setup

3.1   Hardware Configuration

A 4-node Hadoop cluster was set up using Hortonworks HDP 1.3.2 [10]. We were limited to a small cluster because of the feasibility of an academic setup wherein we used the available departmental hardware. Each machine has dual quad-core Intel Xeon processors for a total of 16 hyper-threaded cores per machine, 48 GB RAM and 3.08 TB HDD. All four machines communicate with each other using a gateway machine. The MySQL machine shared the same processor and RAM, but had a 2.05 TB HDD installed. The six machines mentioned here are connected together using a Cisco SG 200-26 26-Port Gigabit Smart Switch.

3.2   Software Configuration

The Hadoop cluster was set up using Hortonworks HDP 1.3.2. The version of Hive used in this study is 0.11, and the version of MySQL used is 5.1.71. Centos 6.4 minimal operating system was used to set up the Hadoop cluster, which ran Hadoop version 1.2.

3.3   Experimental Procedure

There are several benchmarking standards defined to benchmark the performance of Hadoop such as such as Sorting programs (Hadoop Sort Program [17], TeraSort [7]), GridMix [5] and HiBench Benchmarking Suite [12], but none of them have well-defined queries or a schema necessary for evaluating the run time performance of a big data management system such as Hive. BigBench [4] and Hive Performance Benchmark [9] both define a schema and dataset for benchmarking Hive, but Big-Bench is based on the TPC-DS benchmark and provides a larger variety and scale of datasets and queries. While the structured part of BigBench is based on TPC-DS, it also adds several semi-structured and unstructured data components [4]. Since we are dealing with how Hive performs against a relational system, we use the TPC-DS benchmark to analyze the performance of Hive.

TPC-DS (Transaction Processing Performance Council–Decision Support) is a benchmark for evaluating decision support systems. It defines 99 distinct queries that serve a typical business analysis environment [13]. TPC-DS uses a snowstorm schema [13], which is a collection of several snowflake schemas. The schema has been created to model the decision support functions of a retail product supplier [13]. We selected Query 7 [19] from the TPC-DS benchmark as a representative OLAP-style query. It joins 5 tables and contains 4 aggregation operations, 1 group by operation, and 1 order by operation. We modified the original version of the query to remove the "top 100" expression in order to focus on aggregation and filtering over a fact table and several dimension tables. The modified and HiveQL version of the query are as shown below.

The modified SQL query is:

```
select i_item_id,
  avg(ss_quantity) agg1,
  avg(ss_list_price) agg2,
  avg(ss_coupon_amt) agg3,
  avg(ss_sales_price) agg4
from store_sales, customer_demographics, date_dim, item,
promotion
where ss_sold_date_sk = d_date_sk and
  ss_item_sk = i_item_sk and
  ss_cdemo_sk = cd_demo_sk and
  ss_promo_sk = p_promo_sk and
  cd_gender = 'F' and
  cd_marital_status = 'D' and
```

```
   cd_education_status = 'College' and
   (p_channel_email = 'N' or p_channel_event = 'N') and
   d_year = 2001
group by i_item_id
order by i_item_id;
```

Since HiveQL uses joins rather than listing tables using the ',' operator in the FROM clause as in the TPC-DS query above, the revised query is shown below:

```
select i_item_id,
  avg(ss_quantity) agg1,
  avg(ss_list_price) agg2,
  avg(ss_coupon_amt) agg3,
  avg(ss_sales_price) agg4
from store_sales ss join date_dim d on
(ss.ss_sold_date_sk = d.d_date_sk)
join item i on ( ss.ss_item_sk = i.i_item_sk )
join promotion p on (ss.ss_promo_sk = p.p_promo_sk)
join customer_demographics cd on (ss.ss_cdemo_sk =
cd.cd_demo_sk)
  where
  cd_gender = 'F' and
  cd_marital_status = 'D' and
  cd_education_status = 'College' and
  (p_channel_email = 'N' or p_channel_event = 'N') and
  d_year = 2001
 group by i_item_id
 order by i_item_id;
```

The tables mentioned in the above query are defined in both SQL in HiveQL. Since Hive 0.11 does not support variable types such as varchar and date, they are substituted by string and timestamp, respectively.

4   Results and Analysis

4.1   Results

We use dbgen2 [3] the data generator that is provided as a part of the TPC-DS framework to generate datasets of different scales-100 GB, 300 GB and 1 TB (D1, D2 and D3). Tables 1, 2, and 3 display the sizes of datasets used for each experiment and the amount of time taken to load the datasets into Hive and MySQL. Table 4 displays the amount of time taken to execute the query mentioned in the previous section for all the dataset sizes.

Table 1. Amount of time taken to load datasets (100GB)- D1

Table name	Size	Data load time (MySQL)	Data load time (Hive)
customer_demographics	77 MB	5.78s	2.764s
item	56 MB	1.73s	2.045s
promotion	123 KB	0.01s	0.41s
store_sales	39 GB	14h 25m 47.22s	21m 43.907s
date_dim	9.9 MB	0.5s	0.6s

Table 2. Amount of time taken to load datasets (300 GB) – D2

Table name	Size	Data load time (MySQL)	Data load time (Hive)
customer_demographics	77 MB	5.82s	2.507s
Item	72 MB	2.24s	2.271s
Promotion	159 KB	0.03s	0.407s
store_sales	116 GB	1d 19h 42m 48.84s	1h 2m 36.776s
date_dim	10 MB	0.37s	0.718s

Table 3. Amount of time taken to load datasets (1 TB) – D3

Table name	Size	Data load time (MySQL)	Data load time (Hive)
customer_demographics	77 MB	5.74s	3.28s
item	82 MB	2.53s	2.168s
promotion	184 KB	0.02s	0.458s
store_sales	390 GB	6d 3h 17m 20.76s	2h 58m 8.888s
date_dim	10 MB	0.36s	0.686s

Table 4. Query execution times for datasets D1, D2, and D3

Dataset	Original dataset size	Query dataset size	Query execution time (MySQL)	Query execution time (Hive)
D1	100 GB	39 GB	8m 49.18s	4m 12.816s
D2	300 GB	117 GB	31m 59.77s	11m 57.084s
D3	1 TB	390 GB	1h 35m 46.23s	38m 0.41s

4.2   Analysis

From Tables 1-4, we offer two observations and conclusions.

1. Regarding data loading: consider the amount of time taken by both MySQL and Hive to load the item dataset from Tables 1, 2 and 3. While the dataset size is small (D1), MySQL loads data faster than Hive. But as the size of the dataset increases, the difference in time decreases. In D3, Hive is in fact faster in loading the dataset than MySQL. By observing the amount of time taken to load the *store_sales* dataset for the three datasets shown in Tables 1, 2, and 3 it can be observed that for our scenario, Hive loads large datasets faster than MySQL. Since Hive copies the files

verbatim onto a folder on HDFS and does not parse the file [21], and MySQL parses the data file, the difference becomes apparent as the size of the dataset increases. Figures 1 and 2 show a comparison of the amount of time taken to load the *item* and *store_sales* datasets. From the snowstorm schema defined by TPC-DS, *store_sales* is categorized as a fact table, while *item* is categorized as a dimension table [13]. In other words, while the *item* dataset can be categorized as a small/medium scale dataset, with its size ranging between 56-72 MB, the *store_sales* dataset can be categorized as a large dataset, with its size ranging between 39 GB to 390 GB. By considering both these datasets, we are able to analyze how Hive loads datasets of different sizes.

2. Regarding query execution: consider the amount of time taken to execute the query as shown in Table 4. It can be observed that for all the three datasets, Hive executes the query faster than MySQL. Figure 3 shows a comparison between the query execution times for three datasets shown in Table 4. As the size of the dataset increases, the difference in query execution times between MySQL and Hive increases. This difference in query execution speed can be attributed to the fact that a query written in HiveQL is translated into a series of MapReduce jobs as explained in Section 2. Since the query is executed in parallel on different machines based on where the data has been stored by the HDFS, Hive is able to execute the query faster than MySQL.

Based on our studies, we conclude that an organization working with aggregate queries in an RDBMS environment can benefit from scaling up their applications to significantly larger datasets. One limitation, however, is that HiveQL currently only supports equijoins.

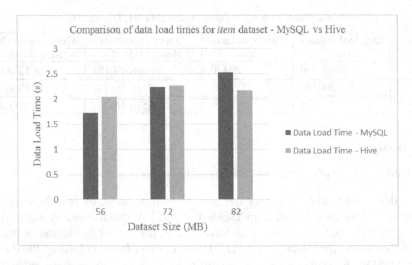

Fig. 1. A comparison of data load times for *item* dataset: MySQL vs. Hive

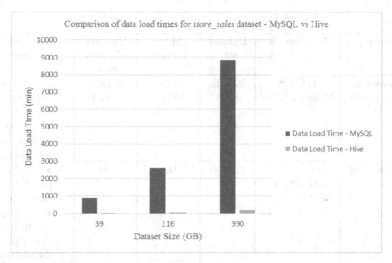

Fig. 2. A comparison of data load times for *store_sales* dataset: MySQL vs. Hive

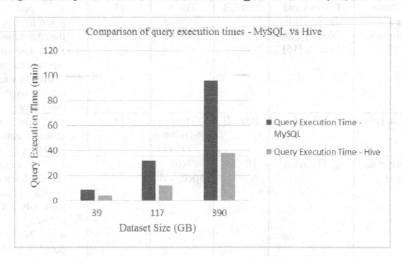

Fig. 3. A comparison of query execution times for MySQL and Hive

5   Related Work

While there have been other studies that have benchmarked the performance of Hive, this study differs from them in terms of the number of nodes used, the version of Hive used, the relational database used, the benchmarking standard used and the size of data used. Table 5 gives a comparison of the different studies conducted on benchmarking Hive and how they differ from our study.

Table 5. Comparison of features with related studies

Study	Benchmark	Dataset size	Hive version	Number of nodes used	Additional Differences
Hortonworks Stinger Initiative [11]	TPC-DS (Query 27, 95)	200GB, 1 TB	0.11, 0.12, 0.13	Not specified	• Not compared to a relational database • Does not consider data load time
Shi et al. [18]	Queries and datasets provided by Pavlo et al. [15]	110 GB	0.6	20	• Not compared to a relational database • Uses queries that are not as complex as the one used in this study
Hive Performance Benchmark [9]	Queries and datasets provided by Pavlo et al. [15]	110 GB	Trunk version 786346	11	• Not compared to a relational database • Uses queries that are not as complex as the one used in this study
Jia et al. [16]	TPC-H	100 GB	Trunk version 799148	11	• Does not consider data load times
Pansare et al. [14]	TPC-H	10 GB	Not specified	4	• Focuses on mid-level data analysis and uses only 10GB dataset • Not compared to a relational database
Gadiraju et al. (current study)	TPC-DS	390 GB	0.11	4	• Compares performance with a relational database • Considers both data load time and query execution time • Focuses on large scale data analysis

6   Future Work

Future performance studies could investigate additional queries as well as increase the number of nodes in the cluster. There are several directions in which research can be conducted on Hive to achieve further improvement. Some of them include:

- Improved connection to the Hive Metastore: one of the issues we observed while working with the cluster is that the Metastore used by Hive to store its metadata is a single point of failure. Once the relational database service running as the Metastore crashes, Hive has no other means of accessing its metadata. There is a need to define a backup mechanism through which Hive can still access its metadata when it is unable to access its Metastore.
- Optimizing performance: while several steps have been taken to ensure query optimization [20] in Hive, there are several ways in which Hive queries can be optimized. Storing statistical data in the form of metadata in the Metastore at column, partition, and table level as suggested by Gruenheid et al. [6] is one way of improving query performance.
- Herodotos et al. [8] conduct research to indicate how placement of data within the HDFS would govern how well a MapReduce job would run. Their model, StarFish [8], defines a means to place data optimally to enhance MapReduce performance. Further research can be conducted to study the efficiency of the StarFish model, and benchmark how the StarFish model would improve the performance of Hive.

Acknowledgements. Thanks to Dr. Thomas Wilson and James Newman for bringing this interesting problem to our attention and to Trajectory HealthCare (www. trajectoryhealthcare.com) for supporting the investigation.

References

1. Baru, C., Bhandarkar, M., Nambiar, R., Poess, M., Rabl, T.: Setting the direction for big data benchmark standards. In: Nambiar, R., Poess, M. (eds.) TPCTC 2012. LNCS, vol. 7755, pp. 197–208. Springer, Heidelberg (2013)
2. Dean, J., Ghemawat, S.: MapReduce: simplified data processing on large clusters. Communications of the ACM 51(1), 107–113 (2008)
3. DSGen v1.1.0, data generation tool for TPC-DS, http://www.tpc.org/tpcds/
4. Ghazal, A., Rabl, T., Hu, M., Raab, F., Poess, M., Crolotte, A., Jacobsen, H.-A.: Big-Bench: Towards an Industry Standard Benchmark for Big Data Analytics (2013)
5. GridMix program. Available in Hadoop source distribution: src/benchmarks/gridmix
6. Gruenheid, A., Omiecinski, E., Mark, L.: Query optimization using column statistics in hive. In: Proceedings of the 15th Symposium on International Database Engineering & Applications, pp. 97–105. ACM (2011)
7. HadoopTeraSort program. Available in Hadoop source distribution since 0.19 version: src/examples/org/apache/hadoop/examples/terasort
8. Herodotou, H., Lim, H., Luo, G., Borisov, N., Dong, L., Cetin, F.B., Babu, S.: Starfish: A Self-tuning System for Big Data Analytics. In: CIDR, vol. 11, pp. 261–272 (2011)

9. Hive Performance Benchmark, https://issues.apache.org/jira/browse/hive-396

10. Hortonworks HDP 1.3.2, http://hortonworks.com/products/hdp/hdp-1-3/#overview

11. Hortonworks Stinger Initiative, http://hortonworks.com/labs/stinger/

12. Huang, S., Huang, J., Dai, J., Xie, T., Huang, B.: The HiBench benchmark suite: Characterization of the MapReduce-based data analysis. In: 2010 IEEE 26th International Conference on Data Engineering Workshops (ICDEW), pp. 41–51. IEEE (2010)

13. Nambiar, R.O., Poess, M.: The making of TPC-DS. In: Proceedings of the 32nd International Conference on Very Large Data Bases, pp. 1049–1058. VLDB Endowment (2006)

14. Pansare, N., Cai, Z.: Using Hive to perform medium-scale data analysis (2010)

15. Pavlo, A., Paulson, E., Rasin, A., Abadi, D.J., DeWitt, D.J., Madden, S., Stonebraker, M.: A comparison of approaches to large-scale data analysis. In: Proceedings of the 2009 ACM SIGMOD International Conference on Management of Data, pp. 165–178. ACM (2009)

16. Running the TPC-H benchmark on Hive, https://issues.apache.org/jira/secure/attachment/12416257/TPC-H_on_Hive_2009-08-11.pdf

17. Sort program. Available in Hadoop source distribution: src/examples/org/apache/hadoop/examples/sort

18. Shi, Y., Meng, X., Zhao, J., Hu, X., Liu, B., Wang, H.: Benchmarking cloud-based data management systems. In: Proceedings of the Second International Workshop on Cloud Data Management, pp. 47–54. ACM (2010)

19. TPC-DS benchmarking standard, http://www.tpc.org/tpcds/spec/tpcds_1.1.0.pdf

20. Thusoo, A., Sarma, J.S., Jain, N., Shao, Z., Chakka, P., Anthony, S., Liu, H., Wyckoff, P., Murthy, R.: Hive: A warehousing solution over a map-reduce framework. Proceedings of the VLDB Endowment 2(2), 1626–1629 (2009)

21. White, T.: Hadoop: The definitive guide. O'Reilly (2012)

A Data Quality in Use Model for Big Data

(Position Paper)

Ismael Caballero, Manuel Serrano, and Mario Piattini

Paseo de la Universidad 4, 13071, Ciudad Real, Spain
{Ismael.Caballero,Manuel.Serrano,Mario.Piattini}@uclm.es

Abstract. Organizations are nowadays immersed in the Big Data Era. Beyond the hype of the concept of Big Data, it is true that something in the way of doing business is really changing. Although some challenges keep being the same as for regular data, with big data, the focus has changed. The reason is due to Big Data is not only data, but also a complete framework including data themselves, storage, formats, and ways of provisioning, processing and analytics. A challenge that becomes even trickier is the one concerning to the management of the quality of big data. More than ever the need for assessing the quality-in-use of big datasets gains importance since the real contribution – business value- of a dataset to a business can be only estimated in its context of use. Although there exists different data quality models to assess the quality of data there still lacks of a quality-in-use model adapted to big data. To fill this gap, and based on ISO 25012 and ISO 25024, we propose the 3Cs model, which is composed of three data quality dimensions for assessing the quality in-use of big datasets: Contextual Consistency, Operational Consistency and Temporal Consistency.

Keywords: Big Data, Data Quality, Quality-in-use model, 3Cs Model.

1   Introduction

If defining data quality was difficult, finding a sound definition for data quality for big data is even worse: there is still not an official definition for big data. Loshin in [1] gathers the definition given by Gartner's IT Glossary: *"Big Data is high-volume, high-velocity, and high-variety information assets that demand cost-effective, innovative forms of information processing for enhanced insight and decision making"*. As [2] states, big data is an umbrella term that covers not only datasets themselves, but also problem space, technologies, and opportunities for enhancing business value.

And precisely, business value is the main reason for what big data can be used for, in fact, analytical projects aimed to extend the meaning of the facts currently happening in business processes in different business cases [1, 3]. In such business cases, regrettably, people in high management tend to think that the larger the big data project is (e.g. the largest amount of data involved in the project), the larger benefits (the soundest knowledge) can be obtained; unfortunately this happens even when they do not know exactly how to address big data concerns nor how to get the maximum benefits from the projects [2].

M. Indulska and S. Purao (Eds.): ER Workshops 2014, LNCS 8823, pp. 65–74, 2014.

So, the first step in any big data project is to encourage high management to lead the project over to buy and deploy sophisticated technology that will not produce any suitable results for the business case at hand [4-6].

Once managers are convinced about the real need of kicking big data projects, they have to deal with the challenges that big data brings in order to achieve an alignment to the reality of the organizations [1]. The challenges have been identified in [7] as being data quality, adequate characterization of data, right interpretation of results, data visualization, real-time view of data vs retrospective view, and determining the relevance of results of projects.

In this paper, we are going to deal with data quality concerns in big data projects independent of which type of project the organization is facing. Our motivation is to define the quality characteristics that the different datasets being used for a specific use should present to fit for such use (quality in use).

Data quality is per se a real challenge although not a myth: all datasets included in big data projects do not necessarily have to lack of quality enough for the task at hand [8]. Anyway, we pose that studying how data quality management for big data has evolved is worthy to research since classical data quality principles cannot further be applied to big datasets due to its new very nature [1]. In this sense, data quality management for big data should prioritize those data quality dimensions really addressing the data quality requirements for the task at hand. Although dealing with internal or external data quality is actually important, sometimes the assessment of these types of quality for big datasets is almost impossible because there may be limited or multiples or even no restrictions on data [9], and consequently these studies are not producing results for developers as relevant as the results provided by the one addressing the levels of data quality-in-use. Unfortunately, not much research has still been conducted for quality-in-use for big data. Even when ISO 25010[10] deals with internal and external quality and quality in-use, and in spite that ISO 25012 [11], which addresses data quality concerns, does not specifically differentiate between internal, external or in-use quality for "traditional" data neither big data. So, there still lacks a quality-in-use model which can be used as a reference to manage data quality in big data.

Our contribution in this paper is precisely "The 3Cs data quality-in-use model for big data" which is to be specifically addressed and customized for big data projects. The 3Cs corresponds to the three kind of consistency required for most of the initiatives in which big datasets are to be integrated for part of a project: Contextual Consistency, Temporal Consistency and Operational Consistency. In the scope of this paper, the concept of consistency of 3C's further specializes the concept of consistency in ISO 25012. For each one of the 3Cs, we will also analyze how the 3Cs are related to the 3Vs that characterize big data, namely, Volume, Velocity and Variety. To the best of our knowledge, the topic has not been previously tackled by others by addressing ISO 25012. The novelty of our proposal is the provision of predefined data quality dimensions sets to be used in specific situation as if they would be quality patterns. The proposal introduces an on-progress research whose results are to be applied to specific kind of big data quality projects, and validated against real case studies.

The remainder of the paper is structured as follows: Section 2 introduces a flash-back motivating how data quality management have evolved over the time. Section 3 presents the proposal and some aspects are further dealt (as the profile for different type of Big Data project). Section 4 presents some conclusions and future work.

2   Flashback: What Has Changed in Data Quality?

This is a question with an easy answer and complex consequences: we are now better communicated and more social than ever. And that makes organizations to reconsider the way in which they can understand their customers, prospect and what influence on them. As soon as somebody provides an opinion for a just bought product, companies become interested in knowing who use their products, what they think about them, and what the markets are emerging [2]. Just to name an example: when we are watching a product in Amazon – with more than 100 million registered members -, we can see a bit below a label showing *"Customers who bought this item also bought...."* and a list containing items that could be of our interest [12]. Analogously, it is possible to find thousand and millions of examples in our day-to-day web experience, overall for data-driven companies that were born digital (e.g. Google), which really know how to gain competitive advantages from their capability of capturing data from users' life through their digital interactions (mobile phones, GPS, tablets, ...) [6]

For achieving this list of suggested items it is necessary to process massive amounts of a combination of structured and unstructured data from both machine-generated and human sources [1]. Whereas this was far away from being done some years ago, today, it is very real. The change that have made it possible is the increase of processing of CPUs, the increase of velocity in communications, the increase of physical storage room at a reasonably low cost, the apparition of ubiquitous devices   [6, 13]. Even more, with the leveraging of cloud computing, and associated commercial solutions, it is even no longer required to buy and deploy an IT infrastructure [3, 14, 15].

These new changes has also dramatically affected to the "classical" vision of data quality. A simple retrospective analysis of the potholes in the road to information quality [16] along with the affected data quality dimensions – see Tab. 1 – reveals that we have shifted from a controllable stability grounded on the "close world assumption" provided by the relational model to the "beautiful and challenging chaos" produced by the coming of large dataset from different sources, at different velocities, and with different formats and representations.

Although the related technologies are changing the market trends [17], and even when data quality has to be now measured in terms of *fitness for purposes* [1], however, we pose that the way to deal with the levels of data quality in big data still remain being the same: management. It is important to not forget that data with adequate levels of quality is produced at the data source [4] and consumed at destination, even when technologies motivated some obvious changes [18-20].

Fundamentally, the changes that are required to face are known as the 3Vs: Velocity (e.g. data coming at real time vs near time or coming in streaming), Volume (e.g. data coming in Terabytes transactions, or in tables or in files) and Variety (e.g. data coming whether in structured or unstructured way) [13]; some other authors also include a fourth V for Veracity [21, 22].

Table 1. Ten potholes on Information Quality ([16])

Potholes	Affected DQ Dimension(s)
#1. Multiples sources of the same information produce different values	Consistency and believability
#2. Information is produced using subjective judgments, leading to bias	Objectivity and believability
#3. Systemic errors in information production lead to loss of information	Correctness, Completeness,
#4.Large Volumes of stored information makes it difficult o access to information in reasonable time	Concise representation, timeliness, value-added, and accessibility
#5. Distributed heterogeneous systems leas to inconsistent definitions, formats and values.	Consistent representation, timeliness, value-added
#6. Non numeric information is difficult to index	Concise representation, Value-added, accessibility.
#7. Automated content analysis across information collection is not yet available	Analysis requirements, consistent representation, relevance, value-added
#8. As information consumers' task and the organizational environment change, the information that is relevant and useful changes, the information that is relevant and useful changes.	Relevance, value-added, Completeness
#9. Easy access to information may conflict with requirements for security, privacy, and confidentiality	Security, accessibility, value-added.
#10. Lack of sufficient computing resources limits access.	Accessibility, value-added.

3   The 3Cs Data Quality-in-Use Model

3.1   ISO 25000 and Quality-in-Use for Big Data

ISO 25000 is the family of standards addressing Systems and Software Quality Requirements and Evaluation (SQuaRE). It provides several divisions: ISO/IEC 2500n – Quality Management, ISO/IEC 2501n – Quality Model, ISO/IEC 2502n- Quality Measurement, ISO/IEC 2503n – Quality Requirements, and ISO/IEC 2504n – Quality Evaluation.

One of the important assumptions introduced in this family of standards is the quality in the lifecycle (see Fig.1). The manufacturing process generates a specific configuration for the internal properties of a product, which are assessed by means of internal quality. This internal quality influences in the external quality; and this latter influence into the quality in use. For software products, ISO 25010 defines an internal/external quality model and a quality in use model. For data, ISO 25012 defines a quality model including some characteristics like accuracy (the extent to which the value of data represent the true value of the attribute in the real world), completeness (the degree to which the number of provided values for expected attributes are enough for the task at hands) or credibility (the degree to which value of data are regarded as true and believable), ... to name a few. This could be enough for traditional data, but Big Data needs a specific quality in use model due to the fact that the business value can be only estimated when data are being used in a specific context of use.

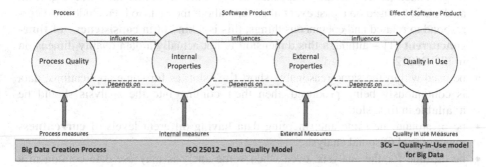

Fig. 1. Quality in the lifecycle (adapted from [10])

3.2   A Quality-in-Use Model for Big Data

We pose that the main data quality characteristics for assessing the level of quality in use of heterogeneous datasets for big data projects is **consistency.** According to Merriam-Webster dictionary, consistency can be defined as *"agreement or harmony of parts or features to one another or a whole"*. From a technical point of view, we reinterpret this definition as the capability of data and systems of keeping the uniformity of specific characteristics when datasets are transferred across the networks and shared by the various applications and systems   [20]. However, it is crucial to clarify that there can exists various types of consistencies: **Contextual Consistency, Temporal Consistency and Operational Consistency**. All these types of consistencies will be influenced by the external data quality -see Tab. 2-. Following, a short description of each one of the types of consistencies is described.

Contextual Consistency refers to capability of datasets to be used within the same domain of interest of the problem independent from any format (e.g. structured vs unstructured), any size, or coming at different velocities. In this sense, it is important that used data (still not exhaustive set of data quality characteristics):

- are relevant to the context: all used data have similar levels of **relevance and consistency** to the task at hand;
- are credible: within the context, analysts performing the analysis should find similar levels of **credibility** in data;

- are unique and semantically interoperable: so the data must be similarly **understandable** by the agents performing the analysis;
- are accurate: within the context, analyst performing the task should find data with similar levels of **semantic accuracy**;
- have been accessed by the same group of people allowed to develop the analysis, so its **confidentially** is assured.

Temporal consistency refers to the fact that dataset are produced by a data generator, used for performing analysis, and understood in a consistent time slot. This has several perceptions, so that, it is important that data in analysis should:

- be generated to refer to facts happened in the same or similar time slot: e.g. if an analysis is focused on a past event, then data about the facts to be include must correspond to related and coetaneous things, this is a kind of in **consistency of time-concurrent** [1] – although this dimension is not actually a data quality dimension in ISO 25012-
- be used within the same reasonably short time slot: as for some applications, data is continuously being produced, then their coming into the analysis should be **available** in time slot;
- be of around the same age: merging data having different levels of **currentness** may not lead to sound analysis;
- be on time for the analysis: even when some analysis may use data coming in a "pay as you go" manner, it is important that all data included have similar level of **timeliness**;
- Be used, when performing some kind of tends analysis, for producing results related to compliant with required future time slots.

Operational Consistency refers to the extent to which dataset can be included in the same analysis, from a technological point of view. So, data in the various datasets should

- be **available, easily recoverable** and **accessible** by analysts;
- be expressed by using similar data types and with the same amount of **precision** and it can be also **portable**;
- be **compliant** to metadata and reference metadata, even when such metadata have different syntactic representation;
- have similar levels of **completeness** so that data can be interoperable;
- have similar level of **precision**;
- have similar level of **efficiency**;
- have similar levels of **traceability**;

The level of quality-in-use of the overall datasets is to be measured based on the 3Cs by combining the ISO 25012 data quality characteristics in a meaningful and representative way. Using the words *"meaningful"* and *"representative"* we want to mean that the combination is case specific according to the very nature of the big data project. In the following section, we are to discuss how each one of the 3Vs impact into the kind of big data project, and hence, in the way of measuring the quality-in-use of the overall datasets.

Table 2. Quality-in-use model for Big Data based on ISO 25012

Data Quality characteristics	Contextual Consistency	Temporal Consistency	Operational Consistency
Accuracy	X		X
Completeness	X		X
Consistency	X	X	X
Credibility	X	X	
Currentness		X	
Accessibility			X
Compliance		X	X
Confidentiality	X		
Efficiency			X
Precision			X
Traceability			X
Understandability	X		
Availability		X	X
Portability			X
Recoverability			X

3.3   Impact of 3Vs on the Measurement of the Quality-in-Use

As known, big data applications consume data from several sources (social network streams, syndicated data streams, news feeds, preconfigured search filters, public or open-sourced datasets, sensor networks, or other unstructured data streams) coming at different velocities and may be having a large variety of formats. We pose that this is especially important when it comes to measure the "big" data quality-in-use dimensions previously presented, since it affects to the definition of the corresponding measurement method. For instance, ISO 25024 [23] propose density measures as measurement method for some of the "regular" data quality characteristics (e.g. semantic accuracy: $X = A/B$, where A is the number of data values semantically accurate and B is the number of data values for which semantically accuracy can be measured). This kind of measurement method must be customized having into account the 3Vs. For example, in the case of semantic accuracy, at the moment of computing the ratio, in order to get a trustful result, one must exactly know: (1) if all data values for which semantically accuracy can be measured are available – volume - (2) if all data values for which semantically accuracy can be measured will be on time to compute the results or if it has to be assume that datasets has to be partitioned in order to plan the computing of the results as data is going into the execution of the algorithm – velocity-, and (3) if the program implementing the analysis algorithm can deal with the heterogeneity of formats (relational vs other non-structured and/or non-relational) – variety-. So, the 3Vs affect directly to the design and implementation of the measurement methods. This is the reason for which, "classical" tools (e.g. data profiling tools) are not enough for the software stack for analytics applications [3], because as McAfee and Brynjolfsson explain in [6], traditional relational databases are ill-suited to work with big data.

In Tab. 3 we briefly describe the impact of 3Vs to definition of the measurement methods for the various data quality characteristics in the 3Cs data quality model.

Table 3. 3Vs affecting to the measurement of 3Cs

	Velocity	Volume	Variety
Contextual Consistency	Consistency, Credibility, Confidentiality	Completeness, Credibility	Accuracy, Consistency, Understandability
Temporal Consistency	Consistency, Credibility, Currentness, Availability	Availability	Consistency, Currentness, Compliance
Operational Consistency	Completeness, Accessibility, Efficiency, Traceability, Availability, Recoverability	Completeness, Accessibility, Efficiency, Availability, Recoverability	Accuracy, Accessibility, Compliance, Efficiency, Precision, Traceability, Availability, Recoverability.

One interesting concern is who (which roles) should be primarily in charge to lead the application of the dimensions of 3Cs data quality model in industrial applications. [2] proposes three specific roles who should work in a big data initiative: data scientist, business analyst and technologist. For the sake of data governability, we pose that technologists should be in charge of assuring adequate levels of operational consistency since they work directly with IT providing datasets; and business analysts and data scientist should be in charge of assuring adequate levels of contextual consistency and temporal concerns, since they work with the domain. Moreover the role of a Chief Data Officers will be necessary in order to coordinate the efforts [24].

4   Conclusions and Future Work

Data quality is a major concern also in Big Data analytics projects. In this paper we have analyzed the reasons that have led us from "traditional" data quality to "big" data quality. One of the first conclusions we raised is that quality-in-use becomes more representative when it comes to measure the level of quality in big datasets composed by several datasets coming from different sources, with probably different formats, and at different velocities.

As part of our reasons, we have proposed the 3Cs Data Quality Model, which is composed of Contextual Consistency, Temporal Consistency and Operational Consistency. These three dimensions are to be measured according to "regular" data quality dimensions defined on each one of the datasets.

Our future work will go through different lines: validating the 3Cs Data Quality Model in real business cases, measuring data quality for big data and establishing the major concerns for "big" data quality by design, this is to say: how to include in the big data analytic projects the corresponding requirement in order to assure the adequate levels data quality for the dimensions in the 3Cs Data Quality Model.

As part of our future work, we plan to further research into how to go deeper in the granularity the corresponding relationship between the "traditional" data quality dimensions and the ones included in the 3Cs Data Quality Model.

Aknowledgement. This work is partially supported by R&D project GEODAS (TIN2012-37493-C03-01), funded by Ministry of Economy and Competitiveness and the Regional Development Fund, FEDER.

References

1. Loshin, D.: Big Data Analytics: From Strategic Planning to Enterprise Integration with Tools, Techniques, NoSQL, and Graph. Elsevier, Walthman (2013)
2. Mantha, B.: Five Guiding Principles for Realizing the Promise of Big Data. Business Intelligence Journal 19, 8–11 (2014)
3. Kambatla, K., Kollias, G., Kumar, V., Grama, A.: Trends in big data analytics. Journal of Parallel and Distributed Computing - In Press - Corrected Proof (2014)
4. Redman, T.C.: Data's Credibility Problem. Harvard Business Review 91, 84–88 (2013)
5. Quality in Progress
6. McAfee, A., Brynjolfsson, E.: Big data: The management revolution. Harvard Business Review 90, 60–68 (2012)
7. CIO INSIGHT
8. Deutsch, T.: Putting big data myths to rest. IBM Data Management Magazine (2013)
9. Howles, T.: Data, Data Quality, and Ethical Use. Software Quality Professional 16, 4–12 (2014)
10. ISO: ISO/IEC 25010, Systems and software engineering - Systems and software Quality Requirements and Evaluation (SQuaRE) - System and software quality models. International Organization for Standardization, Ginebra, Suiza (2011)
11. ISO: ISO/IEC 25012:2008 - Software engineering. Software product quality requirements and evaluation (SQuaRE). Data quality model International Organization for Standarization (2009)
12. Greenberg, P.: Big Data, Big Deal (2012), http://www.destinationCRM.com
13. Russom, P.: Big Data Analytics (2011), ftp://ftp.software.ibm.com/software/tw/Defining_Big_Data_through_3V_v.pdf
14. Buyya, R., Yeo, C.S., Venugopal, S., Broberg, J., Brandic, I.: Cloud computing and emerging IT platforms: Vision, hype, and reality for delivering computing as the 5th utility. Future Generation Computer Systems 25, 599–616 (2009)
15. Armbrust, M., Fox, A., Griffith, R., Joseph, A.D., Katz, R., Konwinski, A., Lee, G., Patterson, D., Rabkin, A., Stoica, I., Zaharia, M.: A view of cloud computing. Commun. ACM 53, 50–58 (2010)
16. Strong, D., Lee, Y., Wang, R.: Ten Potholes in the Road to Information Quality. IEEE Computer, 38–46 (1997)
17. Howard, P.: Market update- Data Quality - Market trends. Bloor (2013)
18. Lundquist, E.: Data Quality Is First Step Toward Reliable Data Analysis. p. 5. QuinStreet, Inc. (2013)
19. Becla, J., Wang, D.L., Lim, K.T.: Report from the 5th workshop on extremely large databases. Data Science Journal 11, 37–45 (2012)
20. Kwon, O., Lee, N., Shin, B.: Data quality management, data usage experience and acquisition intention of big data analytics. International Journal of Information Management (2014)
21. Tee, J.: The Server Side (2013), http://www.theserverside.com/feature/Handling-the-four-Vs-of-big-data-volume-velocity-variety-and-veracity

22. Lukoianova, T., Rubin, V.L.: Veracity roadmap: Is big data objective, truthful and credible? Advances in Classification Research Online 24 (2013)
23. ISO: ISO/IEC CD 25024 - Systems and software engineering – Systems and software Quality Requirements and Evaluation (SQuaRE) – Measurement of data quality
24. Lee, Y., Madnick, S., Wang, R., Wang, F., Hongyun, Z.: A Cubic Framework for the Chief Data Officer: Succeeding in a World of Big Data. MIS Quarterly Executive 13, 1–13 (2014)

Business Intelligence and Big Data in the Cloud: Opportunities for Design-Science Researchers

Odette Mwilu Sangupamba [1], Nicolas Prat[2], and Isabelle Comyn-Wattiau[1,2]

[1] CEDRIC-CNAM, Paris, France
odemwilu@hotmail.com, isabelle.wattiau@cnam.fr
[2] ESSEC Business School, Cergy-Pontoise, France
{prat,wattiau}@essec.edu

Abstract. Cloud computing and big data offer new opportunities for business intelligence (BI) and analytics. However, traditional techniques, models, and methods must be redefined to provide decision makers with service of data analysis through the cloud and from big data. This situation creates opportunities for research and more specifically for design-science research. In this paper, we propose a typology of artifacts potentially produced by researchers in design science. Then, we analyze the state of the art through this typology. Finally, we use the typology to sketch opportunities of new research to improve BI and analytics capabilities in the cloud and from big data.

Keywords: Business Intelligence, Big Data Analytics, Cloud Computing, Design-Science Research, Artifact.

1 Introduction

Business intelligence (BI) helps managers to make informed decisions. BI technology is demonstrated an indisputable support for decision making. BI tools facilitate the presentation of more accurate reporting, improve decision making, enhance customer relationships, and increase revenue. BI must be able to deal with big volumes of data (big data analytics). According to IDC [1], the business analytics software market will grow at a 9.7% compound annual rate through 2017. The growth of the market will be driven in part by the current hype around big data.

Cloud computing also attracts many organizations, because of its potential: ubiquitous, convenient, on-demand network access to a shared pool of configurable computing resources (e.g., networks, servers, storage, applications, and services) [2, 3]. Its objective is to provide innovative services to the request of different types of users. The latter are freed from the underlying infrastructure. Beyond outsourcing, there are two concepts that are highlighted in cloud computing: virtualization and agility. Through the cloud, organizations can acquire IT services without additional intervention or human interaction. According to IDC [4], spending on public IT cloud services alone was estimated a $47.4 billion industry in 2013 and is expected to more than double by 2017. Ultimately, cloud computing enables more efficient BI tasks.

M. Indulska and S. Purao (Eds.): ER Workshops 2014, LNCS 8823, pp. 75–84, 2014.
© Springer International Publishing Switzerland 2014

BI and analytics raise many issues for design-science researchers. This paper focuses more specifically on the deployment of BI on the cloud and big data. The research question addressed in the paper is: what are the research topics on which design-science researchers can contribute regarding BI in the cloud and big data?

Indeed, it is useful for design-science researchers to focus on the definition of new processes and implement new models for BI to take advantage of cloud computing and big data. Given that design-science research leads to the production of artifacts, several researchers made an inventory of potential artifacts. Building on these previous papers, we propose a typology of artifacts that allows us to structure our literature review on BI in the cloud and detect open research questions. Even though business intelligence and big data in the cloud raise many new research issues for the information systems community at large (quantitative and qualitative research, IS economics, design-science research), the present papers focuses specifically on the possible contributions of design-science research.

The remainder of the paper is structured as follows: in the second section, we present our typology of design-science research artifacts. In the third section, we synthesize the current state of research for business intelligence and big data in the cloud. The fourth section describes open research issues and opportunities for design science. The last section introduces a discussion before concluding the paper.

2   Typology of Design-Science Research Artifacts

March and Smith [5] distinguish among four types of artifacts constituting the outputs of design-science research:
-     *Construct*: a conceptualization used to describe problems within the domain and to specify their solutions.
-     *Model*: a set of propositions or statements expressing relationships among constructs.
-     *Method*: a set of steps (an algorithm or guideline) used to perform a task.
-     *Instantiation*: the realization of an artifact in its environment.

This typology of artifacts is widely used, including in the seminal paper by Hevner et al. [6]. However, the typology is sometimes difficult to operationalize, due to the relative fuzziness of the concepts of construct, model, method, and instantiation. Therefore, it is useful to specialize the typology, specifying and defining subcategories for the four categories of artifacts.

Offermann et al. [8] specialize the typology of artifacts, proposing more specific categories. This work provides a useful basis for a classification of the various types of artifacts. However, we claim that this paper lacks some important subcategories of artifacts, some types include a large number of different concepts, and the proposed definitions may lead to confusion. Consequently, we propose our typology of the different types of artifacts (subcategories of the concepts of construct, model, method, and instantiation). This typology is shown in Table 1. For each subcategory, we propose a definition. The references in Table 1 indicate the papers from which the definitions were taken or adapted. Our typology, with precise subcategories and a definition for each subcategory, helps in the identification and characterization of design-science research artifacts. With our typology, design-science researchers can clarify the object of research and reflect on research methods appropriate to this object.

Table 1. Typology of artifacts

Construct	
Language	*A set of concepts, or more generally symbols, rules for combining them (syntax), and rules for interpreting combinations of symbols (semantics) [7].*
Metamodel	*A set of concepts represented in graphical notation, with rules for combining the concepts.*
Concept	*A new concept added to an extant language or metamodel.*
Model	
System design	*A structure or behavior-related description of a system, commonly using some graphical notation and possibly text [8].*
Ontology	*An explicit formal specification of a shared conceptualization [9].*
Taxonomy	*A classification of objects in a domain of interest, based on common characteristics [10].*
Framework	*A logical structure for organizing complex information [11].*
Architecture	*A blueprint representing the fundamental organization of a system embodied in its components, their relationships to each other, and to the environment [12, 13].*
Requirement	*A condition or capability that must be met or possessed by a system [12].*
Method	
Methodology	*A predefined set of steps and guidelines, with associated techniques and tools. It is aimed at, or used by, individuals who work in a discipline [12] [14].*
Guideline	*A suggestion regarding behaviour in a particular situation [8]. Examples: design principles (broad guidelines), heuristics, rules (detailed guidelines) [15].*
Algorithm	*An executable sequence of operations for performing a specific task [8] [12].*
Method fragment	*A method component that can be treated as a separate unit and reused in different contexts [16]. Example: design patterns.*
Metric	*A function that assigns a number or symbol to an entity in order to characterize an attribute or a group of attributes. The value of the metric is called a measure [17].*
Instantiation	
Implemented system	*An implemented software or hardware system. Example: a prototype or finalized tool.*
Example	*Any other concrete materialization of an abstract artifact (construct, model, or method). Examples: the application of a query language to an illustrative scenario, the illustration of a design-theory framework with concrete examples of design theories, the application of a project methodology to a real project.*

In the next sections, we use our typology of design-science research artifacts to synthetize research on BI and big data in the cloud, and identify research opportunities.

3   Current State of Research for Business Intelligence and Big Data in the Cloud

In this section, we summarize the state of the art of BI and big data on the cloud. Then, we analyze the papers through our typology of artifacts. We address this analysis in three themes:

- Data management: includes all artifacts related to representation and manipulation of data in the cloud.
- Service management: describes the potential of cloud services and artifacts relating thereto.
- Security management: describes the issues related to security, privacy, trust, and availability in the cloud.

We propose this categorization because at the heart of BI in the cloud, there is the issue of managing massive amounts of data (big data) and all other services provided by the cloud. Furthermore, security is a major challenge facing the cloud.

3.1   Data Management

Data management has a prominent place in BI. First, it will be necessary to develop new database management systems (DBMS) specifically architectured for BI in the cloud [18]. In addition, big data require developing models and tools capable of analyzing these masses of heterogeneous data that accumulate at high speed. On the one hand, traditional data warehouses can migrate to the cloud warehouse where they will integrate all data structures: documents, spreadsheets, e-mails, images, text and social media content. It is also necessary to think about the integration of big data [19]. Transactional data keep an important role in BI. Big data must be added to the internal data organization for best results of analysis [20]. Also, internal data organizations are structured whereas big data are generally not structured. Hence, the appropriate techniques must be defined.

Several researchers have striven to develop tools from MapReduce and its primitives as Hadoop. Thus, Herodotou et al. [21] developed an *architecture* and a tool called Starfish. Starfish fills a vacuum by allowing different users and Hadoop applications to automatically obtain good performance throughout the life cycle of data in analysis, without the need to understand and manipulate the numerous nodes available. Pedersen et al. [22] introduced the new *concept* of cloud warehouse. In addition, they defined a query *language* called SQLxm. Abadi [18] provided properties that users would appreciate finding in analysis tools. D'Orazio and Bimonte [23] proposed a data *architecture* in the cloud to optimize storage costs and an *algorithm* to convert these structures into Pig data. Chaudhuri et al. [24] presented a BI *architecture* including analysis tools for big data. Analysis tools include many *algorithms* for demand and implementation services as well as resources security. *Methodologies* to parameterize these tools were also implemented [25].

3.2   Service Management

There are six scenarii that illustrate the different service organizations existing in the cloud [26]:

- *Add-on services scenario:* Some components (e.g. components for web search) are selected from the cloud to BI infrastructure.
- *Tool replacement scenario*: The cloud makes available a complete tool, for instance a data mart or OLAP tool. This is SaaS (Software as a Service).
- *Solution provision scenario:* The cloud supports a software and hardware remote solution.
- *Business network scenario*: A solution provider acts within a corporate network. This can be a B2B market or supply chain, for example. The cloud aspect resides in the abstraction of the physical infrastructure that has become virtual.
- *Best-of-breed scenario:* The replacement of the tool is pushed to a higher level to the point where all components of the BI infrastructure are provided by an external supplier.
- *BI mashup scenario*: The BI solution is freely composed from a global market space over the internet.

Some researchers have implemented artifacts related to cloud services. Thus, Fernandez et al. [27] proposed an *architecture* that includes all services that organizations can receive in the cloud to perform their BI tasks. Hoberg et al. [28] established a *framework* according to the four dimensions following: cloud computing characteristics, adoption determinants, governance mechanisms, and business impact. Demirkan and Delen [29] implemented *requirements* and a conceptual *architecture* of service-oriented DSS. Baars and Kemper [26] presented a *framework* of BI in the cloud that can help with identification, combination and finally evaluation of potential BI services.

3.3   Security Management

Resource sharing in the cloud requires measuring more strongly the security level, since security is often considered as the main obstacle to the adoption of cloud computing services. Cloud computing must address the challenges of security, privacy and trust. Data have their physical existence in a given country and are governed by local regulation [29]. These regulations differ from one country to another and may be to the benefit or detriment of cloud customers. In addition, data is managed by an unknown host and customers do not control the use of their data in the cloud. Hence, design-science researchers must define the appropriate techniques.

Thus, Abadi [18] reminded the general principles of security. Many other researchers raise the issue of the cloud challenges. They call for encryption *algorithms* and focus on strengthening security policies for individual users and cloud providers [18] [29] [30].

3.4   Synthesis

Table 2 below synthetizes the state of the art on BI and big data on the cloud, by research theme and type of artifact.

Table 2. Overview of artifacts by subject

		Data management [18][21][22][23] [24][25]	Service management [25][26][27][28][29]	Security man- agement [18][25][29][30]
Construct	Language	covered	not covered	not covered
	Metamodel	not covered	not covered	not covered
	Concept	covered	not covered	not covered
Model	System design	not covered	not covered	not covered
	Ontology	not covered	not covered	not covered
	Taxonomy	not covered	not covered	not covered
	Framework	not covered	covered	not covered
	Architecture	covered	covered	not covered
	Requirement	covered	covered	not covered
Method	Methodology	covered	covered	covered
	Guideline	partly covered	partly covered	partly covered
	Algorithm	covered	covered	covered
	Method fragment	not covered	not covered	covered
	Metric	not covered	not covered	not covered
Instantiation	Implemented system	covered	covered	not covered
	Example	covered	covered	not covered

□ not covered   ▨ partly covered   ■ covered

4 Business Intelligence in the Cloud: Open Issues and Opportunities for Design-Science Research

Table 2 shows that there are many opportunities for design-science research on the topic of BI and big data in the cloud. The cells of Table 2 that are white or grey indicate research opportunities. In Table 3, we present these opportunities. We distinguish between research opportunities identified in the literature and research opportunities identified by us, based on our typology of design-science research artifacts.

4.1 Data Management

In terms of data management, design-science researchers may extend the current research by producing some artifacts, for example:

- A multidimensional *metamodel* helping to design the cloud warehouse could be developed to enable the instantiation of classical multidimensional models in the specific context of the cloud or to bring new constructs enriching these models.
- Data from various sources and of different formats should all be finally consolidated. It is therefore necessary to develop conceptual and logical data models (*system design*).
- Clearer *guidelines* on how to use cloud data will help cloud customers to use the cloud data for the specific purposes of analysis and according to their needs.

Table 3. Overview of opportunities for design-science research

		Data management	Service management	Security management	Capacity management
Construct	Language			░	
	Metamodel	■			
	Concept			■	
Model	System design	░	■		
	Ontology	■	■		
	Taxonomy		■		
	Framework				
	Architecture			■	
	Requirement				■
Method	Methodology				
	Guideline	■	■		
	Algorithm			░	
	Method fragment				
	Metric				
Instantiation	Implemented system	░			
	Example				

■ our proposal ░ proposal from the literature

- *Ontologies* could facilitate the integration of big data. Indeed, big data must be added to transactional data for best results of the analysis. Thus, providers and customers must have the same language. The ontology also facilitates the automation of big data integration.

4.2 Service Management

In the field of service-based computing, the researchers could focus greater attention on the following topics:

- The definition of a business process model (*system design*) could contribute to a better understanding of service requests initiated by users.
- An *ontology* of services needed by organizations will help users to make the choice of services they need from scenarios services offered by the cloud and to share a common language with the cloud provider.
- In order to regulate the demand for services, the implementation of *guidelines* is important since the customer gets services without human interaction with the provider. The *guidelines* will allow users to properly configure the tools at their disposal to access cloud resources.
- The *taxonomy* of cloud services allows users to save time by requesting a service level higher in the hierarchy that covers all their needs rather than choosing several low-level services.

4.3   Security Management

The security domain is not yet sufficiently explored. The cloud raises the challenge of security even higher. Hence, design-science researchers may extend research to develop the following artifacts:

- Encryption *algorithms* for ensuring data security in the cloud.
- Scrambling techniques (*algorithms*) allowing organizations to make available rich amounts of data without risk of disclosure since data are managed by an unknown host and customers do not control the use of their data in the cloud. Thus, these techniques prevent the violation of data privacy in the cloud.

4.4   Capacity Management

Cloud customers must have software and hardware capacity. Even if they are exempt from the details of the underlying infrastructure in the cloud services, they need a high amount of resources in terms of hardware, software and Internet connection. To the best of our knowledge, this topic is not covered by current or past research. Thus, we argue that we need the following artifacts:

- A hardware *architecture* of the cloud is necessary for customers.
- A model of *requirement* to help the cloud customer determine the hardware and software capabilities required given his/her needs.

5   Discussion and Conclusion

BI and big data in the cloud is a recent topic. This topic requires investigation by IS researchers using various methodologies, including quantitative, qualitative and design-science research. This paper has focused on opportunities for design-science research. We have proposed a typology of design-science research artifacts, and used this typology to identify research gaps and opportunities. More specifically, several artifacts must be developed to improve methods, models and tools dedicated to BI in the cloud and allowing users to analyze big data preserving information security. Efforts need to be conducted on logical and physical architecture design models and tools to set analysis in the cloud.

In this article, we have highlighted the services that cloud computing offers to BI to further improve its performance. With the cloud, organizations can gain large amounts of heterogeneous data for analysis (big data). This concept of big data highlights not only the volume of data but also their variety and processing speed.

As BI is growing, traditional models, processes and techniques must be rethought. This situation creates research opportunities for design-science researchers. Based on our typology of artifacts, we have elicited the gaps to be filled by further research. Indeed, our typology allowed us to identify artifacts already implemented in the domain of BI and big data in the cloud, and those to which design-science researchers should dedicate their effort.

References

1. IDC: Worldwide Business Analytics Software 2013-2017 Forecast and, Vendor Shares (2012), http://idcdocserv.com/241689e_sas
2. Cuzzocrea, A., Song, I.-Y., Davis, K.C.: Analytics over Large-Scale Multidimensional Data: the Big Data Revolution! In: Proceedings of DOLAP 2011, pp. 101–104. ACM Press (2011)
3. Pring, B., Brown, R.H., Leong, L., Biscotti, F., Couture, A.W., Lheureux, B.J., Liu, V.K.: Forecast: Public Cloud Services, Worldwide and Regions, Industry Sectors. 2009-2014. Gartner Report (2010)
4. IDC: IDC Cloud, http://www.idc.com/prodserv/FourPillars/mobility/index.jsp
5. March, S., Smith, G.: Design and Natural Science Research on Information Technology. Decision Support Systems 15(4), 251–266 (1995)
6. Hevner, A., March, S., Park, J., Ram, S.: Design Science in Information Systems Research. MIS Quarterly 28(1), 75–105 (2004)
7. Edwards, S., Lavagno, L., Lee, E.A., Sangiovanni-Vincentelli, A.: Design of Embedded Systems: Formal Models, Validation, and Synthesis. Proceedings of the IEEE 85(3), 366–390 (1997)
8. Offermann, P., Blom, S., Schönherr, M., Bub, U.: Artifact Types in Information Systems Design Science-a Literature Review. In: Winter, R., Zhao, J.L., Aier, S. (eds.) DESRIST 2010. LNCS, vol. 6105, pp. 77–92. Springer, Heidelberg (2010)
9. Gruber, T.R.: A Translation Approach to Portable Ontology Specifications. Knowledge Acquisition 5(2), 199–220 (1993)
10. Nickerson, R.C., Varshney, U., Muntermann, J.: A Method for Taxonomy Development and its Application in Information Systems. European Journal of Information Systems 22(3), 336–359 (2013)
11. CIO Council: Federal Enterprise Architecture Framework, version 1.1., Chief Information Officers Council, Washington D.C., USA (1999)
12. ISO/IEC, IEEE: Systems and Software Engineering – Vocabulary, standard ISO/IEC/IEEE 24765:2010(E) (2010)
13. Jarke, M., Loucopoulos, P., Lyytinen, K., Mylopoulos, J., Robinson, W.: The Brave New World of Design Requirements. Information Systems 36(7), 992–1008 (2011)
14. Nunamaker Jr., J.F., Briggs, R.O., De Vreede, G.-J., Sprague Jr., R.H.: Special Issue: Enhancing Organizations' Intellectual Bandwidth: The Quest for Fast and Effective Value Creation. Journal of Management Information Systems 17(3), 3–8 (2000)
15. Hanseth, O., Lyytinen, K.: Design Theory for Dynamic Complexity in Information Infrastructures: the Case of Building Internet. Journal of Information Technology 25(1), 1–19 (2010)
16. Kornyshova, E., Deneckère, R., Salinesi, C.: Method Chunks Selection by Multicriteria Techniques: an Extension of the Assembly Based Approach. In: Ralyté, J., Brinkkemper, S., Henderson-Sellers, B. (eds.) Situational Method Engineering: Fundamentals and Experiences. IFIP, vol. 244, pp. 64–78. Springer, Heidelberg (2007)
17. Purao, S., Vaishnavi, V.: Product Metrics for Object-Oriented Systems. ACM Computing Surveys 35(2), 191–221 (2003)
18. Abadi, D.J.: Data Management in the Cloud: Limitations and Opportunities. IEEE Data Engineering Bulletin 32(1), 3–12 (2009)
19. Bizer, C., Boncz, P., Brodie, M.L., Erling, O.: The Meaningful Use of Big Data: Four Perspectives-Four Challenges. ACM SIGMOD Record 40(4), 56–60 (2011)

20. Chen, H., Chiang, R.H., Storey, V.C.: Business Intelligence and Analytics: From Big Data to Big Impact. MIS Quarterly 36(4), 1165–1188 (2012)
21. Herodotou, H., Lim, H., Luo, G., Borisov, N., Dong, L., Cetin, F.B., Babu, S.: Starfish: A Self-Tuning System for Big Data Analytics. In: Proceedings of CIDR, pp. 261–272 (2011)
22. Pedersen, T.B., Pedersen, D., Riis, K.: On-Demand Multidimensional Data Integration: Toward a Semantic Foundation for Cloud Intelligence. The Journal of Super Computing 65(1), 217–257 (2013)
23. d'Orazio, L., Bimonte, S.: Multidimensional Arrays for Warehousing Data on Clouds. In: Hameurlain, A., Morvan, F., Tjoa, A.M. (eds.) Globe 2010. LNCS, vol. 6265, pp. 26–37. Springer, Heidelberg (2010)
24. Chaudhuri, S., Dayal, U., Narasayya, V.: An overview of Business Intelligence Technology. Communications of the ACM 54(8), 88–98 (2011)
25. Dean, J., Ghemawat, S.: MapReduce: Simplified Data Processing on Large Clusters. Communications of the ACM 51(1), 107–113 (2008)
26. Baars, H., Kemper, H.G.: Business Intelligence in the Cloud? In: Proceedings of PACIS 2010. Association for Information Systems, Paper 145 (2010)
27. Fernández, A., del Río, S., Herrera, F., Benítez, J.M.: An Overview on the Structure and Applications for Business Intelligence and Data Mining in Cloud Computing. In: Uden, L., Herrera, F., Bajo, J., Corchado, J.M. (eds.) 7th International Conference on KMO. AISC, vol. 172, pp. 559–570. Springer, Heidelberg (2013)
28. Hoberg, P., Wollersheim, J., Krcmar, H.: The Business Perspective on Cloud Computing - A Literature Review of Research on Cloud Computing. In: Proceedings of AMCIS 2012, Association for Information Systems, Paper 5 (2012)
29. Demirkan, H., Delen, D.: Leveraging the Capabilities of Service-Oriented Decision Support Systems: Putting Analytics and Big Data in Cloud. Decision Support Systems 55(1), 412–421 (2013)
30. Chaudhuri, S.: What Next? A Half-Dozen Data Management Research Goals for Big Data and the Cloud. In: Proceedings of PODS 2012, pp. 1–4. ACM Press, New York (2012)

From Business Intelligence
to Semantic Data Stream Management

Marie-Aude Aufaure and Raja Chiky

[1] MAS Lab Ecole Centrale Paris, France
marie-aude.aufaure@ecp.fr
[2] ISEP - LISITE, Paris, France
raja.chiky@isep.fr

Abstract. The Semantic Web technologies are being increasingly used for exploiting relations between data. In addition, new tendencies of real-time systems, such as social networks, sensors, cameras or weather information, are continuously generating data. This implies that data and links between them are becoming extremely vast. Such huge quantity of data needs to be analyzed, processed, as well as stored if necessary. In this paper, we will introduce recent work on Real-Time Business Intelligence that includes semantic data stream management. We will also present underlying approaches such as continuous queries and data summarization.

1 Introduction

The main objective of Business Intelligence is to transform data into knowledge for a better decision-making process. The constant growth of data and information, coming from heterogeneous data sources has lead to new ways of interaction and the integration of new models and tools to cope with this heterogeneity. We manipulate more and more unstructured data documents, emails, social networks, contacts that need to be integrated with classical structured data like CRM, data stored in relational databases. We also need more and more interactivity, flexibility, dynamicity and expect the system to be proactive and reactive. Users expect immediate feedback, and want to find information rather than merely look for it. Moreover, the company tends to be organized in a collaborative way, called enterprise 2.0 [23]. All these evolutions induce challenging research topics for Business Intelligence, such as providing efficient mechanisms for a unified access and model to both structured and unstructured data. Semantic technologies are a perfect fit for integrating and matching data. Business Intelligence will integrate collaborative and social software, by combining BI with elements from both Web 2.0 and the Semantic Web. Extracting value from all these data, a crucial advantage for companies, requires business analytics. In order to synthesize information and derive insights from massive, dynamic, ambiguous data, the use of data visualization techniques and visual analytics becomes critical. Business Intelligence is also impacted by big data, and need to account for the volume of data sources as well as the need of response in real-time for extracting value from trusted data.

The rest of this paper is organized as follows. Section 2 describes the new needs in Business Intelligence and present the whole architecture for semantic data stream

M. Indulska and S. Purao (Eds.): ER Workshops 2014, LNCS 8823, pp. 85–93, 2014.

management platform. In Section 3, we present the related work in the area of semantic filtering and continuous queries. Sections 4 and 5 describe the summarizing techniques used in data stream field. Finally, Section 6 concludes this paper and gives an outlook upon future research in this area.

2   From BI to Semantic Data Stream Management

Business Intelligence (BI) refers to a set of tools and methods dedicated to collecting, representing and analyzing data to support decision-making in enterprises. BI is defined as the ability of an organization to take all input data and convert them into knowledge, ultimately, providing the right information to the right people at the right time via the right channel. During the last two decades, numerous tools have been designed to make available a huge amount of corporate data for non-expert users. Business Intelligence is a mature technology, widely adapted, but faces new challenges for incorporating new data such as unstructured data or data coming from sensors or social networks into analytics. A key issue is the ability to analyze in real-time these constantly growing amounts of data, taking their meaning into account. The complexity of BI tools and their interface is a barrier for their adoption. Thus, personalized systems and user modeling [15] have emerged to help provide more relevant information and services to the user. Information visualization and dynamic interaction techniques are key for enhancing the user experience in using such tools.

Traditional BI systems offer tools for structuring and storing data in a data warehouse, in which data are modeled with a multidimensional model representing the analysis axis. Key performance indicators can be computed from this model and restituted to the user in a static dashboard.

These systems can be extended with semantic technologies to capture the meaning of data and new ways of interacting with data, intuitive and dynamic. Semantic technologies [5,12] focus on the meaning of data and are capable of dealing with both unstructured and structured data. Having the meaning of data and a reasoning mechanism may assist a user during his analysis task. The vision of the FP7 CUBIST[1] project was to extend the ETL process to both structured and unstructured data, to semantically store data in a triple store and to provide user-friendly visual analytics capabilities leading to dynamic dashboards. Then, the information provided to the user is not composed of only quantitative values like key performance indicators, but can also integrate qualitative values represented by a graph or a lattice extracted from formal concepts (a formal concept is a set of objects sharing properties; the formal concepts are then organized in a lattice linked together by a relation of inclusion). The user can then navigate into these semantic data through a visual analytic tool [20].

More recently, business intelligence has been impacted by big data and need to take into account the velocity i.e. the ability to provide information or alerts in real-time from streams. With the exponential growth of sensor networks, web logs, social networks and interconnected application components, large collections of data are continuously generated with high speed. These data are called "data streams": there is no limit on the total volume of data and there is no control over the order in which data arrive.

---

[1] CUBIST EU FP7 project: http://www.cubist-project.eu/index.php?id=378

The analysis methods (data mining, machine learning) should self-adapt to these data and process them on the fly in one pass and in the order of their arrival. These heterogeneous data streams [1] are produced in real time and consequently, should be processed on the fly. Then, they are maintained, interpreted and aggregated in the purpose of reusing their semantics and recommending relevant alerts to the targeted stakeholders in order to react to interesting phenomena occurring in the input streams. A precious decision-making value can be enhanced through the semantic analysis of data streams, especially while crossing them with other information sources.

Coming back to semantic technologies, numerous techniques can be used to extract some meaning or knowledge from data sources. Among them, we can cite natural language processing techniques, data mining, machine learning and ontology engineering. These techniques are used to extract patterns or models, to structure data and to transform any information in actionable knowledge. Semantic Web technologies can be used for linking, publishing or searching for data on the web, but also for large-scale structuring and enriching data with the RDF semantic model.

Semantic-based approaches are useful to simplify the integration of heterogeneous data sources by the mean of ontologies and for offering a unified metadata layer. Semantics can also be used for discovering and enriching information, and finally, to provide a unified data access mechanism. Semantics addresses the variety from the 3 V of Big Data (Volume, Variety and Velocity) to generate value from heterogeneous data. The value of data also increases when they can be linked to other data (Linked Data). Semantic technologies can then be seen as a great opportunity to reduce the cost and complexity of data integration.

Figure 1 represents the architecture of a Real-Time BI platform in which structured and unstructured data streams are processed on the fly. In a Real-Time BI platform, multiple heterogeneous data sources can be connected, and data can be static or dynamic.

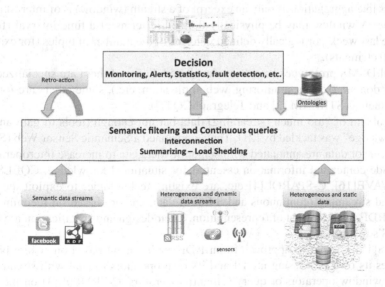

Fig. 1. Semantic real-time BI platform

The static data comes from standard databases or from open data, and does not change or in a minor way. Dynamic data comes as a stream, in a semantic format (RDF for example) or not (raw data). After their capture, data streams and static data are submitted to a set of semantic filters designed to achieve some specific business process. To manage infinite real-time data stream, the platform has to provide the ability to create persistent continuous queries, which allow users to receive new results when they become available. Moreover, In the context of Big Data with a huge volume of data coming in high velocity, the platform provides some summarizing and load shedding techniques [22] that randomly drop data from the streams when the load of the platform increases beyond what it can handle. We introduce in the following sections some research work related to semantic data stream management and summarizing techniques.

3 Semantic Filtering and Continuous Queries

Massive data stream processing is a scientific challenge and an industrial concern. But with the current volumes of data streams, their number and variety, current techniques are not able to meet the requirements of applications. The Semantic Web tools, through the RDF for example, address the problem of heterogeneous data. Thus, the data stream are converted to semantic data stream by using RDF triples extended with a timestamp. To be able to query, filter, or reason on semantic data streams, the query language SPARQL must be extended to include concepts such as windowing, based on previous work in Data Stream Management Systems DSMS.

Data Stream Management Systems (DSMS) [11] are designed to perform continuous queries over data stream. Data elements arrive on-line and stay only for a limited time period in memory. In a DSMS, continuous queries evaluate continuously and incrementally arriving data elements. DSMS use windowing techniques to handle some operations like aggregation as only an excerpt of a stream (window) is of interest at any given time. A window may be physically defined in terms of a time interval (for instance the last week), or logically defined in terms of the number of tuples (for example the last 20 elements).

Several DSMS prototypes have been developed. Some of them are specialized in a particular domain (sensor monitoring, web application, etc.), some others are for general use (such as STREAM [2] and TelegraphCQ [7]).

The problem of "too much (streaming) data but not enough (tools to gain and derive) knowledge" was tackled by [21]. They envisioned a Semantic Sensor Web (SSW), in which sensor data are annotated with semantic metadata to increase interoperability and provide contextual information essential for situational knowledge. CQELS[17], SPARKWAVE[16], C-SPARQL[4] etc. are existing technologies to exploit these semantic and streaming (continuous and infinite) data, and are based on recommended standard RDF, as the format of representation. Their design and specification are based on DSMS's features.

CQELS[17] is a native approach in an RDF environment based on 'white-boxes'. It provides its own processing model and its own operators to deal with streams, for example, window operators or query semantic operators. C-SPARQL[4] on the other hand, uses a 'black-box' approach which delegates the processing to other engines such as stream/event processing engines and SPARQL query processors by translating to their provided languages.

Although almost all the engines are based on the SPARQL Language, there are only a few systems which are able to process big quantity of data on the fly. Moreover, these engines do not feature any tool that would allow them to reduce the processing efforts and improve the processing time. For many applications, we must obtain compact summaries of the stream. These summaries could allow accurate answering of queries with estimates, which approximate the true answers over the original stream [8].

4   Data Summarization

In many fields, we are faced with the ever growing problem of how to manage and analyze large dynamic datasets. Database and data mining researchers often use synopsis (i.e summaries) with great effect to scale up performance on these datasets with a small cost to accuracy. Perhaps the most basic synopsis of a data stream is a sample of elements from the stream. A key benefit of such a sample is its flexibility: other synopses can be built from a sample itself. The rest of this section summarizes the state of the art for data stream algorithms. We will focus primarily on the problems of creating sample structures for a single data stream, in addition, we will also present techniques used in a distributed environment. Most of these summary structures have been considered for traditional databases [6]. The challenge is to adapt some of these techniques to the data stream model.

4.1   Data Stream Sampling

Sampling data streams is based on traditional sampling techniques, but also requires significant new innovations, especially to deal with the problem of infinite length streams. Windowing techniques are used to handle the unlimited nature of data: only an excerpt of a stream (window) is of interest at any given time. A window may be *physical*, defined in terms of a time interval (e.g.: the last week), or *logical*, defined in terms of the number of tuples (e.g.: the last 20 elements). These windows can be fixed with "fixed endpoints", or sliding with "moving endpoints" over time or tuples.

The traditional online algorithm "Reservoir Sampling" was proposed by Vitter in 1985 [24] and is widely used to sample data streams. It produces a sample of fixed size and does not require prior knowledge of data stream length. Reservoir sampling is useful for insertions or updates but not for deletions in the case of a sliding window. The difficulty arises because elements must be removed from the sample as they expire, so that maintaining a sample of a specified size is nontrivial. Several algorithms for handling logical and temporal windows have been developed.

A simple approach was proposed in [3]. The algorithm maintains a reservoir sample for the first window of the data stream. When an element expires, it is replaced with the newly arrived element. This algorithm maintains a uniform random sample for the first window and requires little memory to store the sample, but has the disadvantage of being highly periodic. To handle this, another technique was proposed in [3]. Each new arrival is added to a "Backing sample" with a fixed probability and the sample is generated by down sampling the backing sample. As elements expire, they are removed from the backing sample.

Many other algorithms were developed to be applied to logical windows such as "chain sampling" [3], to temporal windows such as "priority sampling" or for particular use such as "concise sampling" [10]. To the best for our knowledge, all of these techniques sample the data stream individually. Moreover, these techniques exploit neither possibilities of computation in sensors, nor bidirectional communication between the sensors and the central server.

4.2 Distributed Data Stream Sampling

There are many applications where data is continuously produced by a large number of distributed sensors. Adaptive sampling has been developed for these applications to manage limited resources. They aim at conserving network bandwidth and storage memory by filtering out data that may not be relevant in the current context. The data collection rate becomes dynamic and adaptable to the environment.

Most existing adaptive sampling techniques sample data from each source (*temporal sampling*). An adaptive sampling scheme which adjusts data collection rates in response to the contents of the stream was proposed in [13]. A Kalman filter is used at each sensor to make predictions of future values based on those already seen. The sampling interval SI is adjusted based on the prediction error. If the needed sampling interval for a sensor exceeds that is allowed by a specified Sampling Interval range, a new SI is requested to the server. The central server delivers new SIs according to available bandwidth, network congestion and streaming source priority.

In [19], authors present a feedback control mechanism which makes the frequency of measurements in each sensor dynamic and adaptable. Sampled data are compared against a model representing the environment. An error value is calculated on the basis of the comparison. If the error value is more than a predefined threshold, then a sensor node collects data at a higher sampling rate; otherwise, the sampling rate is decreased. Sensor nodes are completely autonomous in adapting their sampling rate.

In [18], authors present a method to prevent sensor nodes to send redundant information; this is predicted by a sink node using an ARIMA prediction model. Energy efficiency is achieved by suppressing the transmission of some samples, whose ARIMA based prediction values are within a predefined tolerance value with respect to their actual values. A similar approach is proposed by Cormode and Garofalakis [9]. Their results show that reduced communication between sensors and the central server can be sufficient by using an appropriate prediction model. A wide range of queries (including heavy hitters, wavelets and multi-dimensional histograms) can be answered by the central server using approximate sketches.

On the other hand, [25] uses a *spatial sampling* technique called backcasting approach. Backcasting operates by first activating only a small subset of sensor nodes which communicate their information to a fusion center. This provides an estimate of the environment being sensed, indicating some sensors may not need to be activated to achieve a desired level of accuracy. The fusion center then backcasts information based on the estimate to the network and selectively activates additional sensors to obtain a target error level. In this approach, adaptive sampling can save energy by only activating a fraction of the available sensors.

5 Summarizing Semantic Data Streams

The growing generated data from web applications is becoming a problem for the processing systems, and the relation between data is causing troubles when attempting to exploit data repositories. Therefore, [14] propose an extension of a real-time request system that allow to reduce processing tasks and memory space requirements. Authors propose the implementation of sampling operators that could be used in conjunction with existing semantic data streams engines considered as a Black Box engine. The sampling methods that have been implemented are: Uniform Random Sampling, Reservoir Sampling and Chain Sampling. Authors propose to extend existing semantic data stream querying engines by creating an external abstraction of the sampling operator as shown in the figure 2.

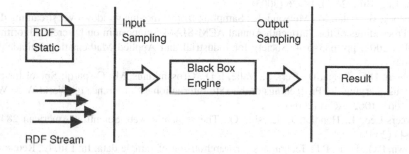

Fig. 2. Adding a sampling operator to semantic data stream management engine

However, this approach as implemented in [14] is only interesting when applied to semantic data streams including only independent RDF triples. The use of such approach is less successful when it comes to treat the data stream of a higher semantic level where RDF triples are linked to form RDF graphs. Indeed, this approach will lead to the destruction of semantic links constituting the structure of these graphs, thus reducing the level of semantics and affecting the data consistency.

6 Conclusion

The interconnection of massive data streams is a scientific challenge and a concrete industrial concern. But with the current volumes of data streams, their velocity and variety, current techniques are not able to meet the requirements of real applications. Yet we believe that this problem can be answered by taking advantage of recent advances in the techniques of querying, summarizing and reasoning on semantic data streams. these techniques are part of the new generation of Real Time Business Intelligence.

The Semantic Web tools, through RDF for example, address the problem of heterogeneous data. Thus, data streams are converted to semantic data streams by using RDF triples extended with a timestamp. To be able to query, filter, or reason on semantic data streams, the SPARQL query language must be extended to include concepts such as continuous queries. Several research prototypes for semantic filtering have been presented recently. However, to the best of our knowledge, none of this work has been concerned about overloading when the semantic data stream management system is not able to handle an overwhelming incoming data. Load shedding techniques and summarization techniques exist in the field of DSMS as we had presented in this paper. The challenge is to adapt these techniques to semantic data streams by losing the least possible links between data.

References

1. Aggarwal, C. (ed.): Data Streams – Models and Algorithms. Springer (2007)
2. Arasu, A., Babcock, B., Babu, S., Datar, M., Ito, K., Motwani, R., Nishizawa, I., Srivastava, U., Thomas, D., Varma, R., Widom, J.: Stream: The stanford stream data manager. IEEE Data Eng. Bull. 26(1), 19–26 (2003)
3. Babcock, B., Datar, M., Motwani, R.: Sampling from a moving window over streaming data. In: Proceedings of the Thirteenth Annual ACM-SIAM Symposium on Discrete Algorithms, SODA 2002, pp. 633–634. Society for Industrial and Applied Mathematics, Philadelphia (2002)
4. Barbieri, D.F., Braga, D., Ceri, S., Valle, E.D., Grossniklaus, M.: C-sparql: Sparql for continuous querying. In: Proceedings of the 18th International Conference on World Wide Web, pp. 1061–1062. ACM (2009)
5. Berners-Lee, T., Hendler, J., Lassila, O.: The semantic web. Scientific American 284(5), 34–43 (2001)
6. Brown, P.G., Haas, P.J.: Techniques for warehousing of sample data. In: Liu, L., Reuter, A., Whang, K.-Y., Zhang, J. (eds.) ICDE, p. 6. IEEE Computer Society (2006)
7. Chandrasekaran, S., Cooper, O., Deshpande, A., Franklin, M.J., Hellerstein, J.M., Hong, W., Krishnamurthy, S., Madden, S.R., Reiss, F., Shah, M.A.: Telegraphcq: Continuous dataflow processing. In: Proceedings of the 2003 ACM SIGMOD International Conference on Management of Data, SIGMOD 2003, pp. 668–668. ACM, New York (2003)
8. Cohen, E., Cormode, G., Duffield, N.: Structure-aware sampling on data streams. In: Proceedings of the ACM SIGMETRICS Joint International Conference on Measurement and Modeling of Computer Systems, pp. 197–208. ACM (2011)
9. Cormode, G., Garofalakis, M.N.: Approximate continuous querying over distributed streams. ACM Trans. Database Syst. 33(2) (2008)
10. Gibbons, P.B., Matias, Y.: New sampling-based summary statistics for improving approximate query answers. In: Proceedings of the 1998 ACM SIGMOD International Conference on Management of Data, SIGMOD 1998, pp. 331–342. ACM, New York (1998)
11. Golab, L., Özsu, M.T.: Issues in data stream management. SIGMOD Rec. 32(2), 5–14 (2003)
12. Hitzler, P., Krtzsch, M., Rudolph, S.: Foundations of Semantic Web Technologies, 1st edn. Chapman & Hall/CRC (2009)
13. Jain, A., Chang, E.Y.: Adaptive sampling for sensor networks. In: Proceeedings of the 1st International Workshop on Data Management for Sensor Networks: In Conjunction with VLDB 2004, DMSN 2004, pp. 10–16. ACM, New York (2004)
14. Jain, N., Pozo, M., Chiky, R., Kazi-Aoul, Z.: Sampling semantic data stream: Resolving overload and limited storage issues. In: DaEng, pp. 41–48 (2013)

15. Kobsa, A.: Generic user modeling systems. In: Brusilovsky, P., Kobsa, A., Nejdl, W. (eds.) Adaptive Web 2007. LNCS, vol. 4321, pp. 136–154. Springer, Heidelberg (2007)
16. Komazec, S., Cerri, D., Fensel, D.: Sparkwave: continuous schema-enhanced pattern matching over rdf data streams. In: Proceedings of the 6th ACM International Conference on Distributed Event-Based Systems, DEBS 2012, pp. 58–68. ACM, New York (2012)
17. Le-Phuoc, D., Dao-Tran, M., Xavier Parreira, J., Hauswirth, M.: A native and adaptive approach for unified processing of linked streams and linked data. In: Aroyo, L., Welty, C., Alani, H., Taylor, J., Bernstein, A., Kagal, L., Noy, N., Blomqvist, E. (eds.) ISWC 2011, Part I. LNCS, vol. 7031, pp. 370–388. Springer, Heidelberg (2011)
18. Liu, C., Wu, K., Tsao, M.: Energy efficient information collection with the arima model in wireless sensor networks. In: GLOBECOM, p. 5. IEEE (2005)
19. Marbini, A.D., Sacks, L.E.: Adaptive sampling mechanisms in sensor networks (2003)
20. Melo, C.A., Mikheev, A., Le Grand, B., Aufaure, M.-A.: Cubix: A visual analytics tool for conceptual and semantic data. In: Vreeken, J., Ling, C., Zaki, M.J., Siebes, A., Yu, J.X., Goethals, B., Webb, G.I., Wu, X. (eds.) ICDM Workshops, pp. 894–897. IEEE Computer Society (2012)
21. Sheth, A., Henson, C., Sahoo, S.S.: Semantic sensor web. IEEE Internet Computing 12(4), 78–83 (2008)
22. Tatbul, N., Çetintemel, U., Zdonik, S., Cherniack, M., Stonebraker, M.: Load shedding in a data stream manager. In: Proceedings of the 29th International Conference on Very Large Data Bases, VLDB 2003, vol. 29, pp. 309–320. VLDB Endowment (2003)
23. Trujillo, J., Maté, A.: Business intelligence 2.0: A general overview. In: Aufaure, M.-A., Zimányi, E. (eds.) eBISS 2011. LNBIP, vol. 96, pp. 98–116. Springer, Heidelberg (2012)
24. Vitter, J.S.: Random sampling with a reservoir. ACM Trans. Math. Softw. 11(1), 37–57 (1985)
25. Willett, R., Martin, A., Nowak, R.: Backcasting: Adaptive sampling for sensor networks. In: Proceedings of the 3rd International Symposium on Information Processing in Sensor Networks, IPSN 2004, pp. 124–133. ACM, New York (2004)

Preface to MReBA 2014

Requirements Engineering (RE) aims to capture the intended system functionality and qualities. In practice, RE activities often fall under the heading of Business Analysis (BA), determining how a business can make use of technology in order to improve its operations, meet targets, and thrive in a competitive economy.

Throughout the years, RE and BA have become much more than just creative learning activities. They are also, and foremost, proven processes that can rely on well defined methods, techniques and tools to handle requirements-related issues for the design of complex socio technical systems in various business contexts. In this context, the use of models in RE and BA allows for a shared perception of requirements and an explicit consideration of business strategy. Moreover, models can ease the transformation towards design, specification, and code, operationalizing strategies through socio-technical systems.

MReBA (Modelling in Requirements and Business Analysis) is a new workshop that builds on RIGiM (Requirements Intentions and Goals in Conceptual Modeling). While RIGiM was specifically dedicated to goal modelling and the use of intentional concepts in RE, MReBa handles any kind of modelling notation or activity in the context of RE or BA.

MReBA aims to provide a forum for discussing the interplay between requirements engineering, business analysis and conceptual modeling. We investigate how conceptual modeling notations and methods, as well as mathematical approaches, help in conceptualizing purposeful systems and business processes. What are the unresolved open questions? What lessons are there to be learnt from industrial experiences? What empirical data are there to support the cost-benefit analysis when modelling requirements? Are there applications domains or types of project settings for which mathematical modelling and conceptual modelling are particularly suitable or not suitable? What degree of formalization, automation or interactivity is feasible and appropriate for what types of participants during requirements engineering and business analysis?

This year, MReBA includes a keynote by Prof. Bill Robinson on Creating Process Models. In addition six high-quality papers are presented, including three full and three short papers.

Each of the submitted papers went through a thorough review process with at least three reviews from our program committee. We thank authors and reviewers for their valuable contributions.

July 2014

Renata Guizzardi
Jennifer Horkoff
Camille Salinesi
Workshop Organizers
MReBA'14

Understandability of Goal Concepts
by Requirements Engineering Experts

Wilco Engelsman[1,2] and Roel Wieringa[2]

[1] BiZZdesign
w.engelsman@bizzdesign.nl
[2] University of Twente
r.j.wieringa@utwente.nl

Abstract. ARMOR is a graphical language for modeling business goals and enterprise architectures. In previous work we have identified problems with understandability of goal-oriented concepts for practicing enterprise architects. In this paper we replicate the earlier quasi-experiments with experts in requirements engineering, to see if similar problems arise. We found that fewer mistakes were made in this replication than were made in the previous experiment with practitioners, but that the types of mistakes made in all the concepts were similar to the mistakes made in our previous experiments with enterprise architects. The stakeholder concept was used perfectly by our sample, but the goal decomposition relation was not understood. The subjects provided explanations for understandability problems that are similar to our previous hypothesized explanations. By replicating some of our earlier results, this paper provides additional support for the generalizability of our earlier results.

1 Introduction

In large organizations the gap between business and IT is usually bridged by an enterprprise architecture (EA). An EA is a high-level representation of the enterprise, used for managing the relation between business and IT and to coordinate IT projects. An EA usually contains models of aspects of the business, of IT applications, of the IT infrastructure aspects and of relations between all of these. In addition, in recent years EA has been used to increase the flexibility of the organization and justify the contribution of EA to business goals. This means that EAs are are not only used to manage the relation between business and IT and to coordinate IT projects, but also to determine the impact of changing business goals on the EA and vice versa.

This requires an extension of EA modelling languages with concepts like goals, and support for tracing business goals to EA. In previous work, we have extended the EA modeling language Archimate [18] with concepts from goal-oriented requirements engineering (GORE) [7]. The extension is called ARMOR, and the result of extending Archimate with ARMOR is called Archimate 2.0. So ARMOR is the GORE part of Archimate 2.0. This paper evaluates the understandability of ARMOR.

M. Indulska and S. Purao (Eds.): ER Workshops 2014, LNCS 8823, pp. 97–106, 2014.

In previous work we have investigated the understandability of the ARMOR extension by two case studies [9] and two quasi-experiments with practicing enterprise architects [8]. The results showed that practitioners find ARMOR very complex and use only a few of the concepts of ARMOR correctly.

To test the generalizability of these findings, we have replicated the experiment with participants of the REFSQ '14 conference that can be considered experts in GORE languages[1]. We additionally asked the subjects for the perceived understandability of ARMOR concepts in an exit survey. The results confirm our earlier findings about understandability problems in goal-oriented notations.

We start with listing the research questions in the next section. Next we describe our research methodology in section 3. Section 4 describes our conceptual framework. The results from the experiment, the exit survey and the comparison with our previous results are described in section 5. Answers to the research questions are summarized in section 7 and section 8 discusses related work. Section 9 describes some implications for practice and further research.

2   Research Problem

In our courses teaching ARMOR to practitioners we saw that there were understandability issues regarding the concepts. Therefore we started to investigate this problem. This work is a replication of our prevous studies. Our research questions are the same as in our previous quasi-experiments, extended with two more questions. We added a question to compare subjects' perception of understandability with the understanding they exhibited during the experiment. We also added a fifth question in which we ask about the comparison across all quasi-experiments.

- Q1: How understandable is the ARMOR language?
- Q2: Which concepts are understood correctly and why?
- Q3: Which concepts are not understood? Why? Does this agree with subjects' perceptions of understandability?
- Q4: What kind of mistakes are made? Why?
- Q5: How much do our findings differ from our previous samples and why?

In all cases, we want to know not only an answer to the journalistic question what is the case, but also the research question why it is the case.

3   Research Methodology

We performed two identical experiments at REFSQ'14 of 90 minutes each. We could not control any information flow from the first experiment to the second experiment, and we depended on the integrity of the participants, all researchers, to refrain from creating such a flow.

---

[1] http://refsq.org/2014/live-experiment/

Table 1. Entry questionnaire

- What is your highest level of completed education?
- What is your daily function?
- How many years of experience do you have in this function?
- How experienced are you with a (any) requirements modeling notation? (select one: I have no experience / I understand the concepts / I can read diagrams / I can create diagrams / I can teach a requirements modeling technique.)

Subjects self-selected into the experiments, and to be able to assess the influence of previous knowledge of GORE concepts, we measured the knowledge and experience of the participants with GORE notations in a short entry-questionnaire (table 1).

Each experiment started with a very short lecture (30 minutes) on ARMOR. Next, the participants had to construct simple goal models of a case. To allow answering the research questions, the case required all ARMOR constructs to model. But to fit the restricted time available for the modeling exercise (50 minutes), the case was very easy compared to the actual real world problems of our previous experiments.

Finally, before leaving the room, each participant filled in an exit questionnaire in which for each of the GORE concepts used in the assignment, it was asked (1) whether they found the concept easy, normal or hard to use, and (2) to optionally explain their answer.

During data analysis, the answers were graded by the first author in the same way as in the previous experiments. The first author compared the used concepts to intended use of the concepts and marked if the concepts were used incorrectly. Results were discussed with the second author.

4   Defining Understandability

In a survey of definitions of understandability of conceptual models, Houy et al. [11] identified five types of definitions: the ability to recall model content, the ability to correctly answer questions about a model,the time needed to answer questions about the model, the ability to solve problems using the model, and the ability to verify a model.These are however measures of model understandability, whereas we are interested in measures of language understandability. An example of a measure of language understandability is the ability of subjects to guess the definition of a language construct by looking at the icons. Caire et al. [5] measured this for i*.

However, these are all measures of passive understanding, whereas we are interested in a more active form of understanding that is closer to the concept of ease of use. How easy is it to construct a model in a language? This concept of understanding is used by, for example, Carvallo & Franch [6] and by Matulevičius & Heymans [13], who measured the number of mistakes made in constructing i* models, and by Abrahao et al., who measured the time needed to build a model [1]. Our concept of understandability is close to the first of these, and we define the understandability of a language construct as *the percentage of users that can use a concept correctly*.

Construct validity is the validity of the operationalizations of a construct. Note that our definition of understandability is close to that of ease of use, and that our results are therefore about a different concept of understandability than that used when studying understandability of a conceptual model. Our definition agrees with that used by other authors [6, 13], but of the two known operationalizations, correctness of use and time to use, we have selected the first one only. This should be taken into consideration when comparing our results with those of others.

5   Observations

There were 18 participants in total, about evenly spread over the two experiments. Two subjects had a bachelor's degree, seven had a master's degree and nine a PhD degree. Furthermore, the majority of the subjects considered themselves experts in requirements engineering in either industry or academia. According to the entry survey 9 out of 18 subjects had the ability to teach requirements engineering notations.

Combining this high level of expertise with the relative simplicity of the assignment, we would not expect any serious understandability problems with GORE notations.

Table 2. Data about correct construct usage by the 18 participants

Practitioner	1	2	3	4	5	6	7	8	9	10	11	12	13	14	15	16	17	18	avg
Stakeholder	100	100	100	100	100	100	100	100	100	100	100	100	100	100	100	100	100	100	100
Influence	94	100			100	100	100	100	100	0		100	100	100					89
Goal	69	100	100	100	100	100	100	100	100	100	100	100	100	0	100	100	100	100	88
Assessment	100	100	85	100	100	100	40	100	100	100	100	100	100	0	100	100	100	100	82
Realization	0	100			100	100	0	100	100	100	100	100	100	33	100		100	100	78
Requirement	0	86		100	100	20	50	100	100	100	67	100	100	100		100	100		73
Driver	0	100	33	100	100	0	100	100	0	100	100	100	50	100	100	100	100	100	71
Decomposition	33	100		0	50	0	12	29	0	25	0	50		100		100	67	0	19

Table 2 lists the ARMOR constructs on the left and summarizes the scores that the subjects received on their assignments. Row *i* column *j* shows the percentage of times that practitioner *i* used concept *j* correctly. The numbers are the percentage of correctly used concepts by each subject. When a subject did not use a concept at all, the corresponding cell is empty. The avg column shows the percentage of users that always used the concept correctly. The rows are ordered from best understood to least understood construct.

Table 3 summarizes the scores of the subjective evaluation of understandability, ordered in the same way as table 2. The numbers are the total number of subjects that found a certain concept easy, normal or hard to use. The final

Table 3. Summary of the exit survey

	Easy	Normal	Hard	Most common explanation
Stakeholder	16	1	1	A very common and well known concept.
Influence	5	7	6	Unknown when to use it.
Goal	6	7	5	Hard to distinguish from driver. Hard to distinguish from requirement. Common concept.
Assessment	7	6	5	Difficult to distinguish from a goal.
Realization	5	5	3	What is a full realization?
Requirement	5	8	5	Very similar to goal. Common concept
Driver	6	9	3	Very difficult to distinguish from a goal.
Decomposition	4	7	7	Unknown when to use it.

column summarizes the most frequently occurring explanations provided by the subjects. We now discuss our findings in detail.

The *stakeholder* concept is based on definitions from TOGAF, i* and Tropos [3, 17, 20]. All subjects used this concept correctly and we conclude that the stakeholder concept is an easy to use concept. This is supported by the subjective evaluation of the exit questionnaire. The explanation the subjects provided is that it is a common concept.

The next best understood construct was that of *influence*, defined in ARMOR as a positive or negative influence of satisfaction of one goal on the satisfaction of another goal. This definition is based the influence concept on i* and Tropos [3,20]. 89% of the subjects used the influence relation correctly, but only 5 out of 18 users found the relation easy to use. Participants found it difficult to choose between the decomposition and influence relation. The most common mistake was also that it was used instead of a decomposition.

ARMOR defines a *goal* as some end that a stakeholder wants to achieve, a definition common in the GORE literature [4, 19, 20]. 89% of the subjects used the goal concept correctly. The subjective evaluation shows that subjects still had a hard time using the concept. They found it hard to distinguish from the concepts of driver and of requirement. This is consistent with the types of mistakes made as sometimes drivers or requirements were stated as goals.

ARMOR defines an *assessment* as the outcome of the analysis of some stakeholder concern, a definition based on that of BMM [4]. 83% of the subjects used the assessment concept correctly. However, subjects found the concept was too close to a goal. This is supported by the types of mistakes made by the subjects, assessments were confused with goals.

ARMOR defines the *realization* relation as a relation that some end that is realized by some means, a definition found too in i* and KAOS [19, 20]. 79% of the subjects used the realization relation correctly. This is consistent with the subjective evaluation, where only three subjects found it hard to use. The most common mistake was that it was used to relate two requirements.

ARMOR defines *requirement* as some end that must be realized by a single component of the architecture, a definition found also in KAOS and GBRAM [2, 19]. 69% of the subjects used the requirements concept correctly. The most common mistake was that goals were modeled as requirement. This is consistent with the explanations the subjects provided, that goals and requirements were difficult to distinguish.

A *driver* in ARMOR is that it is a key interest of a user, a definition that is taken from TOGAF [17]. Only 67% of the subjects used the concept correctly, which is consistent with the subjective evaluation. The subjects found it very similar to the concept of a goal. The most common mistake made was indeed that a goal was modelled as a driver.

The ARMOR concept of a *decomposition* is a combination of concepts from the EA and GORE literature [3, 4, 20]. ARMOR defines it as a some intention that is divided into multiple intention. Only 19% used the decomposition relation correctly. This is consistent with the subjective evaluation where only five users found it easy to use. The subjects found it difficult to choose between decomposition and influence.

Some of the data in table 2 are consistent with the subject evaluations of the exit questionnaire. For example, when a subject subjectively found a concept hard to use, often they would not use the concept all. The subjects provided an explanation that the relations were sometimes hard to identify. We believe that therefore they just picked one. This is also the case with the other concepts which were very similar, for example the goal and requirement concept.

There are also discrepancies. For example, 11 subjects found the decomposition relation not hard to use, but only 3 subjects used the relation correctly. Conversely, only 5 users found the influence relation easy to use, but most participants used it correctly. Apparently, perceived understandability does not coincide with understanding.

6 Discussion

Comparison With Our Previous Results. The level of understanding exhibited by the participants was much higher than in our previous study with practitioners [8]. In our earlier study, only 5 concepts were used correctly by more than half of the practitioners. This agrees with the higher level of expertise of our current group of participants compared to our previous samples.

However, there is a rough correspondence in the orderings of understandability. In our earlier experiment, the concepts of stakeholder and of realization were used correctly by all practitioners. In our current experiment, the concept of stakeholder was used correctly too, but the concept of realization was used incorrectly by some participants, and they perceived some problems in using it. This may be a consequence of the more academic expertise of the subjects.

In all experiments, the concepts of stakeholder, influence, goal and requirement were the best understood (in that order) and the concept of decomposition was the least understood. And in all experiments, participants had trouble distinguishing requirements, assessments and drivers from goals, and participants wondered why all of these concepts are present in the language.

Explanations. Our observations support the explanations of understandability problems listed earlier. The number of concepts in ARMOR is large, making it difficult for novice users to choose among them. Related to this is the second explanation, which is that the semantic distance among some concepts is very small, making it even harder to choose the right concept to use in a modeling problem.

Finally, the distance of ARMOR concepts and the meaning of those concepts in daily practice is large in our previous experiments. This explained problems that practitioners had with assimilating ARMOR concepts. For the academics that participated in the current experiment, this distance is smaller, because they teach GORE concepts or have studied them. This may explain the higher scores that the participants in the current experiment had compared to the practitioners' score in the previous experiments.

One factor that affects the internal validity of these explanations is that the explanation of ARMOR given by the first author may have created understandability problems. However, The first author regularly teaches these concepts to practitioners. And to prepare for the current experiment, he has explained the concepts to university colleagues. This should mitigate the threat that understandability problems have been caused by the instructor rather than by the language.

Generalizability. Our sample is too small to do any statistical inference. Moreover, the participants self-selected in the sample, which may have biased the results. However, given the fact that our sample consisted of GORE experts who chose to do an assignment with a GORE language, we think that other academic subjects would at least have the understandability problems that we observed in our sample.

We replicated the findings of earlier experiments about most understandable and least understandable concepts, and this supports generalizability too.

Moreover, our explanations in terms of the large number of concepts and the small semantic distance among some concepts, and the need of language users to assimilate new concepts to existing knowledge, are stated in general terms. To the extent that these explanations are generalizable, the phenomena that they explain are generalizable too.

Whether our results generalize to other GORE languages, must be determined by repeating this experiment for these other languages. The question whether all semantic constructs present in i* are really needed has been raised earlier by Moody et al. [15], but it has not yet been answered by empirical research.

7 Answers to Research Questions

Q1: How understandable is ARMOR? The last column of table 2 shows the answer to this. Only the stakeholder concept scored 100% an was perfectly understood. However, the only concept that was not clearly understood was that of the decomposition relation, scoring only 19%. The concepts of driver, assessment and goal were very well understood scoring more than 80%. The concepts of requirement, influence and realization were fairly well understood scoring in the 70% range.

Q2: Which concepts are understood correctly and why? Except for the decomposition relation all concepts were understood (scoring more than 55) This can be explained by that most of the concepts are very common concepts.

Q3: Which concepts are not understood correctly and why? There is a gradation in non-understanding, with the decomposition relationship at the bottom. The decomposition relation is very difficult to distinguish from the influence relation.

Q4: What kind of mistakes are made? Why? Does this agree with subjects' perceptions of understandability? The subjects modeled drivers and assessments as goals, and modeled influence relations by means of decomposition relations Explanations were given above. Apparently perceived understandability does not coincide with actual understandability.

Q5: How much do the results differ and why? The results from this study were roughly similar to the results of our previous work. The major difference is that the subjects scored much better than the subjects in our previous experiments This can be explained by the higher expertise level of the current subjects, and the greater simplicity of the assignment compared to the modeling task in the previous experiments.,

8 Related Work

The Business Rules Group has published a model that relates business goals and elements found in EA, called the business motivation model [4], which is now an OMG standard. The difference with ArchiMate is that the BMM provides no concrete modelling notations. It provides plans and guidelines for developing and managening business plans in an organized manner, all related to enterprise architecture.

Stirna et al. describe an approach to enterprise modelling that includes linking goals to enterprise models [16]. However they do not describe concrete modelling notations that are needed to extend existing EA modelling techniques. Jureta and Faulkner [12] sketch a goal-oriented language that links goals and a number of other intentional structures to actors, but not to EA models. Horkhoff and Yu present a method to evaluate the achievement of goals by enterprise models, all represented in i* [10].

An important obstacle to applying GORE to real-world problems is the complexity of the notation. Moody et al. [15] identified improvements for i* and validated the constructs of i* in practice , based on Moody's theory of nottions [14].

Caire et al. [5] also investigated the understandability of i*. They focussed on the ease of understanding of a concept by asking subjects to infer its definition by its visual representation. They had novices design a new icon set for i* and validated these icons in a new case study. This contrasts with our work because they focus on notations and we focus on concepts.

Carvallo & Franch [6] provided an experience report about the use of i* in architecting hybrid systems. They concluded that i* could be used for this purpose for stakeholders and modelers, provided that i* was simplified. Our work extends on these findings. We also found out that related concepts are hard to distinguish (i.e the distinction between driver,assessment,goal, the distinction between requirement and goal and the distinction between decomposition and influence).

Matulevičius & Heymans [13] compared i* and KAOS to determine which language was more understandable. The relevant conclusions for this work were that the GORE languages had ill defined constructs and were there hard to use, GORE languages also lacked methodological guidelines to assist users in using the languages. These conclusions were also found in our work.

9 Implications

9.1 Implications for Practice

ARMOR is part of an Open Group standard [18] and the concepts we investigated in this paper will remain present in the language. However, one practical implication of this paper is that in future training programs we will make a distinction between the recommended minimal concepts such as the concepts of stakeholder, goal, and requirement, and less important concepts, such as those of driver and assessment, that can safely be ignored in practice.

We also have to improve our training material. When we saw that the level of education went up, the number of understandability issues dropped. Somehow we need to compensate some of this with our training material. This can be with practically usable guidelines for the use of the concepts that we do recommend. These guidelines could be tailored to specific experience levels, e.g. develop guidelines for inexperienced participants and different guidelines for experienced participants.

9.2 Future Research

In future work we will focus on the traceability aspects of the ARMOR language. Our design goal was to realize traceability between business goals and enterprise architecture. We want to establish that with a minimalized version this is still achieved. Another interesting connection to explore is the relation with Moody's work on the understandability of notations. That work too seems to point at the need for reducing complexity by reducing the number of concepts to be represented in a language.

References

1. Abrahão, S., Insfran, E., Carsí, J.A., Genero, M.: Evaluating requirements modeling methods based on user perceptions: A family of experiments. Information Sciences 181(16), 3356–3378 (2011)
2. Anton, A.I.: Goal-based requirements analysis. In: Proceedings of the Second International Conference on Requirements Engineering, pp. 136–144. IEEE (1996)

3. Bresciani, P., Perini, A., Giorgini, P., Giunchiglia, F., Mylopoulos, J.: Tropos: An agent-oriented software development methodology. Autonomous Agents and Multi-Agent Systems 8(3), 203–236 (2004)
4. Business Motivation Model: Business motivation model version 1.0. (2007) (September 22, 2009), Standard document: http://www.omg.org/spec/BMM/1.0/PDF
5. Caire, P., Genon, N., Moody, D., et al.: Visual notation design 2.0: Towards user-comprehensible re notations. In: Proceedings of the 21st IEEE International Requirements Engineering Conference (2013)
6. Carvallo, J.P., Franch, X.: On the use of i* for architecting hybrid systems: A method and an evaluation report. In: Persson, A., Stirna, J. (eds.) PoEM 2009. LNBIP, vol. 39, pp. 38–53. Springer, Heidelberg (2009)
7. Engelsman, W., Quartel, D.A.C., Jonkers, H., van Sinderen, M.J.: Extending enterprise architecture modelling with business goals and requirements. Enterprise Information Systems 5(1), 9–36 (2011)
8. Engelsman, W., Wieringa, R.: Understandability of goal-oriented requirements engineering concepts for enterprise architects. In: Jarke, M., Mylopoulos, J., Quix, C., Rolland, C., Manolopoulos, Y., Mouratidis, H., Horkoff, J. (eds.) CAiSE 2014. LNCS, vol. 8484, pp. 105–119. Springer, Heidelberg (2014)
9. Engelsman, W., Wieringa, R.: Goal-oriented requirements engineering and enterprise architecture: two case studies and some lessons learned. In: Regnell, B., Damian, D. (eds.) REFSQ 2011. LNCS, vol. 7195, pp. 306–320. Springer, Heidelberg (2012)
10. Horkoff, J., Yu, E.: Evaluating goal achievement in enterprise modeling–an interactive procedure and experiences. In: Persson, A., Stirna, J. (eds.) PoEM 2009. LNBIP, vol. 39, pp. 145–160. Springer, Heidelberg (2009)
11. Houy, C., Fettke, P., Loos, P.: Understanding understandability of conceptual models - what are we actually talking about? - supplement. Tech. rep., Universitäts- und Landesbibliothek, Postfach 151141, 66041 Saarbräcken (2013), http://scidok.sulb.uni-saarland.de/volltexte/2013/5441
12. Jureta, I., Faulkner, S.: An agent-oriented meta-model for enterprise modelling. In: Akoka, J., et al. (eds.) ER Workshops 2005. LNCS, vol. 3770, pp. 151–161. Springer, Heidelberg (2005)
13. Matulevičius, R., Heymans, P.: Comparing goal modelling languages: An experiment. In: Sawyer, P., Heymans, P. (eds.) REFSQ 2007. LNCS, vol. 4542, pp. 18–32. Springer, Heidelberg (2007)
14. Moody, D.: The "physics" of notations: Toward a scientific basis for constructing visual notations in software engineering. IEEE Transactions on Software Engineering 35(6), 756–779 (2009)
15. Moody, D.L., Heymans, P., Matulevičius, R.: Visual syntax does matter: improving the cognitive effectiveness of the i* visual notation. Requirements Engineering 15(2), 141–175 (2010)
16. Stirna, J., Persson, A., Sandkuhl, K.: Participative enterprise modeling: experiences and recommendations. In: Krogstie, J., Opdahl, A.L., Sindre, G. (eds.) CAiSE 2007. LNCS, vol. 4495, pp. 546–560. Springer, Heidelberg (2007)
17. The Open Group: TOGAF Version 9. Van Haren Publishing (2009)
18. The Open Group: ArchiMate 2.0 Specification. Van Haren Publishing (2012)
19. van Lamsweerde, A.: From system goals to software architecture. In: Bernardo, M., Inverardi, P. (eds.) SFM 2003. LNCS, vol. 2804, pp. 25–43. Springer, Heidelberg (2003)
20. Yu, E.: Towards modelling and reasoning support for early-phase requirements engineering. In: Proceedings of the Third IEEE International Symposium on Requirements Engineering, pp. 226–235. IEEE Computer Society Press (2002)

On the Definition of Self-service Systems

Corentin Burnay[1,2,3], Joseph Gillain[2,3], Ivan J. Jureta[1,2,3],
and Stéphane Faulkner[2,3]

[1] Fonds de la Recherche Scientifique – FNRS, Brussels
[2] Department of Business Administration, University of Namur
[3] PReCISE Research Center, University of Namur

Abstract. Changing requirements are common in today's organizations, and have been a central concern in Requirements Engineering (RE). Over time, methods have been developed to deal with such variability. Yet, the latter often require considerable amount of time to be applied. As time-to-value is becoming a critical requirement of users, new types of systems have been developed to deal more efficiently with changing requirements: the Self-Service Systems. In this paper, we provide an overall discussion about what self systems are, what they imply in terms of engineering, how they can be designed, and what type of questions they raise to RE.

1 Introduction

Information Systems (IS) are becoming central in contemporary organizations, given that they intervene in most, if not all value chain activities. They do so by helping organizations to collect, treat and diffuse data and information, thereby enabling them to know more about, and hopefully influence more precisely and relevantly the business activities. The engineering of IS is the responsibility of systems engineers, which today involves various professions, including requirements engineers (or business analysts), software engineers, system architects, etc. They are expected to define clear and relevant requirements, then engineer, develop, deploy, maintain, and change solutions to satisfy the requirements.

It is well-known that it is hard to get the requirements right [1]. Part of the difficulty comes from the fact that requirements that are available *before* using a system or interacting with its prototype and *after* using it, can, and often are different. The difference comes from various factors, including simply that people learn through experience. Through learning, their expectations change, and so do their requirements. Such issue, of changing requirements, has been a topic of research in adaptive systems and requirements evolution [2].

In this paper, we are interested in one specific approach to deal with requirements changes. We observed it in industry, and our aim is to look at the theoretical issues that arise in relation to it, how it relates to research in Requirements Engineering (RE), and what new issues, if any, it gives rise to.

Specifically, we are interested in the so-called Self-Service Systems. The basic idea is that the system engineers will not produce a system that satisfies all the specific requirements that the various stakeholders may have. Instead, they will

M. Indulska and S. Purao (Eds.): ER Workshops 2014, LNCS 8823, pp. 107–116, 2014.

engineer a system which can, if properly configured *by the users*, satisfy these requirements, whichever they are at system design time, and whichever they may end up being at run-time. If you think of requirements as being represented, as usual in goal-oriented requirements engineering [3,4], as a goal forest, where goals close to roots are abstract and general requirements, and goals close to leaves are more specific requirements, then Self-Service Systems are engineered to satisfy some goals midway in the goal forest, between the leaves and the roots, rather than satisfy the leaves. As we will see later, this view is simplistic, but it gives an initial idea that we build from in the rest of the paper.

We refer to Self-Service Systems as *Selfs* hereafter. We first motivate the use of Selfs in Section 2 and 3. We then provide a more detailed definition of what Selfs are, with examples in Section 4. We discuss how requirements from traditional systems differ from those from Selfs in Section 5. Finally, we suggest that designing a Self raises new challenges for RE in Section 6. We conclude with a discussion about tradeoffs and future works respectively in Section 7 and 8.

2   Illustration - Self-service in Business Intelligence

We observed Self-Service Systems for Business Intelligence (BI). In general, IS for BI gather business data in order to provide information to business decision-makers, under the form of reports, dashboards, or any other relevant output [5,6]. Despite there being frameworks for doing RE of BI systems [7,8], there is a practical difficulty that is hard to overcome in terms of methodology. It can be formulated as follows: the data types and sources, and the information relevant for business decision-making may not be the same at all times, which means that, for example, the content of reports, the analyses applied to data, and so on, need to be changed regularly. In practice, it may be too costly (or take too much time) to have business analysts elicit new requirements on reports and analyses, and propagate these new requirements through the specifications, system architects to architecture, and software engineers to code each time a change occurs.

From the standpoint of those who make and sell BI systems, it may also be more interesting to avoid changing the systems so much, because, for example, it means maintaining systems that become different from each other over time, even if they started from the same set of functionality. Self-Service Systems are a response to this, in that they do not try to satisfy the most specific requirements, but give features whose combinations could satisfy various specific requirements. For example, a Self-Service BI (SSBI) system will have features that allow its users (they can include business analysts as well, not only end-users) to change analyses applied to data, create new reports or change existing ones, and so on.

In [9], SSBI is presented as an important promise of BI, *despite the current difficulties in making those softwares easy to use for business people*. SSBI has been the center of some attention from specialized institutions (e.g. TDWI [10], Gartner [11] or Forrester [12]), which is another clue that business users are actually interested in achieving shorter time-to-value and doing BI on their own.

3   Why Make Self-service Systems?

Selfs are ways to deal with the change of requirements. Instead of making a system that satisfies exactly all of the most specific requirements identified at design-time, we consider these merely as examples of requirements that may arise at run-time, and we engineer features whose combinations can satisfy these anticipated, and perhaps some of the unanticipated run-time requirements.

In fact, the problem with design-time requirements is not that they are changing. In practice, many RE approaches exist, that can be used to identify new requirements [13] or track evolution of existing ones [14,15]. The translation of those requirements into specifications for the system-to-be is not a problem either, as it has also been discussed at length in RE [16]. *The problem is rather on the time it takes to go from there being a new run-time requirement, to the time when the system has been changed to satisfy it.*

In the case of BI systems, the IT department is expected to be very responsive, and to provide quickly adapted solutions to business requirements. This is a generic requirement from BI systems, also known as time-to-value: once a BI system is implemented, users must gain easy and rapid access to information, so that decision making process remains efficient [10]. Traditional RE approaches can appear limited in that regard, because they assume elicitation, modeling, analysis, verification, negotiation, validation, and so on, have to be done for new requirements. This can influence time-to-value negatively.

As a response to delays due to *changing requirements*, Selfs attempt to transfer some of the design responsibility to end-users, who are therefore in charge of understanding what they need, and directly designing what is required to satisfy these needs using a Self. For example, in BI, Self-Service Business Intelligence (SSBI) is used to enable end-users to select some data sources and decide about a visualization tool to view it, all by themselves. Ultimately, they choose what to include in the report that they need the system to make.

Unlike for classical BI systems, SSBI does not require the usual RE processes to occur each time a user has a new requirement. There is therefore a tendency to make systems with generic features, and expect users to combine / configure the latter by themselves, in order to satisfy their new, specific requirements on-demand. They do so with the support of the system, but without the intervention of system engineers. This approach has the main advantage of reducing time-to-value, and hence improving users experience of the BI platform [10].

4   Indirect Requirements Satisfaction

In this section, we suggest and discuss an essential property held by typical requirements of Selfs. We consider that any requirement which satisfies this property can be characterized as a *Self requirement*. The more a system is specified by such Selfs requirements, the more the system can be considered as a Self.

It implies that the distinction between Selfs and non Selfs is not clear cut, and that any system can be placed on a "Self dimension". Besides, Selfs can be distributed or centralized, adaptive or not, agent-based or otherwise, and so on - all such system categorizations are orthogonal to the Self dimension.

To introduce the property in question, it is important to distinguish users from other stakeholders of a Self. The reason lies in the difference between how a Self can satisfy user requirements, and how it can satisfy those of other stakeholders. Just as any system, a Self may satisfy the requirement of a stakeholder who is not a user, e.g., a stakeholder may not be involved in using the system, but may require that the license to use the Self costs below some amount per year. If the annual license costs X, and is smaller than Y (the maximal amount that this stakeholder set), then the system satisfies the requirement. We say that the requirement is *directly* satisfied, *since this stakeholder does not need to invest any more effort in using the system, in order to satisfy that requirement.*

The story is different for most users of Selfs, i.e., individuals who will interact with the system at run-time, precisely in order to satisfy their own requirements. If a system directly satisfies the requirements of its users, then it does not belong to Selfs. It does belong to Selfs, if it satisfies these requirements *indirectly*. We say that a system satisfies a requirement indirectly, if there exists a scenario for using that system, such that if the system is so used, then the requirement will be satisfied, *but that is not the only possible scenario for using that system, and that scenario is not necessarily known by either the users or the system designers.*

It looks like quite a lot of software only indirectly satisfies their users' requirements. An operating system satisfies indirectly a user's requirement to print out a document, if the user needs to find, install, and configure by herself a printer driver. A word processor indirectly satisfies the requirement to format a text according to some formatting guidelines, because it is the user who has to figure out how to use headers, footers, front pages, blank pages, and so on, in order to ensure that the document does indeed follow the guidelines. A web browser, in contrast, looks to be directly satisfying its main requirement, which is to display content on the World Wide Web. But it indirectly satisfies the requirement to play specific kind of video files, if the user has first to find, download and install the relevant plugin.The usual calendar applications satisfy directly the requirements to add events and reminders, invite people to join events, and such. But they only indirectly satisfy the requirement to find the slots that suit everyone, when organizing a meeting. To satisfy that requirement, the user has to find some clever way to use the various existing features in her calendar application.

It is an essential property of Selfs that *the intention in designing them is to satisfy many user requirements indirectly.* The consequence is that a user will have to do the work of finding the appropriate scenario that mobilizes the features of the system, in a way which will satisfy this user's requirements. The scenario should not already built into the system in such a way that a user can, without much effort, activate it. If the intention in designing a system is primarily to enable the indirect satisfaction of many requirements, which were anticipated or unanticipated at design-time, we will say that the system is *undetermined*. We will say that the system is *determined*, if the intention in designing it is to satisfy exactly some specific set of requirements identified at design-time.

Table 1. Examples of Software

	Determined	Undertermined
Business Users	Google Calendar, Microsoft Outlook, Microsoft Word, Skype	Blogger, Joomla, Matlab, QlikView, Excel PowerPivot/View
IT Experts	Visual Paradigm, FileZilla, AVG Anti-Virus, Apache Web Server	MicroStrategy, Pentaho, Symfony Framework, .NET Framework, Java

5 Requirements from Selfs and Non-selfs

In order to analyze the way RE happens in the particular case of Selfs, we first suggest to distinguish between two types of requirements. Then, using this distinction, we provide a more accurate, RE-oriented, definition of Selfs.

We start by distinguishing two kinds of requirements, called Stakeholder Requirements (R_{Stk}) and Derived Stakeholder Requirements (R_{DS}). As their name suggests, we obtain R_{Stk} from stakeholders and through requirements elicitation, which may involve interviews, observation, documentation analysis, and so on. R_{DS} are the requirements that a requirements engineer defines herself, on the basis of R_{Stk}. R_{DS} are made, for example, by refining, decomposing, disambiguating, or otherwise manipulating R_{Stk}, in the aim of identifying such R_{DS} which are operational. A requirement is operational when there is a specification which can be implemented (that is, its implementation is judged feasible), and there are good reasons to believe that, if implemented according to that specification, the resulting system will satisfy that R_{DS}. Various frameworks exist to identify variability in goal models, and could be of particular interest in the identification of R_{DS} [17,18]. We will say that R_{Stk} and R_{DS} together are *Ground Requirements* (R^G), i.e, R^G is the union of R_{Stk} and R_{DS}.

We then distinguish R^G from *Self Requirements* (R^{Self}), which are defined by requirements engineers, in order to ensure that the system has generic features, whose various combinations could satisfy potentially many R^G. For example, the user of a BI system can have the requirement r_1 to "Display average sales margin per product". Such requirement has been elicited explicitly from that business user (through, for example, an interview): r_1 is therefore part of R_{Stk}, and hence of R^G. That requirement provides some direction to derive requirement variants. For instance, r_2, "Display sales revenue repartition per vendors", can be derived from r_1 and is then part of R_{DS}, hence also of R^G.

Selfs are, however, not made to satisfy specifically R^G. Instead, they are made to satisfy a requirement r_3, which is "Be able to *[displaying]* an *[arithmetic function]* over one *[business fact]* for one *[business dimension]*". The latter requirement is such that, if it is satisfied, then both r_1 and r_2 will be, but also potentially many others similar to r_1 and r_2. The requirement r_3 is in R^{Self}. The difference between r_1 and r_3, and between r_2 and r_3, is that r_3 is obtained by looking at r_1 and r_2, and finding what is common to them, in order to formulate a new requirement which, if satisfied, would lead us to conclude that both r_1 and r_2 are satisfiable, provided that the users find out how by themselves.

6   Requirement Engineering for Selfs

6.1   Selfs vs Non-self: An Illustration

Previous RE definition of Selfs offers a support for distinguishing between the design concerns of Selfs and non-Selfs. Consider previous example r_1, where a user wants to "Display average sales margin by product". To obtain such result, the user can use a BI solution, and has two alternatives, called A and B below.

Alternative A: she could use a classical BI system. In that case, she would have to ask the IT to design a report, which shows the average margin by product. This results in the stakeholder requirement r_1 which is part of R^G. One could model that requirement via a goal model such as in Figure 1. With R^G, the IT could decide about the design of a new report, with no room for self-service: user might simply need to select a product to obtain the information she needs. Here, there are no features to select: everything is decided for the user in advance, so that the system can be said to be Determined.

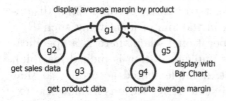
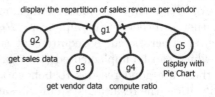

Fig. 1. Goal refinement of r_1 **Fig. 2.** Goal refinement of r_2

As discussed in our Introduction section, the requirements from a BI solution are likely to change rapidly. Previous user could for instance have the new requirement r_2, illustrated with a goal model in Figure 2. To be achieved, that goal would require a new round of elicitation and operationalization, as r_2 would be added to R^G. Based on that new R^G, IT would have to design a new report. This repetitive RE process can increase time-to-value.

Alternative B: The user has access to an SSBI solution, and she is responsible for satisfying her requirements. Suppose that this is a simple spreadsheet software, such as Excel. Let there be a spreadsheet, which satisfies r_3 mentioned earlier. Starting with her first requirement r_1 (Figure 1), the stakeholder could for example select some rows from a data set she judged relevant, sum the cells and divide the result by the count of rows. She could also select all the data, apply a filter to it to keep only the last six months, and compute the average using the function for computing the mean, and so on. This system is Undetermined, as it is up to the stakeholder to find and design a solution to her problem. If a new requirement arises, let's say r_2, there is no need to re-engineer the SSBI solution. The user, or someone helping her, would simply adapt some part of her initial solution to design a new solution that satisfies the new requirement.

6.2   A RE Process Adapted for Selfs

From an RE perspective, Alternative A and B imply different design approaches. This is illustrated in Figure 3. In Alternative A, engineers have to decide about a specification that satisfies the Ground Requirements they elicit from business users. Only R^G is used to design the system-to-be. If R^G changes (due for example to a new variant of a requirement), then engineers must redesign the existing software to satisfy that new set of requirements. In Alternative B, engineers must identify user requirements, and then try to anticipate any other possible requirement. This results in a set of generic requirements R^{Self}. The design based on R^{Self} must offer sufficient features for the user to satisfy by herself the requirements that may appear at run-time in R^G.

Actually, the design of a Self cannot work on R^G since operationalizing R^G would consist in delivering a determined system providing business users with all required features in a single design. It is illustrated in the goal model GV in Figure 4. Identifying Selfs Requirements is more than only taking into account of all possible variability in users requirements. Although possible Self configuration would be able to eventually operationalize each leaf node of GV, a system which directly operationalize all leaf nodes of GV is not a Self. From there on, non-Self systems build from the operationalization of requirements in R^G, while Self systems build from the operationalization of requirements in R^{Self}.

Nonetheless, setting up R^{Self} from R^G is currently still a research challenge. Current methodologies only focus on R^G, i.e. how to gather and model R_{Stk} as well as how to derive R_{SD}. To the best of our knowledge, little attention has been paid as to how R^{Self} can be *abstracted* from R^G.

Notice that Self requirements open the way to some unanticipated uses of the system. Consider the case of MS Word. Word proposes to its user a mailing functionality, in which users are capable of selecting themselves fields, displaying the latter on a form, defining the layout for these fields, etc. Word is therefore

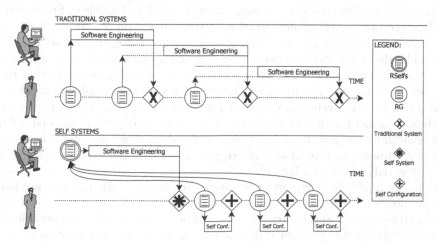

Fig. 3. Comparison of RE process for traditional and Self systems

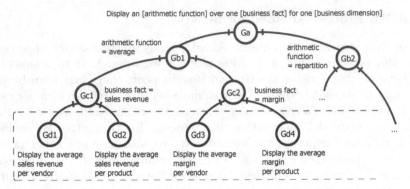

Fig. 4. The goal model GV

somewhere on the Self dimension between pure Selfs and pure non-Selfs, because it satisfies at least one Self requirement, i.e., the user is able to define a mail on her own. A side effect of being a Self system is that users may be creative in using the software, e.g., defining a mailing is not the only way to use the Word functionality. In practice, it could be used in some other, unanticipated, ways.

Imagine for example a professor who wants to create several exercises for her students. Each exercise will be the same except some values and some words which will be changed. For this purpose, she could use the mailing functionality to design a template with print labels, and generate several exercises by giving different values for each label. In this context, she used an Undetermined functionality of Word in order to design her *own solution*. The use of a Self therefore depends on the creativity of its users, and should not be limited to the use cases for which it was initially designed.

7   Challenges of Selfs for Requirements Engineering

Although critical to ensure a Self anticipates as much as feasible of future stakeholders' requirements, the identification of R^{Self} based on R^G (using, for example, an abstraction mechanism) presents some risks. Using the full set of R^{Self} to decide about the specification of a Self can lead to systems with numerous features, and hence to relatively complex Selfs. By complex, we mean that they provide many features to end-users. The problem with the complexity of a Self is that it can be negatively correlated with its usability: end-users, who have relatively low (sometimes no) IT background, may not be capable of understanding and combining the features consistently to build custom solutions. That problem of complexity is typical of Selfs: regular systems avoid such complexity by directly satisfying the specific R^G.

Consider again the requirement of a user who wants to "Display average margin per product". Imagine the user has to satisfy that requirement using a Self. She is given a spreadsheet software such as Microsoft Excel. Excel contains Self requirements because the user is in charge of designing its own solution to compute her average margin from a range of data. In Microsoft Excel, she may have the choice between five, maybe six, features (average, count, sum functions, etc.) to be combined in order to compute an average margin. Imagine the same user is exposed to a new, more complex system, with hundreds of features that could be used to compute that same result. That system would be less usable for the business user. There would be risks that the user gets lost, or uses inappropriately some features of the software, with the ultimate risk that this business user does not satisfy properly her requirements.

This threat is important, and is reflected in existing SSBI solutions, where users are often discouraged because the Self is too complex for them. For example, Weber emphasized that "In an effort to give users what they want, IT sometimes errs on the side of giving users everything" which he claims is a typical problem of SSBI system [19]. SSBI experts also highlighted that "It turns out that most users found the tools too difficult to use. Even when the tools migrated from Windows to the Web, simplifying user interfaces and easing installation and maintenance burdens, it was not enough to transform BI tools from specialty software for power users to general-purpose analytical tools for everyone in the organization." [9]. In that regard, we consider there is a gap in current RE approach to Selfs: designers should not only be interested in creating systems that satisfy the set of requirements R^{Self} (such as in SSBI). They should also account for the fact that Selfs must be usable for business users. Therefore, they should pay attention to the number of feature they provide.

Note finally that research has been conducted to bring variability into software development. One of the most important research regarding variability is Software Product Line Engineering [20]. Although it aims to build a base system which can be customized to particular needs, this customization still requires IT intervention. Moreover, it does not aim to transfer the design responsibility of the users. Consequently, RE is traditionally about R^G and how to derive products which implement sub-parts of R^G. To the best of our knowledge, no research has gone on the business-user intervention in the resolution of R^G.

8   Conclusion and Future Work

In this paper, we provided an overall discussion about the use of Self-Service systems in organizations. We first discussed the rationale for such system, claiming that Selfs are valuable solutions to the problem of changing requirements and long time-to-value for business users. We defined Self-Service systems as being systems which contains operationalization of Self requirements. With such operationalization business users are in charge for configuring themselves the system in order to design their proper solution to some requirements. We then provided a deeper RE perspective on Selfs, by distinguishing between Ground Requirements, obtained requirements elicitation, and Self Requirements, which are requirements to be able to solve other, forthcoming, Ground Requirements. We concluded on a discussion about the trade-off that may appears, during RE for Selfs, between the completeness of a Self platform (in terms of features) and the usability of the latter.

References

1. Brooks Jr., F.P.: No silver bullet - essence and accidents of software engineering. Computer 20, 10–19 (1987)
2. Silva Souza, V.E., Lapouchnian, A., Robinson, W.N., Mylopoulos, J.: Awareness requirements for adaptive systems. In: Proceedings of the 6th International Symposium on Software Engineering for Adaptive and Self-Managing Systems, pp. 60–69. ACM (2011)
3. Dardenne, A., Van Lamsweerde, A., Fickas, S.: Goal-directed requirements acquisition. Science of Computer Programming 20(1), 3–50 (1993)
4. Van Lamsweerde, A.: Goal-oriented requirements engineering: A guided tour. In: Proc. 5th IEEE International Symposium on Requirements Engineering, pp. 249–262 (2001)
5. Golfarelli, M., Rizzi, S., Cella, I.: Beyond data warehousing: what's next in business intelligence? In: Proc. 7th ACM International Workshop on Data Warehousing and OLAP, p. 1 (2004)
6. Negash, S.: Business Intelligence. Communications of the Association for Information Systems 13, 177–195 (2004)
7. Pourshahid, A., Richards, G., Amyot, D.: Toward a goal-oriented, business intelligence decision-making framework. E-Technologies: Transformation in a Connected World, 100–115 (2011)
8. Burnay, C., Jureta, I.J., Faulkner, S.: A Framework for the Operationalization of Monitoring in Business Intelligence Requirements Engineering. Software and System Modeling (SoSym) (in press)
9. Eckerson, W.W.: Performance Dashboards: Measuring, Monitoring, and Managing Your Business. John Wiley & Sons (May 2008)
10. Imhoff, C., White, C.: Self-Service: Empowering Users to Generate Insights. tech. rep., The Data Warehouse Institute, TDWI (2011)
11. Richardson, J., Schlegel, K., Sallam, R.L., Hostmann, B.: Magic quadrant for business intelligence platforms. Core Research Note ... (2008)
12. Evelson, B.: The Forrester Wave: Self-Service Business Intelligence Platforms, Q2 2012, tech. rep., Forrester (2012)
13. Zowghi, D., Coulin, C.: Requirements Elicitation: A Survey of Techniques, Approaches, and Tools. In: Engineering and Managing Software Requirements, pp. 19–46. Springer, Heidelberg (2005)
14. Zowghi, D., Offen, R.: A logical framework for modeling and reasoning about the evolution of requirements. In: Proc. 3rd IEEE International Symposium on Requirements Engineering, pp. 247–257 (1997)
15. Rolland, C., Salinesi, C., Etien, A.: Eliciting gaps in requirements change. Requirements Engineering 9(1), 1–15 (2004)
16. Van Lamsweerde, A.: Requirements engineering: from system goals to uml models to software specifications (2009)
17. Gonzales-Baixauli, B., Prado Leite, J., Mylopoulos, J.: Visual variability analysis for goal models. In: Proceedings of the 12th IEEE International Requirements Engineering Conference, pp. 198–207. IEEE (2004)
18. Liaskos, S., Lapouchnian, A., Yu, Y.: On goal-based variability acquisition and analysis. In: Proc. 14th IEEE International Conference on Requirements Engineering, pp. 79–88 (2006)
19. Weber, M.: Keys to Sustainable Self-Service Business Intelligence. Business Intelligence Journal 18, 18–24 (2013)
20. Pohl, K., Böckle, G., Van Der Linden, F.: Software product line engineering, vol. 10. Springer (2005)

Semantic Monitoring and Compensation in Socio-technical Processes

Yingzhi Gou[1], Aditya Ghose[1,2], Chee-Fon Chang[1], Hoa Khanh Dam[2], and Andrew Miller[1]

[1] Centre for Oncology Informatics
Illawarra Health & Medical Research Institute
University of Wollongong, Australia
{yg452,c03}@uowmail.edu.au
[2] Decision Systems Lab.
School of Computer Science and Software Engineering
University of Wollongong, Australia
{aditya,hoa}@uow.edu.au

Abstract. Socio-technical processes are becoming increasingly important, with the growing recognition of the computational limits of full automation, the growth in popularity of crowd sourcing, the complexity and openness of modern organizations etc. A key challenge in managing socio-technical processes is dealing with the flexible, and sometimes dynamic, nature of the execution of human-mediated tasks. It is well-recognized that human execution does not always conform to predetermined co-ordination models, and is often error-prone. This paper addresses the problem of semantically monitoring the execution of socio-technical processes to check for non-conformance, and the problem of recovering from (or compensating for) non-conformance. This paper proposes a semantic solution to the problem, by leveraging semantically annotated process models to detect non-conformance, and using the same semantic annotations to identify compensatory human-mediated tasks.

1 Introduction

Socio-technical processes, which are executed by synergistic combinations of humans and technological components, have a long history, but have assumed new significance with the current interest in issues such as crowd-sourcing, human computation and gamification. They have also become important as a consequence of the introduction of process automation in settings where human-mediated functionality is critical and indispensable (such as clinical process management, military command and control, or air traffic management). An important aspect of socio-technical processes is that the human-mediated components are fallible, while the machine-mediated components are generally not (although there are critical exceptions). One way in which such fallibility might be manifested is via *structural non-conformance*, where activities are overlooked or executed in the wrong order, or where the wrong activities are executed.

M. Indulska and S. Purao (Eds.): ER Workshops 2014, LNCS 8823, pp. 117–126, 2014.

There is a mature body of work focusing on structural non-conformance (see [1] for a representative reference). Our focus is on the harder problem of *semantic non-conformance*, where we are interested in managing situations where the execution of a process might be structurally correct (the right activities are executed in the right order), but the effects achieved do not conform to what is required by design, potentially due to human errors. For instance, a clinical process might require the administration of an anti-hypertensive medication. The correct execution of this task would require that a nurse should deliver the medication to the patient in question and depart only when the patient has ingested the medication. A semantically non-conformant execution might occur if the nurse delivers the medication to the patient, but does not stay around to confirm that the patient has actually taken it (and the patient happens to not take the medication). In a hospital with a process-aware information system, the nurse might then confirm to the process engine that this task has been completed, leading to a situation where no structural non-conformance would be detected. The fact that this process instance is semantically non-conformant can only be determined by checking the *effects* of the process to ensure that what is expected is actually obtained. Thus, in our example, a blood pressure check later in the day might reveal elevated readings, when the expected readings are lower. This paper addresses the problem of *semantic monitoring* of socio-technical processes, by leveraging process designs that have been annotated with the expected effects at each point. Semantic non-conformance is flagged in settings where the observed effects deviate from the expected ones.

The human-mediated components of socio-technical processes also offer greater flexibility in "fixing" semantic non-conformance via the introduction of human-mediated activities constructed on the fly (generating new machine-mediated functionality, such as a new web service, can often take too long to be able to correct errors in an executing process instance). Thus, in our example, the semantic non-conformance detected via the blood pressure check can be fixed by having the nurse correctly administer the medication as soon as possible. Once this is done, the clinical process instance involving this patient would be restored to a semantically conformant state. This paper also addresses the problem of computing the best "fixes" of this kind, which we shall refer to as *compensations*. The problem is non-trivial. While the common-sense compensation in our running example might be to administer the anti-hypertensive medication as soon as the elevated blood pressure is detected, this might not be possible because of potential interactions between the anti-hypertensive medication and a more recently administered drug. We might thus need to search through the space of possible process re-designs to identify one where the earliest compensation is possible.

In the rest of this paper, we show how semantic annotation of process designs can be leveraged for a machinery for monitoring process execution based on effects (Section 2). We then formalize the notion of compensation and discuss a class of techniques that can be used to compute "optimal" compensations to deal with semantic non-conformance (Section 3). We describe the implementation and empirical evaluation of one of these techniques, with promising results (Section 4).

2   Semantic Process Monitoring

There is a large body of work that explores the use of semantic annotation of business process designs [2,3,4,5,6,7,8,9,10]. A large body of work also addresses the problem of semantic annotation of web services in a similar fashion [11,12,13,14]. Common to all of these approaches is the specification of *post-conditions*, which is what we primarily leverage in defining inter-process relationships. For our purposes, two aspects of the post-conditions (or effects) are important. First, post-conditions should be sensitive to process context, i.e., the post-conditions of a task at a certain point in a process design should reflect not just the effects achieved by executing that task but also the accumulated effects of the prior tasks in the process design that have been executed. Second, non-determinism must be accommodated in relation to post-conditions.

A number of the process annotation approaches referred to above achieve contextualization of post-conditions by using a device originally used in AI planning - add-lists and delete-lists of effects. Others, such as [5] and [8], use a state update operator derived from the literature on reasoning about action. We adopt this approach. The need for permitting non-determinism in effects stems from two observations. First, in any process with XOR-branching, one might arrive at a given task via multiple paths, and the contextualized post-conditions achieved must be contingent on the path taken. Since this analysis is done at design time, we need to admit non-deterministic effects since the specific path taken can only be determined at run-time. Second, many state update operators generate non-deterministic outcomes, since inconsistencies (that commonly appear in state update) can be resolved in multiple different ways. Our approach assumes that each task/activity is annotated with post-conditions (in the implementation presented later, we shall assume them to be unique, as much of the literature does, but this can be easily generalized to admit non-deterministic post-conditions), which are contextualized via a process of *effect accumulation*. We shall assume that all tasks (and their post-conditions) are drawn from an *enterprise capability library*. In this approach, we are able to answer, for any point in a process design, the following question: what will have happened if the process executes up to this point? The answer is a mutually exclusive set of *effect scenarios*, any one of which might describe the actual state of affairs at that point in the execution of the process design. Additional detail on the specific effect annotation and accumulation machinery used in the implementation can be found in Section 4.

We note that when a process is in a state that is (partially) characterized by an effect scenario, the execution of the next task in the model, or the occurrence of the next event, can lead to a very specific set of effect scenarios, determined by the *state update operator* being used. In effect, the process model determines a transition system, which determines how the partial state description contained in an effect scenario evolves as a consequence of the execution/occurrence of the next task (event) specified in the model. We assign each effect scenario appearing in a semantically annotated process model a unique ID (thus if the same partial description applies to a process at different points in its design, it would be assigned a distinct ID at each distinct point). We can thus refer to the *predecessors* (the effect scenarios that can lead to the current scenario via a single state update determined by the next task/event) and *successors* (the scenarios that can be obtained from the current scenario via a single state update determined by the next task/event) of each effect scenario with respect to the transition system implicitly defined by the process design. There are works that have been done on obtaining such effect scenario, such as in [5] and [10], which also suggest that due to different paths at gateways could be taken before a task in a process model, and/or other reasons, there could be multiple effect scenarios associated with the task.

Definition 1. *A* **semantically annotated process model** P *is a process model in which each activity or event is associated with a set of* effect scenarios. *Each effect scenario es is a 4-tuple* $\langle ID, S, Pre, Succ \rangle$, *where S is a set of sentences in the background language, ID is a unique ID for each effect scenario, Pre is a set of IDs of effect scenarios that can be valid* predecessors *in P of the current effect scenario, while $Succ$ is a set of IDs of effect scenarios that can be valid* successors *in P of the current effect scenario.*

A semantically annotated process model is associated with a set of normative traces, each providing a semantic account of one possible way in which the process might be executed.

Definition 2. *A* **normative trace** *nt is a sequence* $\langle \tau_1, es_1, \tau_2, \ldots es_{n-1}, \tau_n, es_n \rangle$, *where*

- *$es_i \ldots, es_n$ are effect scenarios, and for each $es_i = \langle ID_i, S_i, Pre_i, Succ_i \rangle$, $i \in [2..n]$, it is always the case that $ID_{i-1} \in Pre_i$ and $ID_i \in Succ_{i-1}$;*
- *$es_n = \langle ID_n, S_n, Pre_n, \emptyset \rangle$ is the* final effect scenario, *normally associated with the end event of the process;*
- *$es_1 = \langle ID_1, S_1, \emptyset, Succ_1 \rangle$ is the* initial effect scenario, *normally associated with the start event of the process;*
- *Each of $\tau_1, \ldots, \tau_n$ is either an event or an activity in the process.*

We shall refer to the sequence $\langle \tau_1, \tau_2, \ldots, \tau_n \rangle$ *as the* identity *of the trace nt.*

To simplify of the presentation later on, the *es* in the trace, from now, refers to S in the 4-tuple $\langle ID, S, Pre, Succ \rangle$ because ID, Pre, and $Succ$ are meta-information used only to construct normative traces.

Definition 3. *A* **semantic execution trace** *of a process P is a sequence* $\langle \tau_1, o_1, \tau_2, o_2, \ldots, \tau_m, o_m \rangle$ *where each τ_i is either a task or an event, and each o_i is a set of sentences in the background language that we shall refer to as an* observation *that describes (possibly incompletely) the state of the process context after each task or event. We shall refer to the sequence* $\langle \tau_1, \tau_2, \ldots, \tau_m \rangle$ *as the* identity *of the execution trace.*

Note that we do not require each τ_i to belong to the process design P to allow the possibility of actual executions being erroneous. We will, on occasion, refer to a semantic execution trace, simply as an execution trace.

Definition 4. *An execution trace* $et = \langle \tau_1, o_1, \ldots, \tau_m, o_m \rangle$ *is said to be* **non-conformant** *with respect to a semantically annotated process* P *if and only if any of the following hold: (1) There exists an* o_i *in et such that for all normative traces* $nt' = \langle \tau_1', es_1, \ldots, \tau_i', es_i, \ldots \rangle$ *for which the identity of* $\langle \tau_1, o_1, \ldots, \tau_i, o_i \rangle$ *is a prefix of its identity and* $o_j \models es_j$ *for each* $j = 1, \ldots, i - 1$, $o_i \not\models es_i$ *(we shall refer to this as* weak semantic non-conformance*). (2) If we replace non-entailment with inconsistency in condition (1) above, i.e.,* $o_i \cup es_i \models \bot$, *we obtain* strong semantic non-conformance. *In each case, we shall refer to* τ_i *as the* violation point *in the process.*

We only deal with semantic non-conformance in structurally compliant process instances. In other words, we assume that the identity of every semantic execution trace of interest equals the identity of some normative trace of the process.

3 Semantic Compensation

In this section, we formalize the notion of compensation and outline some strategies for computing these. In the following, we will view process instances as semantic execution traces. We will assume that each process is associated with a *goal assertion* g.

Definition 5. *A process instance* $et = \langle \tau_1, o_1, \ldots, \tau_m, o_m \rangle$ *will be referred to as a* **semantically compensated instance** *of a (semantically annotated) process* P *if there exist* τ_i *and* τ_j *in ct, with* $i < j$, *such that* τ_i *is a violation point, and there exists a normative trace* $nt = \langle \tau_1, es_1, \tau_2, \ldots es_{h-1}, \tau_h, es_h, \ldots, \tau_n, es_n \rangle$ *of* P *with an identity for which* $\langle \tau_1, \ldots, \tau_{j-1} \rangle$ *serves as a prefix, such that* $o_k \models es_l$ *for* $k = j, \ldots, m$ *and* $l = h, \ldots, n$. *As well, it must be the case that* $o_m \models g$. *We shall refer to* τ_j *as the* compensation point. *The compensation point must be a task and not an event.*

Definition 6. *Given a semantically compensated process instance* $et = \langle \tau_1, o_1, \ldots, \tau_m, o_m \rangle$ *of* P *with a compensation point* τ_j, *a* **compensation** *is a process design* P' *for which the completion of* τ_{j-1} *serves as the start event and* $\langle \tau_j, o_j, \ldots, \tau_m, o_m \rangle$ *is a valid normative trace. Every normative trace associated with* P' *must end in an effect scenario* es *such that* $es \models g$, *where* g *is the goal associated with the original process* P.

This definition of compensation is fairly general. More specifically, we are interested in *optimal compensations*, driven by the following intuitions. We prefer earlier compensations. In other words, we aim to ensure that as few system states as possible deviate for the normative process design (noting that a later compensation will necessarily mean that there would be more states between the violation point and the compensation point). We also prefer to minimize deviation of the overall semantically compensated process instance from the semantic "intent" of the original process design. These preferences can lead to competing pulls. We might in some situations be able to introduce an earlier compensation, but the compensation, while ensuring conformance from subsequent steps (assuming no other steps deviate), might lead to greater changes in the system states than a potential later compensation.

Computing a compensation thus requires that we identify a process design which permits us to complete the currently executing process instance from the compensation point onwards in a manner that gives us a complete semantic execution trace that is as close as possible to the normative trace that would have been executed has there been no violation. The occurrence of a violation entails that we are only able to identify a prefix of this normative trace (the part that is actually executed prior to the violation). Given that multiple normative traces associated with the process design may share that prefix, we do not actually know which of these we would have actually executed had there been no violation. One way to compute the compensation is to identify that process design (or designs) which would minimize deviation from this set of normative traces (by picking one that minimizes the distance to the either the closest, or the farthest normative trace). This requires a distance measure to assess the distance between an execution trace and a normative trace. This distance measure must take into account both structural similarity (e.g., the number of activities in common between the two traces) and semantic similarity (e.g., the extent to which a set of observed assertions agree with an effect scenario). We describe an implementation with one such distance measure in the next section.

4 Implementation and Evaluation

In this section, we outline one specific implementation of the general framework for semantic process monitoring and compensation described above and present some preliminary empirical results. We note that the general framework could be instantiated in multiple ways (indeed the space of alternative design decisions is very large) and we do not suggest that this particular implementation is to be preferred to other possible ones (such claims can only be made after a series of substantive comparative studies). However, this particular implementation provides an adequate basis for making a preliminary determination of whether this approach is practical.

We use a machinery for semantic annotation of business process designs represented in BPMN. We omit details here for brevity but these can be found in [5]. It uses a syntactic state update operator based on the Possible Worlds Approach (PWA) [15]. The choice of this particular operator is mainly a matter of convenience (and adequate for assessing feasibility), while other operators, such as one based on the Possible Models Approach (leveraged by [8]) could also be used. We assume that a process model, semantically annotated using this machinery, is provided as input.

To measure the structural distance between a pair of sequences of activities/events, we use the *Levenshtein Distance* $lev(a, b)$ where $a = \langle a_1, \ldots, a_n \rangle$ and $b = \langle b_1, \ldots, b_m \rangle$.

For semantic distances, we define a simple distance function $\phi(es, o)$ where es is an effect scenario and o is a set of observations. We note that many, potentially more sophisticated schemes for measuring semantic distance exist, but this is adequate for preliminary analysis. In the following, V_{strong} computes the number of assertions in an effect scenario that contribute to strong semantic non-conformance (as in Definition 3), while V_{weak} computes the number of assertions that contribute to weak semantic non-conformance. We leverage a background knowledge base KB that contains, amongst others, domain and compliance constraints.

$$V_{strong} = \{e | e \in es, o \cup KB \models \neg e\}$$
$$V_{weak} = \{e | e \in es, o \cup KB \not\models e, e \notin V_{strong}\}$$
$$\phi(es, o) = w_{strong} \times |V_{strong}| + w_{weak} \times |V_{weak}|$$

where, w_{strong} and w_{weak} are weights. If all observations reveal complete state descriptions, then weak violations do not apply. We can focus attention solely on strong or weak violations by appropriately setting the corresponding weights.

We measure the distance between a normative trace $nt = \langle a_1, es_1, \ldots, a_n, es_n \rangle$ and a semantic execution trace $et = \langle b_1, o_1, \ldots, b_m, o_m \rangle$ using the following function:

$$J(nt, et) = \sum_{i=1 \ldots n} \min_{j=1 \ldots m} (w_1 \times \phi(es_i, o_j) + w_2 \times lev(\langle a_1, \ldots, a_i \rangle, \langle b_1, \ldots, b_j \rangle))$$

where w_1 and w_2 are the weights for each distance.

Our prototype takes a semantically annotated business process and a capability library as inputs, then generates a set of all normative traces. We simulate a normative execution trace and randomly insert a violation in it. Once a violation is detected, the compensation computation machinery initiates a search for a sequence of activities from the capability library that can constitute a valid completion of the current partially complete process instance and that guarantees that it terminates in a goal-satisfying state. The prototype performs an exhaustive constructive search. Every candidate partial extension of the current process instance is evaluated for compliance with the KB. In the event of non-compliance, the search backtracks and evaluates an alternative extension. Our evaluation uses a propositional language for representing effects and the KB. Effect accumulation, goal satisfaction and compliance checking require the use of a theorem prover - in our prototype, the SAT4J SAT solver (modified to generate all maximal consistent subsets) is used for this purpose. We apply the effect accumulation machinery to generate a semantic trace from each of the valid task sequences identified by the search procedure. This gives us a set of semantically compensated process instances which are then ranked according to the nearest distance to a valid normative trace (i.e., for each process instance, we compute the shortest distance to any valid normative trace, and the instance with shortest distance amongst all appears at the top of the ranking, and so on). We limit each task in the capability library to be used only once in a semantically compensated process instance.

In the evaluation, we manually design 5 distinct semantically annotated process models with variations in the number of activities, gateways (we only use

Table 1. Evaluated Process Models

Process Model ID	Complexity of Process			Complexity of Semantic Annotation			Complexity of Knowledge Base	
	Total Number of Activities and Events	Length of Paths in the Model (Min/Max)	Number of Gateways (split and merge)	Size of Propositional Vocabulary	Length of Task Post-conditions (Min/Max)	Length of Effect Scenarios (Min/Max)	Number of Clauses in the Knowledge Base	Number of Activities in Capability Library
1	6	6/6	0	3	1/2	1/3	3	4
2	12	12/12	0	13	1/7	7/13	3	10
3	9	6/7	2	13	2/7	7/13	9	7
4	9	7/7	6	5	1/3	1/5	1	17
5	9	7/7	6	13	1/7	7/10	9	10

Table 2. Best Evaluation Result

Process Model ID	Location of Violation in Process	Shortest distance between process instance and normative trace	Goal Compliance	Time to compute best compensation(mm:ss:SSS)
1	Beginning	10	NO	00:00:199
1	Middle	10	NO	00:00:038
1	End	3	YES	00:00:085
2	Beginning	114	NO	10:00:206
2	Middle	30	NO	00:00:019
2	End	1	YES	00:14:817
3	Beginning	30	NO	04:53:580
3	Middle	30	NO	00:00:009
3	End	2	NO	00:00:034
4	Beginning	9	YES	01:55:569
4	Middle	6	YES	00:16:785
4	End	7	YES	00:04:986
5	Beginning	38	NO	00:00:010
5	Middle	17	NO	00:00:018
5	End	2	NO	00:00:102

XOR gateways), complexity of the knowledge base and effect scenarios etc (note that these cannot be randomly generated). These dimensions of the 5 process model are summarized in Table 1. We then identify the quality of solutions generated within a 10 minute time bound and report these results in Table 2. The table only shows summaries of the best compensated process instances from multiple runs of evaluation (violations are randomly generated).

Analysis of the results: The results we obtain here are only modestly encouraging. We note that none of the minimum distances for the compensated process instances are 0, but this is not a negative (any violation will lead to a non-zero distance). The location the violation is clearly important. A violation at the beginning of a process presents a much larger search space than a violation later in the process. The more complex the semantic annotations are, the longer it takes to compute compensations (which is not surprising). Process models 4 and 5 are structurally identical, but 5 has semantic annotations that are significantly more complex than those of 4. As a result, we are able to compute a goal-satisfying compensation from process 4 within the time-bound, but not for process 5. In general, not all of the "closest" process instances are goal compliant. Many socio-technical processes of interest have durations far greater than 10 minutes, hence the fact that we are able to compute goal-satisfying compensations for many (if not all) of the processes is actually encouraging. This suggests that with a higher time-bound, we might find even better and more goal-satisfying compensations, while still being able to compensate quite early in these long-duration processes.

5 Related Work

Cook et al. [16] offer a process validation framework, which involves comparing the event stream from the process model against the event stream from the log using string distance metrics. Rozinat and van der Aalst [1] developed the Conformance Checker as part of the ProM framework which, given a process design and a collection of its event log from execution, determines whether the process execution behavior reflects the designed behavior. Different from [1] and [16], our semantic conformance checking assumes that the instance of executed process is structurally correct. A number of proposals for goal-oriented process management exist [17,18]. Klein and Dellarocas [19] present a knowledge-based approach to exception detection and handling in work-flow systems. They define an exception as "any deviation from an 'ideal' collaborative process that uses the available resources to achieve the task requirements in an optimal way" [19]. In their exception management approach, the participant of an enacted process will be notified when there is an exception with the exception types and associated exception handler processes proposed by the work-flow designer, so that the participants are able to modify the instance of the process to resolve the exception and allow the process to continue. Our approach does not require that exceptions handlers be written for every possible exception.

6 Conclusion

In this paper we present a novel framework for semantic monitoring and compensation of business processes, leveraging semantic annotations of process designs. We identify some abstract strategies for implementing such a framework, and then present a concrete implementation. The evaluation of the implementation suggests that there is modest room for optimism that such an approach would be viable in practice.

References

1. Rozinat, A., van der Aalst, W.: Conformance checking of processes based on monitoring real behavior. Information Systems 33(1), 64–95 (2008)
2. Fensel, D., Facca, F., Simperl, E.: Web Service Modeling Ontology. In: Semantic Web Services, pp. 107–129. Springer (2011)
3. Fensel, D., Lausen, H., Polleres, A., Bruijn, J., Stollberg, M., Roman, D., Domingue, J.: Enabling Semantic Web Services: The Web Service Modeling Ontology. Springer (2006)
4. Hepp, M., Leymann, F., Domingue, J., Wahler, A., Fensel, D.: Semantic business process management: A vision towards using semantic Web services for business process management. In: IEEE International Conference on e-Business Engineering, pp. 535–540. IEEE (2005)
5. Hinge, K., Ghose, A., Koliadis, G.: Process SEER: A tool for semantic effect annotation of business process models. In: Proceedings of the 13th IEEE International EDOC Conference. IEEE Computer Society Process (2009)

6. Di Pietro, I., Pagliarecci, F., Spalazzi, L.: Model checking semantically annotated services. IEEE Transactions on Software Engineering 38, 592–608 (2012)
7. Smith, F., Proietti, M.: Rule-Based Behavioral Reasoning on Semantic Business Processes. In: Proceedings of the 5th International Conference on Agents and Artificial Intelligence, pp. 130–143. SciTePress (2013)
8. Weber, I., Hoffmann, J., Mendling, J.: Beyond soundness: On the verification of semantic business process models. Distributed and Parallel Databases 27, 271–343 (2010)
9. Di Francescomarino, C., Ghidini, C., Rospocher, M., Serafini, L., Tonella, P.: Semantcally-aided business process modeling. In: Bernstein, A., Karger, D.R., Heath, T., Feigenbaum, L., Maynard, D., Motta, E., Thirunarayan, K. (eds.) ISWC 2009. LNCS, vol. 5823, pp. 114–129. Springer, Heidelberg (2009)
10. Ghose, A., Koliadis, G.: Auditing Business Process Compliance. In: Krämer, B.J., Lin, K.-J., Narasimhan, P. (eds.) ICSOC 2007. LNCS, vol. 4749, pp. 169–180. Springer, Heidelberg (2007)
11. Martin, D., et al.: Bringing semantics to web services: The OWL-S approach. In: Cardoso, J., Sheth, A.P. (eds.) SWSWPC 2004. LNCS, vol. 3387, pp. 26–42. Springer, Heidelberg (2005)
12. Meyer, H.: On the Semantics of Service Compositions. In: Marchiori, M., Pan, J.Z., de Sainte Marie, C. (eds.) RR 2007. LNCS, vol. 4524, pp. 31–42. Springer, Heidelberg (2007)
13. Montali, M., Pesic, M., van der Aalst, W.M.P., Chesani, F., Mello, P., Storari, S.: Declarative specification and verification of service choreographiess. ACM Transactions on the Web 4, 3:1–3:62 (2010)
14. Smith, F., Missikoff, M., Proietti, M.: Ontology-Based Querying of Composite Services. In: Ardagna, C.A., Damiani, E., Maciaszek, L.A., Missikoff, M., Parkin, M. (eds.) BSME 2010. LNCS, vol. 7350, pp. 159–180. Springer, Heidelberg (2012)
15. Ginsberg, M.L., Smith, D.E.: Reasoning about action I: A Possible World Approach. Artificial Intelligence 35(2), 165–195 (1988)
16. Cook, J.E., Wolf, A.L.: Software process validation: quantitatively measuring the correspondence of a process to a model. ACM Transactions on Software Engineering and Methodology 8(2), 147–176 (1999)
17. Ghose, A., Koliadis, G.: Actor eco-systems: From high-level agent models to executable processes via semantic annotations. In: Proceedings of the 31st Annual International Computer Software and Applications Conference, vol. 02, pp. 177–184. IEEE Computer Society, Washington, DC (2007)
18. Koliadis, G., Vranesevic, A., Bhuiyan, M., Krishna, A., Ghose, A.K.: A combined approach for supporting the business process model lifecycle. In: Proceedings of the, Pacific Asia Conference on Information Systems, pp. 1305–1319 (2006)
19. Klein, M., Dellarocas, C.: A knowledge-based approach to handling exceptions in workflow systems. Computer Supported Cooperative Work 9, 399–412 (2000)

Modeling Regulatory Compliance
in Requirements Engineering

Silvia Ingolfo[1], Alberto Siena[2], and John Mylopoulos[1]

[1] University of Trento, via Sommarive 7, Trento, Italy
[2] FBK-Irst, via Sommarive 18, Trento, Italy
{ingolfo,jm}@unitn.it,siena@fbk.eu

Abstract. A large and rapidly growing number of laws is impacting software systems world-wide. For each one of them, software designers need to ensure that their system, new or legacy, complies with the law. Establishing compliance requires the ability to identify which laws are applicable, what are the different ways to comply, and whether given requirements for a software system comply. In this short paper we give an overview of ongoing work on Nòmos 3, a modelling language tailored to modelling laws and requirements. Nòmos 3 models can be translated into a formal specification that supports automated compliance analysis.

Keywords: Requirement engineering, regulatory compliance, modeling language.

1 Introduction

In the last decades, software systems have increasingly gained attention of governmental agencies for the risks they introduce in case of mishap (stolen data, cyber-attacks, and more). In response, governments have passed new laws and regulations to foresee and prevent conceivable adverse conditions. The impact on business of ensuring compliance to laws is high: in the financial domain the U.S. Government Accountability Office estimates a $2.9 billion expense over five years [1] to implement the Wall Street Reform and Consumer Protection Act. In the Healthcare domain, organizations have spent $17.6 billion over a number of years[2] to align their systems and procedures to HIPAA, the Health Insurance Portability and Accountability Act. The challenge for software engineers is to understand and analyze the various ways systems can achieve stakeholder requirements, while complying with applicable laws.

Different solutions have been proposed in requirement engineering to support the analyst in aligning requirements with the law. Some approaches are based on natural language processing techniques, and focus on direct extraction of

---

[1] http://blogs.wsj.com/economics/2011/03/28/
gao-implementing-dodd-frank-could-cost-2-9-billion/
[2] Medical privacy - national standards to protect the privacy of personal health information. Office for Civil Rights, US Dept. of Health and Human Services, 2000.

M. Indulska and S. Purao (Eds.): ER Workshops 2014, LNCS 8823, pp. 127–132, 2014.

legal requirements from legal documents [1, 6]. Some goal-oriented approaches have also been proposed. Ghavanati et al. [4] have extended the Goal-oriented Requirement Language to manage law and identify which requirements are not aligned. Darimont et al. [2] have used KAOS for the representation of elements extracted from legal texts. Siena et al. [10] have introduced a 'dedicated' modeling language to provide a legal extension for the i* framework. In the community of Multi-Agent Systems (MAS), norms are generally treated as agents' behavioral constraints and the typical problem addressed in this area include the definition and derivation of these rules [3, 7]. [11] takes an interesting social perspective of MAS and proposes formal model for governance that provides similar type of compliance analysis similar to ours, in the domain of Socio Technical System with autonomous agents. However most of these approaches are difficult to apply to requirement engineering because of their heavy-weight formal approach.

In our earlier work we have introduced Nòmos 2, a modelling language that supports formal reasoning about alternative ways to comply with a given law [9]. Nòmos 2 relies on the intuition that laws generally establish norms (i.e., duties and rights) expressed in terms of conditions for compliance to, but also applicability of a given norm. Nòmos 2 adopts a modelling approach, which on one hand is less expressive (hence more user-friendly) than others, but on the other hand eases the integration with RE practices. Its viability in solving real world size problems is confirmed by a scalability study [8]. We are currently working on Nòmos 3, an extension of Nòmos 2 that introduces the concepts of goal (for modelling requirements) and roles for modelling both social roles (e.g., a manager, a professor) and legal ones (e.g., a data processor for a privacy law) [5]. Moreover, *compliance* with a norm in Nòmos 2 was evaluated with respect to a norm's applicability condition and satisfiability condition (*how to* comply with the norm), while Nòmos 3 takes into consideration the role who has to obey the norm.

The main objective of this progress report is to sketch the main ingredients of Nòmos 3. We show how to link models of the requirements (i*) with model of the law, and w.r.t. [5], we offer a more detailed glimpse of the types of reasoning it needs to support in order to establish compliance of goals relative to a set of applicable laws.

The objective is achieved by illustrating Nòmos 3 and its reasoning capabilities for evaluating compliance by answering questions like: given a set of requirements, which norms apply? which norms are violated? how do I comply with a given norm? who is responsible for a norm?

2   Nòmos 3

Nòmos 3 [5] is a modelling language for representing legal provisions, such as laws and regulations, and reasoning about the compliance of requirements — represented in terms of goals [12]. Nòmos 3 the language (see figure 1) uses the following primitive concepts:

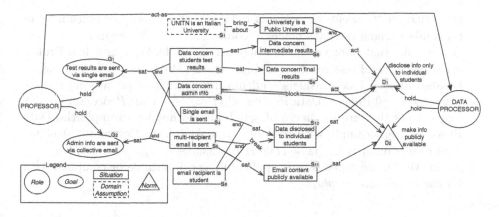

Fig. 1. Example of a Nòmos 3 model

- Situation: a state of affairs; e.g., s_3 = "Data concern administrative information"
- Goal: a desired state of affairs; e.g., g_1 = "Tests results are sent via single email"
- Domain Assumption: a state of affairs that is assumed in the fulfillment of a goal or compliance with a norm; e.g., "UNITN is an Italian University"
- Norm: a right or duty that somebody has; e.g., D_1 "Duty to disclose scholastic data, such as marks, only to the student owner"
- Role: has an associated Goal (Social Role, such as "Professor") or an associated Norm (Legal Role, such as "Data Processor"); the goals/norms associated to a role are to be fulfilled/complied with by any agent who plays the role.

Basic relationships between concepts allow for the expression of:

- Situations that can satisfy/negate Goals/Situations (*satisfy/break*). For example, when "Multi-recipient email is sent" is satisfied, then "Email content publicly available" is also satisfied ($s_5 \xrightarrow{\text{sat}} s_{11}$).
- Situations that can make a Norm applicable/not applicable (*activate/block* relation) or make a Norm satisfied/not satisfied (*satisfy/break*). For example, when "Data concern intermediate results" and "The University is a public University", then it applies the duty D_1 to disclose information only to individual students (($s_7 \wedge s_8$) $\xrightarrow{\text{act}} D_1$); when the data concern administrative info the duty does not apply ($s_3 \xrightarrow{\text{block}} D_1$). This duty is satisfied when data are disclosed to individual students ($s_{10} \xrightarrow{\text{sat}} D_1$)
- Goals and Domain Assumptions that can bring-about Situations (relation *brings-about*), for example the domain assumption "UNITN is a public University in Italy" brings about the situation "University is an Italian Public University"
- Situations that can be assigned to a specific role (*reserved*) in order to model responsibility. For example (not shown in figure 1) in data-privacy laws,

the situation "Consent for personal data is given" is only responsibility of the subject whom the data belong ("*consent*..." $\xrightarrow{reserved}$ *subject*).

- Social Roles that want Goals, and play a Legal Role. For example a Professor wants to send test results via single email (*Professor* $\xrightarrow{hold}$ G_1) and — because Privacy Law considers students information as private data — he plays the Legal Role of 'Data Processor' (*Prof* $\xrightarrow{act-as}$ *DataProcessor*)
- Legal Roles that are in charge of satisfying Norms; for example the Data Processor must comply with the duty to make information about students final results publicly available (*DataProcessor* $\xrightarrow{hold}$ D_2)
- Norms that make other Norms applicable, not applicable or complied with (*endorse, derogate, imply*)

3   Reasoning

Compliance in Nòmos 3 is established through reasoning. Initial values are assigned to input nodes of the model: Situations, which are observed or hypothesized to be satisfied (i.e., the state of affair that they represent holds: ST), not satisfied (the state of affair that they represent does not hold: SF) or undefined (it is not known whether the state of affairs that they represent holds or not: SU). Relationships propagate the values across the model and allow the analyst to perform different types of analysis: Norms and Roles will receive values through the relations, and from the evaluation of these values a compliance assessment is formulated. In particular, compliance evaluation of norms involves: (a) the identification of applicable Norms (Situations that make a Norm applicable); (b) satisfied Norms (Situations that make a Norm satisfied); and (c) Legal Roles, who have fulfilled their responsibilities (Situations that should be satisfied by a Role). Depending on these three conditions — norm's applicability, satisfiability and role fulfillment — a norm is evaluated as compliant, non-compliant. Moreover, taking into account the uncertainty of some Situations holding, a norm can also be evaluated as tolerated or inconclusive. For example an initial assignment to the Situations in the example of figure 1, can be that of UNITN evaluating the requirements of a new software managing student results. The scenario allowing a Professor to notify the results is represented by having s_1, s_2, s_4 hold.

Reasoning is implemented by means of forward and backward analysis algorithms. In forward analysis, input values are propagated across the model, and the resulting knowledge is reported (norms complied/violated and roles complying or not).

With this type of analysis it is possible to answer questions like (*Given a set of requirements*), *which norm apply?, which norm are complied?, which roles in the domain are subject to which norms?, which roles in the domain comply?*. For example, given a set of Situations holding/not holding, values are propagated from Situations to norms and to roles, so that norms compliance can be evaluated. Similarly, in backward analysis, a desired knowledge is queried (a compliance value for some norms) and solutions matching the query are reported (sets of situations holding/not-holding). In the example of UNITN, propagation of values results in having s_7, s_8, s_9 also satisfied, which make both D_1 and D_2 applicable. Since the two applicable norms are not satisfied — which would require s_{10} and s_{11} to hold — they are not complied with. Since the Social Role of 'Professor' plays the Legal Role of Data Processor, and the Data Processor holds two norms that are applicable in the scenario, the Professor is the social role subject to the norms. Since the two norms held by the Legal Role of 'Data processor' are not complied with, the Social Role of Professor is also not compliant.

In backward analysis, an explicit query is given (e.g., specific norms and roles complied with), and an exhaustive backward search is done to find an assignment satisfying the query. With this type of analysis it is possible to answer questions like *How do I comply with a specific Norm?*, *Which goals contribute to the violation a specific Norm?*, *How does a legal role comply with the norm it holds.*

In the example of UNITN, for example complying with D_1 requires the norm to be satisfied, and this is true when situation "Data are disclosed to individual student"(s_{10}) holds. s_{10} is in turn satisfied when s_4 and s_6 hold, but not if s_5 holds too $((s_5 \land s_6) \xrightarrow{\text{break}} s_{10})$. An assignment to the situations satisfying the norm would be in having s_1, s_4, s_6, s_8 holding: UNITN is a public university, a single email is sent, the recipient of the mail is a student, and data concern intermediate results.

The information gathered through these types of analysis can be used by the requirement analyst for different purposes. In the example above, the assignment of the situations satisfying the norm can be used by the analyst in order to identify new elements to include — like the domain assumption about the university being a public one (if not present) — or how to revise the initial goal so that it does not violate the applicable norm $g_1' =$ "Test results *about intermediate results* are sent *to students* via single email" (where now $(s_4 \land s_6 \land s_8) \xrightarrow{\text{sat}} g_1$).

4   Conclusions and Future Work

In this short paper we have presented on-going work on Nòmos 3, a modeling language for evaluating compliance of a set of requirements to a fragment of law. We represent requirements by means of Goals and the Social Roles who want them, and we represent the law in terms of Norms, Legal Roles holding the norms, and Situations making the norms applicable or satisfied. We have described the main concepts and relations of our language with a small illustrative example related to the compliance of a set of goals with some norms.

Current work-in-progress is concerned with including in our language the concept of delegations between social roles, and reasoning on whether the compliance condition is maintained. Our future work will be dedicated in developing a tool-supported methodology for the revision of a set of requirements in order to help the analyst amend requirements that do not comply with a given law.

Acknowledgments. This work has been supported by the ERC advanced grant 267856 "Lucretius: Foundations for Software Evolution" (April 2011 – March 2016).

References

1. Breaux, T.D., Vail, M.W., Antón, A.I.: Towards Regulatory Compliance: Extracting Rights and Obligations to Align Requirements with Regulations. In: IEEE Conf. Req. Eng. – RE 2006 (2006)
2. Darimont, R., Lemoine, M.: Goal-oriented analysis of regulations. In: ReMo2V, held at CAiSE 2006 (2006)
3. Derakhshan, F., Bench-Capon, T., McBurney, P.: Dynamic assignment of roles, rights and responsibilities in normative multi-agent systems. Journal of Logic and Computation 23(2), 355–372 (2013)
4. Ghanavati, S., Amyot, D., Peyton, L.: Towards a framework for tracking legal compliance in healthcare. In: Krogstie, J., Opdahl, A.L., Sindre, G. (eds.) CAiSE 2007. LNCS, vol. 4495, pp. 218–232. Springer, Heidelberg (2007)
5. Ingolfo, S., Jureta, I., Siena, A., Perini, A., Susi, A., Mylopoulos, J.: Nòmos 3: Legal compliance of roles and requirements. In: ER 2014 (2014)
6. Maxwell, J., Anton, A.: Developing production rule models to aid in acquiring requirements from legal texts. In: RE 2009, pp. 101–110 (2009)
7. Sadri, F., Stathis, K., Toni, F.: Normative kgp agents. Comput. Math. Org. Theor. 2006, 101–126 (2006)
8. Siena, A., Ingolfo, S., Perini, A., Susi, A., Mylopoulos, J.: Automated reasoning for regulatory compliance. In: Ng, W., Storey, V.C., Trujillo, J.C. (eds.) ER 2013. LNCS, vol. 8217, pp. 47–60. Springer, Heidelberg (2013)
9. Siena, A., Jureta, I., Ingolfo, S., Susi, A., Perini, A., Mylopoulos, J.: Capturing variability of law with Nòmos 2. In: Atzeni, P., Cheung, D., Ram, S. (eds.) ER 2012 Main Conference 2012. LNCS, vol. 7532, pp. 383–396. Springer, Heidelberg (2012)
10. Siena, A., Mylopoulos, J., Perini, A., Susi, A.: Designing law-compliant software requirements. In: Laender, A.H.F., Castano, S., Dayal, U., Casati, F., de Oliveira, J.P.M. (eds.) ER 2009. LNCS, vol. 5829, pp. 472–486. Springer, Heidelberg (2009)
11. Singh, M.P.: Norms as a basis for governing sociotechnical systems. ACM Trans. Intell. Syst. Technol. 5(1), 21:1–21:23 (2014)
12. Yu, E.: Towards modelling and reasoning support for early-phase requirements engineering. In: Proc. IEEE International Symposium on Requirements Engineering, RE 1997, pp. 226–235 (January 1997)

Automated Completeness Check in KAOS

Joshua C. Nwokeji[1], Tony Clark[1], Balbir Barn[1], and Vinay Kulkarni[2]

[1] Middlesex University, London, UK
Hendon the Burroughs, NW4 4BT
{J.Nwokeji,T.N.Clark,B.Barn}@mdx.ac.uk
[2] Tata Consultancy Services, India
{vinay.vkulkarni}@tcs.com

Abstract. KAOS is a popular and useful goal oriented requirements engineering (GORE) language, which can be used in business requirements modelling, specification, and analysis. Currently, KAOS is being used in areas such as business process modelling, and enterprise architecture (EA). But, an incomplete or malformed KAOS model can result to incomplete and erroneous requirements analysis, which in turn can lead to overall systems failure . Therefore, it is necessary to check that a requirements specification in KAOS language are complete and well formed. The contribution at hand is to provide an automated technique for checking the completeness and well-formed-ness of a requirements specification in KAOS language. Such a technique can be useful, especially to business or requirements analysts in industries and research, to check that requirements specification in KAOS language is well formed.

1 Introduction

Requirements engineering (RE) is a core imperative in systems development, this is because it has the ability to cripple the entire system if incomplete or erroneous [4]. In fact, the vast majority of systems failures have been attributed to incomplete or erroneous requirements specification and analysis [2,18]. Goal oriented requirement engineering (GORE) refers to various requirements engineering methods, which uses goals, and other categories of intentions, to analyse and specify the requirements of a system [20]. Among varieties of competing GORE languages such as i* [19], GBRAM [1], and BMM [14], KAOS [3,8,11,12,15,17] is one of the most popular and widely used languages [8].

In order to facilitate a well formed requirements specification in KAOS language, we contribute by developing a tool that can be used to check the completeness of a requirements model in KAOS language. This tool is an extension of our previous work reported in [13], where we developed a comprehensive meta-model and a graphic editor (Ktool) for requirements specification in KAOS.

The rest of this paper is structured as follows: In Section 2 we describe a motivating example and use it to explain certain concepts of the KAOS language. This is also used as a case study for demonstrating the completeness check in KAOS. Section 3 gives a brief description of the KAOS framework. Related work is briefly explained in Section 4. In Section 5, the tooling process is described and a conclusion is given in Section 6.

M. Indulska and S. Purao (Eds.): ER Workshops 2014, LNCS 8823, pp. 133–138, 2014.

2   Motivating Example

We describe a motivating example below, and use to explain the various concepts in Kaos and to demonstrate completeness check in Kaos. Consider the requirement analysis of a *card payment system* for Bank xyz. Bank xyz provides point of sale (POS) services to vendors, via wireless routers. A router can be encrypted but slow (E1), or unencrypted but fast (E2). Vendors sell products to customers but must upload daily transactions to Bank xyz. The bank desires to protect all transactions from hacker, who steal smart card information from customers.

3   KAOS

KAOS is a GORE language that uses the concepts of goals, actors and other intentional elements to elaborate, specify, model and analyse the requirements of a system [8] [10]. A goal is a statement that describes the intentions of a given actor in a system, *e.g.*, *steal credit card information* [5]. A *parent* goal may be decomposed, or *refined*, into *child* sub-goals [12]; a *leaf* goal has no children. A leaf goal that has a clear criteria for its satisfaction is called a *requirement*, else it is called an *expectation*. A KAOS goal model is said to be *complete* when all leaf goals are assigned to agents-active entities, machine or human, in a system [15]. KAOS is a composite language/framework consisting of a *Goal, Object, Operation* and *Responsibility* models [8,15]. More details about the KAOS model and its elements can be found in [3, 8, 11–13, 15, 17].

4   Related Work

In the past, various approaches have been used to check the completeness of KAOS model. For instance, the use of *pre, post, and trigger conditions* based on temporal logic has been proposed in [16], while the *goal question metric (GQM)* has been proposed in [7]. Although these approaches can be useful, they involve some sort of rigour or formality, which can be difficult and thus discourage systems or business analysts from using them. However, our approach is different, we aim to provide a conceptual method that can be easier to use and less rigorous when compared with other methods. To achieve this, we consolidate the KAOS *elaboration criteria* proposed in [16], the *completeness criteria* proposed in [15], and the *GQM* in [7] into three *completeness checks* itemized below, and implement a tool that automates them:

- **Completeness Criteria 1**: All goals must be refined until they become either leaf goals (expectations and requirements) or domain property.
- **Completeness Criteria 2**: All leaf goals must be assigned to agents.
- **Completeness Criteria 3**: All agents, especially machine or software agents, must be assigned to operations.

In the following Sections we explain the processes involved in automating these checks.

5   Automating the Completeness Criteria

The tool that automates these completeness criteria is implemented by integrating a set of constraints, defined in epsilon validation language (EVL), with our graphics editor (Ktool) developed with the eclipse modelling framework (EMF). The processes and steps involved in implementing our graphics editor (Ktool) have been described in our previous publications [13], and thus will not be repeated in this paper. The epsilon validation language (EVL) is a similar language to the object constraint language (OCL) and a part of the eclipse epsilon family of languages [1], that provides a technique for defining a set of constrains on a model. These constraints can then be used for validation or checking the well formed-ness of the model [9]. The eclipse modelling framework (EMF) is an integrated development platform commonly used for model driven requirements engineering to develop software systems and modelling languages. The steps involved in EVL constraints with a graphic editor in EMF have been described in details in [6], and can be summarised as follows: First, we create an integration plug in into our graphics editor. Secondly we set the dependencies. Then we define the three completeness criteria as a set constraints and saved them as *.evl. Finally we bind these constraints to the editor and test each of them with the case study defined in Section 2. Each of these criteria is described in details in the sections below.

5.1   Completeness Criterion 1

Completeness criterion 1 ensures that all goals are refined to leaf goals, *i.e* expectations and requirements, or domain property. For the sake of page limitation, part of the EVl constraint that checks this criterion is shown in the listing below:

```
1    context Goal{
2      constraint ToLeaf{
3      check: Refinement.all.exists
4       (g|g.froma.isKindOf(And) or
5       g.froma.isKindOf(Or) and
6       g.toa.isKindOf(Requirement) or
7       g.toa.isKindOf(Expectation) or
8       g.toa.isKindOf(DomainInvariant) or
9       g.toa.isKindOf(DomainHypothesis))
10       message:"The " + self.name +
11       " should be refined into a leaf Goal" }}
```

The term *context* in Line 1 is an EVL keyword that shows the model element where the constraint is defined, in this case *goal*. The *constraint* keyword in Line 2 specifies that the name of the constraint is *ToLeaf*, while the *check* keyword in Line 3 defines the algorithm for the constraint. The *message* keyword in Line 10 shows the output message if the *check* is not satisfied. To demonstrate completeness criterion 1, we use our *Ktool* to construct a simple Kaos model of the case

---

[1] https://www.eclipse.org/epsilon/

study described in Section 2. As shown in Figure 1a, the root goal -*G1:provide excellent point of sale (POS) services* of Bank xyz is refined into subgaols-*SG1: secure transaction, and SG2:successful transaction*. The completeness or well formed-ness of this model can be checked by clicking on the *validate button* in the Ktool. As shown in Figure 1a, when the *validate* command is executed, our tool checks if this Kaos model satisfies the constraints for *completeness check 1*. If this is true, there will be no error sign in the *context* model element or in the *problem dialogue box*. But if false, as in this case, an error signs will appear in the *context* model elements, in this case, *G1, SG1, and SG2*. This will be accompanied by error messages, displayed in the *problem dialogue box*. The error message, *"The ¡Goal¿ G1 , and The ¡SubGoals¿ SG1, and SG2-should be refined into a leaf Goal"*, indicates that the model is incomplete and malformed and indicates why it is so.

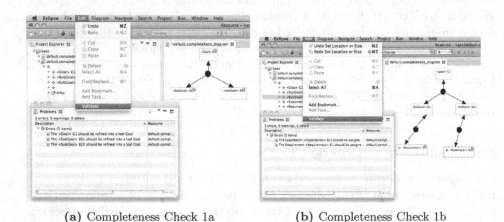

(a) Completeness Check 1a   (b) Completeness Check 1b

Fig. 1. Completness Check 1

For this model to satisfy completeness criterion 1, we refine the subgoals *SG1 and SG2* into leaf goals, and then revalidate the model. The result of the revalidated model is shown in Figure 1b. The error signs have moved from *G1, SG1, and SG2* to *R1 and Ex1*. This means that although the first completeness criteria has been satisfied, the model is not yet complete because the second and third completeness criteria have not been satisfied.

5.2   Completeness Criteria 2

In *completeness criterion 2*, each leaf goal must be assigned to at least one *agent*. The EVL constraint for this is available on request. The error messages and signs in Figure 1b shows that the leaf goals have not been assigned to agents, thus completeness criteria 2 has not been satisfied.

To satisfy completeness criterion 2, we simply assign two agents to the leaf goals and then re-validate the model. The validated model shown in Figure 2a

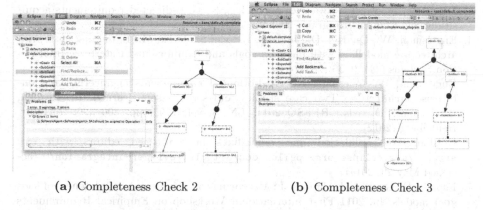

(a) Completeness Check 2   (b) Completeness Check 3

Fig. 2. Completeness Checks 2 and 3

shows that completeness criteria 2 has been satisfied. However the model is not yet complete because completeness criteria 3 has not been satisfied.

5.3   Completeness Criterion 3

Completeness criterion 3 can be satisfied when each agent, especially machine or software agent, is assigned to an operation. The EVL constraint that checks this criteria is available on request. To satisfy completeness criterion 3, we assign an peration: OP1, to the agent and revalidate the model. The result as shown in Figure 2b is a complete KAOS model without of error signs and error messages. Thus this model is presumed complete.

6   Conclusion and Future Work

This paper presents a technique that can allow business analysts in industry or research to automatically check the well formed-ness of a KAOS model. A major advantage of this approach is that it shield users from formal and mathematical approach, which analysts from non-mathematical background may find difficult to use. In addition, it is based on conceptual modelling techniques, which can allow users to specify ad check the well formed-ness of a systems requirement in terms of its modelling elements or concepts. This tool is still at the pilot stage, and has only been demonstrated with a basic KAOS model. We are still working on it, so that it can support a more complex kAOS model. Our future work will focus on testing this tool with a more complex KAOS model, and extending it's usability with other GORE languages.

References

1. Anton, A.: Goal-based requirements analysis. In: ICRE, pp. 136–144 (1996)
2. Baccarini, D., Salm, G., Love, P.E.D.: Management of risks in information technology projects. Industrial Management & Data Systems 104(4), 286–295 (2004)

3. Dardenne, A., van Lamsweerde, A., Fickas, S.: Goal-directed requirements acquisition. Sci. Comput. Program. 20(1-2), 3–50 (1993)
4. Engelsman, W., Quartel, D., Jonkers, H., van Sinderen, M.: Extending enterprise architecture modelling with business goals and requirements. Enterprise Information Systems 5(1), 9–36 (2011)
5. Engelsman, W., Wieringa, R.: Goal-oriented requirements engineering and enterprise architecture: Two case studies and some lessons learned. In: Regnell, B., Damian, D. (eds.) REFSQ 2011. LNCS, vol. 7195, pp. 306–320. Springer, Heidelberg (2012)
6. Epsilon. Live validation and quick-fixes in gmf-based editors with evl, https://www.eclipse.org/epsilon/doc/articles/evl-gmf-integration/ (accessed May 29, 2014)
7. Espada, P., Goulao, M., Araujo, J.: Measuring complexity and completeness of kaos goal models. In: 2011 First International Workshop on Empirical Requirements Engineering (EmpiRE), pp. 29–32 (August 2011)
8. Heaven, W., Finkelstein, A.: Uml profile to support requirements engineering with kaos. IEE Proceedings Software 151(1), 10–27 (2004)
9. Kolovos, D., Rose, L., Paige, R., Polack, F.A.C.: The epsilon book. Structure 178, 1–10 (2010)
10. Lapouchnian, A.: Goal oriented requirement engineering: An overview of the current research (2005)
11. Matulevicius, R., Heymans, P.: Analysis of kaos meta-model: Technical report (2005)
12. Monteiro, R., Araujo, J., Amaral, V., Goulao, M., Patricio, P.M.B.: Model-driven development for requirements engineering: The case of goal-oriented approaches. In: Machado, R., Faria, J.P., Silva, A. (eds.) 8th International Conference on the Quality of Information and Communications Technology (QUATIC 2012). Quality of Information and Communications Technology, vol. 8, pp. 75–84. IEEE Computer Society (September 2012)
13. Nwokeji, J.C., Clark, T., Barn, B.S.: Towards a comprehensive meta-model for kaos. In: 2013 International Workshop on Model-Driven Requirements Engineering (MoDRE), pp. 30–39 (2013)
14. OMG. Business motivation model (2010)
15. Respect-IT. A kaos tutorial (2007)
16. van Lamsweerde, A., Letier, E.: Handling obstacles in goal-oriented requirements engineering. IEEE Transactions on Software Engineering 26, 978–1005 (2000)
17. Werneck, V.M.B., de Padua Albuquerque Oliveira, A., do Prado Leite, J.C.S.: Comparing gore frameworks: i-star and kaos. In: Ibero-American Workshop of Engineering of Requirements, Val Paraiso, Chile (July 2009)
18. Yeo, K.T.: Critical failure factors in information system projects. International Journal of Project Management 20(3), 241–246 (2002)
19. Yu, E.: Modeling strategic requirement for process reengineering (1995)
20. Yu, E., Giorgini, P., Maiden, N., Mylopoulos, J.: Social modeling for requirement engineering: an introduction (2009)

Practical Goal Modeling for Enterprise Change Context: A Problem Statement

Sagar Sunkle, Hemant Rathod, and Vinay Kulkarni

Tata Research Development and Design Center
Tata Consultancy Services
54B, Industrial Estate, Hadapsar
Pune, 411013 India
{sagar.sunkle,hemant.rathod,vinay.vkulkarni}@tcs.com

Abstract. Modern enterprise need to rapidly respond to changes. Goal modeling techniques are intuitive mechanisms that help in modeling and analyzing rationale behind enterprise's response to change. In spite of their intuitiveness, there are several challenges that need to be addressed for their practical adoption and application. We present a problem statement based on real world case study and possible ways in which these challenges can be addressed.

Keywords: Goal Modeling, Strategy Making, Organizational Hierarchy, Course of Action.

1 Introduction

Modern enterprises need to respond to multiple change drivers such as evolving market conditions, technology obsolescence and advances, and regulatory compliance among others. These changes affect what the enterprise is doing, how it is doing it, and more importantly why it is doing it in a certain way. In other words, response to change drivers tends to result in systemic changes across business, IT, and infrastructure dimensions of an enterprise. Our organization often gets involved in engagements where we need to help enterprises respond to changes while maintaining a bridge between strategic goals and operational execution.

Toward this end, we have been exploring application of goal/intentional modeling techniques to enterprise change context [1, 2]. Considerable research already exists around goal modeling issues, and while results are promising, our ongoing explorations have led us to several questions about efficient and effective use of these techniques for enterprise decision/strategy modeling and decision/strategy execution. In this paper, we put forth our observations and a problem statement. Our purpose is to bring out practical problems in the application of goal/intentional modeling techniques. Note that it is not the purpose of this paper to survey intentional modeling in particular or goal-oriented requirements engineering (GORE) techniques in general, nor is it to indicate specific merits or demerits. Rather, we solicit feedback with regards how best to use these techniques in enterprise change context.

The paper is arranged as follows. Section 2 presents the problem statement using high level details of an ongoing case study where we continue to explore intentional

M. Indulska and S. Purao (Eds.): ER Workshops 2014, LNCS 8823, pp. 139–144, 2014.

modeling for enterprise strategy making and execution. The key questions of what to model, how to model it, and how to use what is modeled are elaborated in Section 3. In Section 4, we briefly draft a set of requirements toward practical application of goal modeling in enterprises and conclude the paper.

2   Industrial Problem Statement

We are exploring intentional modeling for analyzing possible alternatives toward achieving varied goals of a merger. The merger took place between two wealth management banks. The merged entity faced the following problems- can it achieve the strategic goal of revenue increment over a period of time (specifically, tripling merger initiator bank's revenue and gross margin over five years) in the face of changes induced by the merger to its structure and behavior?, in doing so how can it ensure that responses to various changes are rooted in reasonable practices?, and how to respond optimally to the changes during post-merger integration execution? The most important change is to the products and services portfolio with potentially similar products and services from both the banks. Second most important change is to its branch operations since branches have to be consolidated. These have implications on workforce integration, data migration, and technology infrastructure capacity enhancement. All of these changes affect the application portfolio consisting of products and other IT applications, and must be rationalized in accordance with the chosen responses to the rest of changes.

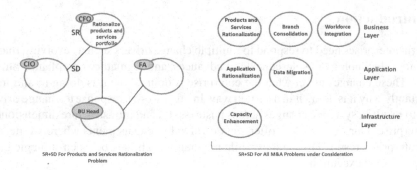

Fig. 1. Goal Models for Each Problem to be Solved in Merger Case Study

From the goal modeling perspective, we treated each of the above situations as an individual problem to be solved. We created a set of strategic rationale (SR) and strategic dependency (SD) models for individual problems. Figure 1 shows just the key actors involved in response to the doubled products and services portfolio. We do not show details of SR and SD because they are not necessary for the intended discussion. Figure 1 shows all such models and which specific enterprise dimension/layer the change scenario affects. Correspondingly, key actors differ for whom SR models are created with solution as the hard goal and desirable qualities of the solution as the soft goals in each case.

Although, such a treatment of merger as a change driver and change responses as individual problems to be solved is intuitive, several concerns emerged as we continue to explore goal modeling. These are mainly along the lines of what needs to be modeled for conceptualization and modeling of strategy, how to model it, and how to practically apply what was modeled. We elaborate each of these next.

3   Key Questions in Practical Application of Goal Modeling

3.1   What to Model?

Organizational Hierarchy. Within intentional and other GORE techniques there are elaborate ways of explicating organization hierarchy. But there is a fundamental difference in the treatment of strategic goals, their reinterpretation at tactical level, and their implementation at operational level in real world and the way this situation is represented using intentional modeling for analysis purposes. In practice, while top management comes up with strategic goals, a complete course of action till operationalization is either not modeled or is difficult model, if at all. Strategic goals percolate down the organization hierarchy. Individual units interpret the initiatives in their local context and set local goals to be operationalized. Ongoing operations contribute to individual unit goals which in turn are supposed to contribute to strategic goals. This is illustrated on the left of Figure 2. Intentional modeling proposes to capture all relevant roles/actors whose contribution is necessary for realization of a (root) goal irrespective of which level of organization hierarchy they belong to as shown on right of Figure 2. This implies that before goal modeling techniques are applied in enterprise change context, some way of imitating and improving the enterprise strategy modeling process needs to be arrived at.

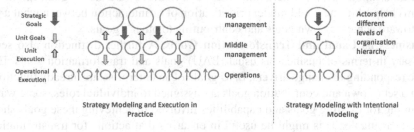

Fig. 2. Strategy Modeling and Execution in Practice vs. using Intentional Modeling

Ownership and Contributions. Furthermore, using intentional modeling, we arrived at SR and SD models of chief financial officer (CFO), chief information officer (CIO), business unit head (BU Head), and financial advisor (FA) roles. Once a course of action is chosen across these roles, various tasks will be handed over to several other roles/actors, for instance, while CIO might have been modeled as performing integration of product applications for products chosen by CFO (i.e., CFO's team as it were), product application integration is handed over down the hierarchy to program managers, project leaders, till the requirements of product application integration are actually implemented by developers. This is a rough hierarchy of roles, but essentially top level management should and generally does focus on strategic aspects rather than tactical and operational realizations. The question when using existing goal modeling

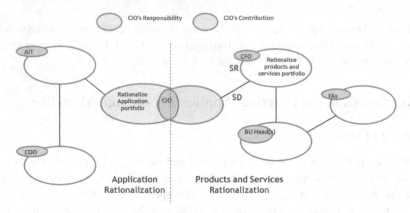

Fig. 3. Reconciling Ownership and Contributions of a Role

techniques is, how deep the organizational hierarchy should the actors be modeled yet keeping ties with the way strategy modeling and execution takes place in practice.

A role in a organization hierarchy partakes in the solution of problems which are the responsibility of other roles. At the same time, the same role may also be responsible for solution to a problem that the role owns. We encountered this situation as we divided the problem of goal modeling for merger into sub-problems, where several similar roles naturally repeated in solution to individual problems. For instance, in Figure 3, CIO contributes to CFO's goal of products and services rationalization in terms of integrating applications of newly product mix. At the same time, CIO is responsible for application rationalization where other roles contribute toward CIO's goal. Intuitively, it seems helpful if one could model prioritization of or interaction between what a role does toward achieving own goals and contributing to other's goals.

Business as Usual and Transformation Goals. A further distinction also seems necessary in terms of business as usual (BAU) goals and transformation goals. Even before responding to change drivers, BAU goals of an enterprise are already functional. When a set of own and contribution goals are assigned to individual roles, some way of accounting for existing goals and capabilities involved in achieving these goals should be made available. This might be useful in ensuring that actions for transformational goals are not hurting BAU goals.

Motivations, Assumptions, and Course Corrections. Several GORE techniques provide the facility to model and analyze various facets of goals [3]. In practice, (change) drivers are often recognized by stakeholders, an assessment is conducted following which goals and policies are arrived at [4]. Several assumptions are made during assessment of drivers. Such assumptions are also implicit when capturing qualitative aspects of alternative courses of actions. For instance, in intentional modeling, the contributions links from various elements to soft goals originate from observations or assumptions on domain expert's part. We believe that an explicit representation of these concepts is necessary mainly because incorrect assumptions often lead to unexpected results. Also, even as a course of action suggested by goal evaluation is taken, it might be necessary to make course correction if the environment of the enterprise or its internal capabilities change or if the assumptions behind prevalent course of action were proved to be incorrect. This indicates that some sort of historic trace of assumptions, course of action taken, key environmental and internal factors, and the results that ensued may be kept and referred to in order to be able to change assumptions and correct the course of action in operation.

3.2 How to Model It?

The question of who builds or helps build goal models in practice is very hard. As discussed earlier, in practice a person in a specific set of roles may have the necessary depth and breadth of domain knowledge that is vital in interpreting goals and coming up with alternative courses of actions to choose from. Ideally, a modeler well versed in given goal modeling technique could interview/discuss/observe such domain experts to build goal models. In practice, unless there is awareness about and concerted effort aimed at making and managing goals models over a pre-determined period of time (presumably till change initiative is complete), it is quite difficult to make goal models practically applicable.

3.3 How to Make Use of What Is Modeled?

Recent research in goal evaluation techniques suggests that depending on particular syntax of given goal modeling technique and semantics of evaluating alternatives, different techniques rank same alternative differently [5]. Therefore, it is suggested that goal modeling should be used for domain exploration and communication. We find this suggestion practical, because goal modeling encourages coming up with alternatives toward achieving goals [6] which may not be thought of in the absence of goal models. Still, the result in [5] is interesting, because it essentially removes prescriptive abilities of goal models and therefore makes them as good as descriptive models. We believe that if goal modeling practice was followed strictly, the correlation between the recorded rationale, the course of action taken, and results that ensued may be used to influence a future course of action.

4 Toward More Practical Goal Modeling

Goal models are difficult to create for complex enterprise change contexts, and may not be able to rigorously suggest a prescriptive course of action toward achievement of a goal [5]. Still they intuitively seem to be useful. We believe that their practical adoption requires further research along following directions-

1. Some goal-related concepts should be explicated [7] based on their practical relevance, such as assumption(s) involved in taking a particular course of action, assessment which lead to goals and in some cases to policies [8] and so on.
2. Our observations on keeping track of decisions taken, assumptions and assessments made, indicate that goal models should be created and maintained over the entire lifecycle of change initiative. This requires research in *goal model lifecycle management*.
3. A clear distinction between a role's/actor's own goals and actions toward achieving other role's/actor's goals, and between BAU and transformational goals seems

necessary. Existing work in [9–12] could be used to specialize analysis algorithms to bring out the differences.

4. Based on seriousness in adoption of goal models, awareness and requisite tooling for goal modeling should be focused on, and may be made part of goal lifecycle management as suggested above. This may help ensure that goal models for imminent change drivers may be rapidly developed either by domain experts themselves or with the help of existing goal model repository.

In this paper, we put forth our observations and discussed problems we continue to face in using goal models in enterprise change context. We also suggested possible ways in which practical application of goal models makes sense. While solutions to individual problems may already have been proposed in intentional and GORE literature, in concert treatment seems necessary. We would like to get further feedback on key challenges mentioned as well as input on how to make goal model lifecycle management a reality.

References

1. Sunkle, S., Kulkarni, V., Roychoudhury, S.: Intentional Modeling for Problem Solving in Enterprise Architecture. In: Hammoudi, S., Maciaszek, L.A., Cordeiro, J., Dietz, J.L.G. (eds.) ICEIS (3), pp. 267–274. SciTePress (2013)
2. Sunkle, S., Roychoudhury, S., Kulkarni, V.: Using Intentional and System Dynamics Modeling to Address WHYs in Enterprise Architecture. In: Cordeiro, J., Marca, D.A., van Sinderen, M. (eds.) ICSOFT, pp. 24–31. SciTePress (2013)
3. Quartel, D.A.C., Engelsman, W., Jonkers, H., van Sinderen, M.: A Goal-Oriented Requirements Modelling Language for Enterprise Architecture. In: EDOC, pp. 3–13. IEEE Computer Society (2009)
4. Quartel, D., Engelsman, W., Jonkers, H.: ArchiMate ® Extension for Modeling and Managing Motivation, Principles and Requirements in TOGAFT™ (October 2010)
5. Horkoff, J., Yu, E.S.K.: Comparison and Evaluation of Goal-oriented Satisfaction Analysis Techniques. Requir. Eng. 18(3), 199–222 (2013)
6. Lapouchnian, A., Mylopoulos, J.: Capturing Contextual Variability in i^* Models. In: de Castro, J.B., Franch, X., Mylopoulos, J., Yu, E.S.K. (eds.) iStar. CEUR Workshop Proceedings, vol. 766, pp. 96–101. CEUR-WS.org (2011)
7. Regev, G., Wegmann, A.: Where do Goals Come from: the Underlying Principles of Goal-Oriented Requirements Engineering. In: RE, pp. 353–362. IEEE Computer Society (2005)
8. OMG: Business Motivation Model - Version 1.1. (May 2010)
9. Mao, X., Yu, E.: Organizational and Social Concepts in Agent Oriented Software Engineering. In: Odell, J.J., Giorgini, P., Müller, J.P. (eds.) AOSE 2004. LNCS, vol. 3382, pp. 1–15. Springer, Heidelberg (2005)
10. Yu, E.S.: Social Modeling and i*. In: Borgida, A.T., Chaudhri, V.K., Giorgini, P., Yu, E.S. (eds.) Conceptual Modeling: Foundations and Applications. LNCS, vol. 5600, pp. 99–121. Springer, Heidelberg (2009)
11. Kavakli, E.: Goal-Oriented Requirements Engineering: A Unifying Framework. Requir. Eng. 6(4), 237–251 (2002)
12. Almeida, J.P.A., Guizzardi, G.: A Semantic Foundation for Role-Related Concepts in Enterprise Modelling. In: EDOC, pp. 31–40. IEEE Computer Society (2008)

Preface to QMMQ 2014

Quality assurance has been and still is a very challenging issue within the Information Systems (IS) and Conceptual Modeling (CM) disciplines. This ongoing research encompasses theoretical aspects including quality definition and quality models, and practical/empirical aspects such as the development of methods, approaches and tools for quality measurement and improvement. Research can be general or focused on specific application domains, such as web application quality, data warehouse quality, requirements model quality, model transformations quality, etc.

Although research contributions are highly diverse and relevant, they are not adopted by practitioners as useful solutions to reach better developed solutions.

Nowadays, with the development of web technologies and the growth of collected and exploited data volumes (or to exploit), IS and CM communities are faced to new challenges. They have to envision new perspectives to the problem of evaluating quality in IS.

The 1st Quality of Modeling and Modeling of Quality workshop held in conjunction with the 33rd International Conference on Conceptual Modeling aims to provide a space for fruitful exchanges involving both researchers and practitioners having a variety of interests such as: data quality, information quality, system quality as well as models, methods, processes and tools for managing quality. The aim of the workshop was twofold: firstly, to provide an opportunity for researchers and industry developers working on various aspects of information systems quality to exchange research ideas and results and discuss them; secondly, to promote research on information systems and conceptual model quality to the broader conceptual modeling research community attending ER 2014.

The workshop addresses the two main following topics :

- *Modeling of quality*: covering approaches and solutions for quality management. Despite a growing interest in quality at the early stages of systems development there is no agreement on a clear definition of what quality models are and which purposes they target.
- *Quality of modeling*: including data quality, data models quality, quality of notations, etc. .

The workshop attracted 8 papers from over 6 countries and the program committee finally selected 4 high quality papers. We would like to thank all the authors who submitted papers to our workshop. We would also like to thank program committee members and all the referees who gave up their valuable time to review the papers and help in proposing the workshop program. Finally, our thanks go out to organizing committee of ER2014 for recognizing the relevance of this workshop and ER2014 workshop chairs for their helpful work.

Samira Si-Said Cherfi, CNAM, France
Oscar Pastor, Universidad Politècnica de Valencia, Spain
Charlotte Hug, University Paris 1 Panthéon-Sorbonne, France

A Superstructure for Models of Quality

David W. Embley[1], Stephen W. Liddle[2], and Scott N. Woodfield[1]

[1] Department of Computer Science
[2] Information Systems Department
Brigham Young University, Provo, Utah 84602, USA
{embley,woodfiel}@cs.byu.edu, liddle@byu.edu

Abstract. With additional quality modeling features added to conceptual models, computers could play a greater role in ensuring a higher level of quality in the information we model. For information-discovery applications, these additional conceptual modeling features should automatically accommodate certainty and conflicting information, support evidence-based research, automate collaboration, and provide research guidance. To address these issues, we propose a superstructure that adds four additional abstraction layers to typical conceptual models: a knowledge layer, an evidence layer, a communication layer, and an action layer. We show by a running example the benefits these abstraction layers provide for increasing the quality of the information being modeled.

Keywords: Conceptual modeling continuum, abstraction hierarchy for conceptual modeling, evidence-based conceptual modeling, information-discovery applications, automated collaboration, research guidance, and uncertainty.

1 Introduction

Improving quality is a means to an end—not an end in and of itself. To improve quality, we need to know how it relates to our end goal. For systems whose end goal is the discovery of correct information in the face of uncertainty, conceptual models can play two quality roles: They can (1) reliably model the information discovered and (2) reliably model the meta-information that supports reasoning and communication about the discovered information and guides users in resolving uncertainties.

Suppose, for example, that we wish to have reliable information about human intergenerational ancestry to check hypotheses about inherited diseases or to trace our roots and better understand ourselves in our historical context. Then our end goal is to discover and then correctly populate a conceptualization of ancestral information. Ideally, the conceptual model itself needs to be able to (1) reflect reality, (2) allow for contradictory assertions, (3) organize evidence to support and refute assertions, (4) gather, disseminate, and reason about assertions, and (5) guide users in resolving contradictions and adjusting assertions with the end goal of having as many discovered assertions as possible, all of which are correct.

M. Indulska and S. Purao (Eds.): ER Workshops 2014, LNCS 8823, pp. 147–156, 2014.

Our end goal for information-discovery applications is an accurate model of reality—a quality model. To achieve this end, we need a model of quality, which for our information-discovery application is one that allows us to represent the relevant meta-information about the reality we seek to model. The combination is the superstructure we propose. To improve the quality of models, we investigate models of quality. We base our investigation on Meadow's continuum [1].[1] Meadow's continuum provides ever-higher levels of conceptualization, taking raw symbols from data to meaning and even wisdom. The first four layers are concerned with quality models (the information being modeled), while the last three are concerned with model quality (the meta information used to ensure the quality of the information being modeled).

Meadow's seven conceptual layers, renamed to better fit our needs, are:

Quality of Models:
1. Symbols: to represent and record information.
2. Classes: to classify and provide semantics for symbols.
3. Information: to relate and constrain class instances.
4. Knowledge: to allow for conflicting assertions and supporting documentation.

Models of Quality:
5. Evidence: to organize supporting evidence and automate evidentiary logic.
6. Communication: to send and receive information without distortion or loss.
7. Action: to provide automated guidance for user behavior.

2 Conceptualization Superstructure

Figures 1 and 2 are conceptual-model diagrams, which we use to illustrate our superstructure. In the subsections below, we explain the components of these diagrams that pertain to each of the seven layers and how these components provide an increase in power over each preceding layer.

As an illustration of the superstructure, we show how the increase in power helps a doctor determine the pain management regimen for his patient, Laura Williams. The proper regime depends on whether there is a genetic disposition to opioid addiction. An important indicator is whether two or more of Laura's parents, grandparents, or great-grandparents were alcoholics. Laura knows her mother was not an alcoholic nor was anyone on her father's side, but she knows little about her maternal ancestors since her mother died when she was three.

2.1 Symbols

Conceptualization: The symbol layer has no conceptual-modeling features. It is merely a collection of symbols: text files and digitized documents and images. The cloud in Figure 1 represents a collection of symbols.

Example: Laura's maternal grandmother is Mary Turner. Laura has a transcribed copy of Mary's diary stored as a text file—symbols. She also has a

---

[1] Others (e.g., [2] and [3]) have proposed similar hierarchies of conceptualization.

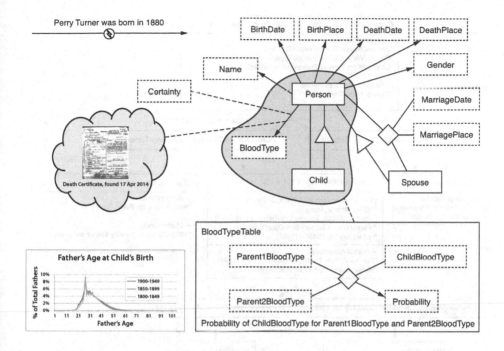

Fig. 1. Conceptualization of First Six Layers

scanned death certificate for Mary's husband, Bill Turner, stored as an image—symbols. Entries in the diary mention Bill's blood type as "A". The death certificate gives Bill's birth date, full name, and cause of death—cirrhosis of the liver, which implies that she has one ancestor who was alcoholic. She now needs help to determine whether either of Bill's parents were alcoholic.

Superstructure Motivation: At the symbol level, the computer is unable to provide any assistance. While easily understood by humans, text documents and images are difficult for machines to organize and process. Further, with no semantic information, the symbol "A" appearing in the diary adjacent to the phrase "Blood Type" has no meaning.

2.2   Classes

At this level we are able to classify symbols and place them into classes—the named rectangles in Figure 1. The dashed-border rectangles are lexical classes whose members are symbols, often short strings of characters such as "AB-" for *BloodType*. The solid-border rectangles are nonlexical classes whose members are object identifiers. A so-called *data frame* [4] provides the semantics for each class. Figure 3 shows a data frame for the *BloodType* class. Note that it defines the expected external representation for blood types and context keywords that indicate that symbols such as "A-" are blood types, not grades or something else. Like abstract data types, data frames have I/O methods and other opera-

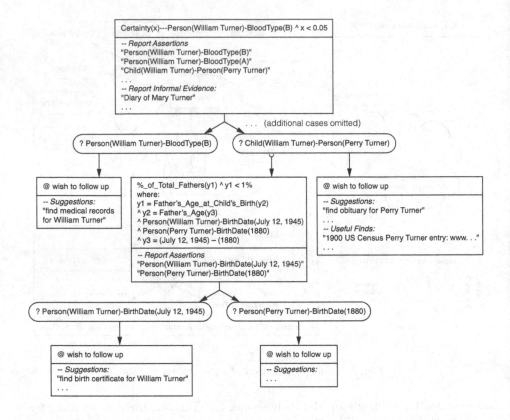

Fig. 2. Generated Action Conceptualization (partial)

tions. Operators may also include expected phrase templates used to indicate the applicability of an operation. Data frames for nonlexical classes contain object-existence rules, which state that when an instance of some specified lexical class is recognized, an instance of a corresponding nonlexical class exists (e.g., when a *Name* instance is seen, a corresponding *Person* object exists).

Example: Some of Laura's information can now be classified. Using representation and context information in the *BloodType* data frame, a computer can identify the symbol "A" as a *BloodType*. Similarly, the computer can also extract the symbol "July 12, 1945" as a date and "William Turner" as a person's name.

Superstructure Motivation: Even with this information the computer can do little to assist Laura in determining who Bill's parents are and whether they are alcoholic. At the *Class Layer* the computer can classify information but cannot record how the instances in one class relate to instances in another class. We cannot associate the object identifier for "William Turner" in the class *Person* with his name, date of birth, and blood type.

BloodType
external representation: \b(A|A+|A−|B|B+|B−|AB|AB+|AB−|O|O+|O−)\b
context keywords: \b[Bb]lood\s[Tt]ype\b
input method: BloodTypeToString
output method: StringToBloodType
operator methods:
    CanDonateTo(x: BloodType, y:BloodType) **returns** (Boolean)
      external representation: \b[Cc]an\s.{0,30}{x}\sdonate\sto\s.{0,30}{y}
      end;
  end;

Fig. 3. Data Frame for Blood Type

2.3 Information

Conceptualization: All typical conceptual modeling features are included at this level: classes, relationships, generalization/specialization, and cardinality constraints. In Figure 1, lines connecting object-set classes represent relationship sets (e.g., *Person-BloodType*). Lines with triangles represent *isa* abstractions (e.g., *Child-isa-Person*). Decorations on lines express cardinality constraints (e.g., the arrowhead on *Person-BloodType* designates a functional constraint, limiting a person to at most one blood type). Furthermore, at this level, we retain and expand data-frame semantics to full extraction ontologies [4], which allows a computer to "read" text—extract information from text and populate conceptualizations. When the *Person* object-existence rules fire, for example, not only is an object identifier added to *Person* and the string added to *Name*, but a relationship between the instances is also added to the *Person-Name* relationship set. Similarly, with extraction-ontology recognizers for phrases that represent relationships, it is possible to automatically "read" information from semi-structured documents like an OCRed version of the death certificate.

Example: For our story, we now have Bill's blood type "A", birth date "July 12, 1945", and father "Perry Turner" with his birth date "1880". Laura is excited because further research shows that Perry was a teetotaler. Because she only has one ancestor with an apparent alcohol problem she concludes that she is probably not susceptible to opioid addiction. Unfortunately, what the computer "says" with its conclusion-based model at this level of the conceptualization superstructure could be invalid—a potential life threatening mistake.

Superstructure Motivation: At the information layer, models must be valid—all constraints must hold—but in historical research we often have conflicting information. Further, the computer has no principled way to associate explanations and justifications with assertions.

2.4 Knowledge

Conceptualization: This layer allows for invalid models, unstructured meta-information for justification, and soft constraints for expressing likelihood. In Figure 1, the dashed line connecting the cloud with the *Person-BloodType* relationship set designates a set of links between relationship instances and unstructured

Person(x_1)-BloodType(x_2), Person(x_3)-BloodType(x_4), Person(x_5)-BloodType(x_6),
Child(x_1)-Person(x_3), Child(x_1)-Person(x_4),
Probability(x_7)_of_ChildBloodType(x_2)_for_Parent1BloodType(x_4)_and_Parent2BloodType(x_6),
$\Rightarrow$ Certainty(x_7)---Person(x_1)-BloodType(x_2)

Fig. 4. Inference Rule for Obtaining Certainty for Blood Type

meta-information. Distributions like the "Father's Age at Child's Birth" in Figure 1 represent soft constraints. "Violation" of a soft constraint does not make a model instance invalid but suggests some assertions are unlikely. Since the *Knowlege Layer* permits conflicts, we can define valid models without weakening constraints. We can, for instance, record two birth mothers for a child without having to reduce the quality of the model, which can still declare that there is at most one mother for a child.

Example: With birth dates in 1880 and 1945, Perry Turner was apparently 65 years old when Bill was born, and the computer can use the distribution "Father's Age At Child's Birth" to suggest to Laura the unlikelihood that Perry is Bill's father. Armed with this computer-provided insight, Laura digs deeper and discovers a medical form stating that Bill has blood type "B". Since we can violate constraints, we can add this assertion while retaining the assertion that Bill's blood type is "A". Furthermore, we can attach a scanned image of the medical form as justification that Bill has blood type "B".

Superstructure Motivation: It would be nice if the computer could assist Laura in resolving these seeming contradictions. Unfortunately, since the evidence is informal, the computer cannot reason about it.

2.5 Evidence

Conceptualization: This layer of our superstructure allows justifying meta-information to be formally organized as a conceptual-model instance. In Figure 1, the *BloodTypeTable* is a populated conceptual-model instance yielding the probability of a child's blood type being x when its parents have blood types y and z. In Figure 1, a dashed line connects the blood-type table to a conceptual-model subcomponent in which the information to compute the probability resides. Since the justifying meta-information is formal, the computer can reason with it as the datalog-like rule in Figure 4 shows. The inference rule in Figure 4 yields for each relationship instance in *Person-BloodType* its *Certainty* as recorded in the *BloodType* table. These results can be added as a formal *Certainty* justification as Figure 1 shows.

Example: Laura looks for and finds a medical record documenting that Perry Turner and his wife have blood type "A", but the computer tells her that there is a 0% chance that their son Bill has blood type "B". Thus something is wrong.

Superstructure Motivation: Information becomes more valuable and better validated when we share it with others. We can easily do this by encoding the information in human readable form and sending it. The human receiver must then read, understand, and manually store it in their own machine. It would

model structure:

Probability[1:*] of ChildBloodType[1:*] for Parent1BloodType[1:*] and Parent2BloodType[1:*];

ChildBloodType, Parent1BloodType, Parent2BoodType --> Probability;

end;

model instance:

Probability(.9375) of ChildBloodType(A) for Parent1BloodType(A) and Parent2BloodType(A);

Probability(.0625) of ChildBloodType(O) for Parent1BloodType(A) and Parent2BloodType(A);

...

end;

Fig. 5. Model Structure and Instance Data

be better if the source machine could directly communicate with the receiving machine.

2.6 Communication

Conceptualization: To communicate on its own, the computer must be able both to write/send and receive/read information. In Figure 1 the arrow with a lightning bolt in the center shows the computer receiving a message from some unknown source. Our proposed superstructure has three forms of communication.

1. When a statement of fact is sent, a previously agreed-upon format is used to decode the message—a common form of communication that only works if the sender and receiver agree on the format and semantics.
2. With extraction ontologies [4] the receiver can read, decode, and store facts; how well this works depends on how well the extraction ontology's recognizers can read.
3. If the sender and receiver are using the same conceptual model, both the statements of fact and the corresponding sub-model can be shared. In Figure 5 we demonstrate this using a model-equivalent programming language [5]. The textual model structure represents the *BloodTypeTable* in Figure 1, including its functional constraint, and the model-instance statements populate the model structure.

Example: In our example Laura remembers that Perry Turner may have been too old to be William Turner's father. She asks William Turner's sister, who is still alive, when Perry Turner was born. The reply comes as the message in Figure 1, "Perry Turner was born in 1880", which can be read using extraction-ontology technology and which confirms the fact that Perry was born in 1880. The question Laura asked was based on the assumption that Perry Turner was Bill's father. A better question would have been, "Is Perry Bill's father?"

Superstructure Motivation: Although helped by the computer to some extent, Laura has been on her own to decide what to do. Could a computer have provided her with the relevant information and, more importantly, could it have guided her reasoning and search for additional relevant information?

2.7   Action

Conceptualization: At this level of abstraction, we add object-behavior modeling along with object-interaction modeling and object-relationship modeling [6]. We represent object-behavior models with multi-threaded, enhanced state/transition diagrams as Figure 2 shows. Interestingly, we observe here that for fact-discovery applications as in our running example, useful object-behavior models can be generated automatically, rather than being specified by an expert in the field.

Example: Having reasoned (based on the inference rule in Figure 4) that the *Certainty* of *Person(William Turner)-BloodType(B)* is highly unlikely, the computer generates the object-behavior model in Figure 2 as follows:

- The trigger in the first transition in Figure 2 is the conclusion of the inference rule in Figure 4. In the action part of the first transition the *Reported Assertions* are the antecedent predicates of the inference rule with their variables bound to the instances for which the 0% certainty was derived, and the *Reported Informal Evidence* is the informal information in the cloud linked to these instances.
- Since if the conclusion is wrong, one or more of the antecedent assertions must be wrong, the computer can generate the subsequent states of the first transition as hypotheses to be considered. (Figure 2 shows only two of the six subsequent hypothesis states.)
- The @ *wish to follow-up* transitions depend on Laura's deciding to activate them. The provided *Suggestions* in these transitions are automatically generated if the conceptual modeler has included them in the formal evidence model and linked them as meta-information to the hypothesis relationship sets in question. The provided *Useful Finds* also come automatically if, knowing what to look for from the *Suggestions* list, the computer can send a query to a service such as `FamilySearch.org` or `Ancestry.com` and retrieve an image of a document that the computer suggests should be sought.
- Finally, when a constraint applies, as does the soft constraint in Figure 1 for the *? Child(William Turner)-Person(Perry Turner)* hypothesis in Figure 2, the computer generates a trigger that fires when the condition holds. The transition's action is to report assertions and informal evidence and then generate subsequent hypothesis states as explained previously.

Being guided by the computer-generated research plan, Laura follows up on the hypothesis that William Turner is not Perry Turner's child by searching for obituaries. She finds one for Perry and one for William Turner. Neither suggested a *Person-Child* relationship between the two. However, Laura also finds an obituary of a Steven Turner in which a William Turner was the son of Steven, and Steven was the son of Perry. The article stated that Steven Turner, a well known alcoholic, had died in a car accident. William Turner had been raised by his grandparents! Now Laura has found that two ancestors had suffered from apparent alcohol addictions, and she and her doctor now believe she may have a genetic disposition for opioid addiction.

Table 1. Matrix of Implementation Status

Feature	Status	Feature	Status
Comprehensive conceptual models	yes	Data frames	yes
Extraction ontologies	yes	Contradictory information	yes
Probability/likelihood data	no	"Soft" constraints	no
Informal evidence	partial	Formal evidence	partial
Communication support	yes	Action specification generation	no
Action specification execution	yes	Component integration	partial

3   Implementation Status

Our running example is reminiscent of the medical appointment scheduling example of Berners-Lee et al. when they first proposed the Semantic Web [7]. Indeed, our application fits well with the Semantic Web vision. However, as with the Semantic Web, even though a great deal has already been accomplished, there is still much to be done. The lower layers in our proposed superstructure—Symbols, Classes, Information, and Knowledge—tend to be thoroughly implemented, while the upper layers—Evidence, Communication, and Action—show a good amount of progress but need more work. Over the years we have implemented numerous software projects that support the proposed superstructure. Most of these projects fit within a Java-based graphical workbench that runs as a desktop application. Table 1 summarizes our implementation status.

We have implemented a comprehensive object-oriented conceptual model (OSM), data frames, and an ontology-based extraction system, OntoES, that works with high precision and recall in ontologically narrow domains [4]. Our workbench supports editing both schema and data-layer information within OSM, and we are able to communicate this information both graphically and textually (see Figures 1 through 5) and in an interchange-friendly XML format we call OSM-X. We can both manually and automatically (e.g. via OntoES) annotate assertions based on unstructured source documents, and we capture full linkage information between assertions and their supporting sources. This forms the basis for the evidence layer in our superstructure. Though our front-end tools do not yet support this, our OSM-X storage format allows for arbitrary user comments about annotations and assertions. We have implemented tools to execute state/transition diagrams (e.g. Figure 2): (1) automatically when fully formal triggers and actions are present [5] and (2) synergistically with the user's help for cases where triggers and actions may be informal or semi-formal [8]. We have not yet implemented the automatic generation of state/transition diagrams as explained in Section 2.7. While we have experimented with various types of uncertain data, we have not yet implemented "soft" constraints in our current toolset. Because we have a tool that converts our proprietary OSM-X interchange format to RDF/OWL, we are able to use Semantic Web reasoning tools like Jena to perform various kinds of automated inferencing [9] (e.g. for the rule in Figure 4). In addition to implementing additional features, we also need to better integrate some of the components in our toolset.

4   Concluding Remarks

Our superstructure includes both "models of quality" and "quality of models." The first four layers of the superstructure address models of quality: we can model our observations of the real world accurately with hard and soft constraints and ADT data frames, and we can allow our models to accept uncertain and conflicting assertions as we discover them. The last three layers address the quality of models: we can analyze the quality of the assertions in our models and improve them. The evidence layer enables computer-assisted reasoning and finding hard and soft constraint violations; the communication layer supports automated information collection both about the assertions and the evidence supporting the assertions; and the action layer supports improving the quality of the data in our conceptualizations and our search for truth under the guidance of an automated expert. Although developing our superstructure is a massive undertaking, we are well along in its implementation.

Meadow adds a last layer that he calls "Wisdom," and which we interpret to mean the proper application of knowledge based on truth (via evidence), communication, and action. It is our hope that the superstructure we propose here can more effectively enable us to proceed wisely—from our story, for example, to avoid placing Laura in a potentially life-threatening medical regimen.

References

1. Meadow, C.T.: Text Information Retrieval Systems. Academic Press, Orlando (1992)
2. Zins, C.: Conceptual approaches for defining data, information, and knowledge. Journal of the American Society for Information Science and Technology 58(4) (February 2007)
3. Rowley, J.: The wisdom hierarchy: Representations of the DIKW hierarchy. Journal of Information Science 33 (2007)
4. Embley, D.W., Campbell, D.M., Jiang, Y.S., Liddle, S.W., Lonsdale, D.W., Ng, Y.-K., Smith, R.D.: Conceptual-model-based data extraction from multiple-record web pages. Data & Knowledge Engineering 31(3), 227–251 (1999)
5. Liddle, S.W.: Object-Oriented Systems Implementation: A Model-Equivalent Approach. PhD thesis, Department of Computer Science, Brigham Young University, Provo, Utah (June 1995)
6. Embley, D.W., Kurtz, B.D., Woodfield, S.N.: Object-oriented Systems Analysis: A Model-Driven Approach. Prentice Hall, Englewood Cliffs (1992)
7. Berners-Lee, T., Hendler, J., Lassila, O.: The semantic web. Scientific American 36(25), 34–43 (2001)
8. Jackson, R.B.: Object-Oriented Requirements Specification: A Model, A Tool and a Technique. PhD thesis, Brigham Young University (1994)
9. Park, J.S., Embley, D.W.: Extracting and organizing facts of interest from OCRed historical documents. In: Proceedings of the 13th Annual Family History Technology Workshop, Salt Lake City, Utah, USA (March 2013)

A Quality Management Workflow Proposal for a Biodiversity Data Repository

Michael Owonibi and Birgitta Koenig-Ries

Friedrich Schiller University, Ernst-Abbe-Platz 2,
07743 Jena, Germany
{Michael.Owonibi,Birgitta.Koenig-Ries}@uni-jena.de

Abstract. The importance of quality-assured data in scientific analysis necessitates the inclusion of data quality management (DQM) functionality in research data repositories in addition to their primary role of data storage, sharing and integration. Typically, the DQM workflow in data repositories is fixed and semi-automated for datasets whose structure and semantics is known a-priori, however, for other types of datasets, DQM is either manual or minimal. In comparison, classical DQM methodology (especially in data warehousing research) has established standard, typically manually undertaken, DQM procedures for different types of data. Therefore, our proposal aims at customizing and semi-automating the classical DQM procedures for bio-diversity data repositories. As opposed to reviewing scientific contents of the data, we focus on technical data quality. Our proposed workflow includes DQM criteria specification, client and server-side validation, data profiling, error detection analysis, data enhancement and correction, and quality monitoring.

1   Introduction

Data Quality Management (DQM) is extremely important in science because the value of a research depends on the quality of its data. Situations where data quality problems become obvious very late can set back a research for a considerable period of time as data recapture may be impossible or prohibitively costly. DQM and the implications of poor data quality for enterprise data have long been studied. However, despite these early works, it is only rather recently, that the immense importance of DQM for research data has been equally broadly acknowledged.

According to [1],"error is a fundamental dimension of data because it is inescapable". Also, [2] suggested that unless extraordinary efforts have been taken, a field error rate of 1-5% should be expected. Errors can occur in different stages of data management such as collection, digitization, documentation, archiving, transfer, analysis, integration, and presentation. So, there is a need for continuous DQM in order to prevent, detect, correct and monitor both the potential for and the existing data errors.

The responsibility for DQM rests on the creator, the custodian and the consumer of a data [3]. Pursuant to this, data centers and repositories, in addition to their primary role of data storage, sharing and integration, attempt to apply DQM procedures to ensure that their dataset holdings meet relevant data quality standards. Extensive

M. Indulska and S. Purao (Eds.): ER Workshops 2014, LNCS 8823, pp. 157–167, 2014.
© Springer International Publishing Switzerland 2014

DQM is automatically carried out in data repositories and data integration centers which manage and integrate data whose schema and semantics are known a priori. The schemas of data managed by these data centers are either standardized or custom-defined. Examples of such data repositories and integration centers include GBIF[1], ALA[2], GBW[3]. In contrast, there are repositories which curate structured tabular data-sets (e.g. csv, spreadsheets) with arbitrary user-defined schemas, whose semantics is not known to the repository e.g. Pangaea[4], BExIS[5], KNB[6], and some data journals. As far as we know, none of these carry out rigorous data quality assurance automatically. Some, e.g. Pangaea perform extensive data quality assurance manually, and some others e.g. BExIS automatically perform data schema check, and manually check the contents of the dataset. Some repositories peer-review the datasets they are curating, while some others do not carry out any form of DQM [4]. This is often based on the assumption that the data creators are best placed to judge their data quality. However, according to [5], this assumption is usually wrong because many researchers lack good DQM skills.

Over the years, there have been contributions to DQM research from many disciplines. Most notably among these is the data warehousing community. They mostly focus on DQM within the Extract-Transform-Load (ETL) procedure for different data types whose schema and semantics may not have been known a priori. However, this is typically manually undertaken - a painstakingly labor intensive process. Therefore, we propose a workflow for semi-automatically performing DQM on datasets in a biodiversity-related data repository by exploiting the synergy of DQM principles used, most especially, in biodiversity data integration centers, and the data warehousing research.

2   Data Quality Management Overview

In the literature, data quality is widely referred to as "fitness of data for use" [6]. This definition, however, is not universally accepted: On the one hand, [7] believe that it is too restrictive and argue for a definition that includes fitness for potential uses. On the other hand, [8] believe the definition is describing the "usability" of the data as opposed to the quality which should be "the extent to which the data actually represents what it purports to represent". There is, however, agreement, that data quality needs to be regarded along different dimensions. [9] presented the four most important dimensions namely accuracy, completeness, consistency, and timeliness.

---

[1] Global Biodiversity Information Facility is an organization that focuses on making scientific data on biodiversity available via the Internet. (http://www.gbif.org/).

[2] Atlas of Living Australia is a data repository for Australian plants, animals, and fungi (www.ala.org.au/).

[3] GBW- Garden BirdWatch (http://www.bto.org/volunteer-surveys/gbw).

[4] Aims at archiving, publishing and distributing global change research data (www.pangaea.de/).

[5] BExIS - Biodiversity Exploratories Information System (See Section 4).

[6] KNB - Knowledge Network for Biocomplexity (https://knb.ecoinformatics.org/).

Motivated by the ETL requirements, significant efforts have been put into creating generic DQM systems, as opposed to subject-themed procedures. In this regard, [10] surveyed existing tools and workflows with respect to their comparative strengths and functionalities. Most of the tools surveyed are integrated with ETL for data warehousing and are developed for enterprise data. The DQM workflow presented typically consists of data entry, extraction, profiling, rules creation, analysis, cleansing, transformation, standardization, reporting, and monitoring. Although the number of tools has increased since the survey by [10] was made, they still share the same principles. In addition, a classification of error detection techniques by [6] is presented below:

- *Deterministic Tests*: Consist of hard constraints and business rules which indicate the validity of a data value.
- *Probabilistic Tests:* Involve the analysis to detect possible errors (outliers, duplicates, and other anomalies) in a dataset using different forms of statistics. This is based on the logic that errors are likely to appear as deviation from a pattern. [11] presents a survey of different types of outlier detection analysis. [12] provides guidelines on selection of the univariate outlier detection methods based on data properties such as symmetry, normality of distribution etc. Multivariate outliers detection tests (i.e. the simultaneous analysis of several variables to detect extreme values in a relationship) are much more complicated.
- *Semantics Based Approach*: By transforming the data into an ontology and reasoning on it, this technique detects errors by identifying entries in the data contradictory to the knowledge represented in some other ontology [13].
- *Data Mining*: Extends the probabilistic test by attempting to discover rules, patterns, and relationships in data before searching for the deviations from it [11].
- *Visualization*: Extends other methods by using different forms of graphics to represent the data and error [14].

3   Biodiversity DQM – Species Occurrence Data Example

Biodiversity research aims at measuring and understanding biological diversity and the mechanisms underlying it. The research objects range from microorganisms to landscapes, and the research questions from ecological to economical. Thus, supporting such a multi-disciplinary field of study, biodiversity data repositories contain different types of data including structured tabular data, geospatial data, genetic sequencing data etc. This paper, however, focusses on structured tabular data- the most widely used biodiversity data format and one that is particularly challenging with respect to DQM. This structured textual data could be standardized or unstandardized. Relatively, DQM is easier for standardized data; however, it is unrealistic to enforce a standard schema and standard, restrictive data types due to the following reasons.

- The wide range of biodiversity disciplines and questions addressed.
- Autonomy of researchers (with respect to data collection and recording).
- Relatively slow speed of data collection and documentation standardization.

These reasons make DQM more necessary and simultaneously, difficult.

In this section, we present the DQM procedure for one type of standardized biodiversity dataset - species occurrence data, typically presented using the Darwin Core[7] Standard. This data is arguably the most common type of biodiversity data, and several error detection and data cleaning procedures have also been developed for it. The most common types of error associated with this data are geocoding and species identification errors [3]. Geocoding errors include latitude-longitude inversion, incomplete coordinates, wrong coordinate system, numerical sign confusion, unrecorded datum, units misinterpretation (e.g. degree vs. radian) etc. Species identification errors often include inconsistent data values, misspellings, redundancy, taxonomic incompleteness, missing data, non-atomic data etc. [3]. These errors are typically detected using deterministic tests, and probabilistic tests.

Similarly, several tools exist for managing data quality of species occurrence data right from the data entry, through error detection and correction, to data enhancement and standardization. Some tools assist with managing the whole process while others focus on a particular DQM task. For instance, tools for species geo-location entry and cleaning include Biogeomancer[8], Geolocate[9]. Similarly, Spoutlier[10], Diva-gis[11], and some R-statistical[12] packages can be used to detect species outliers. Tools for parsing species names, validating them against a taxonomic list, and finding the most similar scientific names include Nameparser[13], Namefinder[14], and Checklist bank[15]. Darwin Core Archive Validator[16] and Darwin Test[17] can be used to validate records of a species occurrence dataset with respect to some listed errors. Furthermore, OpenRefine[18] now has an extension called TaxRefine[19] which is used for cleaning biodiversity data.

An important application which can be used for improving the quality of wildlife datasets whose structure is not standardized or predefined is the NBN Record Cleaner. According to [15], the tool "validates" data against a set of built-in rules. These rules, which are maintained by relevant experts, can specify, for example, where a species can be found at a given time of the year. One drawback of this application is that the rules are only based on species name, location and time. Therefore, error detection

---

[7] A body of data standards establishing a vocabulary of terms to facilitate the discovery, retrieval, and integration of data about organisms (http://www.tdwg.org/standards/450/).

[8] Species Occurrence DQM Tools - Biogeomancer (http://www.gbif.org/resources/2852).

[9] Geolocate (http://www.museum.tulane.edu/geolocate/).

[10] Spoutlier (http://splink.cria.org.br/).

[11] Diva-gis (http://www.diva-gis.org).

[12] R-statistical packages (http://www.r-project.org/).

[13] Nameparser (http://tools.gbif.org/nameparser/).

[14] Namefinder (http://tools.gbif.org/namefinder/).

[15] Checklist bank (https://github.com/gbif/checklistbank).

[16] Darwin core archive validator (http://tools.gbif.org/dwca-validator/).

[17] Darwin Test (http://www.gbif.es/darwin_test/Darwin_Test_in.php).

[18] OpenRefine (http://openrefine.org/).

[19] TaxRefine (https://github.com/gaurav/taxrefine).

and correction is not possible for other variable types not containing that information. Also, the application can validate only datasets containing information about the UK.

A sample biodiversity research project that shows the value of combining different types of error detection techniques in their DQM is the Garden BirdWatch. According to [16], their DQM uses both statistical data, based on observation databases, and ontological a-priori knowledge about the application domain, which in their case, is birds and their characteristics, places, and times. It also uses historical data of species observation to error-check new observations. However, their DQM is restricted to a specific type of dataset with a schema pre-defined by the project.

4   Biodiversity Exploratories Information System (BExIS)

One of the repositories from which the requirements towards DQM are derived and on which the prototype DQM is being implemented is called BExIS (Biodiversity Exploratories Information System). It is the data repository of the Biodiversity Exploratories project [17] - a long-term, interdisciplinary research platform. The Biodiversity Exploratories' goal is to further the understanding of the relationship between biodiversity, land use and management, and ecosystem processes. In this respect, different types of data are collected from various biodiversity related disciplines. Every researcher can define their own schema for their data. Up to now, only the data schema is checked at data upload time. Every other form of validation is done manually, hence, the motivation to include a semi-automatic DQM.

5   Data Quality Management Overview

As indicated, the motivations for this DQM proposal are the need for
- flexible, configurable DQM tools for handling the large variety of biodiversity data. This include data from subjects like phenology, morphology, traits, environment, ecological functions and processes, land use, food webs, chemical diversity, forestry, biodiversity interactions etc.
- easy-to-use, semi-automatic DQM tools for researchers who are typically non-experts in DQM, to replace manual DQM performed by experts.

Therefore, we propose a workflow (Fig. 1) that combines existing procedures, methods, and algorithms for providing an ideal and practical DQM system. We believe that this will encourage and/or enforce good DQM practices by the DQM stakeholders.

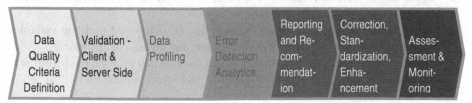

Fig. 1. Proposed Workflow for DQM in Biodiversity Repository

The *data quality criteria definition component* allows the data owner to specify criteria for validating and detecting errors in the data. Based on the DQM criteria specified, a user would be able to download Microsoft Excel templates with macros for performing a guided data entry and validation before dataset upload. At upload time, the dataset will be *validated* against some of the user-specified DQM criteria. Afterwards, *data profiling* which generates a description of the components of the dataset using various statistical metrics will be carried out. Following this will be the *error detection analytics*. A *report* of data profiling and the possible errors based on the data analytics will then be sent to the data owner. The *correction and enrichment component* which will be based on the report comes thereafter. Finally, the data quality will be continuously *monitored* in the light of newer data and models. We provide below the details of what some of these components should be capable of doing.

5.1   Data Quality Criteria Definition

In BExIS, whose conceptual model is presented in [18], the data structure (schema) for a dataset must be created in the system before data upload. During the data structure creation, a set of criteria including the system data type and data unit is specified for each variable in the dataset. For DQM, the data structure is extended with the following DQM criteria which must be specified at data structure creation.

Deterministic Test Specifications: These are the integrity constraints specifications and we broadly classify them into two based on their complexity.

Simple Integrity Constraint: This comprises constraints on the data type, data length/size, primary key, null property, uniqueness, regex pattern, series definition function, and domain value ranges. The series definition specified through a simple function will be used to detect missing values and determine the completeness of the dataset. Similarly, the domain value range types to be supported by the system include simple numeric range, simple function definition, simple flat list, hierarchical list (e.g. SKOS[20]-based list). These lists can be defined in the metadata, another dataset, or externally in some standard list e.g. biodiversity-related thesauri, taxonomies, controlled vocabularies, etc. Examples of external standard lists are provided in [19].
Business rules constraints: This is the second component of the deterministic specifications. The supported rules are broadly classified based on their complexity below:

- Simple single-variable rules where the rule is composed of one variable, a scalar value and one comparison operator.
- Simple multi-variable rule where the rule can be composed multiple variables and scalars and only one comparison operator, and no logical operator.
- Conditional variable dependencies in which the rule can be composed from several variables, scalars, comparison operators and logical operators.

---

[20] SKOS - Simple Knowledge Organization System.

With these rule sets, users, especially DQM experts, will be able to define re-usable rules templates that can be applied by data creators to their datasets.

Probabilistic Tests' Indicators Specifications: Besides the deterministic rules, indicators and information that can be used in deriving outliers, incomplete records and dataset, and duplicated records will also be specified. These include:

- Variables in other quality assured datasets which are similar to a variable in the dataset being uploaded. The variable in the quality assured datasets can thus act as the baseline to which the new variable is compared while looking for outliers.
- Dependent variables either within a dataset or across several datasets. This will assist in determining multi-variate outliers.
- Related datasets, which will guide the data mining process in searching for relationships between variables which will later be the used for outlier detection.
- Conditional weighted matching rules as proposed in [20], which can be used to compute the degree of matching of the records. For instance, in trying to determine whether two trees records in the datasets are the same, the species name, height, distance from each other, etc. can be given as weights and then used in the computing how closely the objects match.
- Thresholds for fuzzy matching of values and records in duplicate detection.
- Variables indicating completeness. We define dataset completeness as even distribution of records of the dataset along the domain range of one or more specified variable. Thus, any un-evenness along the variable(s) range, e.g. missing time period in a time series, can be caught and reported.

Variable Annotation: The variables in a dataset will also be mapped to corresponding elements of a data standard or to some concept in an ontology supported by the repository. For the supported standards, the repository managers will define DQM checklists. Using the mappings to the standards, a set of deterministic and probabilistic data quality criteria can be generated for variables based on the predefined checklist. For instance, if a species name variable in the dataset is be mapped to the species name variable in the Darwin Core Standard, then, a set of deterministic specifications will be generated based on a checklist which predefined for species name element in Darwin Core Standard. Similarly, semantic annotation can be used to validate the data; however, this is momentarily beyond the scope of our planned implementation.

5.2   Error Detection Analysis

The validation procedure during upload will only detect errors based on the deterministic specifications. Thus, using the probabilistic tests' indicator specifications and the results of data profiling (which is carried out after validation), the data is analyzed to detect errors not caught during validation. This analysis is divided into the following.

Probabilistic Analysis: This consists primarily of

Outlier detection analysis: Several generic subject-agnostic models which can potentially be used to detect outliers have been specified; some as presented by [11] include extreme value analysis, probabilistic and statistical models, linear models, proximity-based models, information theoretic models, high-dimensional detection models etc. According to [12], the model to use depends on the properties of the data, and this can be obtained during data profiling or by data mining procedures. Similarly, there are subject-specific outlier detection algorithms. For instance, [3] provided a list of the commonly used outlier detection algorithms in species occurrence data in geographic and environmental space. These include the use of climate models, clustering techniques based on Euclidean distance, principal components analysis of climate layers, Climatic envelope method etc. The inputs for these subject-specific outlier detection algorithms would be mapped to some set of predefined standard elements in the repository, and an algorithm would be used if the variables of a dataset can be mapped to the all predefined standard elements upon which the input to the algorithm is based.

Duplicate detection analysis: The basis for this analysis is that duplicate exists because of different representation of a term e.g. misspellings and synonyms. Thus, the analysis here would use value comparison algorithms to find terms that are likely referring to the same object. Various value comparison algorithms such as exact, standardized exact, soundex, abbreviation, partial name, jaro-wrinkler, levenshtein, etc [20] will be used in detecting multiple representations of a value. Also, conditional weighted matching rules [20] will be applied, and if the result of comparison of two objects is above a specified threshold, then, they can be return as likely duplicates.

Missing values: For the detection of missing records, the variables indicating completeness would be analyzed for evenness during this phase, and un-evenness will be considered as data gap. An obvious challenge is the quantification of evenness for continuous data as opposed to categorical data. Hence, we consider only a considerable deviation from the even distribution of the data as indication of missing records.

Data Mining: The aim of data mining in this analysis is to

- Detect rules or constraints which have not been specified by the owners by analyzing the patterns in the data and finding deviations to these detected rules and constraints, i.e., likely errors. For example, a data type, or data series definition, or standard used can be detected and assumed for a variable if most of the values in the variable conform to it. The deviations to the detected rules and constraints are therefore reported as likely anomalies.
- Detect related and similar datasets and variables and use the detected relationships and similarities to detect outliers in the data. The related datasets can be obtained by analyzing the primary data and / or metadata.

Other Analysis: The other analysis consists of the following

Lexical Errors / Cryptic terms: This will depend very greatly on the language used and the vocabularies in a research field. Nevertheless, terms used in the dataset must have been defined earlier, either in a dictionary, standard, controlled vocabularies or in the metadata. Analysis here will detect terms not in the terms previously defined, and terms in the pre-defined terms that closely matches the undefined terms.

Non-atomic variable detection: This will involve analysis of the values in a variable vis-à-vis their usage in other datasets, standards, dictionary, thesauri, and concatenation symbols. There is a chance that this can assist in determining if a variable is atomic or it can be split.

6   Implementation and Evaluation

The implementation of the DQM module of our data repository management application (BExIS) is ongoing with the various components of the workflow at various stages of development. Some of these, e.g., dataset validation (based on deterministic specifications) and profiling, have already been integrated into our production system. On a non-technical level (for the implemented components), the user feedback has been positive as many of the errors not handled by typical spreadsheet programs are easily discovered within our DQM framework.

A thorough evaluation of the DQM system and its components is planned once it is fully operational. Aspects that will be included are the error detection accuracy, performance, and usability. Since BExIS – and thus its DQM module – is not just a research prototype, but a system that is productively being used by a significant number of researchers, we will be able to do not only a lab-based evaluation but a real-life, comprehensive user study, which will then be used as input for further improvements of the module. The evaluation will be performed in the BExIS instance run for the Exploratories. Results can be compared to data quality management in instances of BExIS used by other research consortia that do not yet contain the DQM module.

7   Conclusion

Many of the repositories which curate structured tabular data with arbitrary user-defined schema do not typically have an automatic way of quality assuring the data, and many scientists lack good data quality management skills. On the one hand, biodiversity data repositories and integration centers with pre-defined data schema have automatic ways of checking for errors. And on the other hand, there are well established workflows for managing quality of data with arbitrary schema in ETL procedure in data warehousing. Therefore, we propose a semi-automatic DQM workflow that combines existing procedure, methods, and algorithm in discipline-agnostic and biodiversity-related data quality management research. While the components of this workflow (as well as the workflow) are not new, we customize their usage for the DQM requirements of a research data repository. At the same time, we semi-automate the process such the data creator will only have to interact with the DQM system at data structure design time and at data correction time.

Overall, the workflow uses a combination of hard and soft rules and constraints, statistical analysis, data mining, data standards, and biodiversity models to semi-automatically detect and correct current and potential anomalies in data. We believe that this will encourage good DQM practices by the data creators and repositories.

Acknowledgments. We would like to thank the members of the Biodiversity Exploratories for making their data available via our data repository, BExIS.

Further, we thank Christiane Fischer giving support through the central office, the Local Management Team, and Markus Fischer, Eduard Linsenmair, Dominik Hessenmöller, Jens Nieschulze, Daniel Prati, Ingo Schöning, François Buscot, Ernst-Detlef Schulze, Wolfgang W. Weisser and the late Elisabeth Kalko for their role in setting up the Biodiversity Exploratories project. Among these, special thanks are due to Jens Nieschulze and Ernst-Detlef Schulze for initiating and developing BExIS for the first years of the Exploratories. The work has been (partly) funded by the DFG Priority Program 1374 "Infrastructure-Biodiversity-Exploratories" (BR 2315/7-2).

References

1. Chrisman, N.R.: The Error Component in Spatial Data. In: Maguire, D.J., Goodchild, M.F., Rhind, D.W. (eds.) Geographical Information Systems, vol. 1, pp. 165–174. Longman Scientific and Technical, Principals (1991)
2. Redman, T.C.: Data Quality for the Information Age. Artech House, Inc., Boston (1996)
3. Chapman, A.D.: Principles of Data Quality, version 1.0. Report for the Global Biodiversity Information Facility, Copenhagen, pp. 1–58 (2005)
4. Costello, M., Michener, W., Gahegan, M., Zhang, Z., Bourne, P.: Biodiversity data should be published, cited, and peer reviewed. Trends in Ecology & Evolution 28(8), 454–461 (2013), doi:10.1016/j.tree.2013.05.002
5. Swan, A., Sheridan, B.: To Share or Not to Share: Publication and Quality Assurance of Research Data Outputs. A report for the Research Information Network. School of Electronics & Computer Science, University of Southampton (2008), http://www.rin.ac.uk/system/files/attachments/To-share-data-outputs-report.pdf (Online: Accessed February 2014)
6. Sadiq, S.: Handbook of Data Quality. Springer (2013)
7. English, L.P.: Improving Data Warehouse and Business Information Quality: Methods for Reducing Costs and Increasing Profits. John Wiley & Sons, Inc., New York (1999)
8. Chisholm, M.: Data Quality is Not Fitness for Use, http://www.information-management.com/news/data-quality-is-not-fitness-for-use-10023022-1.html (Online: Accessed February 2014)
9. Batini, C., Cappiello, C., Francalanci, C., Maurino, A.: Methodologies for data quality assessment and improvement. ACM Comput. Surv. 41(3), 1–52 (2009)
10. Barateiro, J., Galhardas, H.: A Survey of Data Quality Tools. Datenbank-Spektrum 14, 15–21 (2005)
11. Aggarwal, C.C.: Outlier Analysis. Springer Publishing Company, Incorporated (2013)

12. Seo, S.: A review and comparison of methods for detecting outlier in univariate data sets. PhD thesis. University of Pittsburgh, Department of Biostatistics (2006)
13. Fürber, C., Hepp, M.: Ontology-Based Data Quality Management - Methodology, Cost, and Benefits. In: 6th Annual European Semantic Web Conference (ESWC 2009), Heraklion, Greece, May 31-June 4 (2009)
14. Malik, W.A., Unwin, A., Gribov, A.: An Interactive Graphical System for Visualizing Data Quality - Tableplot Graphics. In: Loracek-Junge, H., Weihs, C. (eds.) Proceedings of the 11th IFCS Conference Classification as a Tool for Research, pp. 331–339. Springer, Berlin
15. Ball, S., French, G.: NBN Record Cleaner user guide, V.1.0.8.3, https://data.nbn.org.uk/recordcleaner/documentation/NBNRecordCleanerUserguide.pdf (Online: Accessed February 2014)
16. Hyvönen, E., Alonen, M., Koho, M., Tuominen, J.: BirdWatch—supporting citizen scientists for better linked data quality for biodiversity management. In: Workshop on Semantics for Biodiversity (S4BIODIV), ESWC, Montpellier, France. CEUR Workshop Proceedings (2013)
17. Lotz, T., Nieschulze, J., Bendix, J., Dobbermann, M., König-Ries, B.: Diverse or uniform? - Intercomparison of two major German project databases for interdisciplinary collaborative functional biodiversity research. Ecological Informatics 8, 10–19 (2012)
18. Chamanara, J., König-Ries, B.: A conceptual model for data management in the field of ecology. Ecological Informatics (2013), http://dx.doi.org/10.1016/j.ecoinf.2013.12.003
19. Marine Metadata Interoperability Project: Ontologies and Thesauri References. 3, https://marinemetadata.org/conventions/ontologies-thesauri (Online: Accessed February 2014)
20. Oracle Warehouse Builder User's Guide, 11g Release 1 (11.1) (2009), http://docs.oracle.com/cd/B28359_01/owb.111/b31278.pdf (Online: Accessed February 2014)

Applying a Data Quality Model to Experiments in Software Engineering

María Carolina Valverde[1], Diego Vallespir[1], Adriana Marotta[1],
and Jose Ignacio Panach[2]

[1] Universidad de la República, Montevideo, Uruguay
{mvalverde,dvallesp,amarotta}@fing.edu.uy
[2] Departament d'Informàtica, Universitat de València,Valencia, España
joigpana@uv.es

Abstract. Data collection and analysis are key artifacts in any software engineering experiment. However, these data might contain errors. We propose a Data Quality model specific to data obtained from software engineering experiments, which provides a framework for analyzing and improving these data. We apply the model to two controlled experiments, which results in the discovery of data quality problems that need to be addressed. We conclude that data quality issues have to be considered before obtaining the experimental results.

Keywords: data quality, software engineering, controlled experiments.

1 Introduction

Empirical Software Engineering collects data for predictions, discoveries, or to determine the effectiveness and impact of use in new techniques and strategies [14]. Data collected during the experimental activities becomes the primary source to obtain the experimental results. These results are assumed to be trusted, and the research community as well as the professionals use them to make decisions. However, the quality of the data used in the software engineering experiments is seldom questioned or analyzed, as Data Quality (DQ) issues have not received the attention it deserves in this area [16]. Thus, the quality of the experimental results could be unknown [13,14].

DQ research area has focused basically on defining different DQ aspects, as well as on proposing techniques, methods and methodologies for measuring and dealing with DQ problems [3,4], [7]. In many research areas, data producers and consumers have recognized DQ issues as an important matter that needs to be considered and attended [5], [8].

The importance of the DQ used by empirical studies has been recognized and studied in the last few years [13,14,15,16,17,18], [30,31]. According to Liebchen, there seems to be an increase over time in the amount of works that consider DQ issues, suggesting that the community is giving more attention to DQ [14]. In the few cases that DQ is considered, the analysis of the quality of the data is normally ad-hoc; i.e. nor a systematic neither a repeatable method is used. In order to change this situation, we propose a framework adapted specifically to this field of study: Experiments in

M. Indulska and S. Purao (Eds.): ER Workshops 2014, LNCS 8823, pp. 168–177, 2014.
© Springer International Publishing Switzerland 2014

Software Engineering (ESE). To achieve this, we develop a DQ model and a systematic, disciplined and structured approach (that uses this model) in order to analyze and improve DQ in ESE that involves humans as subjects. Our DQ model defines DQ metrics that are based on techniques proposed in the DQ area [3,4,5,6,7].

In this work, we apply our DQ model to the data of two controlled experiments. We present the application of the model as well as the results obtained by applying the proposed DQ metrics. We found that data used by ESE present DQ problems that need to be addressed before obtaining the experimental results.

The paper is structured as follows. Section 2 presents a DQ meta-model as the conceptual base for our model. Section 3 describes the experiments we used to evaluate our model. Section 4 presents the DQ model and metrics. Section 5 shows the application of a DQ metric. Section 6 presents the results obtained by applying the defined DQ metrics to the experiments presented. Finally, section 7 compares related work, and section 8 presents the conclusions.

2   Background: Data Quality Meta-model

DQ is generally defined as "fitness for use" [9], [14,15], if data is suitable for its use or purpose. As the use of the data depends on every context, its quality will be evaluated in function of its specific purpose [4]. DQ is a multifaceted concept, as it is defined as a function of the dimensions it describes. Each dimension represents a different aspect (or facet) of DQ [3,4,5,6,7].

Our approach is based on a DQ meta-model [32] that includes the following concepts: a *quality dimension* is a concept that captures one facet of DQ, a *quality factor* represents a particular aspect of a DQ dimension. A dimension is seen as the join of factors having the same aim. A *quality metric* is a quantifiable instrument that defines the way a quality factor is measured, and will indicate the presence of a DQ problem. Finally, a *measurement method* is a process that implements a metric. As the same factor can be measured with different metrics, the same metric can be implemented with different methods. DQ measurement can be done at different levels of granularity: cell (attribute value for a given tuple), tuple, column, table or even database.

We have chosen the most widely referenced DQ dimensions and their definitions according to [3,4,5,6,7]:

- *Accuracy*. Specifies how accurate and valid the data is. It indicates if a correct association between the Information System (IS) states and the real world objects exist. Three quality factors are proposed. **Semantic accuracy** refers to how close is a real world value to its representation in the IS. **Syntactic accuracy** indicates if a value belongs to a valid domain. **Precision** refers to the detail level of the data.
- *Completeness*. Specifies if the IS contains all the important data, with the required scope and depth. It indicates the IS capacity to represent all the significant states of the reality through two factors. **Coverage** refers to the portion of real world objects that are represented in the IS, while **density** refers to the amount of missing data.
- *Consistency*. Specifies if the semantic rules are satisfied in the IS. An inconsistency exists when more than one state in the IS is associated with the same object in

the real world. There are different kinds of integrity restrictions. **Domain restrictions** refer to rules about the attributes values. **Intra-relation restrictions** refer to rules that must be satisfied by one or more attributes in the same relation, while in the **inter-relation rules** the attributes entailed are from different relations.

- *Uniqueness*. Specifies the duplication level of the data through two factors. **Duplication** occurs when the same entity is duplicated exactly, while **contradiction** occurs when the entity is duplicated with contradictions.
- *Representation*. Considers the consistent and concise representation of the data in the IS, and the extent in which data is always represented in the same format and structure. We consider the factors *data format* and *data structure*.
- *Interpretability*. Refers to the documentation and metadata available in order to correctly interpret the meaning and properties of the IS. We consider two factors, *ease of understanding* and *metadata*.

3   Experiments Description

In order to validate the DQ model defined in this work through a proof of concept, we have applied the DQ model to data collected from two executed experiments in Software Engineering. These experiments are briefly presented in this section.

The experiments aim to compare the Model-Driven Development (MDD) paradigm [12] versus a traditional software development method. MDD proposes focusing all analysts' effort on building a conceptual model that abstractly represents the system. The code is automatically generated through transformation rules. In a traditional development method, the code is manually implemented. The following variables are defined: *Software Quality:* degree of success after applying test cases; *Effort:* time spent to develop the system; *Productivity:* quality-effort ratio; *Satisfaction*: range of values from 1 to 5 (1: totally unsatisfied, 5:totally satisfied).

Subjects of the experiment are master students from the Technical University of Valencia. We have 2 sessions of 2 hours per development method (MDD and traditional) and 2 problems (P1 and P2) to develop a Web application from scratch.

The experiment starts with a demographic questionnaire that subjects have to fill in on paper to identify their background. Next, we apply the traditional development treatment to all the subjects. The experimenter records the start and end session times, and then calculates how much time each subject spent to develop the system (per session and total). Once the session has finished, each subject must fill in a satisfaction questionnaire. Finally, experimenters check the quality of the systems developed through test cases and write down the results. Each test case is defined as a sequence of items. We consider that a test case is fulfilled when every item is passed. The test cases as well as the items result have two possible values: success (1) or failure (0). All the data collected during the experiment is recorded in spread sheets. Finally, the process is repeated to apply the MDD treatment.

The experiment was carried out twice with the same design. The base experiment was executed in 2012 with 26 subjects, while the replication in 2013 had 20 subjects. In the replication, we extend the problems to increase the difficulty. This new version of the problems is divided into 3 exercises (parts) such a way the first exercise is the same problem used in the base experiment and exercise 2 and 3 are extensions. At the end of each exercise, subjects have to write down on a paper the time spent to finish it. The experimenter then copies these data in the spread sheets.

4   Data Quality Model for Software Engineering Experiments

A DQ model represents DQ concepts (such us dimensions, factors and metrics) and the relation between them, which are defined for a specific domain. We define a DQ model for the ESE domain, you can find DQ models for other domains in [10,11]. This model provides a framework for the analysis and assessment of DQ. Fig. 1 shows how our DQ model is defined from the DQ meta-model presented in Section 2.

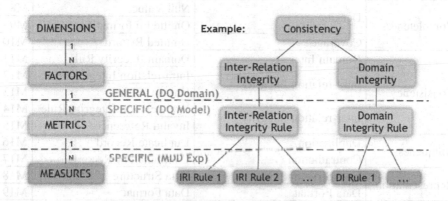

Fig. 1. DQ model defined and its application

Our model defines a set of DQ metrics that can be applied to ESE data, and are based on the DQ concepts presented in Section 2. They are shown in Table 1. We define the metrics by induction, as they are applied to specific experiments (from the particular) and adjusted such a way they could be applied to any ESE data collection (to the general). This model is the result of successive refinements to previous developed models [1,2]. DQ problems are classified as follows.

- *Data Errors (DE)*: correspond to errors in the data that (whenever possible) need correction.
- *Questionable Value (QV)*: in this case it is not possible to assure if the DQ problem corresponds to a real data error (examples of these are *outliers*). It is necessary to compare data and reality in order to know if a data error exists.
- *Improvement Opportunities (IO)*: correspond to suggestions of aspects that could be improved in order to prevent the occurrence of a DQ problem in the future.

Due to space restrictions, it is not possible to present every metric. In the next section, we show the definition and results of a particular DQ metric of our model.

We choose the metric "Inter-relation Integrity rules" (M14), as it corresponds to a DQ aspect that is not generally addressed in ESE data. In Section 6 we present the results of the application of the whole DQ model to the experiments.

Table 1. DQ Metrics

DQ Dimension	DQ Factor	DQ Metric	Id
Accuracy	Syntactic Accuracy	Out of Range Value	M1
		Lack of Standardization	M2
		Embedded Value	M3
	Semantic Accuracy	Inexistent Record	M4
		Incorrect Record	M5
		Out of Referential Value	M6
	Precision	Lack of Precision	M7
Completeness	Density	Null Value	M8
		Omitted Information	M9
	Coverage	Omitted Record	M10
Consistency	Domain Integrity	Domain Integrity Rule	M11
	Intra-relation Integrity	Intra-relation Integrity Rule	M12
		Unique Value	M13
	Inter-relation Integrity	Inter-relation Integrity Rule	M14
		Invalid Reference	M15
Uniqueness	Duplication	Duplicate Record	M16
	Contradiction	Contradictory Record	M17
Representation	Data Structure	Data Structure	M18
	Data Format	Data Format	M19
Interpretability	Ease of understanding	Ease of understanding	M20
	Metadata	Metadata	M21

5   Data Quality Metric Example: Inter-relation Integrity Rule

This metric is implemented through integrity rules involving attributes that belong to different relations, and that must be satisfied in the database. Its measurement is defined as the verification of rules satisfaction in the data. The result unit is a Boolean value, indicating if the object measured presents a DQ problem (0) or not (1). Its granularity is at cell level.

In order to apply this metric to the experiments, rules are defined with the experiment responsible. We define 6 rules for the base experiment and 9 for the replication, but only 3 are presented here.

1. *Test case result will be 1 (success) if and only if each of its items result is 1. Otherwise, the test case result will be 0.*
2. *Total execution time is the sum of the time spent in the two working sessions.*
3. *Time spent in making the first exercise has to be less or equal than the total execution time (only for the replication).*

We measure the three cases presented through formulas implemented in a spreadsheet that verifies rules satisfaction. "Rule 1" was not satisfied in any of the experiments. In the base experiment, we found 2 test case records where one of its items result was 0 but the test case result was 1. We discovered that the item involved was not considered to calculate the final result, so it was not necessary to take corrective actions.

In the replication experiment, we found 2 test case records whose items results did not exist, but the test case result had a value (1 or 0). Both cases correspond to data errors. The subjects had not implemented the functionality being tested, so the test case result should have been a null value. This DQ problem impacts on the experimental results obtained (regarding the variable *software quality*).

"Rule 2" was satisfied in both experiments. "Rule 3" was only applied to the replication experimental data, where it was not satisfied. We found 6 records where the time spent in making the first exercise was longer than the total execution time. In 4 cases, it did not exist one of the session time values. Note that these cases were also found by the metric "Omitted Information". Thus, the total execution time only considered the time of one session, making the exercise time longer. This data error has to be corrected because it impacts on the results obtained (regarding the variable *effort*). In the remaining cases, the difference was by less than 3 minutes.

6   Results

Table 2 shows the DQ value obtained for each metric applied. It is calculated as the aggregation of the DQ values obtained by applying the metric to the corresponding data. We applied 16 out of the 21 DQ metrics that are defined in the model (Table 1). We validated with the experiment responsible that the application of the remaining 5 metrics was not necessary for these experiments. Whereas in the base experiment the metrics were applied on 47 different domain objects, in the replication they were applied on 59. The amount of measurements is higher in the second case because more data are collected. As a result of applying our model, we found that in the base experiment 9 of the metrics showed the presence of a DQ problem that needs attention. These DQ problems correspond to 13 different objects. In the replication 10 metrics showed the presence of DQ problems, corresponding to 17 objects. Only 7 of the DQ problems found are common to both cases.

When possible, an automatic measurement method is applied (68% in the base experiment and 75% in the replication), through the implementation of formulas in a spreadsheet. When the measurement is subjective or it involves the comparison with data extracted from the real world, a manual method is used (26% in the base experiment and 22% in the replication). Remaining metrics 6% and 3% respectively, were not implemented since they require a great amount of time from the experimenters.

We propose preventive actions for every case in which a DQ problem was found in order to prevent its occurrence in future experiences. We then classified the DQ problems found. Table 2 shows which metrics correspond to each classification.

- *Data Errors (DE)*. In the base experiment, we found data errors for 4 of the 9 metrics. However, no corrective actions were taken. This is because the data affected by the quality problems were not used as a base to obtain the experimental results.
  In the replication, we found 4 data errors. For 2 of them corrective actions were taken (1 described in the previous section). In the remaining cases it was not possible to apply corrections because real data was omitted and could not be known.
- *Questionable Value (QV)*. We found questionable values for 2 of the metrics in the base experiment and 2 in the replication. These cases correspond to unusual values. We did not identify any possible corrective actions after validation with the experiment responsible.
- *Improvement Opportunities (IO)*. We propose specific improvement opportunities for 3 subjective metrics in the base experiment and for 4 subjective metrics in the replication, all referred to the data structure, format and storage.

Table 2. Results of applying the DQ Metrics to the experiments

DQ Metric Id	DQ Value - Base	DQ Problem	# Data - Base	DQ Value - Repl.	DQ Problem	# Data - Repl.
M1	0.968	QV	7	0.988	QV	5
M2	0.941	DE	8	1.000		
M3	0.692	DE	16	1.000		
M5	1.000			1.000		
M7	1.000			1.000		
M8	1.000			0.959	DE	9
M9	1.000			0.800	DE	9
M10	0.996	DE	1	0.933	DE	4
M11	1.000			1.000		
M12	0.971	QV	3	0.963	QV	3
M14	0.857	DE	20	0.926	DE	13
M16	1.000			1.000		
M18	Regular	IO		Regular	IO	
M19	Acceptable			Regular	IO	
M20	Regular	IO		Regular	IO	
M21	Regular	IO		Regular	IO	

As Table 2 shows, the quantity of data with a DQ problem is low. This might be mainly because of the low amount of data collected during the experiment. However, the experimental results could anyway be affected due to the DQ problems found, regardless of the amount of data.

We can see some differences between the results obtained in each case, even though collected data are almost the same. While in the base case no corrective actions were taken, in the replication we found errors in data used to obtain the experimental results that needed correction. Contrary to the replication, in the base case the DQ analysis was carried out after the experimental statistical analysis. Thus, as the amount of data is low, the experimenters could have applied some manual corrections during the analysis. However, this "ad-hoc" method cannot assure that the DQ problems will be found, as it depends on the person who is making the analysis (his knowledge and abilities), as well as on the complexity and amount of data. Neither has been established a systemic way to perform the DQ analysis, so it cannot be repeated in future experiences.

Another difference is in the metric with the lowest DQ value. While the first case corresponds to data entered by the subjects (M3), the second one is an omission in a calculation that made the experimenter. Moreover, the improvement in the metrics M2 and M3 is because preventive actions were taken during the replication.

The results obtained show that the application of the DQ model proposed to the experimental data allows the identification of DQ problems that could otherwise be ignored. Even though the data analyzed is of low complexity, the application of the DQ metrics uncovers the existence of bad quality data, as showed in the example presented. It is important to analyze and improve the quality of the data used, so that the experimental results can be trusted.

7   Related Work

The importance of the quality of data used by empirical studies has been acknowledged and assessed in the last years [13,14,15,16,17,18], [30,31], mostly due to the impact that it may have on the decisions taken. Some papers explicitly emphasize the importance of DQ in empirical software engineering datasets, as data imperfections can have unwanted impact on the data analysis and might lead to false conclusions [14], [16], [25]. However, we did not find in the literature any study that specifically analyses the quality of the data which source is a controlled experiment in Software Engineering, as we present in this work.

On the other hand, the results of a systematic literature review carried out by Liebchen and Shepperd [14,15] show that only 1% of analyzed papers explicitly consider noise or DQ as an issue, not necessarily proposing solutions. Even though the majority of the publications in the review recognize its importance (138 out of 161), little work has been done to deal with DQ problems. Liebchen also suggests the development of unified DQ protocols for the empirical software engineering community, since none of the works found proposes or applies one. Our DQ model aims to address this absence, by proposing a DQ framework including the definition of DQ metrics that could be applied to ESE, in order to assess and improve its quality.

Bachman [13], [17], [28] analyzed DQ characteristics of closed and opened software projects source, finding that all projects contain DQ issues. These issues may have a major impact on empirical software engineering research results. Bachman defines a DQ framework and metrics to evaluate and analyze DQ software projects, but he does not state that it could be applied to experimental data.

Three literature reviews were carried out in this particular topic, showing interest and concern about how researchers are dealing with DQ problems [13,14], [30]. They all conclude that empirical software engineering community should pay more attention to this issue, which has long been neglected according to the results

We also found another set of related works that analyze the quality in software engineering historic datasets [19,20,21,22,23,24], [26,27], [29]. In these works, software project, process and product data are collected, stored, and then used to analyze strategies and methodologies, construct heuristics or prediction models, or apply statistical techniques. The works found also agree on the great significance of assessing the quality of the data used, as they have an impact on the obtained results.

8   Conclusions

We present a DQ model that can be applied to ESE data. This model defines DQ metrics as the instrument to measure the quality of the data and identify DQ problems. We show how to apply the DQ metrics defined in two controlled experiments. We found that experimental data has DQ problems, and that they can impact on the results of the experiment.

Our model allows us to predefine metrics for DQ in ESE, being an important contribution to both DQ and ESE communities. The introduction of a DQ analysis previous to the experimental statistical analysis motivates the consideration of DQ aspects that are not normally addressed by ESE researchers and could otherwise be neglected.

Our ultimate goal is to define a DQ model such that it can be useful for any ESE. As future work we will apply our approach to other experiments with a higher number of subjects and data. This way, our systematic approach will probably find a higher amount of DQ problems. As a result of these new applications we aim to adjust (again) our DQ model and achieve its generalization for the ESE domain.

References

1. Valverde, C., Grazioli, F., Vallespir, D.: A study of the quality of data gathered during the use of personal software process. In: Proceedings JIISIC 2012. Lima, Peru (2012)
2. Valverde, C., Vallespir, D., Marotta, A.: Data quality analysis in software engineering experimental data. In: Proceedings CACIC 2012, Argentina, pp. 794-803 (2012)
3. Batini, C., Scannapieco, M.: Data Quality: Concepts, Methodologies and Techniques. Springer, Heidelberg (2006)
4. Strong, D.M., Lee, Y.W., Wang, R.Y.: Data quality in context. Communications of ACM 40, 103–110 (1997)
5. Pipino, L., Lee, Y.W., Wang, R.Y.: Data quality assessment. Communications of ACM 45(4), 211–218 (2002)
6. Wang, R.Y., Strong, D.M.: Beyond Accuracy: What Data Quality Means to Data Consumers. Journal of Management Information Systems 12(4), 5–33 (1996)
7. Scannapieco, M., Catarci, T.: Data quality under a computer science perspective. Archivi & Computer 2, 1–15 (2002)
8. Redman, T.: Data Quality for the Information Age. Artech House (1996)
9. Crosby, P.B.: Quality without tears: The art of hassle free management. McGraw-Hill, New York (1984)
10. Moranga, M.A., Calero, C., Piattini, M.: Comparing different quality models for portals. Online Information Review 30(5), 555–568 (2006)
11. Etcheverry, L., Marotta, A., Ruggia, R.: Data Quality Metrics for Genome Wide Association Studies. In: DEXA Workshops, pp. 105–109 (2010)

12. Embley, D.W., Liddle, S., Pastor, Ó.: Conceptual-Model Programming: A Manifesto. In: Handbook of Conceptual Modeling, pp. 3–16. Springer (2011)
13. Bachmann, A.J.E.: Why Should We Care about Data Quality in Software Engineering? Ph.D. thesis, University of Zurich (2010)
14. Liebchen, G.A.: Data Cleaning Techniques for Software Engineering Data Sets. Ph.D. thesis, Brunel University (2010)
15. Liebchen, G.A., Shepperd, M.: Data sets and data quality in software engineering. In: Proceedings PROMISE 2008, pp. 39–44. ACM, New York (2008)
16. Liebchen, G.A., Twala, B., Shepperd, M., Cartwright, M., Stephens, M.: Filtering, robust, filtering, polishing: Techniques for addressing quality in software data. In: ESEM 2007, Madrid, Spain, pp. 99–106 (2007)
17. Bachmann, A., Bernstein, A.: When Process Data Quality Affects the Number of Bugs: Correlations in Software Engineering Datasets. In: MSR 2010, pp. 62–71. IEEE Computer Society, Cape Town (2010)
18. Chen, K., Schach, S.R., Yu, L., Offutt, J., Heller, G.Z.: Open-source change logs. Emp. Softw. Eng. 9(3), 197–210 (2004)
19. Liebchen, G.A., Shepperd, M.: Software productivity analysis of a large data set and issues of confidentiality and data quality. In: Proceedings of METRICS 2005 (2005)
20. Bachmann, A., Bernstein, A.: Software process data quality and characteristics - a historical view on open and closed source projects. In: IWPSE-Evol 2009, Amsterdam, The Netherlands, pp. 119–128 (2009)
21. Basili, V., Weiss, D.: A methodology for collecting valid software engineering data. IEEE Transactions on Software Engineering 10(6), 728–738 (1984)
22. Kim, S., Zhang, H., Wu, R., Gong, L.: Dealing with Noise in Defect Prediction. In: Proc. of ICSE 2011, Honolulu, Hawaii, pp. 481–490 (2011)
23. Strike, K., Emam, K.E., Madhavji, N.: Software Cost Estimation with Incomplete Data. IEEE Trans. on Software Engineering 27(10), 890–908 (2001)
24. Aranda, J., Venolia, G.: The secret life of bugs: Going past the errors and omissions in software repositories. In: ICSE 2009, pp. 298–308 (2009)
25. Liebchen, G.A., Twala, B., Shepperd, M., Cartwright, M.: Assessing the quality and cleaning of a software project data set: An experience report. In: Proceedings of EASE 2006. British Computer Society (2006)
26. Cartwright, M.H., Shepperd, M.J., Song, Q.: Dealing with Missing Software Project Data. In: Proceedings of METRICS 2003, p. 154. IEEE Computer Society, Australia (2003)
27. Rodriguez, D., Herraiz, I., Harrison, R.: On software engineering repositories and their open problems. In: RAISE (2012)
28. Bachmann, A., Bird, C., Rahman, F., Devanbu, P., Bernstein, A.: The Missing Links: Bugs and Bug-Fix Commits. In: ACM SIGSOFT / FSE 2010. ACM, USA (2010)
29. Wu, R., Zhang, H., Kim, S., Cheung, S.: ReLink: recovering links between bugs and changes. In: Proceedings of the 19th ACM SIGSOFT, Szeged, Hungary (2011)
30. Bosu, M.F., MacDonell, S.G.: Data quality in empirical software engineering: A targeted review. In: Proceedings of EASE 2013, pp. TBC. ACM Press, Brazil (2013)
31. Bosu, M.F., MacDonell, S.G.: A Taxonomy of Data Quality Challenges in Empirical Software Engineering. In: Australian Software Engineering Conference, pp. 97–106 (2013)
32. Etcheverry, L., Peralta, V., Bouzeghoub, M.: Qbox-Foundation: A Metadata Platform for Quality Measurement. In: DKQ 2008 in EGC 2008, Sophia-Antipolis, France (January 2008)

Towards Indicators for HCI Quality Evaluation Support

Ahlem Assila[1,2], Káthia Marçal de Oliveira[1], and Houcine Ezzedine[1]

[1] L.A.M.I.H. – UMR CNRS 8201
UVHC, Le Mont Houy, 59313 Valenciennes Cedex 9, France
assila.ahlem@gmail.com,
{Kathia.Oliveira,Houcine.Ezzedine}@univ-valenciennes.fr
[2] S.E.T.I.T. – Université de Sfax, Tunisie

Abstract. The current variety of existing approaches for HCI quality evaluation is marked by a lack of the integration of subjective methods (such as the questionnaire method) and objective methods (such as the electronic informer method) for supporting in making an evaluation final decision. Over the past decades, different researches have been interested to define various quality criteria with their measures. However, the lack in determining how to integrate qualitative with quantitative data leads us to specify new indicators for HCI quality evaluation. This paper aims at defining and constructing quality indicators with their measures related relatively to existing quality criteria based on ISO/IEC 15939 standard. These indicators allow the integration of qualitative and quantitative data and provide a basis for decision making about the quality of the HCI relatively to the evaluation quality criteria. This paper presents a proposal for defining and constructing quality indicators and it highlights a proposed example. A feasibility study of using a quality indicator is presented by the evaluation of traffic supervision system in Valenciennes (France) as a part of CISIT-ISART project.

Keywords: Human-Computer Interface (HCI), HCI evaluation, integration, measures, indicator, qualitative, quantitative, criteria.

1   Introduction and Background

The evaluation of interactive system interfaces consists in ensuring that the users are able to carry out their tasks effectively with responding to their requirements and needs [14]. Several HCI (Human-Computer Interface) quality evaluation methods and tools have been proposed. Some of them are based on subjective methods to extract qualitative data such as questionnaire and/or interview methods [17]. Others urge the importance to objective methods to extract analytic and quantitative data such as the electronic informer method [15]. However, all these methods do not perform the same measuring procedures. Many authors have argued for employing various methods so that these methods supplement each other rather than compete [1]. Nevertheless, the variability of these methods (subjective and objective) features and drawbacks poses a challenge to effectively integrate them. This integration is an important issue in order to obtain better coverage of design problems and to support evaluators in decision making during processing the various results.

M. Indulska and S. Purao (Eds.): ER Workshops 2014, LNCS 8823, pp. 178–187, 2014.
© Springer International Publishing Switzerland 2014

Over the past decades, different researches have been interested to define various quality criteria with their measures to support evaluation and they adapted it into existing methods [3][13]. These measures are designed to be operational parameters that can be computed by consistent means that are agreed on and reliably understood [6].

With the aim of supporting the evaluators in making an evaluation final decision based on heterogeneous evaluation results, we present in this paper a proposal of defining and constructing quality indicators based on the ISO/IEC 15939 standard.

The reminder of the paper is organized as follows. Section 2 presents an overview about HCI evaluation. Section 3 explains our proposal of defining quality indicators for HCI quality evaluation based on the ISO/IEC 15939 standard and it highlights a proposed example. Section 4 presents a feasibility study of using a quality indicator. Section 5 draws conclusions and future works.

2   Overview about HCI Evaluation

Several research efforts about HCI quality evaluation have been established. They concern various methods and approaches [15] [4]. These approaches can be categorized into three categories: (1) approaches based on subjective methods. These methods are focused on the capture of the users' attitudes and judgments after a direct interaction between users and the evaluated system (such as the questionnaire method, e.g. CSUQ [11]), (2) approaches based on objective methods which are based on capturing analytic data without direct interaction with users (such as the electronic informer method, e.g. EISEval electronic informer [15]), and (3) approaches that combined both subjective and objective methods. Recent researches have investigated the possibility of employing different methods to improve evaluation results. They have suggested combinations of various evaluation methods for improving evaluation [1] [4] [10]. Indeed, these approaches attempt generally to combine methods in a separate manner. Furthermore, they did not consider the possibility to combine the evaluation data with an integrated and complementary form for supporting evaluators in decision making. There is still a lack to determine how effectively integrate qualitative with quantitative evaluation results extracted from various existing evaluation tools.

A proposal of quality indicators will be presented in the next section.

3   Defining Quality Indicators for HCI Quality Evaluation Based on ISO/IEC 15939 Standard

3.1   Proposed Approach

Motivation.
The use of subjective with objective evaluation methods provides evaluators with various and heterogeneous results which make difficult their processing task. These results include qualitative and quantitative data extracted respectively from highly cited HCI quality questionnaires (e.g. [11]) and from others existing tools (e.g. [15]). In this paper, we focus on the issue of supporting evaluators in decision making about

the quality of HCI based on these heterogeneous evaluation results. We propose an approach for the integration of these data with a complementary manner. Our proposal is based on defining and constructing new indicators with their related measures relatively to existing quality criteria (e.g. ISO 9241-11 criteria [9]) based on ISO/IEC 15939 standard [8]. The proposed indicators aim to integrate qualitative and quantitative evaluation data based on a proposed mapping model used for extracting and defining measures. They aim also to provide a basis for decision making about the quality of the HCI relatively to quality criteria in order to support evaluators in the detection of quality problems, Figure 1.

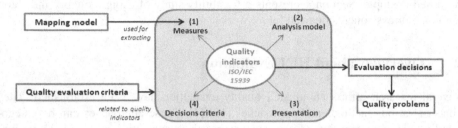

Fig. 1. The proposed approach

As defined by the ISO/IEC 15939 [8] standard, an indicator is a measure providing estimation or evaluation of specified attributes. These attributes are quantified based on the type of measurement method which can be subjective or objective. This measure is characterized by a set of other measures which can be of two types: the base measures and the derived measures [8]. The selection of the used measures that specify the indicator is related to the information needs (the purpose to be achieved using the indicator) and it is realized by specifying an analysis model. In addition, an indicator presents a tool for supporting decision making [8].

The definition and construction of indicators are based on a Measurement Information Model specified by ISO/IEC 15939 standard. It presents a structure linking the needs to the relevant entities to the attributes of concern [8]. This model also describes how the relevant attributes are quantified and converted to indicators that provide a basis for decision making (for more details see [8]).

By adopting the ISO/IEC 15939 standard, we are interested to determine how define quality indicators based on the integration of qualitative with quantitative evaluation data. We propose a quality indicator definition process depicted in the Figure 2.

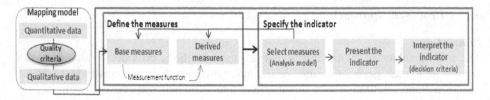

Fig. 2. The proposed process of a quality indicator definition

As illustrated in this figure, there are two steps: (1) the definition of the measures related to the indicator and (2) the specification of the indicator.

The Definition of Measures Related to a Quality Indicator.

The specification of the information need presents the purpose to be achieved using an indicator. The proposed quality indicators aim to make decisions about the quality of the HCI relatively to each quality criteria based on the integration of qualitative with quantitative evaluation data.

Before specifying a quality indicator, we are interested to define their related measures (base and derived measures) by taking into account the defined information need. Based on the ISO/IEC 15939 standard a base measure is a measure defined in terms of an attribute and the method for quantifying it [8]. A derived measure is a measure that is defined as a function of two or more values of base measures [8].

To determine these measures based on our purpose, we are preceded by a deep study for defining a mapping model that combines qualitative with quantitative data based on the evaluated quality criteria. This mapping model allows specifying the required attributes and the base measures used when constructing each indicator. It links each qualitative data with the appropriate quantitative data in a complementary manner. Figure 2 includes briefly an illustration of the proposed mapping model.

As the proposed mapping model integrates and synthesizes the data issued from different evaluation tools, it exploits different tools that have been developed to facilitate and to automate a variety of quality evaluation aspects (e.g. the functional and ergonomic aspects).

The tools related to the qualitative data are the questionnaires for inspecting users' satisfaction degree toward the evaluated interface. Based on a broad literature review, we have selected the CSUQ questionnaire [11] among 23 of the most known and the most validated tools. The choice of CSUQ [11] compared to the others questionnaires is due to various factors (e.g. it is a successful record of practical and academic applications in its original, etc. [2]).

To perform a quantitative evaluation, we chose two tools respectively related to the functional and ergonomic aspects of interactive systems interfaces. The first tool is a generic and configurable electronic informer named EISEval (Environment for Interactive System Evaluation) [15]. It allows capturing and analyzing automatically HCI information and it generates different attributes such as the rate of completion of a task, time of task execution, etc. The second tool is an ergonomic guidelines inspector [9] that aids for ergonomic quality evaluation of interactive systems. It is based on different graphical components attributes such as the writing size, the writing color, the informational density, etc. [4].

Table 1 illustrates some examples of the obtained mapping results of qualitative and quantitative data extracted from the specified evaluation tools. These results present the attributes (e.g. task, interface) and the base measures associated to quality criteria (e.g. the rate of completion of a task related to the effectiveness criterion [9], the images density related to the informational density criterion [3]). For the qualitative data (questions), we have defined as a base measure 'the question response' which takes a value of the applied scale of the questionnaire (e.g. from 1 to 7). This measure is varied from an indicator to another based on the specified quality criteria.

Table 1. Results examples of the mapping model

Quality criteria	Mapped data	
	Qualitative data	Relative quantitative data
Effectiveness: **ISO 9241-11**	It is simple to use this system Strongly agree 1 2 3 4 5 6 7 Strongly disagree	The rate of completion of a task
Informational density: **Bastien and Scapin criteria**	It is easy to find the information I needed Strongly agree 1 2 3 4 5 6 7 Strongly disagree	Workload density Images density Components dimension

These results are the base to define two quality indicators relatively to each quality criteria (the effectiveness and the informational density criteria).

In addition to the base measures, the ISO/IEC 15939 gives the importance to derive new measures based on the specified base measures. The specification of the derived measures is based on the combination of two or more base measures by applying a set of measurement functions. The construction of derived measure aims to group a set of base measures into a unique derived measure to be used by the indicator.

Specify and Interpret the Quality Indicator for Supporting Decision Making.
After specifying the measures related to a quality indicator relatively to a quality criterion, we defined an analysis model that specify the selected measures used by the indicator. Based on the ISO/IEC 15939 standard, this model describes an algorithm to be applied that combined the base and/ or derived measures.

Generally, each indicator uses one or more derived measures, and those measures in turn use one or more base measures. Therefore, some base measures can be specified in different indicators [12]. For our proposed quality indicators, we proposed an analysis model that crosses the qualitative base measure (the question response) with quantitative base/derived measure to perform the integration between qualitative and quantitative data as specified into the defined mapping model.

The presentation and the interpretation of each indicator based on their combined measures are crucial for supporting evaluators in decision making. These decisions are considered based on a set of applied rules. These rules are founded to interpret the combined measures defined by the analysis model.

The interpretation of the quality indicators is a necessary phase; however, there is an intensified need to determine firstly how presenting it in order to make the evaluation decisions. Our quality indicators are presented graphically to provide evaluators a significant visualization format for better illustration of measures. After a deep study about the possible used charts, we have decided to choose the point cloud chart as one of the adequate chart to illustrate the evaluation results for some quality indicators. This type of chart is primarily intended to relate different variables into a point cloud and to check their relationships [5]. We have called this chart the evaluation results curve. For each indicator, the proposed curve illustrates the distribution of the results relatively to the combined measures. This style of curve is generally characterized by the addition of a line of linear fit that allows clarifying the correlation between the data. Mathematically, this line of linear fit is characterized by an linear equation with the form of $Y = aX+b$ where (1) 'X' and 'Y' are respectively the variables values of the abscissa axis (it concerns the quantitative base/derived measure values) and the ordinate axis (it concerns the values of the measure of question response), (2) 'a' is the slope of the line, and (3) 'b' is the intercept value. Furthermore, this linear equation is characterized by a correlation coefficient that clarifies the correlation between the data. This coefficient is always between 0 and 1. More than it tends to 1, the more it proves that the relationship between the data is good [5].

To interpret the indicator, we have illustrated their defined rules into a curve named trend line reference curve (an example of this chart will be presented in the next section). It illustrates the adopted shape of the point cloud that will be compared to the evaluation results curve for making evaluation decisions. This comparison is illustrated using the principle of the superposition between the two curves. It allows verifying if the evaluation is good based on generated correlation coefficient. This principle aims to propose an aid for interpreting the obtained results. For each indicator, we propose a set of decision criteria based on defined rules. These rules will be schematizing into the evaluation results curve in order to identify the possible groups of the point cloud relatively to each rule and as a results, to make evaluation decisions (see the example treated in the next section that schematizes six defined rules).

After specifying the basic principles of our proposed approach for defining quality indicators, we present in the next section a detailed example.

3.2   An Example of a Quality Indicator

In this section, we describe a detailed description of an example of a quality indicator named 'Effectiveness of completion of tasks in a HCI' relatively to the effectiveness quality criteria [9], Table 2.

Table 2. Indicator of the effectiveness of completion of tasks in a HCI based on the ISO/IEC 15939 Standard

Information Need	Evaluate the quality of HCI relatively to the effectiveness quality criterion
Attributes	1- Tasks to be realized for a session
Base Measures	1- The rate of completion of a task for a session: VT 2- The tasks number to be executed: TN 3- The question response : Resp 4- The users number: UN
Derived Measures	1- The rate of completion of tasks per user: RTT 2- The rate of users responses per question: Rresp
Measurement Functions (relatively to each derived measure)	1- For RTT: Divided the sum of the rate of the completion of a task for a session per user by the total tasks number to be executed 2- For Rresp: For each question, calculate the number of users who chosen the same response and divided it by the total users number
Indicator Name	Effectiveness of completion of tasks in a HCI.
Analysis model	This indicator combines two measures (the RTT derived measure and the Resp base measure). It aims to present them in complementary manner for making evaluation decisions.

Table 2. (*Continued.*)

Measures interpretation	For the RTT measure, the highest proportion is better (since the best proportion of the rate of completion of tasks per user is 100%). While, for Resp (question response) measure the smallest value is better (since value 1 is the strongly agree). We have deduced that more the RTT measure is high and more the Resp measure is small is better. Based on this deduction, we define two rules: (1) More than the RTT measure is high (tends to 100%), more than the Resp measure is small (tends to the value 1: strongly agree), and (2) more than the RTT measure is small (tends to 0), more than the Resp measure is high (tends to the value 7: strongly disagree).Based on the combination between these two rules, we obtained the Trend line reference curve for the effectiveness indicator. Mathematically, this curve (straight line) is characterized by negative slope with a correlation coefficient (noted r^2) equal to 1.
Decisions criteria	Based on the defined rules, there exist three possible cases: **Case 1:** When the slope of the linear fit line of the evaluation results curve is negative (downtrend line) and the correlation coefficient tends to 1: Valid curve and valid evaluation We interpret the two measures into various stats as follow: If Resp equal to 1, 2 or 3→ Satisfaction / If Resp equal 4,5, 6 or 7 → Dissatisfaction If RTT between [0%, 50%]→ Failure/ If RTT between [50%, 70%]→ Partial success/ If RTT between [70%, 100%]→ Success Based on these measures' interpretation, we identified six rules for describing the distribution of the point cloud of the evaluation results (figure below): 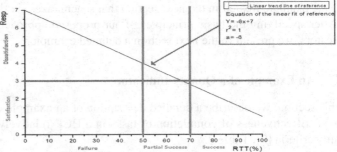 • IF (Satisfaction and Failure)→ there are problems which can be related to users or HCI, this required revisions. • IF (Dissatisfaction and Failure) → there are problems on the HCI, this required revisions. • IF (Satisfaction and Partial success) → the evaluated HCI are partially effective. • IF (Dissatisfaction and Partial success) → there are problems on the HCI, this required revisions • IF (Satisfaction and Success) → the evaluated HCI are effective • IF (Dissatisfaction and Success) → there are problems related to users, revisions are recommended. **Case2:** When the slope of the linear fit line of the evaluation results curve is negative (downtrend line) and the correlation coefficient tends to 0: Valid curve but the evaluation is not valid→an analysis phase is recommended with taken into account the users' profiles. **Case3:** When the slope of the linear fit line of the evaluation results curve is positive (uptrend line): Invalid curve→ there are problems that required revisions of the evaluated interfaces

In the next section, we present a feasibility study of using an example of one of the proposed quality indicators.

4   Feasibility Study: Evaluating a Traffic Supervision System

The main goal of this section is not to evaluate a user interface itself, but to demonstrate the feasibility of the proposed approach for the evaluation of a user interface. Thus, we base this section on only one indicator 'the effectiveness indicator'.

We have applied our approach for evaluating a traffic supervision system named the information assistance system. It is an interactive system based on agent designed to help the regulator to oversee the public transport network [14].

During our experiment, to evaluate the effectiveness of completion of tasks, we have proposed a preliminary evaluation scenario consisting of four phases: the first was the specification of the evaluation (the experimental scenario, the choice of users and the experimental protocol), the second was the capture of the evaluation data using the experimental devices (for the effectiveness indicator, we used the EISEval electronic informer and the CSUQ questionnaire), the third phase was the calculation of derived measures values associated to each indicator based on the captured data and the fourth was the presentation and the interpretation of indicator results.

During our evaluation, the user acted as a network regulator to execute an experimental scenario that involved a set of tasks defined by the evaluator. Various tasks can be performed using this system. We propose an experimental scenario made up of four tasks. The choice of these tasks is based on the fact that they are linked to the different system interfaces.

The recommendations on the choice of the number of subjects are very abundant and varied [16]. According to [7], during the evaluations of interactive systems, the evaluator appeals generally ten subjects per user profile. Hence, our experiment was made up in laboratory by 10 subjects to evaluate the effectiveness quality criterion of the information assistance system. The population of the evaluation has an average age of 25 years. We have considered a unique category of users' profiles (students). All of them are PhD or master students in computer sciences and sports sciences that have good skills in computer sciences at the University of Valenciennes. These users are not experimented in this task (the network supervision). They have never manipulated such systems. We chose novice users in order to better detect design problems related to the IAS.

Figure 3 illustrates the obtained evaluation results of the effectiveness indicator example for making evaluation decisions. It presents the distribution of subjects' results relatively to the combined qualitative and quantitative measures (Resp measure and the RTT measure). This curve shows how qualitative and quantitative measures values are crossed between them. It identifies also the areas that characterized the defined rules (see Table 2) specified for decision making support.

As specified in Table 2, the trend line reference curve of the effectiveness indicator is characterized by negative slope (down trend line) with a correlation coefficient (noted r2) equal to 1. The evaluation results curve (Figure 3) is generated using OriginPro Tool. It indicated the distribution of a point cloud that presents the subjects results after crossing the qualitative measure (Resp) with their associated quantitative measure (RTT). We obtained a down linear fit. Mathematically, this curve is characterized by a negative slope equal to -0.08 with a correlation coefficient equal to 0.6. Based on our indicator decisions (Table 2), we are in the first case. This coefficient indicates a good correlation between the two measures. This proves us that the evaluation results curve is well defined and that our evaluation is valid. Also, this curve allows visualizing and identifying groups of cloud points relatively to their location areas. It allows checking if these groups are nearby the trend line of reference curve.

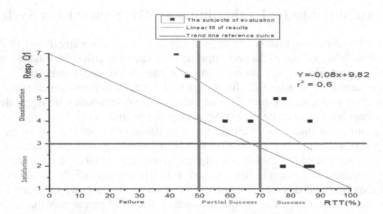

Fig. 3. The superposition of the evaluation results curve and the trend line reference curve for the effectiveness indicator

Based on our figure, we distinguish that the cloud points are distributed on four areas (dissatisfaction and partial success, dissatisfaction and failure, satisfaction and success, dissatisfaction and success).

We note that only one group is superimposed on the trend line reference curve. It is located in the area of 'satisfaction and success' with few point cloud relatively to the others points cloud which are distributed into the others areas as shown in the figure above. This proves that users are not satisfied by system although they have performed their tasks. The dissatisfaction of the majority of subjects shows that users found difficulties using the HCI when performing tasks. This confirms the existence of problems related to realizations of some tasks. We deduce that the system interfaces have problems and require revisions in order to improve its effectiveness in terms of tasks execution.

The defined evaluation decisions present the basis to support evaluators in decision making about the quality of HCI relatively to the evaluation quality criteria. It indicated the preliminary interpretations that will be improved for giving more detailed interpretations.

5   Conclusion and Perspectives

In this paper, we have focalized at resolving the problem of the integration of qualitative and quantitative data based respectively on subjective and objective evaluation methods. A proposal of indicators for supporting HCI quality evaluation was presented in this paper. It allows crossing qualitative and quantitative data extracted from different evaluation tools. These indicators provide a basis of decision making about the quality of HCI relatively to the evaluation quality criteria. A feasibility study is presented to demonstrate the applicability of the use of the proposed approach for supporting decision making.

As future works, various experiments will be done to ensure the validation of our approach, define a catalog of indicators for HCI quality evaluation support and implement our proposal into a new quality evaluation tool.

References

1. Al-Wabil, A., Al-Khalifa, H.: A Framework for Integrating Usability Evaluations Methods: The Mawhiba Web Portal Case Study. In: The International Conference on the Current Trends in Information Technology (CTIT 2009), Dubai, UAE, pp. 1–6 (2009)
2. Assila, A., de Oliveira, K.M., Ezzedine, H.: Towards qualitative and quantitative data integration approach for enhancing HCI quality evaluation. In: Kurosu, M. (ed.) HCI 2014, Part I. LNCS, vol. 8510, pp. 469–480. Springer, Heidelberg (2014)
3. Bastien, J.M.C., Scapin, D.: Ergonomic Criteria for the Evaluation of Human Computer interfaces. Technical Report n° 156, Institut Nationale de Recherche en Informatique et en Automatique, France (1993)
4. Charfi, S., Ezzedine, H., Kolski, C.: RITA: A Framework based on multi-evaluation techniques for user interface evaluation, Application to a transport network supervision system. In: ICALT, May 29-31, pp. 263–268. IEEE, Tunisia (2013) ISBN 978-1-4799-0312-2
5. Hardin, M., Hom, D., Perez, R., Williams, L.: Quel diagramme ou graphique vous convient le mieux? Copyright Tableau Software, Inc. (2012)
6. Hartson, H.R., Andre, T.S., Will, R.C.: Criteria for evaluating usability evaluation methods. International Journal of Human-Computer Interaction, vol 15(1), 145–181 (2003)
7. Hwang, W., Salvendy, G.: Number of people required for usability evaluation: the 10 2 rule. Commun. ACM 53(5), 130–133 (2010)
8. ISO/IEC 15939 Systems and software engineering — Measurement process (2007)
9. ISO/IEC. ISO 9241-11 Ergonomic requirements for office work with visual display terminals (VDT) s- Part 11 Guidance on usability. ISO/IEC 9241-11: 1998(E)
10. Kerzazi, N., Lavallée, M.: Inquiry on usability of two software process modeling systems using ISO/IEC 9241. In: CCECE, pp 773–776 (2011)
11. Lewis, J.R.: IBM computer usability satisfaction questionnaires: Psychometric evaluation and instructions for use. IJHCI (7), 57–78 (1995)
12. Monteiro, L., Oliveira, K.: Defining a catalog of indicators to support process performance analysis. Journal of Software Maintenance and Evolution: Research and Practice 23(6), 395–422 (2010)
13. Nielsen, N.: Engineering, Usability. Morgan Kaufmann Publishers Inc., San Francisco (1993)
14. Trabelsi, A., Ezzedine, H.: Evaluation of an Information Assistance System based on an agent-based architecture in transportation domain: first results. International Journal of Computers, Communications and Control 8(2), 320–333 (2013)
15. Tran, C., Ezzedine, H., Kolski, C.: EISEval, a Generic Reconfigurable Environment for Evaluating Agent-based Interactive Systems. International Journal of Human-Computer Studies 71(6), 725–761 (2013)
16. Whiting, M.A., Haack, J., Varley, C.: Creating realistic, scenario-based synthetic data for test and evaluation of information analytics software. In: Proc. Conference on Beyond Time and Errors: Novel Evaluation Methods For information Visualization, A Workshop of the ACM CHI 2008 Conference, Florence, Italy, pp. 1–9 (2008)
17. Yang, T., Linder, J., Bolchini, D.: DEEP: Design-Oriented Evaluation of Perceived Usability. International Journal of Human Computer Interaction, 308–346 (2012)

Preface to SeCoGIS 2014

Recent advances in information technology have changed the way geographical data were originally produced and made available. Nowadays, the use of Geographic Information Systems (GIS) is not reserved anymore to the specialized user. GISs are emerging as a common information infrastructure, which penetrates into more and more aspects of our society. The technological drift implies a profound change in mentality, with a deep impact on the way geographical data needs to be conceptualized. New methodological and data engineering challenges must be confronted by GIS researchers in the near future in order to accommodate new users' requirements for new applications.

The SeCoGIS workshop intends to bring together researchers, developers, users, and practitioners with an interest in all semantic and conceptual issues in GISs. The aim is to stimulate discussions on the integration of conceptual modeling and semantics into various web applications dealing with spatio-temporally referenced data and how this benefits end-users. The workshop provides a forum for original research contributions and practical experiences of conceptual modeling and semantic web technologies for GIS, fostering interdisciplinary discussions in all aspects of these two fields and highlighting future trends in this area. The workshop is organized in a way to stimulate interaction amongst the participants.

This edition of the workshop received 10 submissions, from which the Program Committee selected 3 very high quality full papers corresponding to an acceptance rate of 30%. Another 3 very good papers were also accepted as short papers which will also be presented and published in the proceeding of the workshop. The authors of the accepted papers are world-wide distributed, making SeCoGIS a truly international workshop. A keynote talk and all the accepted papers are organized in three sessions. The first session is dedicated to a keynote. The second session is focused on the semantic based qualitative movement and network analysis and the third session is organised around semantic based spatiotemporal databases design and analysis.

We would like to express our gratitude to the Program Committee members for their qualified work in reviewing papers, the authors for considering SeCoGIS as a forum to publish their research, and the ER 2013 organizers for all their support.

July 2014

Mir Abolfazl Mostafavi
Andrea Ballatore
Esteban Zimanyi
Program Chairs
SeCoGIS 2014

Towards a Qualitative Representation of Movement

Jing Wu[1,2], Christophe Claramunt[2], and Min Deng[1]

[1] Department of Geo-Informatics, Central South University, Changsha, China
[2] Naval Academy Research Institute, Lanvéoc-Poulmic,
BP 600, 29240 Brest Naval, France
{jing.wu,claramunt}@ecole-navale.fr, dengmin028@yahoo.com

Abstract. Over the past few years there have been several attempts to model and represent the spatial and temporal properties of moving entities. Several semantic and computational frameworks have been developed to track and analyze moving object trajectories, but there is still a need for a qualitative reasoning support at the abstract level. The research presented in this paper introduces a qualitative approach for representing and reasoning about moving entities. The model combines topological relations with qualitative distances over a spatial and temporal framework. Several basic movement configurations over dynamic entities are identified as well as movement transitions.

Keywords: Movement, topological relations, qualitative distances.

1   Introduction

Movement is a vital element of all organisms and many spatio-temporal processes that happen in large- and small-scale spaces. In particular, comprehending and modeling movement is still an important domain of research interest for geographic information science (GIS). A better understanding of movement patterns is a key issue for many GIS application areas such as behavioral ecology [1], human mobility [2], traffic management [3] and environmental hazards [4]. Several recent research has developed qualitative reasoning formalisms for the representation of moving objects (some references here taken from our list of references: e.g., [5, 8, 15-17]). The research presented in this paper suggests a relatively different approach, by taking a relative point of view of the movement of two given entities, movement being considered by giving a particular importance on the boundary of the one that might be considered as predominant or as a reference. This specific property is relevant for example in indoor spaces, when analyzing the trajectory of a moving object with respect to a given bounded room or place, or when analyzing in a large-scale space the movement of an object with respect to a region. A moving human has for example to pass through a door when moving from one room to another. When modeling such activities, the relativity of these processes is a factor that matters, for instance the qualitative

M. Indulska and S. Purao (Eds.): ER Workshops 2014, LNCS 8823, pp. 191–200, 2014.
© Springer International Publishing Switzerland 2014

location of a human with respect to a given room (is he inside or outside?), and when integrating time his overall behavior with respect to this room (is he leaving or approaching this room?). These two examples illustrate the motivation behind our approach that will be more formally developed in the next sections.

More precisely, our approach explores a modeling representation of movement based on an integration of qualitative topological and distance relationships. We intend to provide an intuitive set of modeling primitives that support the qualitative representation of movement, with the potential advantage of providing a systematic tool for investigating and reasoning qualitative movements. The approach is complemented by a systematic representation of possible configurations, a tentative qualification of possible natural language expressions of the different cases identified, and a modelling of conceptual transitions.

The remainder of this paper is organized as follows. Section 2 briefly reviews related work on the qualitative modeling of movement. Section 3 introduces the basic principles of our approach and a series of qualitative topological and distance-based primitives that model the movement between a moving entity and a reference entity. Section 4 presents movement transitions and finally section 5 concludes the paper and draws some conclusions.

2   Related Work

Several authors have proposed some general conceptual frameworks for representing complex geographic phenomena as a hierarchy of events, processes, and state, and where implicitly the concept of movement is closely related to a process [5,6]. In the context of our paper, the relative movement of a given entity can be informally defined as a change of some qualitative spatial properties with respect to a reference entity. Explicitly, such a notion of movement has been studied by qualitative spatial reasoning approaches, this section briefly discusses related works.

Galton [7] modeled a movement as an event and interpreted motion primarily as change in position. A qualitative theory of movement was introduced and developed more completely in [8]. Time was modeled using either instants or intervals with an ordering relation, the representation of space was based on regions and $RCC8$ relations [9], while moving entities can be rigid or non-rigid. The semantics behind moving entities can be also derived from natural language expressions. Stewart Hornsby and Li [10] explored how textual documents that contain movement verbs and terms can be mapped to elementary abstractions that include source, destination, route, direction, distance, start time, end time, and duration properties. Pustejovsky and Moszkowicz [11] developed a computational semantics for motion as expressed in natural languages, based on a temporal logic.

Kurata and Egenhofer [12] extended the 9-intersection (9I) calculus [13] to the 9I⁺ calculus, where the concept of a directed line is introduced to represent the trajectory of a moving entity. Further, Shi and Kurata [14] explored the modeling of motion concepts with different configurations between a directed line and a region.

In order to model the relative movement between two moving entities considered as moving points, the Qualitative Trajectory Calculus [15] studies the configurations that qualify the relative position in time of two moving points, and identifies some basic movements such as moving towards or moving away from. Besides, relative directions and velocity are also considered. Noyon *et al.* [16] developed a relative-based modeling approach that integrates the concept of location, speed and acceleration to qualify the relative motion of two rigid entities, as also perceived and represented by natural language expressions.

Muller [17] introduced a modeling framework that combines *RCC*8 relations with a temporal algebra, and derived a theory of motion based on mereo-topology. The algebra developed gives a set of six motion classes: leave, hit, reach, external, internal and cross, that can be associated to natural language expressions. However, the approach developed is not precise enough to characterize some specific movements where distance between the entities considered matters. In a recent work, Gottfried [18] modeled the relative movement of pairs of moving rigid entities by taking into account directional information and relative movement. This allows to derive 16 atomic motion patterns that hold between two rigid entities, but non rigid entities are not considered.

This brief review shows that qualitative formalisms have a long standing tradition as methods to bridge the gap between formal and linguistic descriptions of movement. Some of these models considered moving objects as points [15,16], while others as representations for studying changes of spatial configurations [14,18]. Other approaches combined qualitative spatial relations with temporal relations in order to derive some sets of configurations that contain a dynamic semantics [8,17,19]. The research presented in this paper differs to previous approaches in several aspects. Firstly, we take into account the role of the entities boundaries when observing the relative behavior of two given entities. This allows to characterize more precisely the relative spatial configurations and evolution of two entities. Secondly, modelling over time the distance between the entities considered favors the identification of a series of possible configurations qualified by natural language expressions.

3   Qualitative Representation of Movement

The relative movement of two entities in space and time is modeled using qualitative topological relationships and the evolution of their relative distances. We consider simply connected planar regions in the Euclidean plane. The configurations identified corresponds to monotonic and continuous movements valid over a given temporal of time as suggested by Allen [20]. We assume that the boundaries of the entities modeled are well-defined, as well as the topological relationships and relative distance between them. Most of the configurations identified are formally defined and mapped to linguistics constructs when appropriate.

3.1 Spatio-temporal Primitives

In order to model motion in qualitative terms a primitive movement is firstly formally defined from a given $RCC8$ relation valid over an interval of time T. The relative spatial relations between two given entities are modeled using the $RCC8$ algebra and the eight jointly exhaustive and pairwise disjoint relations and denoted as follows: disconnected (DC), externally connected (EC), partial overlap (PO), equal (EQ), tangential proper part (TPP) and its inverse ($TPPI$), and non-tangential proper part ($NTPP$) and its inverse ($NTPPI$).

The relative distance denoted as D between a moving entity A and a reference entity B over a time interval T is the second property taken into account to for example distinguish between whether an entity A moves toward or away from an entity B. The relative distance between an entity A and an entity B denoted d at a given time t is modeled as the minimum distance between the boundary of A and the boundary of B. This relative distance can be calculated whatever the relative location of the entities A and B: whether A is outside, on the boundary or inside B. Let us model some basic relative distance configurations of two given entities A and B over a given interval of time T:

- d_{ext+} denotes that D is continuously increasing outside B over a given temporal interval T (i.e, for all t of T)
- d_{ext-} denotes that D is continuously decreasing outside B over a given temporal interval T
- $d_{ext=}$ denotes that D is constant outside B over a given temporal interval T
- d_0 denotes that D is null over a given temporal interval T
- d_{int+} denotes that D is continuously increasing inside B over a given temporal interval T
- d_{int-} denotes that D is continuously decreasing inside B over a given temporal interval T
- $d_{int=}$ denotes that D is constant inside B over a given temporal interval T

3.2 Classification of Movement

The movement is classified into three categories according to the relative location of a moving entity with respect to a reference entity. Over a given temporal interval T a moving entity will be either outside, on the boundary, or inside a reference entity.

3.2.1 Movement Outside a Reference Entity

Let us first consider the configuration where a moving entity A is disconnected from a reference entity B. Three categories of movements can be distinguished: Approach (AP), Leave (LV) and AroundOutside (AO) over a given temporal interval T. During that time interval T, the $RCC8$ relation is DC, and the relative distance can be either increasing, decreasing or constant (d_{ext+}, d_{ext-} and $d_{ext=}$, respectively). More formally:

- $Approach((A, B), D, T)$: A moving entity A is approaching a reference entity B over a time interval T, as shown in Fig. 1a. For all $t \in T$, $DC(A, B)$ holds and the distance relationship D is decreasing outside B over T:

$$Approach((A, B), D, T) \equiv Holds(DC(A, B), d_{ext-}, T)$$

- $Leave((A, B), D, T)$: A moving entity A is leaving a reference entity B over a time interval T, as shown in Fig. 1b. For all $t \in T$, $DC(A, B)$ holds and the distance relationship D is increasing outside B over T:

$$Leave((A, B), D, T) \equiv Holds(DC(A, B), d_{ext+}, T)$$

- $AroundOutside((A, B), D, T)$: A moving entity A is either moving around or static outside a reference entity B over a time interval T, as shown in Fig. 1c. For all $t \in T$, $DC(A, B)$ holds and the distance relationship D is constant outside B over T:

$$AroundOutside((A, B), D, T) \equiv Holds(DC(A, B), d_{ext=}, T)$$

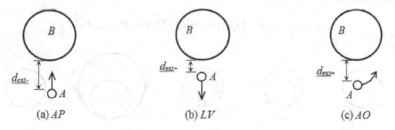

Fig. 1. Movement outside a reference entity

3.2.2 Movement on the Boundary of a Reference Entity

When an entity A is moving on the boundary of a reference entity B over a time interval T, five different categories of movements are identified: *Touching (TI)*, *Overlapping (OI)*, *CoveringBy (CB)*, *Covering (CI)* and *Equaling (EI)*, in which *CB* and *CI* are a pair of inverse movements. The relative distance D between them is d_0, and five topological relationships apply: *EC, PO, TPP, TPPI* and *EQ*. More formally the basic movements identified are as follows:

- *Touching((A, B), D, T)*: A moving entity *A* is touching outside the boundary of a reference entity *B* over a time interval *T*, as shown in Fig. 2a. For all $t \in T$, *EC(A, B)* holds and the relative distance *D* is d_0 over *T*:

$$Touching((A, B), D, T) \equiv Holds(EC(A, B), d_0, T)$$

- *Overlapping((A, B), D, T)*: A moving entity *A* is overlapping the boundary of a reference entity *B* over a time interval *T*, as shown in Fig. 2b. For all $t \in T$, *PO(A, B)* holds and the relative distance *D* is d_0 over *T*:

$$Overlapping((A, B), D, T) \equiv Holds(PO(A, B), d_0, T)$$

- *CoveringBy((A, B), D, T)*: A moving entity *A* is touching inside the boundary of a reference entity *B* over a time interval *T*, as shown in Fig. 2c. For all $t \in T$, *TPP(A, B)* holds and the relative distance is d_0 over *T*:

$$CoveringBy((A, B), D, T) \equiv Holds(TPP(A, B), d_0, T)$$

- *Covering((A, B), D, T)*: A moving entity *A* is touching outside the boundary of a reference entity *B* over a time interval *T*, as shown in Fig. 2d. For all $t \in T$, *TPPI(A, B)* holds and the relative distance *D* is d_0 over *T*:

$$Covering((A, B), D, T) \equiv Holds(TPPI(A, B), d_0, T)$$

- *Equaling((A, B), D, T)*: A moving entity *A* equals a reference entity *B* over a time interval *T*, as shown in Fig. 2e. For all $t \in T$, *EQ(A, B)* holds and the relative distance *D* is d_0 over *T*:

$$Equaling((A, B), D, T) \equiv Holds(EQ(A, B), d_0, T)$$

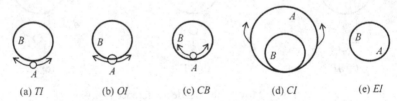

(a) *TI*   (b) *OI*   (c) *CB*   (d) *CI*   (e) *EI*

Fig. 2. Movement on the boundary of a reference entity

3.2.3   Movement Inside a Reference Entity

When an entity *A* moves inside a reference entity *B* over a time interval *T*, there are six categories of movements: *MovetoInterior (MI)*, *MovetoBoundary (MB)*, *AroundInside (AI)*, *EmbracingMoveOutside (EMO)*, *EmbracingMovetoBoundary (EMB)*, and *EmbracingAroundOutside (EAO)*, in which *MI* and *EMO*, *MB* and *EMB*, *AI* and *EAO* are three pairs of inverse movements, respectively. Those disjoint configurations are derived from six relative distance behaviors over a given temporal of time: d_{int+}, d_{int-}, $d_{int=}$, d_{ext+}, d_{ext-}, and $d_{ext=}$. Similarly the spatial configurations valid are *NTPP* or

NTPPI when respectively an entity *A* is either inside a reference entity *B*, and conversely. More formally the basic movements identified are as follows:

- *MovetoInterior((A, B), D, T)*: When a moving entity *A* is *NTPP* to a reference entity *B* and leaving the boundary of *B* over a time interval *T*, we say that *A* is moving to the interior of *B*, as shown in Fig. 3a. For all $t \in T$, *NTPP(A, B)* holds and the relative distance *D* is increasing inside *B* over *T*:

$$MovetoInterior((A, B), D, T) \equiv Holds(NTPP(A, B), d_{int+}, T)$$

- *MovetoBoundary((A, B), D, T)*: When a moving entity *A* is *NTPP* to a reference entity *B*, and *A* is moving to the boundary of *B* over a time interval *T*, we say that *A* is moving to the boundary of *B*, as shown in Fig. 3b. For all $t \in T$, *NTPP(A, B)* holds and the relative distance *D* is decreasing inside *B* over *T*:

$$MovetoBoundary((A, B), D, T) \equiv Holds(NTPP(A, B), d_{int-}, T)$$

- *AroundInside((A, B), D, T)*: When a moving entity *A* is *NTPP* to a reference entity *B*, and *A* is either moving around the boundary of *B* or static relative to *B* over a time interval *T*, we say that *A* is around inside *B*, as shown in Fig. 3c. For all $t \in T$, *NTPP(A, B)* holds and the relative distance *D* is constant inside *B* over *T*:

$$AroundInside((A, B), D, T) \equiv Holds(NTPP(A, B), d_{int=}, T)$$

- *EmbracingMoveOutside((A, B), D, T)*: When a moving entity *A* is *NTPPI* to a reference entity *B*, and *A* is moving outside *B* over a time interval *T*, we say that *A* is embracing *B* and moving outside *B*, as shown in Fig. 3d. For all $t \in T$, *NTPPI(A, B)* holds and the relative distance relationship *D* is increasing outside *B* over *T*:

$$EmbracingMoveOutside((A, B), D, T) \equiv Holds(NTPPI(A, B), d_{ext+}, T)$$

- *EmbracingMovetoBoundary((A, B), D, T)*: When a moving entity *A* is *NTPPI* to a reference entity *B*, and *A* is moving to the boundary of *B* over a time interval *T*, we say that *A* is embracing *B* and moving to the boundary of *B*, as shown in Fig. 3e. For all $t \in T$, *NTPPI(A, B)* holds and the relative distance *D* is decreasing outside *B* over *T*:

$$EmbracingMovetoBoundary((A, B), D, T) \equiv Holds(NTPPI(A, B), d_{ext-}, T)$$

- *EmbracingAroundOutside((A, B), D, T)*: When a moving entity *A* is *NTPPI* to a reference entity *B*, and *A* is either moving around or static outside of *B* over a time interval *T*, we say that *A* is embracing *B* and moving around outside *B*, as shown in Fig. 3f. For all $t \in T$, *NTPPI(A, B)* holds and the relative distance *D* is constant outside *B* over *T*:

$$EmbracingAroundOutside((A, B), D, T) \equiv Holds(NTPPI(A, B), d_{ext=}, T)$$

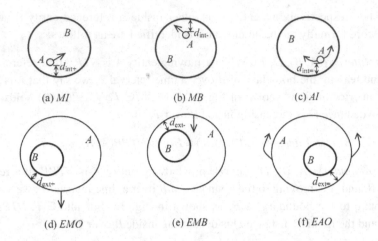

Fig. 3. Movement inside a reference entity

4   Conceptual Neighbor Diagram

Conceptual neighbors provide additional reasoning capabilities to anticipate future movements and to develop reasoning mechanisms in case of incomplete knowledge. It was formally studied based on conceptual neighbor diagram, as initially developed for temporal reasoning [21]. A crucial factor in the definition of a conceptual neighborhood diagram is the continuity of possible transformations. Galton [8] has studied the valid transitions by his theory of dominance and the constraints imposed by the constraint of continuity, which restricts admissible changes.

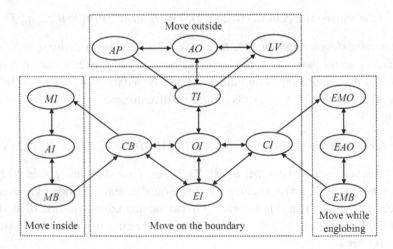

Fig. 4. Conceptual neighbor diagram for movements

The conceptual neighbor diagram that can be derived from primitive movements identified in the previous section is shown in Fig. 4. Two movements are conceptual neighbors, if there is a continuous transition between them without any intermediary movement. A bidirectional arrow indicates that the relationships on each side can be directly transformed into the other by a continuously transition. A one-way arrow shows the direction of the transition. Consider for example the qualitative distinction between *MovetoBoundary* (*MB*) and *Leave* (*LV*). A change from *MB* to *LV* must pass from the movements on the boundary, since a relative distance cannot change directly from d_{int-} to d_{int+} without passing by d_0.

5   Conclusion

This paper introduces a modelling approach for the representation of primitive movements between dynamic entities. The model is based on two complementary qualitative primitives: *RCC*8 relations and qualitative distances. The framework developed favors the identification of a series of movement primitives that qualify the relative movements of two evolving entities, as well as movement transitions. The model is preliminary and still should be extended by the integration of additional qualitative and quantitative properties such as direction relations or velocities. Further work will be oriented to the study of sequences of movement and patterns that emerge from a group of moving objects. We also plan to validate our approach by prototype developments applied to human and robot navigations in indoor spaces.

Acknowledgements. Jing Wu's research was funded by the Fundamental Research Funds for the Central Universities of Central South University and Open Research Fund Program of Key Laboratory of Digital Mapping and Land Information Application Engineering (GCWD201206), State Bureau of Surveying and Mapping.

References

1. Raffaeta, A., Ceccarelli, T., Centeno, D., Giannotti, F., Massolo, A., Parent, C., Renso, C., Spaccapietra, S., Turini, F.: An Application of Advanced Spatio-Temporal Formalisms to Behavioural Ecology. GeoInformatica 12, 37–72 (2008)
2. González, M.C., Hidalgo, C.A., Barabási, A.L.: Understanding Individual Human Mobility Patterns. Nature 453, 779–782 (2008)
3. Mouza, C., Rigaux, P.: Mobility Patterns. GeoInformatica 9, 297–319 (2005)
4. Sinha, G., Mark, D.M.: Measuring Similarity between Geospatial Lifelines in Studies of Environmental Health. Journal of Geographical Systems 7, 115–136 (2005)
5. Peuquet, D.J.: It's about Time: A Conceptual Framework for the Representation of Temporal Dynamics in Geographic Information Systems. Annals of the Association of American Geographers 84, 441–461 (1994)
6. Yuan, M.: Representing Complex Geographic Phenomena in GIS. Cartography and Geographic Information Science 28, 83–96 (2001)

7. Galton, A.: Towards a Qualitative Theory of Movement. In: Kuhn, W., Frank, A.U. (eds.) COSIT 1995. LNCS, vol. 988, pp. 377–396. Springer, Heidelberg (1995)
8. Galton, A.: Qualitative Spatial Change. Oxford University Press, Oxford (2000)
9. Randell, D.A., Cui, Z., Cohn, A.G.: A Spatial Logic Based on Regions and Connection. In: Proceedings of the Third International Conference on Knowledge Representation and Reasoning, pp. 165–176. Cambridge, Massachusetts (1992)
10. Stewart Hornsby, K., Li, N.: Conceptual Framework for Modeling Dynamic Paths from Natural Language Expressions. Transactions in GIS 13(s1), 27–45 (2009)
11. Pustejovsky, J., Moszkowicz, J.L.: The Qualitative Spatial Dynamics of Motion in Language. Spatial Cognition & Computation 11, 15–44 (2011)
12. Kurata, Y., Egenhofer, M.: The 9+-Intersection for Topological Relations between a Directed Line Segment and a Region. In: Gottfried, B. (ed.) 1st Workshop on Behavioral Monitoring and Interpretation, TZI-Bericht, vol. 42, pp. 62–76. Technogie-Zentrum Informatik, Universität Bremen (2007)
13. Egenhofer, M., Franzosa, R.: Point-set Topological Spatial Relations. International Journal of Geographical Information Science 5, 161–174 (1991)
14. Shi, H., Kurata, Y.: Modeling Ontological Concepts of Motions with Two Projection-Based Spatial Models. In: 2nd International Workshop on Behavioral Monitoring and Interpretation, vol. 396, pp. 42–56. Kaiserslautern, Germany (2008)
15. Van de Weghe, N.: Representing and Reasoning about Moving Objects: A Qualitative Approach. Phd thesis, Ghent University, Belgium (2004)
16. Noyon, V., Claramunt, C., Devogele, D.: A Relative Representation of Trajectories in Geographical Spaces. Geoinformatica 11, 479–496 (2007)
17. Muller, P.: A Qualitative Theory of Motion Based on Spatio-Temporal Primitives. In: Cohn, A.G., Schubert, L., Shapiro, S.C. (eds.) Principles of Knowledge Representation and Reasoning, pp. 131–141. Morgan Kaufmann, San Francisco (1998)
18. Gottfried, B.: Interpreting Motion Events of Pairs of Moving Objects. GeoInformatica 15, 247–271 (2011)
19. Praing, R., Schneider, M.: Modeling historical and future spatio-temporal relationships of moving objects in databases. In: Proceedings of the 16th ACM Conference on Information and Knowledge Management, Lisbon, Portugal, pp. 183–192 (2007)
20. Allen, J.: Maintaining Knowledge about Temporal Intervals. Communications of the ACM 26, 832–843 (1983)
21. Freksa, C.: Temporal Reasoning Based on Semi-Intervals. Artificial Intelligence 54, 199–227 (1992)

Lagrangian Xgraphs: A Logical Data-Model for Spatio-Temporal Network Data: A Summary

Venkata M.V. Gunturi and Shashi Shekhar

Dept of Computer Science & Engineering,
University of Minnesota, Minneapolis, USA
{gunturi,shekhar}@cs.umn.edu

Abstract. Given emerging diverse spatio temporal network (STN) datasets, e.g., GPS tracks, temporally detailed roadmaps and traffic signal data, the aim is to develop a logical data-model which achieves a seamless integration of these datasets for diverse use-cases (queries) and supports efficient algorithms. This problem is important for travel itinerary comparison and navigation applications. However, this is challenging due to the conflicting requirements of expressive power and computational efficiency as well as the need to support ever more diverse STN datasets, which now record non-decomposable properties of n-ary relations. Examples include travel-time and fuel-use during a journey on a route with a sequence of coordinated traffic signals and turn delays. Current data models for STN datasets are limited to representing properties of only binary relations, e.g., distance on individual road segments. In contrast, the proposed logical data-model, Lagrangian Xgraphs can express properties of both binary and n-ary relations. Our initial study shows that Lagrangian Xgraphs are more convenient for representing diverse STN datasets and comparing candidate travel itineraries.

1 Introduction

Increasingly a variety of spatial-temporal datasets representing diverse properties of a transportation network over space and time (STN datasets) are becoming available. Examples include temporally detailed (TD) roadmaps [1] that provide travel-time for every road-segment at 5 minute granularity, traffic signal timings and coordination [2], map-matched GPS tracks annotated with engine measurement data (e.g., fuel consumption) [1,3], etc. Given a collection of such STN datasets and a set of use-case queries, we aim to build a unified logical data-model across these datasets which can express a variety of travel related concepts explicitly while supporting efficient algorithms for given use-cases. The objective here is to explore the trade-off between expressiveness and computational efficiency. Such a unified logical data-model would enable richer results by allowing query algorithms to access and compare information from multiple datasets simultaneously.

Value of STN Datasets: Collectively, STN datasets capture a wide assortment of travel-related information, e.g., historic traffic congestion patterns, "fuel efficiency index" of different road segments, emerging commuter driving preferences,

M. Indulska and S. Purao (Eds.): ER Workshops 2014, LNCS 8823, pp. 201–211, 2014.

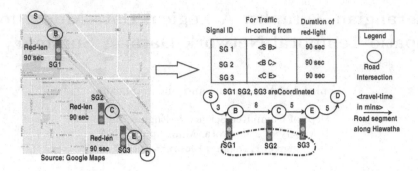

Fig. 1. Coordinated traffic signals [7] (best is color)

etc. Such information is not only important for routing related use-cases, e.g., comparison of alternative itineraries and navigation, but also valuable for several urban planning use-cases such as traffic management and analysis of transportation network. According to a 2011 McKinsey Global Institute report, annual savings of about $600 billion could be achieved by 2020 in terms of fuel and time saved [4] by helping vehicles avoid congestion and reduce idling at red lights or left turns. Preliminary evidence on the potential of STN datasets include the experience of UPS which saves millions of gallons of fuel by simply avoiding left turns and associated engine-idling when selecting routes [5]. Similarly, other pilot studies with TD roadmaps [6] and congestion information derived from GPS traces [3] showed that indeed, travelers can save up to 30% in travel time compared with approaches that assume a static network. Thus, it is conceivable that immense savings in fuel-cost and green-house gas emissions are possible if other consumers avoided hot spots of idling, low fuel-efficiency, and congestion, potentially leading towards 'eco-routing' [1].

Challenges: Modeling a collection of STN datasets is challenging due to the conflicting requirements of expressive power and computational efficiency. In addition, the growing diversity of STN datasets requires modeling a variety of concepts accurately. For instance, it should be convenient to express all the properties of a n-ary relation in the model. A route with a sequence of coordinated traffic signals is a sample n-ary relation. Properties measured over n-ary relations cannot always be decomposed into properties over binary relations. Consider the following scenario of signal coordination on a portion of Hiawatha Ave in Minneapolis (shown in Figure 1). Here, the traffic signals SG1, SG2 and SG3 control the incoming traffic from segments S-B, B-C, and C-E (and going towards D) respectively. Now, the red-light durations and phase gap among traffic signals SG1, SG2 and SG3 are set such that a typical traveler starting at S and going towards D (within certain speed-limits) would typically *wait only at SG1*, before being smoothly transferred through intersections C and E *with no waiting at SG2 or SG3*. In other words, in this journey initial waiting at SG1 renders SG2 and SG3 wait free. If the effects of immediate spatial neighborhood are referred to as local-interactions, e.g. waiting at SG1 delaying entry into segment B-C, then we this would be referred to as a *non-local interaction* as SG1 is not in

Road	Typical Travel Time
S-B	3mins
B-C	8mins
C-E	5mins
E-D	5mins

Signal	Incoming Traffic	Outgoing Traffic	Max Delay
SG1	S-B	B-C	90secs
SG2	B-C	C-E	90secs
SG3	C-E	E-D	90secs

Journeys with non-local interactions	Typical travel-time Experienced
S-B +delay at SG1	3 mins --- 4 mins 30 sec
S-B +SG1+ B-C +SG2	11 mins -- 12 mins 30 sec
S-B +SG1+ B-C +SG2+ C-E +SG3	16 mins -- 17 mins 30 sec

(a) Related Work   (b) Our approach

Fig. 2. Related work and our approach for holistic travel-time shown in Figure 1

immediate spatial neighborhood of C-E (controlled by SG2) and E-D (controlled by SG3).

Travel-time measured on a typical journey with non-local interactions (e.g. a journey from S to D in Figure 1) cannot be decomposed to get typical experiences on individual segments. Consider again the above sample journey from S to D in Figure 1. Here, the total travel-time measured on a typical journey from S to D would not include any waiting at intersections C (signal SG2) and E (signal SG2). This is, however, *not true* as a traveler starting intersection C (or E) would typically wait for some time SG2 (or SG3). We refer to this kind of behavior, where properties (e.g. travel-time) measured over larger instances (e.g. a route) loose their semantic meaning on decomposition, as *holism*. For our previous example, we say that the total travel-time measured over the route S-B-C-E-D was behaving like a *holistic property*.

Limitations of Related Work. Current approaches for modeling STN datasets such as time aggregated graphs [8], time expanded graphs [9], and [10,11] are most convenient when the property being represented can be completely decomposed into properties of binary relations. In other words, they are not suitable for representing the previously described holistic properties of n-ary relations. Consider again our previous signal coordination scenario. The related work would represent this using following two data structures: one containing travel-time on individual segments (binary relations) S-B, B-C, C-E, and E-D; the second containing the delays and the traffic controlled by signals SG1, SG2, and SG3 (also binary). However, this is not convenient as non-local interactions affecting travel-times on some journeys (e.g. S-B-C-E-D) are not expressed explicitly. Note that this representation would have been good enough if SG1, SG2 and SG3 were not coordinated.

Our Approach: In contrast, our approach can support n-ary relations better by modeling non-local interactions on journeys more explicitly. Figure 2(b) illustrates the spirit of our logical data-model for the previous signal coordination scenario. The first entry in the figure corresponds to travel-time experienced on a journey containing road segment S-B (3 mins) and delay at SG1 (max delay 90 secs). This would be between 3 mins and 4 mins 30 secs (no non-local interactions in this case). Next we would store travel-time experienced on the journey containing road segment S-B (3mins) , delay at SG1 (max delay 90secs), segment B-C (8mins) and delay at SG2 (max 90secs) as between 11 mins and 12 mins 30 secs. Notice that we did not consider the delay caused by SG2 due

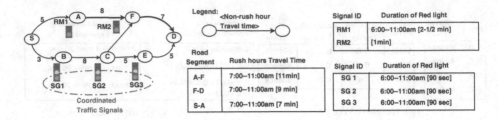

Fig. 3. Sample TD roadmap and traffic signal data

to non-local interaction from SG1. This process continues until all the possible non-local interactions are covered.

Contributions: This paper makes the following contributions: (1) Elucidate valuable routing-related concepts, e.g. reference frame and type of properties, captured in STN datasets, (2) Propose a logical data-model called *Lagrangian Xgraphs* for these concepts, (3) Propose an abstract data type for Lagrangian Xgraphs, and (4) Illustrate Lagrangian Xgraphs through a sample scenario.

Scope and Outline: The scope of the paper is limited to routing-related use-cases (e.g. comparison of travel itineraries and navigation) only. The rest of the paper is organized as follows: Section 2 describes the STN datasets considered in this paper. Section 3.1 presents the routing-related concepts captured in these datasets. Our proposed logical data-model, Lagrangian Xgraph model, and its abstract data types are described in Section 3.2. We illustrate Lagrangian Xgraphs in Section 3.3. Finally, Section 4 concludes the article with a brief look at future work.

2   Description of STN Datasets

Consider the sample transportation network shown in Figure 3 (on the left). Here, the arrows represent road segments and labels (in circles) represent an intersection between two road segments. Location of traffic signals are also annotated in the figure. On this network, we consider three types of STN datasets: (a) temporally detailed (TD) roadmaps [1], (b) traffic signal data [2], and (c) annotated GPS traces [1,3]. These datasets record either historical or evolving aspects of certain travel related phenomena on our transportation network. TD roadmaps store historical travel-time on road segments for several departure-times in typical week [1]. For simplicity, TD roadmap data is illustrated in Figure 3 by highlighting the morning (7:00am – 11:00am) travel-time only on segments A-F, F-D and S-A. The travel-times of other road segments in the figure are assumed to remain constant. The figure also shows the traffic signal delays during the 7:00am – 11:00am period. Additionally, traffic signals SG1, SG2 and SG3 are coordinated for a journey from S to D.

Another type of STN dataset considered in this paper are the map-matched and pre-processed [12] GPS traces. These are typically also annotated with data from engine computers to get richer datasets illustrating fuel economy of the route. We refer to them as annotated GPS traces. Each trace in this dataset is represented as a sequence of road-segments traversed in the journey along with its corresponding schedule denoting the exact time when the traversal of a particular segment began. GPS traces can potentially capture the evolving aspect of our system. For instance, if segment E-D (Figure 3) is congested due to an event (a non-equilibrium phenomenon), then travel-time denoted by TD roadmaps may no longer be accurate. In such a case, a traveler may prefer to follow another route (say C-F-D) which other commuters may be taking to reach D.

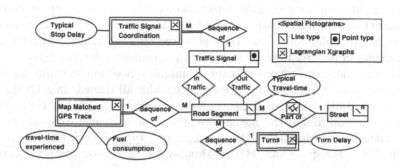

Fig. 4. Conceptual model of a transportation network with spatial pictograms

Figure 4 provides a conceptual model of the transportation network using pictogram enhanced ER diagram [13,14]. Our model primarily contains streets, road segments and traffic signals as entity types. Additionally, we have turns, traffic signal coordination and GPS traces as weak entity types. One may observe that the attributes of these weak entity types form our previously described STN datasets. More detailed conceptual models for transportation networks (containing many more entity types and relations) have been proposed in the literature [15]. We have simplified our model in order to focus on the previously mentioned weak entity types.

Usually entities like road segments, traffic signals and streets are modeled using basic shapes like lines, points and line-strings (see spatial pictograms in Figure 4). These basic shapes are then queried using a logical data implemented through Open Geodata Interchange Standard (OGIS) operators. However, this approach is not suitable for use-cases that involve comparing candidate routes or itineraries (e.g. fastest path queries). As a solution, spatial [10,11] and spatial-temporal [8] network models were developed which implement these concepts through graphs where each edge contains only two entities (a binary relation). However, as described earlier, this approach is not suitable for modeling holistic properties of n-ary relations, although they can represent decomposable properties of n-ary relations. To this end, we propose a novel logical data-model called Lagrangian Xgraphs which is capable of modeling both holistic and decomposable properties.

3 Lagrangian Xgraphs

3.1 Desired Routing-Related Concepts to Be Modeled

STN datasets capture routing-related concepts along two dimensions: (i) frame of reference, (ii) nature of property recorded (see Figure 5).

Frame of Reference: For the first dimension, datasets are assembled with either *Eulerian* or *Lagrangian* reference frame shown upfront. In Eulerian reference frame, the phenomenon is observed through fixed locations in the system [16]. For a transportation network, this view corresponds to a stationary observer sitting on a side of a freeway (loop detectors or traffic observatory). By contrast, Lagrangian frame of reference corresponds to the perspective of an traveler driving along a particular route [16]. Data collected through annotated GPS traces is Lagrangian in nature. Both Eulerian and Lagrangian reference frames can be thought of as means to represent a set of unique space-time coordinates in the transportation network. Generally, we can consider all records in STN datasets as certain attributes associated with these space-time coordinates. For example, a data record containing the measurement 5 mins as travel-time on the road S-A at 9:00am on a Monday (TD roadmaps) of a typical week has the physical location of S-A for space and 9:00am-Monday for time coordinate respectively. Travel-time in TD-roadmaps shows Eulerian frame upfront, whereas in a annotated GPS trace it shows Lagrangian frame upfront.

Nature of Property: Under Eulerian or Lagrangian frame of reference, the property being recorded can be either *decomposable* or *holistic*. A decomposable property when re-constructed for a larger instance (e.g. route) by joining values for smaller instances (at appropriate space-time coordinates) retains its correctness. Distance measured from a GPS trace (Lagrangian frame) or as measured through maps (Eulerian frame) is a decomposable property. Other examples include, travel-time obtained from loop detectors, signal delays (red light duration) at individual traffic signals as set by traffic managers.

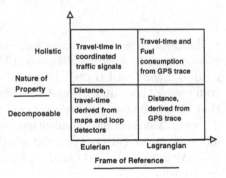

Fig. 5. Taxonomy of concepts

Decomposable properties can be further classified as deterministic or non-deterministic. Properties which can be expressed clearly from a start-point are termed as deterministic. Travel-time as captured in TD roadmaps is deterministic as given a departure-time (in a typical week), TD roadamps will provide a unique travel-time for a road-segment. In contrast, traffic signal delays are non-deterministic unless the absolute start-time of their cycles is known. In other words, given a departure-time on a route, we cannot determine (at least in current datasets) the precise delay to be experienced at a signal.

On the other hand, holistic properties are properties when measured over a large instance cannot be broken down into corresponding values for smaller instances through space-time decomposition. This is due to presence of non-local interactions. Apart from our earlier example with coordinated traffic signals, travel-time (and fuel consumption) experienced by a commuter on a road-segment, as derived from his/her annotated GPS trace, is holistic in nature. Here, the travel-time experienced would depend on his/her initial velocity gained *before* (a non-local interaction) entering the particular road-segment under consideration. Travel-time of the commuter is deterministic as we can exactly measure its value from start of journey. By contrary, travel-time through a series of coordinated traffic signals is non-deterministic.

It is important to note that 'data-collection' reference frame may be different from 'querying' reference frame. For instance, travel-time recorded in TD roadmaps shows Eulerian frame upfront. Whereas, routing queries on the same TD roadmaps (and other STN datasets) would be more meaningful through Lagrangian frame of reference [17]. The interoperability of Eulerian and Lagrangian frame of reference allows for the 'querying' and 'data-collection' reference frames to be different. In other words, data recorded in one frame can be easily queried from (or converted to) another reference frame [16].

3.2   Proposed Logical Model

Given a collection of STN datasets measured over a time horizon $\mathcal{H}$, we formally define a Lagrangian Xgraph $(\mathcal{L}a\mathcal{X})$ as an ordered set of Xnodes $(\mathcal{X}v)$, Xedges $(\mathcal{X}e)$ and a time horizon parameter $\mathcal{H}$, i.e., $\mathcal{L}a\mathcal{X} = (\mathcal{X}v, \mathcal{X}e, \mathcal{H})$.

Xnodes: For any network system under consideration, Xnodes $\mathcal{X}v_i \in \mathcal{X}v$ represent the underlying entities at specific space-time coordinates.

Xedges: are used to express a 'as-traveled' or 'typical-experience-in-travel' relationship among a set of Xnodes. More formally, $\mathcal{X}e^i = \{\mathcal{X}v_s, \mathcal{X}v_1, \ldots, \mathcal{X}v_k, \mathcal{X}v_{d1}, \mathcal{X}v_{d2}, \ldots, \mathcal{X}v_{dj}\}$. Here, the first Xnode $(\mathcal{X}v_s)$ and the last set of Xnodes $(\mathcal{X}v_{d[1\ldots j]})$ correspond to the instance of the first and the last entities participating in the relation and are marked separately for ease.

Taxonomy of Xedges: Xedges as defined above are further categorized according to: (a) spatial relationship between the first $(\mathcal{X}v_s)$ and last set of Xnodes $(\mathcal{X}v_{d[1\ j]})$ and (b) property being modeled is deterministic or non-deterministic. Figure 6 shows the proposed classification. Primarily, we classify an Xedge as: (i) shoot-Xedge, (ii) flower-Xedge, (iii) stem-Xedge or, (iv) bush-Xedge. The first and last Xnodes in both shoot-Xedges and flower-Xedges belong to entities which are spatially immediate neighbors. Thus, they would be used for modeling decomposable properties. In a shoot-Xedge, each entity is present for a single time and thus, can model deterministic properties. Flower-Xedges allow one entity to be

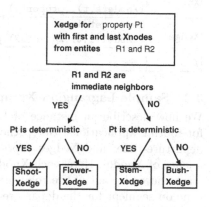

Fig. 6. Taxonomy of Xedges

represented for multiple time coordinates and thus, can be used to model non-deterministic properties (e.g. individual signal delays).

By contrast, both stem-Xedges and bush-Xedges allow the first and last Xnode(s) to be separated physically. This physical separation allows both stem and bush-Xedges to represent holistic properties. Bush-Xedges are useful for non-deterministic properties since they allow one entity to be represented at multiple time coordinates. Stem-Xedges are employed for deterministic properties since each entity is present only for one time coordinate.

Abstract Data Type: Access operators for Lagrangian Xgraphs define the basic logical units of work during information retrieval for queries. Table 1 shows an illustrative set of access operators for Xnodes and Xedges. In the table we use (s,t) to denote the Xnode representing an entity at a particular space-time coordinates.

Access operators for Xnodes retrieve information on Xedges which are incident on a particular Xnode. For example, the operation Xnode.decom_successors (Xnode(s,t), property) retrieves all the Xedges whose first Xnode is Xnode(s,t) and represent a decomposable property. Similarly, get_holistc_successors(Xnode(s,t), property) returns Xedges representing a given holistic property from Xnode(s,t).

Access operators for Xedges require the following parameters for retrieval: (1) the first Xnode (Xnode(s1,t) in Table 1); (2) the last Xnode; (3) the property. Here, the time coordinate of the last Xnode (Xnode(s2) in Table 1) may not always be precisely defined before hand. Based on the information retrieved, we would know the time coordinate of last Xnode(s2). Lastly, we also have an operator Xroute which can successively join Xedges to create a route as would be experienced by a person traveling on that route.

Table 1. Access operators for Lagrangian Xgraph

Category	Decomposable	Holistic
Xnode	Xnode.decom_successors (Xnode(s,t), property)	Xnode.holistc_successors (Xnode(s,t), property)
Xedge	Xedge.get_decom (Xnode(s1,t),Xnode(s2),property)	Xedge.get_telecon (Xnode(s1,t),Xnode(s2),property)
Xroute	Xroute.glue(an Xedge)	

3.3   Sample Lagrangian Xgraph

We now describe an instance of Lagrangian Xgraphs modeling STN datasets for routing applications. Here, Xnodes represent the road segments at multiple departure-times and Xedges express the experience of a traveler among a sequence of Xnodes. Here, each Xnode is associated with information such as: (a) start and end point of the road-segment, (b) departure-time, (c) typical travel-time on segment for the departure-time (from TD roadmaps), (d) lower bound on travel-time, and other information depending on application requirements. Due to space limitation we only illustrate Xedges for travel-time experienced in a sequence of coordinated traffic signals.

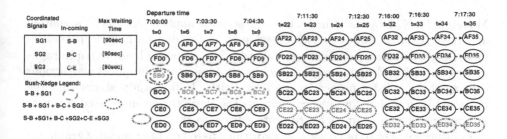

Fig. 7. First and last Xnodes for journey through a series of coordinated signals

Coordinated traffic signals: Consider again our previous example of coordinated signals SG1, SG2 and SG3 in Figure 3. Here, we will represent typical experiences of journeys through these signals starting from S at 7:00:00am. Given that signal delays are non-deterministic and travel-time experienced in a sequence of coordinated traffic signals is holistic, we would use bush-Xedges. Figure 7 illustrates bush-Xedges for some journeys at 30secs temporal granularity. We have bush-Xedges for following journeys: (a) start at S and travel to the beginning of segment B-C (after SG1), (b) start at S and travel to the beginning of segment C-E (after SG2), (c) start at S and travel to the beginning of segment E-D (after SG3).

For case (a), the bush-Xedge would include (SB0) and (BC6, BC7, BC8 and, BC9) as Xnodes for the first ($\mathcal{X}v_s$) and last Xnodes ($\mathcal{X}v_{d[1\ j]}$). Intuitively, this Xedge means that a typical journey starting from S at 7:00am along S-B (SB0 in the Figure) can start traversing road segment B-C at times 7:03:00 (no wait at SG1, BC6 in Figure), 7:03:30 (30secs wait at SG1, BC7 in the Figure), 7:04:00 or 7:04:30 (90secs wait at SG1, BC9 in the Figure). Similarly, in case (b), we would have SB0 and (CE22, CE23, CE24, CE25) as the first and last Xnodes. Internally, this would include the Xnodes (BC6, BC7, BC8 and, BC9) (not shown in Figure to maintain clarity). Other bush-Xedges can be defined in a analogous way. Similarly, there would be other bush-Xedges representing journeys starting at beginning of B-C (after SG1).

Discussion: Other related work for modeling STN data includes literature on conceptual models for spatio-temporal data [18], moving objects [19,20] and hypergraphs [21,22]. Studies focusing on conceptual models alone [18] do not model routing-related concepts such as Lagrangian reference frame. Though, studies done on moving objects represent the Lagrangian history of an object. They are not suitable for modeling TD roadmaps and traffic signal data. Furthermore, Lagrangian Xgraphs differ from both general hypergraphs [22], which represent subsets of nodes without any reference frame and directed hypergraphs [21] which directly connect a set of sources to a set of destinations.

4   Conclusion and Future Work

Modeling STN datasets is important for societal applications such as routing and navigation. It is however challenging to do so due to holistic properties increasingly being captured in these datasets. The proposed Lagrangian Xgraphs addresses this challenge at logical level by expressing the non-local interactions causing these holistic properties more explicitly. Initial study shows that the proposed Lagrangian Xgraphs can express the desired routing-related concepts in a manner which is amenable to routing frameworks.

In future we plan to build routing algorithms based on Lagrangian Xgraphs for diverse routing use-cases and perform extensive evaluation via real datasets. Further, we also plan to engage with transportation domain experts to incorporate more aspects reflecting common practices in traffic engineering and management into the model.

Acknowledgment. This work was supported by: NSF IIS-1320580 and 0940818; USDOD HM1582-08-1-0017 and HM0210-13-1-0005; IDF from UMN. We would also like to extend our thanks to Kim Koffolt for improving the readability of this paper. The content does not necessarily reflect the position or the policy of the government and no official endorsement should be inferred.

References

1. Shekhar, S., Gunturi, V., Evans, M.R., Yang, K.: Spatial big-data challenges intersecting mobility and cloud computing. In: MobiDE, pp. 1–6. ACM (2012)
2. Liu, H., Hu, H.: Smart-signal phase ii: Arterial offset optimization using archived high-resolution traffic signal data. Technical Report CTS 13-19, Intel. Trans. Sys. Inst., Center for Transportation Studies, Univ. of Minnesota (April 2013)
3. Yuan, J., et al.: T-drive: driving directions based on taxi trajectories. In: Proc. of the SIGSPATIAL, pp. 99–108. ACM (2010)
4. Manyika, J., et al.: Big data: The next frontier for innovation, competition and productivity. McKinsey Global Institute (May 2011), http://goo.gl/AA8DS
5. Lovell, J.: Left-hand-turn elimination. NY Times (December 9, 2007)
6. Demiryurek, U., Banaei-Kashani, F., Shahabi, C.: A case for time-dependent shortest path computation in spatial networks. In: Proc. SIGSPATIAL. ACM (2010)
7. Koonce, P., et al.: Traffic signal timing manual. Technical Report FHWA-HOP-08-024, US Dept of Trans. Federal Higway Admin. (June 2008)
8. George, B., Shekhar, S.: Time-aggregated graphs for modelling spatio-temporal networks. J. Semantics of Data XI 191 (2007)
9. Köhler, E., Langkau, K., Skutella, M.: Time-expanded graphs for flow-dependent transit times. In: Möhring, R.H., Raman, R. (eds.) ESA 2002. LNCS, vol. 2461, pp. 599–611. Springer, Heidelberg (2002)
10. Hoel, E.G., Heng, W.-L., Honeycutt, D.: High performance multimodal networks. In: Medeiros, C.B., Egenhofer, M., Bertino, E. (eds.) SSTD 2005. LNCS, vol. 3633, pp. 308–327. Springer, Heidelberg (2005)
11. Güting, R.H.: Graphdb: Modeling and querying graphs in databases. In: Proc. of the 20th International Conference on Very Large Data Bases, pp. 297–308 (1994)

12. Zheng, Y., Zhou, X.E. (eds.): Computing with Spatial Trajectories. Springer (2011)
13. Shashi: Spatial pictogram enhanced conceptual data models and their translation to logical data models. In: Intl. Works. on Integrated Spatial Databases, Digital Inages and GIS, pp. 77–104. Springer, Heidelberg (1999)
14. Bedard, Y.: Visual modeling of spatial databases: Towards spatial PVL and UML. Geoinformatica 53(2) (1999)
15. Shekhar, S., et al.: Data models in geographic information systems. Commun. ACM 40(4) (April 1997)
16. Batchelor, G.: An introduction to fluid dynamics. Cambridge Univ. Press (1973)
17. Gunturi, V.M.V., Nunes, E., Yang, K., Shekhar, S.: A critical-time-point approach to all-start-time lagrangian shortest paths: A summary of results. In: Pfoser, D., Tao, Y., Mouratidis, K., Nascimento, M.A., Mokbel, M., Shekhar, S., Huang, Y. (eds.) SSTD 2011. LNCS, vol. 6849, pp. 74–91. Springer, Heidelberg (2011)
18. Parent, C., et al.: Spatio-temporal conceptual models: Data structures + space + time. In: Proc. of the Intl. Symp. on Adv. in GIS, pp. 26–33. ACM (1999)
19. Tøssebro, E., Nygård, M.: Representing topological relationships for spatiotemporal objects. GeoInformatica 15(4), 633–661 (2011)
20. Fileto, R., Krüger, M., Pelekis, N., Theodoridis, Y., Renso, C.: Baquara: A holistic ontological framework for movement analysis using linked data. In: Ng, W., Storey, V.C., Trujillo, J.C. (eds.) ER 2013. LNCS, vol. 8217, pp. 342–355. Springer, Heidelberg (2013)
21. Gallo, G., Longo, G., Pallottino, S., Nguyen, S.: Directed hypergraphs and applications. Elsevier, Discrete applied mathematics 42(2), 177–201 (1993)
22. Berge, C.: Graphs and Hypergraphs. Elsevier Science Ltd (1985)

Efficient Reverse kNN Query Algorithm on Road Network Distances Using Partitioned Subgraphs

Aye Thida Hlaing, Htoo Htoo, and Yutaka Ohsawa

Graduate School of Science and Engineering, Saitama University

Abstract. Reverse k-nearest neighbor (RkNN) queries in road network distances require long processing time in most conventional algorithms because these require kNN search on every visited node. In this paper, we propose a fast RkNN search algorithm that runs using a simple materialized path view (SMPV). In addition, we adopt the incremental Euclidean restriction (IER) strategy for fast kNN queries. In the SMPV used in our proposed algorithm, distance tables are constructed only inside of an individual partitioned subgraph, therefore the amount of data is drastically reduced in comparison with the conventional materialized path view (MPV). According to our experimental results using real road network data, our proposed method showed 100 times faster in processing time than conventional approaches when POIs are sparsely distributed on the road network.

1 Introduction

Recently, efficient reverse k-nearest neighbor (RkNN) query algorithms have been researched with increased attention. This type of query is required in a wide variety of applications, including facility management, taxi allocation, location-based services, advertisement distribution, and GIS; however, most existing algorithms are based on the Euclidean distance. In contrast, in location-based services (LBS), queries based on road network distances are required. Some literature [1] [2] proposes algorithms applicable to road network distance, however, those require long processing time. Therefore, in this paper, we propose an efficient algorithm to obtain RkNN in road network distances.

When a set of POIs P and a query point q are given, an RkNN query finds the POIs for which q is included in their kNN; i.e.

$$\text{R}k\text{NN}(q) = \{p \in P | d(p,q) \leq d(p, p_k(p))\}$$

where $p_k(p)$ is the k-th NN of p, and $q \in P$ in an usual mono-chromatic RkNN.

A simple approach for the RkNN query is to find kNN for every POI in P in advance. By searching kNN in advance, RkNN of q is easily found to search the entry that q is included in kNNs. The cost of this naive method is bounded by $O(n^2)$ when the number of POI is n. Several algorithms have been proposed to reduce the cost in Euclidean space; however, researches for queries in road network distances have limitedly focused, and these methods require

M. Indulska and S. Purao (Eds.): ER Workshops 2014, LNCS 8823, pp. 212–217, 2014.

long processing time, especially when POIs are sparsely distributed on the road network or when k is large.

In this paper, we propose a fast R*k*NN query algorithm for road network distances using the simple materialized path view (SMPV) data [3]. This algorithm runs on SMPV and refers to the SMPV tables to obtain road network distances for pairs of terminal points. The proposed algorithm is two or three order of magnitude faster in searching R*k*NN than conventional algorithms when POIs are sparely distributed on the road network, and the processing time is stable and independent of the density of the POI.

2   Basic Method for R*k*NN Search

In this section, we describe a basic method for R*k*NN search on road networks presented by Yiu et al., [1], and problem points of the method.

Lemma 1. *Let q be a query point, n be a road network node, and p be a POI which satisfies $d_N(q, n) > d_N(p, n)$. For any POI $p'(\neq p)$ whose shortest path to q passes through n, $d_N(q, p') > d_N(p, p')$. That means p' is not an RNN of q.*

This Lemma is proved in [1]. Here, $d_N(a, b)$ denotes the road network distance between two points on the road network, a and b.

Fig. 1 shows a simple road network. Here, the circles show the nodes on the road network and the squares show POIs. The numbers at edges show costs (e.g., lengths) of edges. In the following, we assume the case that the query point q is on node a.

When we focus on node d, the NN of d is e and that of e is f; hence, a (i.e. the query point q) is not the NN of e. When we substitute n for d, p for e, and p' for f in Lemma 1, we obtain the relations $d_N(a, d) > d_N(e, d)$ and $d_N(a, f) > d_N(e, f)$. This characteristic can be used to prune the search area on the road network.

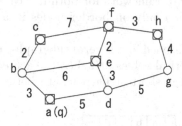

Fig. 1. Example of a road network

Yiu et al. [1] proposed the Eager algorithm and Lazy algorithm based on Lemma 1 and a branch-and-bound approach. In the Lazy algorithm, it is necessary to investigate wide area of nodes, and the processing time is apt to be longer than Eager algorithm. Hence, the rest of the paper focuses on the Eager algorithm to compare with our proposed method.

In the Eager algorithm, road network nodes are visited from q to surrounding nodes in a method similar to that of in Dijkstra's algorithm. When a query point q is on node a in Fig. 1, node b is visited first because it is the nearest node from q. Then, at most number of k NNs of b is searched within the distance, $D = d_N(b, a)$. This function is called RANGENN (n, q, D). In the previous query, c is found as the NN of b.

Next step is to verify that each found POI by RANGENN (n, q, D) is truly RkNN of q or not. This can be done by checking q is included in kNN of the POI (in this case, c). This function is called VERIFY (c, k, q) and returns true when q is included in the kNN of c; otherwise, it returns false. For the simplicity, we assume k is 1 in the rest of this section. In this example, the result of VERIFY $(c, 1, q)$ is true; therefore, c is determined as the RNN of q.

The next visited node is d (the second nearest node from q); thus, RANGENN $(d, q, 5)$ is issued and e is obtained as the NN of d. To check whether e is an RNN of q, VERIFY $(e, 1, q)$ is issued; however, false is obtained in this case. Hence, the edges beyond d are safely pruned. At this time, there is no search path left; therefore, the search processing is terminated.

In Yiu's Eager algorithm, Dijkstra's algorithm is applied for VERIFY (p, k, q) and RANGENN (n, q, D). When the density of POIs is high and the search area is small, this algorithm is completed quickly. In contrast, when the density is low or k is large, the processing time becomes very long because the search area becomes large. The problems of the Eager algorithm are (1) the RANGENN and VERIFY functions require long processing time and (2) RANGENN is invoked for every visited road network node, thus times of repeatedly invoked becomes numerous times.

3   RkNN Query Algorithm on Partitioned Subgraph

To address problems in the Eager algorithm, we present the following two proposals: (1) to adapt an IER framework for both RANGENN and VERIFY and (2) to run the Eager algorithm only on border nodes in a simplified materialized path view (SMPV) [3].

A road network is partitioned into several subgraphs. Fig. 2 shows an example of a subgraph. The numerical values attached to each edge show the weights of the edges. Fig. 3 shows the shortest path length between every pair of border

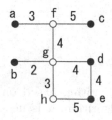

	a	b	c	d	e
a	0	9	8	11	15
b	9	0	11	6	10
c	8	11	0	13	17
d	11	6	13	0	4
e	15	10	17	4	0

	a	b	c	d	e
f	3	6	5	8	12
g	7	2	9	4	8
h	10	5	12	7	5

Fig. 2. A subgraph   **Fig. 3.** BBDT   **Fig. 4.** IBDT

nodes. The lengths are calculated by traveling inside the subgraph; therefore, these values are not always global shortest path lengths. If there is no connected path between a pair of nodes inside the subgraph, infinity is assigned. We refer to this table as a border-to-border distance table (BBDT).

Fig. 4 shows the inner-to-border node distance table (IBDT), which shows the distance from an inner node to a border node. This table is used to retrieve the distance from an inner node as the starting point to a border node.

When the points are included in a same cell, the distance between two points cannot be determined by these tables. In such case, the distance is calculated by A* algorithm. When two points are included in a cell, the distance between two points is apt to small. Therefore, the A* algorithm runs fast in such case.

The most time-consuming step in the Eager algorithm by Yiu et al. is to perform RANGENN at every expanded node. In the proposed algorithm, RANGENN is invoked only on the border nodes of the subgraphs to alleviate this problem.

When a query point q is given, the cell in the SMPV structure that q belongs to is determined and the POIs belonging to the subgraph are searched. Let this POI set be P. Each element in P is checked whether q is an RkNN of the border node or not. This procedure is the same as VERIFY (p, k, q) in the Eager algorithm; VERIFY (p, k, q) searches kNNs of each $p \in P$, and then if q is included in the kNN set, q is decided as a RkNN of p. Though, this check requires a wide-area search and is not exclusive to only a subgraph, it can be efficiently performed using SMPV by IER.

Fig. 5 shows the example of a subgraph in which q is a query point and p is a POI included in the subgraph. For the simplicity, one NN search is considered in this case. By searching for the NN of p, q is obtained as the result. Therefore, p is an RNN of q. Consequently, p is added to the result set.

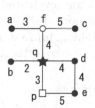
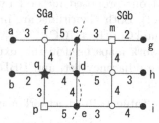

Fig. 5. Processing in a cell where q is included   **Fig. 6.** Border node expansion

Then, the search area is enlarged to the neighboring subgraph. For each border node b_i, the distance from q to b_i is obtained by referencing the IBDT of the subgraph. Thereafter, a record is composed and inserted into priority queue PQ; the record is composed as

$$< dist, n, prev, cid >$$

where *dist* is the road network distance between q and the respective border node, *prev* is the previous node on the shortest path from q to n, and *cid* is the cell ID to which n belongs. The first record inserted into PQ is as follows.

$$< d_N(q, b_i), b_i, q, cid >$$

For example, for node a of Fig. 5, the record $< 7, a, q, cid >$ is inserted into PQ.

Next, the RkNN search starts. When a record is dequeued from PQ, the search propagates to the neighboring subgraphs. In Fig. 6, the subgraph SGa is the cell in which query point q is included and SGb is a neighboring subgraph. When a record r is dequeued from PQ and $r.n$ is the border node d, POIs in SGb are searched. In this subgraph, a POI m is included. The kNNs of m are searched, and if q is included in the kNN set, m is added to the result set. Otherwise, m is ignored. This subgraph can be visited several times from different border nodes. Therefore, SGb is marked as visited subgraph to avoid duplicate searches.

In the next step, RANGENN is invoked from the border node b_i to find candidate POIs. If the result set is not empty, VERIFY is invoked to check whether each POI is truly an RkNN of q. If the result of VERIFY is true, the POI is added to the result set. If the size of the result set returned from RANGENN is smaller than k, there can exist other RkNNs on the path through this node $v.n$, and still cannot prune the search. Therefore, new records from b_i to the other border nodes in the subgraph are created and inserted into PQ.

4   Experimental Results

We evaluated our proposed method by comparing with the Eager algorithm presented in [1]. Both algorithms are implemented in Java and evaluated on a PC with an Intel Core i7-4770 CPU (3.4GHz) and 32 GB memory. Table 1 shows the road network maps used in this experiment. In this table, *Adj.List* shows the size of the adjacency list, and BBDT and IBDT are the size of the tables described in [3].

Table 1. Road network maps used in the experiments

map name	# of nodes	# of edges	area size	Adj. List	BBDT	IBDT
MapA	16,284	24,914	168 km^2	1.5MB	1.1MB	4.1MB
MapB	109,373	81,233	284 km^2	6.8MB	4.5MB	17.4MB

We generated several POI sets on the road network nodes by pseudo-random sequences, changing density D. For example, $D = 0.01$ indicates that a POI exists on every 100 links.

Fig. 7 shows the processing time when the density of POI (D) varies. Fig. 7(a) and 7(b) show the results for MapA and MapB respectively. In the figures, the horizontal axis shows D and the vertical axis shows the processing time in seconds. k was fixed to 5. The processing time of the Eager algorithm increases sharply when the density is low. On the other hand, the proposed algorithm

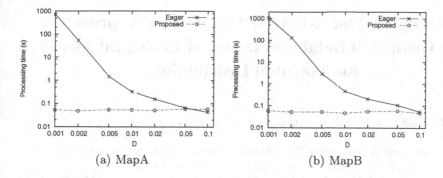

Fig. 7. Processing time for varying D value

remains low even in that case. When the density of POI is high, the Eager algorithm performed well because the size of the search area decreases with the increase in the density. The proposed algorithm shows stable characteristics independent of the probability.

5 Conclusion

In this paper, we proposed an RkNN query algorithm using the simple distance materialization approach suitable for LBS.

In the proposed method, the RANGENN procedure is performed only on border nodes. This limitation drastically reduces the total times of invoking RANGENN . In addition, IER adaptation to the RANGENN and VERIFY procedures contributes to reduce the overall processing time. Consequently, the proposed method performs RkNN search well on a road network significantly, especially when the distribution of the POIs is sparse or k is large.

Acknowledgments. The present study was partially supported by the Japanese Ministry of Education, Science, Sports and Culture (Grant-in-Aid Scientific Research (C) 24500107).

References

1. Yiu, M.L., Papadias, D., Mamoulis, N., Tao, Y.: Reverse nearest neighbor in large graphs. IEEE Transaction on Knowledge and Data Engineering 18(4), 1–14 (2006)
2. Cheema, M.A., Zhang, W., Lin, X., Zhang, Y., Li, X.: Continuous reverse k nearest neighbors queries in Euclidean space and in spatial networks. VLDB Journal 21, 69–95 (2012)
3. Hlaing, A.T., Htoo, H., Ohsawa, Y., Sonehara, N., Sakauchi, M.: Shortest path finder with light materialized path view for location based services. In: Wang, J., Xiong, H., Ishikawa, Y., Xu, J., Zhou, J. (eds.) WAIM 2013. LNCS, vol. 7923, pp. 229–234. Springer, Heidelberg (2013)

Using the Model-Driven Architecture Approach for Geospatial Databases Design of Ecological Niches and Potential Distributions

Gerardo José Zárate[1], Jugurta Lisboa-Filho[1], and Carlos Frankl Sperber[2]

[1] Departamento de Informática, Universidade Federal de Viçosa, Viçosa, MG, Brazil
gerardo.zarate.m@gmail.com, jugurta@ufv.br
[2] Departamento de Biologia Geral, Universidade Federal de Viçosa, Viçosa, MG, Brazil
sperber@ufv.br

Abstract. An ecological niche is defined by an array of biotic and abiotic requirements that allow organisms to survive and reproduce in a geographic area. Environmental data from a region can be used to predict the potential distribution of a species in a different region. Potential geographic distributions are useful in predicting the extent of invasive species, preventing economic and ecological damages. Many formalisms for modeling geospatial information have been developed over the years. The most notable benefit of these formalisms is their focus on a high-level abstraction of reality, leaving unnecessary details behind. This paper presents the stages of the Model-Driven Architecture approach for the design of database, with geospatial capabilities, for niches and potential geographic distributions. We take advantage of the UML GeoProfile formalism for geospatial databases, which is capable of modeling geographic and environmental data.

Keywords: Geospatial database modeling, MDA, Potential Geographic Distributions, Ecological Niche.

1 Introduction

Joseph Grinnell introduced the concept of ecological niche in 1917 [1]. Grinnell defined a species' ecological niche as its habitat requirements, i.e., the environmental variables that allow the survival and reproduction of a species [2]. George Hutchinson proposed a similar definition; he defined the ecological niche as an n-dimensional hypervolume determined by species requirements [3]. Dimensions of the hypervolume can be biotic interactions or abiotic conditions in which a species can survive and reproduce [4]. Nevertheless, the number of dimensions in a hypervolume is potentially infinite. Dimensions such as temperature and soil characteristics can be easy to collect, while other variables like the diet of an organism are, in some cases, not accessible. Additionally, certain dimensions can be irrelevant to determine the ecological niche [4, 5]. Notice that, an environmental niche is constructed only by abiotic conditions [6].

M. Indulska and S. Purao (Eds.): ER Workshops 2014, LNCS 8823, pp. 218–227, 2014.

On the other hand, potential geographic distributions refer to regions that have the appropriate set of environmental conditions for a species to live and reproduce. New approaches to calculate potential geographic distributions are mathematical algorithms that use environment data and occurrences of a species to make predictions [7]. Inputs for these algorithms are a set of occurrence data in an occupied area (GIS vector points, i.e., longitude–latitude coordinates), and environmental variables for both occupied and evaluated area (GIS coverage layers). Outputs, on the other hand, are either regions with suitable conditions in which species are present (but there is no evidence of this), or regions with suitable conditions where organisms are not present (both of them GIS coverage layers) [7, 8]. One of the most adopted algorithms to predict geographic distributions is the Genetic Algorithm for Rule-Set Production (GARP) [9]. The GARP algorithm uses occurrence and environmental data from the occupied area to produce a set of rules that define the dimensions of the species' ecological niche, i.e., the n-dimensional hypervolume. Next, the set of rules is projected onto the environmental variables of areas of interest (evaluated areas) to produce the potential geographic distribution of those areas [7, 8].

The ecological niche and potential geographic distributions are fields of study in Ecology that have been of major research interest in the last years [10]. Still, few researches take into consideration the construction of dedicated databases for niches and potential distributions [5]. Modern Database Management Systems (DBMS) have capabilities to store geospatial information including geographic objects and environmental phenomena. Nevertheless, before creating a database, it is convenient to model the required entities and relationships in a conceptual model that can later be transformed into a database schema. The aim of this paper is to describe the stages of a Model-Driven Architecture (MDA) for the design of geospatial database of environmental niches and potential geographic distributions. The rest of this paper is structured as follows: Section 2 overviews related studies. Section 3 offers a summary of geospatial databases formalisms. Section 4 presents the MDA stages for designing geospatial database for environmental niches and potential geographic distributions. Additionally, Section 4 briefly describes an implementation of the data schema in a DBMS. Finally, Section 5 provides some final considerations.

2   Related Work

Previous works have attempted to provide means to model niche and geographic distribution information [5, 7, 11, 12]. This section summarizes prior efforts found in the literature. Although it does not involve conceptual modeling of geospatial databases, the work in [7] emphasizes the importance of databases in GIS applications stressing their storage capabilities. Moreover, it provides a six-step guide for using ecological niche data to predict potential geographic distributions using the GARP algorithm. Finally, it describes how environmental variables are handled in GIS applications, highlighting the selection of the appropriate GIS data types.

The authors of [11] developed a tool that helps ecologists to design databases. The focus of their research is to simplify the design process for ecologists with no experience in database theory. They provided previously created templates that help overcome common errors while identifying relationships between entities. Models created in their tool can later be exported to a DBMS like MySQL. The major drawback is the lack of support for geospatial capabilities. Entities cannot be labeled as points, lines, polygons or fields; contrary to conceptual models like PVL or UML GeoProfile. Even if not directly related to ecological niches or potential distributions, the work in [11] is a valuable effort because it recognizes the importance of databases for ecologists.

The work in [12] presents guidelines for representing ecological niches in a conceptual model. According to the authors, traditional ER and Object-oriented models fail to represent the granularity of an ecological niche. They propose an ontological engineering approach to model ecological data. Despite the fact that there is no reference to ecological niche theory, the focus of their study is modeling the relationships between humans and their environment. Again, there is no support for geospatial capabilities.

Finally, the author of [5] provides an overview of the principal concepts related to ecological niches and presents an Object-Role Modeling (ORM) diagram of the ecological niche. The proposed ORM diagram includes entities such as species, fundamental niche, realized niche, hypervolumes and conditions. The work in [5] is an attempt to model ecological niches based on the concepts first introduced by Grinnell and Hutchinson from a database conceptual standpoint. Similar to [11] and [12], it does not offer geospatial capabilities entities of the schema.

3   Formalisms for Modeling Geospatial Databases

One of the major elements of a GIS is the database in which information is stored [7]. Modern DBMS, such as Oracle and PostgreSQL (with the PostGIS expansion), offer capabilities to manage geospatial data and provide additional benefits like security, redundancy or user control access. Database designing has three basic stages: conceptual, logical and physical [13]. The conceptual stage produces conceptual data schemas that represent a high-level abstraction of entities and the relationships between them. The major benefit of using conceptual models is their independence of implementation details. Bédard and Paquette were the first to create a conceptual model (formalism) dedicated to model geospatial databases. They proposed a geospatial extension of the Entity-Relationship formalism [14]. Since then, various formalisms for geospatial databases have been proposed or expanded. The works in [15] and [16] offer a summary of the most important formalism.

We decided to use the UML GeoProfile formalism for its capabilities to model both geographic (geographic objects) and environmental data (continuous fields). Fig. 1 shows the pictograms used in UML GeoProfile to represent geospatial phenomena. Additionally, UML GeoProfile supports international standards like the Geographic Information of the International Organization for Standardization (ISO) and the Open Geospatial Consortium (OGC). Moreover, UML GeoProfile adopts a Model-Driven Architecture (MDA) approach to develop databases schemas in separate stages [17]. Further information on UML GeoProfile, the ISO standards and MDA can be found in [17,18, 19].

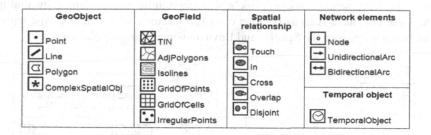

Fig. 1. Pictograms used in UML GeoProfile

4   Modeling Environmental Niches and Potential Distributions Using MDA

The MDA approach is a design technique that emphasizes the use of models in the software development process [19]. In MDA, software is first modeled in a Computation Independent Model (CIM); CIM models are later transformed to a Platform Independent Model (PIM). The third stage of the process is the Platform Specific Model (PSM), which is later converted to implementation code. Benefits of using the MDA approach include reduction in system development time and increase in the abstraction levels in which designers can work [17]. In this section, we describe the three MDA stages of data schema for Environmental Niches and Potential Geographic Distributions. We also present an implementation of the data schema in PostgreSQL and PostGIS.

4.1   CIM Level

The work in [20] proposed a conceptual data schema for environmental niches and potential geographic distributions using UML GeoProfile (schema proposed by the same authors of this paper). As mentioned in [17], conceptual data schemas created using UML GeoProfile are equivalent to CIM levels in MDA. The three packages in Fig. 2 represent the CIM level. Here, we summarize the explanation of the conceptual data schema proposed in [20]. Notice that in the CIM the focus is which (not how) geospatial features will be implemented; this is accomplished using the GeoProfile stereotypes [19].

The "Environmental Niche" package covers the classes and associations of an environmental niche. The Occupied Area class is related to various instances of the Occurrence class, which represents organisms of a species. Notice the topological relationship between the two classes marked with the Inside stereotype, i.e., and organism must be inside an area. In some cases an organism can be spotted in two or more areas in a different time, this is solved by assigning the Temporal Object stereo-type to the Occurrence class. The niche's hypervolume is represented by multiple instances of the Niche Axis association class (dimension), which cannot exist without the association between the Species and Environmental Variable classes.

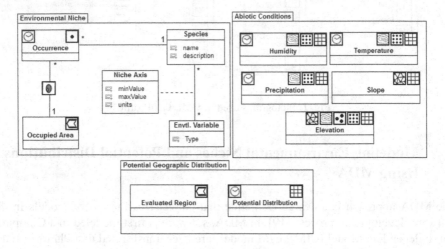

Fig. 2. MDA CIM level for Environmental Niches and Potential Distributions

The Abiotic Conditions package provides an example of the possible representation of the environmental data (coverage layers) that serves to construct a hypervolume. Notice the presence of the Temporal Object stereotype in some classes, meaning that certain abiotic conditions can vary over time, e.g., the monthly average temperature of a region. Finally, the Potential Geographic Distribution package shows the classes related to distribution projections. The Evaluated Region class represents the boundaries of the area in which the distribution is projected. The Evaluated Region and Potential Distribution classes are not associated because they belong to different views [20].

4.2   PIM Level

The next level of abstraction is the PIM level, which is still independent of any implementation technologies. The transformation process from CIM to PIM consists in the inclusion of identifiers that differentiates the instances of a class and the use of standard ISO types [17, 18]. UML GeoProfile stereotypes change to ISO data types, e.g., the Polygon stereotype is transformed to a GM_Surface attribute. Fig. 3 shows the PIM abstraction level of the proposed schema. Notice that classes with multiple representations in the CIM level now contain a geometry attribute for each representation. For a complete reference of ISO standard types and their UML GeoProfile equivalent refer to [17] and [18].

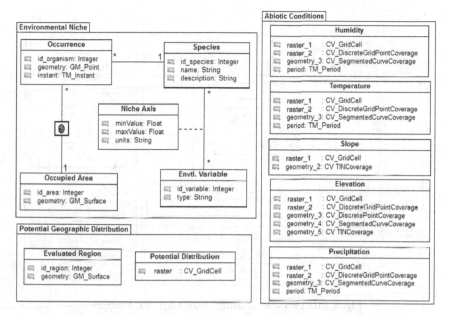

Fig. 3. MDA PIM level for Environmental Niches and Potential Distributions

4.3   PSM Level

PSM is the lowest MDA level and it is the one closer to the real implementation. In this case, for a PSM model it is necessary to use a technology capable of storing geospatial phenomena. Some wide known technologies are Oracle Spatial and the PostGIS geographic extension of PostgreSQL, both able to store and manage geospatial data. Fig. 4 exhibits the PSM level of the proposed schema using PostgreSQL and PostGIS. The PSM level presents implementation details like the use of Primary and Foreign Keys. Notice the use of PostgreSQL specific basic data type such as INTEGER or CHARACTER VARYING. ISO standard geospatial types are transformed to PostGIS implementations. The GM_Surface and GM_Point ISO types are transformed to the generic GEOMETRY type. For a complete reference of PostGIS, including guidelines to implement on how to use the GEOMETRY and RASTER and types, refer to the documentation available at http://postgis.net/documentation.

4.4   Implementation

We implemented the PSM level in PostgreSQL; tables in the schema can be created and used in a straightforward manner, i.e., using basic SQL statements. Code 1 shows the create statements to define the Occupied Area and Occurrence tables. Notice that additional fields were included in the table for Occupied Area to store a name and a description.

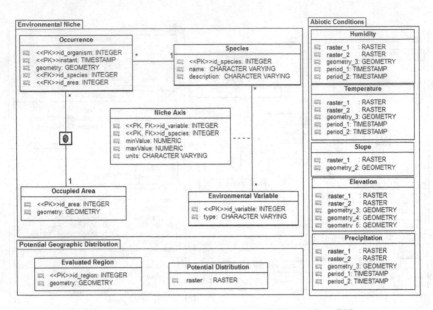

Fig. 4. MDA PSM level using PostgreSQL and PostGIS

```
CREATE TABLE public.occurrence(
  id_organism INTEGER NOT NULL,
  id_species INTEGER,
  id_area INTEGER,
  instant TIMESTAMP WITHOUT TIME ZONE,
  geom GEOMETRY(POINT),
  CONSTRAINT occurrence_pkey
      PRIMARY KEY (id_ organism, instant),
  CONSTRAINT occurrence_id_area_fkey FOREIGN KEY
      (id_area) REFERENCES public.area (id_area),
  CONSTRAINT occurrence_id_species_fkey FOREIGN KEY
      (id_species) REFERENCES public.species (id_species)
);
CREATE TABLE public.occupied_area(
  id_area INTEGER NOT NULL,
  name CHARACTER VARYING,
  description CHARACTER VARYING,
  geom GEOMETRY(MULTIPOLYGON),
  CONSTRAINT area_pkey PRIMARY KEY (id_area)
);
```

Code 1. SQL code to create table for Occurrence and Occupied Area

Tables with geospatial information require the usage of special tools to insert information in them. These tools include shp2pgsql, which is capable of transforming Shapefiles to the GEOMETRY type, and raster2pgsql to convert raster images to the RASTER type. Both shp2pgsql and raster2pgsql can be used via command in a computer console, or as a part of an external application in conjunction with a programming language. Fig. 5 shows an example of the usage of the tool shp2pgsql via command in a computer console and Code 2 displays how to use raster2pgsql in combination with the programming language PHP.

```
C:\>shp2pgsql -W LATIN1 shpFileArea.shp public.shptemp | psql -U postgres
-d nichedb -h localhost -p 5432_
```

Fig. 5. Usage of shp2pgsql via command

Columns of the RASTER type need constraints to maintain the integrity of the information in regards of spatial references system and block size, among others. Given that many types of raster images can be stored in a single table, it is fundamental to drop and add the constraints while storing information in the table. The PostGIS functions DropRasterConstraints and AddRasterConstraints serve to remove and add the constraints before and after the storage of the raster image.

```
$sql="SELECT DropRasterConstraints ('rTable','rast')";
$result=pg_query($testdb, $sql);
$ret=shell_exec("raster2pgsql -s 4236 img.asc -F -a public.rTable > file.sql");
$sql=file_get_contents("file.sql");
$result=pg_query($testdb, $sql);
$sql="SELECT AddRasterConstraints ('rTable','rast')";
$result=pg_query($testdb, $sql);
```

Code 2. Storing a raster image in PostGIS using PHP (partial implementation)

Additionally, the topological relationship between the Occupied Area and Occurrence classes is covered with the PostGIS function ST_Contains(GEOMETRY A, GEOMETRY B), which checks if GEOMETRY A contains GEOMETRY B. Further documentation on how to use shp2pgsql, raster2pgsql and other PostGIS tools and function is available at http://postgis.net/documentation.

As a demonstration of the functionality of the data schema, we projected the potential distribution of a Brazilian tree species using the software openModeller [21]. Occurrences were obtained from GBIF.org (www.gbif.org) and environmental layers from WorldClim (http://www.worldclim. org/bioclim). Fig. 6 displays two projections made using the algorithms GARP (a) and Climate Space Model (b) [22]. Occurrence data, environmental layers and both potential distributions were later stored in the proposed schema created in PostgreSQL using PostGIS tools. Notice that all occurrences were checked with ST_Contains on the occupied area in the storage process.

5   Concluding Remarks

This paper presented the development of a data schema of ecological niches and potential geographic distributions of species using the MDA approach. The CIM level was previously modeled using the UML GeoProfile [20]. The CIM model was transformed into a PIM model that follows the ISO standards described in [18], and then the PIM was translated into a PSM model linked to PostgreSQL and PostGIS specifications of geospatial data. For the transformation processes, we followed the guidelines presented in [17] and the ISO standards in [18]. We also presented an implementation of the data schema using PostgreSQL and PostGIS. We showed how to use PostGIS tools to store data in geospatial tables. The data schema can be implemented in other DBMSs with geospatial capabilities like Oracle; this might require further research of Oracle geospatial types and tools. The data schema presented can help ecologists to start their projects related topics involving niche-based potential geographical distributions. Future work includes the development of a tool that simplifies the usage of PostGIS tools to those who are not familiar with computer consoles and programming codes.

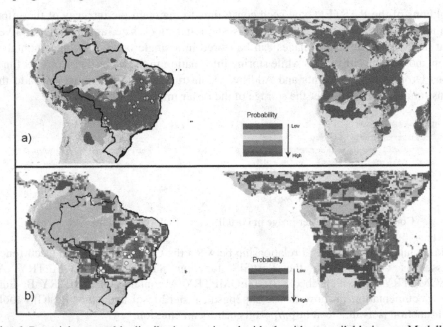

Fig. 6. Potential geographic distributions projected with algorithms available in openModeller. Algorithms used: GARP (a) and Climate Space Model (b). Marked points represent the occurrences used. The same occurrences were used in the two algorithms.

Acknowledgment. This project is partially financed by CAPES, OAS, CNPq and FAPEMIG.

References

1. Chase, J.M., Leibold, M.A.: Ecological niches: linking classical and contemporary approaches. University of Chicago Press (2003)
2. Grinnell, J.: The niche-relationships of the California Thrasher. The Auk 34(4), 427–433 (1917)
3. Hutchinson, G.: Concluding remarks. Cold Spring Harbour Symposium on Quantitative Biology 22, 415–427 (1957)
4. Polechová, J., Storch, D.: Ecological niche. Encyclopedia of Ecology 2, 1088–1097 (2008)

5. Keet, C.M.: Representations of the ecological niche. In: WSPI 2006: Contributions to the Third International Workshop on Philosophy and Informatics, pp. 75–88 (2006)
6. Soberón, J.: Grinnellian and Eltonian niches and geographic distributions of species. Ecology letters 10(12), 1115–1123 (2007)
7. Blackburn, J.K.: Integrating geographic information systems and ecological niche modeling into disease ecology: a case study of Bacillus anthracis in the United States and Mexico. In: Emerging and Endemic Pathogens, pp. 59–88. Springer, Netherlands (2010)
8. Roura-Pascual, N., Suarez, A.V., Gómez, C., Pons, P., Touyama, Y., Wild, A.L., Peterson, A.T.: Geographical potential of Argentine ants (Linepithema humile Mayr) in the face of global climate change. Proceedings of the Royal Society of London. Series B: Biological Sciences 271(1557), 2527–2535 (2004)
9. Stockwell, D.: The GARP modelling system: problems and solutions to automated spatial prediction. Int. Journal of Geographical Information Science 13(2), 143–158 (1999)
10. Peterson, A.T., Soberon, J.: Species distribution modeling and ecological niche modeling: getting the concepts right. Natureza & Conservação 10(2), 102–107 (2012)
11. McIntosh, A., Cushing, J.B., Nadkarni, N.M., Zeman, L.: Database design for ecologists: Composing core entities with observations. Ecological informatics 2(3), 224–236 (2007)
12. Semwayo, T.D.T., Berman, S.: Representing ecological niches in a conceptual model. In: Wang, S., et al. (eds.) ER Workshops 2004. LNCS, vol. 3289, pp. 31–42. Springer, Heidelberg (2004)
13. Lisboa-Filho, J., Sampaio, G.B., Nalon, F.R., Borges, K.A.D.V.: A uml profile for conceptual modeling in gis domain. In: Proceedings of the International Workshop on Domain Engineering at CAiSE, Hammamet, Tunisia, pp. 18–31 (2010)
14. Bédard, Y., Paquette, F.: Extending entity/relationship formalism for spatial information systems. AUTO-CARTO 9, 818 827 (1998)
15. Pinet, F.: Entity-relationship and object-oriented formalisms for modeling spatial environmental data. Environmental Modelling & Software 33, 80–91 (2012)
16. Miralles, A., Pinet, F., Bédard, Y.: Describing spatio-temporal phenomena for environmental system development: An overview of today's needs and solutions. International Journal of Agricultural and Environmental Information Systems (IJAEIS) 1(2), 68–84 (2010)
17. Lisboa-Filho, J., Nalon, F.R., Peixoto, D.A., Sampaio, G.B., Borges, K.A.: Domain and Model Driven Geographic Database Design. In: Domain Engineering, pp. 375–399. Springer, Heidelberg (2013)
18. Brodeur, J., Badard, T.: Modeling with iso 191xx standards. In: Encyclopedia of GIS, pp. 705–716. Springer, US (2008)
19. Mellor, S.J., Scott, K., Uhl, A., Weise, D.: Model-driven architecture. In: Bruel, J.-M., Bellahsène, Z. (eds.) OOIS 2002. LNCS, vol. 2426, p. 290. Springer, Heidelberg (2002)
20. Zárate, G.J., Lisboa-Filho, J., Sperber, C.F.: Conceptual modeling for environmental niches and potential geographic distributions using UML GeoProfile. In: International Conference on Advanced Geographic Information Systems, Applications, and Services, Barcelona, pp. 31–37 (2014)
21. De Souza, M.E., De Giovanni, R., Ferreira, M., Sutton, T., Brewer, P., Scachetti, R., Lange, D., Perez, V.: openModeller: a generic approach to species' potential distribution modelling. GeoInformatic 15, 111–135 (2011)
22. Robertson, M.P., Caithness, N., Villet, M.H.: A PCA-based modelling technique for predicting environmental suitability for organisms from presence records. Diversity and Distributions 7, 15–27 (2001)

OMT-G Designer: A Web Tool for Modeling Geographic Databases in OMT-G

Luís Eduardo Oliveira Lizardo and Clodoveu Augusto Davis Jr.

Computer Science Department – Universidade Federal de Minas Gerais
Belo Horizonte, Brazil
{lizardo,clodoveu}@dcc.ufmg.br

Abstract. Data modeling tools are useful in software development and in database design. Some advanced modeling tools available in the market go beyond the data modeling process and allow the generation of source code or DDL scripts for RDBMSs based on the modeled schema. This work presents OMT-G Designer, a web tool for modeling geographic databases using OMT-G, an object-oriented data model for geographic applications. The tool provides various consistency checks on the integrity of the schema, and includes a function that maps OMT-G geographic conceptual schemas into physical schemas, including the necessary spatial integrity constraints. The tool was developed using free software and aims to increase the practical and academic uses of OMT-G, by providing an open and platform-independent modeling resource.

Keywords: OMT-G, Geographic Information Systems, Geographic Software Design, Spatial Database Modeling.

1 Introduction

Most data modeling activities nowadays use data modeling tools, aiming at software development and database design. Such tools reduce the development effort with a variety of features that provide the generation of source code and scripts for some database management systems (DBMS). There are many modeling tools available in the market, directed towards various data models, with a variety of features and prices, including commercial and free software.

However, although some commercial modeling tools can be adapted for geographic database design, we notice that certain aspects are lacking, such as the treatment of spatial integrity constraints. Even though spatial database extensions have functions that would allow the implementation of the necessary constraints, manually programming constraint verification code with them is often tedious and repetitive, due to the lack of a specific support for such constraints in the DDL. Furthermore, semantic aspects can make it hard to automatically decide on the more adequate constraint implementation style, based on resources such as checks, assertions, and triggers. We covered this subject in previous work, first defining the means for extracting spatial integrity constraints from a geographic schema [1], and later creating a framework to generate code for

M. Indulska and S. Purao (Eds.): ER Workshops 2014, LNCS 8823, pp. 228–233, 2014.

that purpose [2], always based on OMT-G, an object-oriented UML-based data model for geographic applications [3]. Now, we merged these results into a Web-based modeling tool, so that more people can freely experiment and learn the subtle aspects of spatial data modeling, while generating useful code. This paper introduces OMT-G Designer[1], a Web-based free software tool developed for modeling geographic databases in OMT-G. It allows users to create geographic conceptual schemas and to map them to Oracle Spatial SQL schemas.

The remainder of this paper is structured as follows. Section 2 describes related work. Section 3 describes OMT-G Designer. Section 4 presents a brief example of use. Finally, Section 5 presents our conclusions and lists future work.

2   Background and Related Work

The special nature of spatial data modeling has been noticed many years ago [4]. In the late 1990s and early 2000s, much work was directed towards creating and adapting existing models in order to accommodate the needs of geographic database design. We mention, for instance, Modul-R [5], GISER [6], GeoOOA [7], and GMOD [8], all of which are proposals of spatial data models.

A decade later, the most active initiatives are UML-based. UML-GeoFrame [9], for instance, proposes using the extensiveness features of UML in order to accommodate spatial representations, geographic and topological relationships, and other modeling primitives. CASE tools have been proposed for UML-GeoFrame [9], based on previously existing free software, but leaving the mapping towards a physical implementation in charge of the modeler.

OMT-G (*Object Modeling Technique for Geographic Applications*) is an object oriented data model for the design of geographic applications and geographic database systems. It provides primitives for modeling the geometric shape and location of geographic objects, supporting spatial and topological relationships, "whole-part" structures, networks, and multiple representations of objects and spatial relationships. Due to space limitations, we will not present OMT-G's notation in detail here. For more information on the model, and for more detailed examples, see OMT-G Designer's site[1]. OMT-G considers eleven representation alternatives for geographic data: six for geo-objects (*point, line, polygon, network node, uni-* and *bi-directional network arc*), and five for geo-fields (*isolines, tesselation, triangulation, sampling* and *planar subdivision*). Relationships include *simple association, spatial relationship, spatial aggregation, arc-node network relationship, generalization/specialization,* and *conceptual generalization,* which allows modeling multiple representations for geographic objects. OMT-G is also UML-based [3], but opted for a modified notation and established a basis for the extraction of spatial integrity constraints [1].

Based on OMT-G's definitions, we created methods to automate the mapping from a geographic conceptual schema to a physical schema, materialized as a script of table-creation statements and the associated spatial integrity constraints, implemented as checks, assertions and triggers. OMTG2SQL is a

---

[1] http://aqui.io/omtg

conceptual-physical mapping procedure introduced by Hora et al. [2]. Currently it supports mapping an OMT-G schema formatted in XML and generates a data definition language (DDL) file, a dynamic controls file and a static controls file, currently following Oracle Spatial's syntax. The DDL file contains statements for creating tables, primary and foreign keys, spatial indexes and geometric constraints for the spatial classes. The static and dynamic control files implement spatial and non-spatial integrity constraints. The dynamic control file contains triggers that check the consistency of topological relationships, generalizations and user-defined spatial integrity constraints. The static control file contains functions to check the integrity of network relationships, spatial aggregations and geo-field classes. Code is generated from templates, which can be adapted and modified to accommodate other spatial DBMSs, considering that the spatial function sets in current OGC-compliant DBMSs are quite similar. Due to space limitations, we will not present the code templates in more detail (see [2]).

OMT-G Designer, detailed in the next section, is the first tool that fully supports the OMT-G model up to the mapping to a spatial DBMS, by means of a Web-based modeling interface that implements consistency checks on the schema as it is created, and by incorporating OMTG2SQL.

3   OMT-G Designer

OMT-G Designer's interface has three main parts: the *tool palette*, the *menu* and the *canvas* (Figure 1). The menu allows users to export their project to SQL, to import from and export to XML and also to print the schema. In the canvas, users develop their schema, adding classes and relationships chosen from the tool palette. Relationships, selected at the tool palette, can be inserted by clicking over the source class and dragging a line to the target class. Class and relationship attributes can be edited by double-clicking on the primitive.

Following OMT-G semantics, some constraints apply to class diagrams, and our tool blocks invalid design constructions, as follows. **Aggregations:** Spatial aggregation cannot be used if conventional classes are involved; **Associations:** Simple associations can occur between classes of any representation type, but spatial associations only occur between georeferenced classes; **Conceptual generalizations:** The superclass must be non-geographic; **Generalizations:** Superclass and subclasses must be of the same representation type; **Networks:** Network relationships are only allowed between node and arc classes, or without nodes in a recursive relationship on the class that represents network segments.

When a project is exported to SQL, an XML file containing an encoding of the schema is generated. This file is sent to the server to be validated and processed by OMTG2SQL, which maps the user's conceptual schema to Oracle Spatial. The resulting code files are zipped and sent to the client for downloading. The same occurs when the schema is exported as an XML file for future importing. When a schema is imported from a XML file, the file is first sent to the server to be validated, and is later rendered by the browser on the client's side.

4   Example

Figure 1 shows a schema fragment for a bus transportation network (nodes at bus stops and unidirectional arcs corresponding to route segments) that serves a set of school districts. A conventional class holds the attributes for the bus line. The schema embeds spatial integrity constraints for (1) the network relationship (each route segment must be related to two bus stops), (2) a "contains" relationship (bus stops cannot exist outside of a school district), and (3) the geometry of route segments and school districts (lines and polygons must be simple, i.e., with no self-intersections).

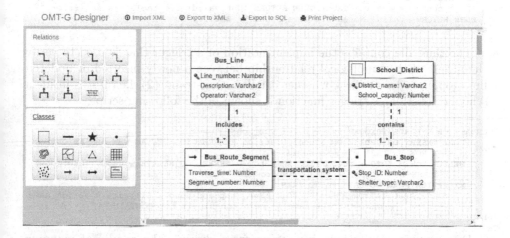

Fig. 1. OMT-G Designer's interface with a sample schema fragment

After exporting the schema to SQL, three files are supplied. The first one contains DDL statements for creating the necessary tables and indexes, along with commands to update Oracle's spatial metadata table, as shown next:

```
-- Create table Bus_Stop
CREATE TABLE Bus_Stop (
  Stop_ID NUMBER(null,1), Shelter_type VARCHAR2(5), geom MDSYS.SDO_GEOMETRY,
  CONSTRAINT pk_Bus_Stop PRIMARY KEY (Stop_ID));
-- Insert the geom column of Bus_Stop into metadata table USER_SDO_GEOM_METADATA
INSERT INTO USER_SDO_GEOM_METADATA (TABLE_NAME, COLUMN_NAME, DIMINFO, SRID)
  VALUES ('Bus_Stop', 'geom', MDSYS.SDO_DIM_ARRAY(
    MDSYS.SDO_DIM_ELEMENT('X', -180.000000000, 180.000000000, 0.005),
    MDSYS.SDO_DIM_ELEMENT('Y', -90.000000000, 90.000000000, 0.005)), '29100');
-- Create the spatial index on geom column of Bus_Stop
CREATE INDEX SIDX_Bus_Stop ON Bus_Stop(geom)
  INDEXTYPE IS MDSYS.SPATIAL_INDEX PARAMETERS('SDO_INDX_DIMS=2,LAYER_GTYPE=POINT');
```

The second file contains PL/SQL code to verify constraint (1), i.e., the consistency of the network relationship. A function (val_network_Bus) checks connections at the endpoints of arcs, which must coincide with nodes. If the result is not exactly one node, an error message is generated and stored in a special table for future reference, as follows:

```
-- Validate the network between the Bus_Route_Segment and Bus_Stop
CREATE OR REPLACE FUNCTION val_network_Bus_Bus BEGIN
  FOR reg IN (SELECT rowid, geom FROM Bus_Route_Segment) LOOP
    p_geom_initial_vertex := get_point(reg.geom);
    p_geom_final_vertex := get_point(reg.geom, SDO_UTIL.GETNUMVERTICES(reg.geom));
    BEGIN SELECT rowid INTO p_rowid_initial_vertex FROM Bus_Stop WHERE MDSYS.
        SDO_EQUAL(geom, p_geom_initial_vertex) = 'TRUE'; END;
    BEGIN SELECT rowid INTO p_rowid_final_vertex FROM Bus_Stop WHERE MDSYS.
        SDO_EQUAL(geom, p_geom_final_vertex) = 'TRUE'; END;
  END LOOP;
  FOR reg IN (SELECT rowid FROM Bus_Stop) LOOP
    BEGIN SELECT a.rowid INTO p_rowid_point FROM Bus_Route_Segment a, Bus_Stop n
        WHERE (MDSYS.SDO_EQUAL(n.geom, get_point(a.geom)) = 'TRUE' OR MDSYS.
        SDO_EQUAL(n.geom, get_point(a.geom, SDO_UTIL.GETNUMVERTICES(a.geom))) = '
        TRUE') AND reg.rowid = n.rowid AND rownum <= 1; END;
  END LOOP;
  IF (p_contains_error = TRUE) THEN RETURN 'Not valid! See table Spatial_Error.';
  ELSE RETURN 'Valid! No errors were found.'; END IF;
END;
```

The third file contains the implementation of a trigger that is used to verify the nature of the topological relationship between a newly inserted or updated bus stop, in order to check whether it follows constraint (2), i.e., if it is inside a school district. This trigger function is shown in the following script:

```
-- Validate the topological relationship between Bus_Stop and School_District
CREATE OR REPLACE TRIGGER val_top_rel_Bus_Sch
  BEFORE INSERT OR UPDATE ON School_District REFERENCING NEW AS NEW OLD AS OLD
  FOR EACH ROW DECLARE w_rowid rowid; BEGIN
    SELECT rowid INTO w_rowid FROM Bus_Stop w WHERE SDO_RELATE(w.geom, :NEW.geom,
        'MASK=contains') = 'TRUE' AND rownum <= 1;
    EXCEPTION WHEN NO_DATA_FOUND THEN
        RAISE_APPLICATION_ERROR(-20001, 'Bus_Stop and School_District District_name
        = '||:NEW.District_name||' relationship is not CONTAINS');
END;
```

Due to space limitations, we refrain from showing the results of mapping more complex integrity constraints, such as the validity of spatial aggregations and the consistency of planar subdivision classes. Ideally, such constraints could be implemented using direct SQL statements, but current spatial DBMSs only count on geometric and topological functions, and lack statement variations to implement the constraints directly at the DDL statement.

5   Conclusion

We have presented OMT-G Designer, a Web-based modeling tool for the OMT-G model. Our intention is to disseminate the use of OMT-G further and to support current users of the model in the task of implementing their schemas in a spatial DBMS. OMT-G Designer is able to prevent some modeling mistakes that commonly occur when a user is learning to model, and provides support for the implementation of spatial integrity constraints in the physical schema, usually a tiresome and demanding task. As a result, OMT-G Designer is currently intended as an educational tool, with which modelers can learn more about the intricacies of spatial data modeling.

A number of features remain to be implemented as future work. First, as previously mentioned, OMT-G Designer can be expanded to support mapping to PostGIS 2.0 and other physical schemas, in addition to Oracle Spatial. Second, OMT-G defines two more diagrams as part of the modeling process, the transformation and presentation diagrams [3]. These diagrams respectively allow for the design of transformation processes between representations, and for the specification of visualization parameters for the spatial data. Including such diagrams would allow the tool to automatically generate code for representation-transformation triggers, and to create visualization parameter files for popular GIS software, such as QGIS project files, or for Web publishing using application servers such as GeoServer. Furthermore, we intend to enhance the tool with code to support online collaborative work, thereby allowing multiple users to work on the same project at the same time.

Acknowledgments. The second author acknowledges CNPq (308678/2012-5) and FAPEMIG (CEX-PPM-00518/13), Brazilian agencies in charge of fostering research and development, for supporting this work.

References

1. Davis Jr., C.A., Borges, K.A.V., Laender, A.H.F.: Deriving spatial integrity constraints from geographic application schemas. In: Rivero, L.C., Doorn, J.H., Ferraggine, V.E. (eds.) Encyclopedia of Database Technologies and Applications., pp. 176–183. IGI Global (2005)
2. Hora, A.C., Davis Jr., C.A., Moro, M.M.: Generating XML/GML schemas from geographic conceptual schemas. In: Proceedings of the IV Alberto Mendelzon Workshop on Foundations of Data Management (AMW) (2010)
3. Borges, K.A.V., Davis Jr., C.A., Laender, A.H.F.: OMT-G: an object-oriented data model for geographic applications. GeoInformatica 5(3), 221–260 (2001)
4. Friis-Christensen, A., Tryfona, N., Jensen, C.S.: Requirements and research issues in geographic data modeling. In: Proceedings of the 9th ACM International Symposium on Advances in Geographic Information Systems, GIS 2001, pp. 2–8. ACM, New York (2001)
5. Bédard, Y., Caron, C., Maamar, Z., Moulin, B., Vallière, D.: Adapting data models for the design of spatio-temporal databases. Computers, Environment and Urban Systems 20(1), 19–41 (1996)
6. Shekhar, S., Coyle, M., Goyal, B., Liu, D.R., Sarkar, S.: Data models in geographic information systems. Communications of the ACM 40(4), 103–111 (1997)
7. Kosters, G., Pagel, B.U., Six, H.W.: GIS-application development with GeoOOA. International Journal of Geographical Information Science 11(4), 307–335 (1997)
8. Oliveira, J.L., Pires, F., Medeiros, C.B.: An environment for modeling and design of geographic applications. GeoInformatica 1(1), 29–58 (1997)
9. Lisboa Filho, J., de Freitas Sodré, V., Daltio, J., Rodrigues Júnior, M.F., Vilela, V.: A CASE Tool for Geographic Database Design Supporting Analysis Patterns. In: Wang, S., Tanaka, K., Zhou, S., Ling, T.-W., Guan, J., Yang, D.-q., Grandi, F., Mangina, E.E., Song, I.-Y., Mayr, H.C., et al. (eds.) ER Workshops 2004. LNCS, vol. 3289, pp. 43–54. Springer, Heidelberg (2004)

A Model of Aggregate Operations for Data Analytics over Spatiotemporal Objects

Logan Maughan, Mark McKenney, and Zachary Benchley

Department of Computer Science, Southern Illinois University Edwardsville,
Edwardsville, IL USA 62026
{lmaugha,marmcke,zbenchl}@siue.edu

Abstract. In this paper, we identify a conceptual framework to explore notions of spatiotemporal aggregate operations over moving objects, and use this framework to discover novel aggregate operators. Specifically, we provide constructs to discover temporal and spatial coverage of a query window that may itself be moving, and identify quantitative properties of entropy relating to the motion of objects.

1 Introduction

Spatiotemporal datasets represent a valuable resource for business, industry, government, and scientific entities. Specifically, spatiotemporal data in the form of moving objects encode useful information in the form of spatial location, extent, and temporal variance that is independent of traditional thematic data that may be associated with the objects. For example, a moving region (i.e., a region that changes shape and/or position over time) might represent the aggregate position of a cluster of vehicles traveling along a highway. Despite the sensor data providing information, the spatial and temporal characteristics of the moving region provide information as well; information such as the relative speed of the region, the ability of the group to maintain proximity (forcing a smaller region), and the change of the shape of the group over time (presumably impacted by traffic). Furthermore, if many such moving regions exist in a database, aggregates of this information may be computed to gain large-scale data analysis. Aggregate operations could identify areas of greatest movement activity, areas forcing the most regions to become thin and stretched, or areas forcing the greatest or least amount of dispersion of vehicles in a group.

In this paper, we i) identify novel constructs to quantify spatiotemporal interactions of moving objects with query windows that provide insights into the duration and rate of qualitative change of such interactions, ii) we present a novel conceptual framework for discovering and classifying new types of queries over moving objects, and iii) we identify novel aggregate operations based on the discovered queries for use in large scale analytics of moving objects.

2 Related Work

Aggregate operations on spatiotemporal databases have been studied via two main approaches. The first approach uses spatial operations on spatial data to

M. Indulska and S. Purao (Eds.): ER Workshops 2014, LNCS 8823, pp. 234–240, 2014.
© Springer International Publishing Switzerland 2014

generate traditional numeric data, which is then aggregated [3]. In this paper, we are concerned about spatiotemporal aggregates that operate on purely spatial and temporal properties of moving objects, and not the related attribute values. The other approach has focused on discovering aggregate information of objects in query windows, such as the maximum or minimum count of spatiotemporal objects in a query window over time [9,2,5]. The operations presented in this paper differ from those in that we are aggregating spatial and temporal values derived from the intersection of moving objects and irregular query windows.

Much work has been done in the literature to identify and define spatiotemporal data types and operations to form spatiotemporal algebras [1,7,8]. The traditional spatial types consist of complex points, lines, and regions. A complex point can contain multiple individual points, a complex line can contain multiple lines that may branch, and a complex region is defined as a closed area that may contain multiple faces and holes: for example, Italy can be represented as a region with its mainland and islands each forming a face in the region, and the area where Vatican City lies forming a hole that does not belong to Italy [6]. A *moving object* is defined as a mapping from time to instances of a traditional spatial type, resulting in a type that changes position and shape over time, but that defines a valid spatial type at every time instant. Moving types form 3-dimensional structures when plotted in two spatial dimensions and a temporal dimension; for example, a moving region forms a volume in 3-dimensional space in which space forms the first two dimensions, and time the third.

3   Definitions

For the purposes of this paper, a *spatial object* is a point, line, or region and the type of all valid spatial objects is denoted as the set $[S]$ [6]; a *moving object* is a moving point, moving line, or moving region as defined in [1] and the set $[M]$ represents the type of all valid moving objects. A *query window* is an instance of a moving object such that the type of query windows is equivalent to $[M]$. The type of time is $[T] = \mathbb{R}$. We are concerned with interpreting the interaction of a query window and a set of moving objects in order to compute aggregate operations relating to the spatial and temporal properties of moving objects.

The intersection of a moving object and a query object defines a *motion window*. For example, Figure 1a depicts a moving region with its motion indicated by the arrow, and a 1-dimensional query window that the moving region crosses as it progresses through time. Figure 1b shows a 3-dimensional representation of the moving region and the query window, with space as the first two dimensions and time as the third dimension, as they exist over a time interval. The motion window, the intersection of the moving region and the query window, is shown as the vertical oval contained in the query window.

The function $extract : [M] \times [T] \to [S]$ takes the spatial object at a given time instant from a moving object. Let m be a moving object that interacts with a query window q for a time interval from t_0 to t_1, and let w be the motion window defined by the intersection of m and q. For $t_i, t_j | t_0 \leq t_i <$

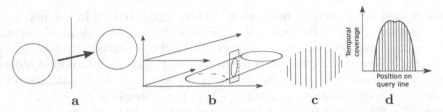

Fig. 1. Visualizations of a moving region, a query window, and their interactions

$t_j \leq t_1$ and $a = extract(w, t_i)$ and $b = extract(w, t_j)$, the symmetric difference $a - b$ indicates the portion of the query window in the time interval (t_i, t_j) in which m was involved in a topological transition with q; in other words, the moving object made a qualitative change with respect to its topology at the query window over that time interval. For example, the boundary of the motion window in Figure 1b depicts the points in space and time when the boundary of the moving region transitioned from being disjoint with the query window to being in contact with the motion window. The area inside the motion window depicts the points in space and time when the interior of the moving region is in contact with the query window. We denote the concept of the transition of the topological relationship between a moving object and a query window *topological transition entropy (TTE)*. The rate of TTE that occurs over a time interval, the *topological transition entropy rate (TTER)* is a quantifiable measure of the rate of topological transition of a moving object over a query window. A value for a TTER is implicitly represented in a motion window. Details on computing measures of TTER are discussed in the following sections.

4   Conceptual Framework

The example used in Section 3 to introduce the notion of TTER utilized a moving region and query window defined as a moving line that was static in terms of space over a time interval (i.e., the moving line did not actually move in the spatial dimensions across the interval). Because the query window is defined as a moving line, it can move through space over time; thus, we have two possible query scenarios that may affect the notion of the TTER across a query line: a query window that is spatially static or spatially dynamic. In general, we can manipulate concepts of space and time to identify four combinations of the space/time states (the states being *static* and *dynamic*) that a query window of any dimension can conform to. In Section 5, we explore the implications of each of the four space/time state combinations in terms of the semantic meaning of query windows that fit each category, the implications in terms of TTER computations, and the meaning of queries for each category.

5   Implications for Queries

Static Space and Static Time (SS): The static space/static time combination for a query window describes a situation in which an n-dimensional query window is fixed in both space time. This corresponds to traditional window queries in which a user may ask "return the portions of all moving regions in a database that intersect with query window q at time t". Aggregate operations available in this situation involve finding the area in the query window that is covered by the highest or lowest number of objects, as defined in [4], among others.

Static Space and Dynamic Time (SD): Static space/dynamic time (SD) queries occur when a query window is held constant in space, but allowed to exist across a time interval; the example discussed in Section 3 and illustrated in Figure 1 corresponds to this type of query. This type of query is useful, for example, to a user who wishes to discover the area along a line segment which is covered for the longest time by a moving region. The query line is spatially static, but is projected through time for the duration of a user-defined interval. Figure 1 depicts an example scenario in which a region moves over time across a query line. The interaction of the query line and the object may be computed by sampling the object at the query line at discrete time intervals, or by computing the motion window induced by the interaction of the object and the query line.

The motion window induced by a query object and a query line encodes two useful pieces of information: i) the duration of coverage of the query window by the moving object, and ii) the TTE of the moving object as the query window progresses in time. The duration of coverage across the query line is computed by recording the height of the motion window in the temporal dimension. Coverage duration is most intuitively represented as a graph, such as Figure 1d for the motion geometry in Figure 1b, which we denote the *coverage duration graph*.

The TTER for the motion window in Figure 1b is most intuitively described from a discritized point of view. Consider the sampled interaction of a moving region and query window in Figure 1c: the TTER between each successive sampled interaction of the moving object and query window in Figure 1b is computed as the difference in the length of adjacent samples in Figure 1c. In essence, the amount of topological transition of the moving object across the query line is embodied in the difference of lengths, in this case, of adjacent sampled lines of the motion window. From a continuous point of view, the transitional entropy rate at any instant is computed from a motion geometry by summing the absolute value of the slope of the boundary of the motion geometry in the vertical direction wherever it intersects a specified time instant. In the general case, the motion window may be a 3D line, 3D surface, or volume depending on the dimensionality of the input moving object and query window. Thus, the general form of the computation of TTER at a particular time instant t for a motion window is the sum of the absolute values of the partial derivative in the z direction of the function describing the boundary of the motion geometry at all points at which the boundary of the motion geometry is defined at $z = t$.

For the SD case, two types of operations are implied for a query window coupled with a single object: i) the duration of the interaction of the moving object and query window defined as the height in the z direction at all points of the resulting motion window, and ii) the TTER of the object in the motion window defined as the 1st order derivative in the z direction of all points on

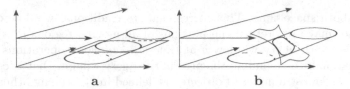

Fig. 2. Examples of a DS and DD query window

the boundary of the motion window. Clearly, the TTER can be aggregated for a single motion window to find the average TTER, the area of max TTER, or the area of minimum TTER. In the case of applying these operations to sets of moving regions, aggregate operations are available that are currently not possible in systems: the area representing the max/min/avg amount of temporal coverage of a set of moving objects over a query window, and the area representing the max/min/avg amount of TTER for a set of moving objects over a query window. To compute the aggregate operations, the motion windows computed from each object are projected out of time into a map of regions such that each region represents a constant time coverage or TTER, depending on the query type. The procedure in [4] is then used to compute the appropriate aggregate operation.

Dynamic Space and Static Time (DS): The dynamic space/static time (DS) combination of a query window is a rather non-intuitive concept. Essentially, a query window is allowed to exist at multiple spatial locations at a single instant in time. One can conceptualize the query as a SD query in which the roles of the moving object and the query window are reversed. Figure 2a illustrates a situation in which a query window defined by a line segment that is projected through space creates a motion window with a moving region. Again, the moving object can be a moving point, line or region, and the query window can be defined as a point, line, or region projected through space. The types of queries available in this construction are similar to the queries available in the DS construction, except that the motion window in the DS construction includes a temporal component, while the query windows in the SD construction represent spatial components. Thus, instead of time coverage and TTER, the DS construction provides concepts of space coverage and spatial transition entropy rate (STER). Essentially, the query types, and associated aggregates are constructed in the same manner, but are taken in a spatial direction. Because time is one-dimensional, time coverage and TTER are computed only in the vertical direction. The corresponding concepts of space coverage and STER can be taken in any spatial direction. The concept of space coverage as defined as time coverage in a spatial dimension, is not new; however, the concept of STER is novel. The STER in a spatial dimension provides a quantitative value describing the irregularity of a moving object's boundary at a specific time instant. For example, a region whose boundary is star shaped, or that has numerous concavities will have a higher STER value than a square.

Dynamic Space and Dynamic Time (DD): The dynamic space/dynamic time (DD) combination of a query window and a moving object describes the case in which the query window is essentially allowed to be a moving object, that is, it is allowed to change over both space and time. For example, a query window might represent a cold front that moves over time, and query objects may be areas of pollution that are moving due to wind, thus the user is interested in discovering the areas of greatest movement in the pollution regions as they interact with the cold front. Because the DD construction allows a query window to move over time, the concepts of temporal coverage and TTER once again apply. Figure 2b depicts a moving region, a query window defined by a moving line, and the motion window induced by the scene. The coverage duration of the region by the query window at any point p in space is defined as the length of the intersection of a vertical line extending in the temporal dimension at point p and the motion window. Furthermore, the temporal coverage can be taken along the surface of the motion window to more closely align with the SD construct. Similarly, spatial coverage can be computed using a spatial dimension.

Similar to temporal coverage, two options exists for computing the TTER. A user can compute the TTER in the z direction for each time instant along the boundary of the motion window, resulting in a TTER representing only the changes along vertical movement. More interesting is the case when the TTER is taken along a direction parallel to the motion window; such a computation provides entropy values along the query window. Finally, because change occurs in the spatial dimension in the DD case, STER values may be computed as well.

6 Conclusion

We introduced the concepts of coverage duration, TTER and STER, and systematically explored their interpretations by manipulating the spatial and temporal components of query windows. The result are new operations and aggregates that are not possible given existing query constructs in spatiotemporal databases.

References

1. Güting, R.H., Böhlen, M.H., Erwig, M., Jensen, C.S., Lorentzos, N.A., Schneider, M., Vazirgiannis, M.: A Foundation for Representing and Querying Moving Objects. ACM Trans. Database Syst. 25(1), 1–42 (2000)
2. Lazaridis, I., Mehrotra, S.: Progressive approximate aggregate queries with a multi-resolution tree structure. SIGMOD Rec. 30(2), 401–412 (2001)
3. Lopez, I., Snodgrass, R., Moon, B.: Spatiotemporal aggregate computation: a survey. IEEE Transactions on Knowledge and Data Engineering 17(2), 271–286 (2005)
4. McKenney, M., Olsen, B.: Algorithms for fundamental spatial aggregate operations over regions. In: Proceedings of the ACM SIGSPATIAL BigSpatial, pp. 55–64 (2013)
5. Papadias, D., Kalnis, P., Zhang, J., Tao, Y.: Efficient olap operations in spatial data warehouses. In: Proceedings of SSTD (2001)
6. Schneider, M., Behr, T.: Topological relationships between complex spatial objects. ACM Trans. Database Syst. 31(1), 39–81 (2006)
7. Wolfson, O., Sistla, P., Xu, B., Xu, J., Chamberlain, S.: Domino: Databases for moving objects tracking. SIGMOD Rec. 28(2), 547–549 (1999)

240   L. Maughan, M. McKenney, and Z. Benchley

8. Worboys, M.F.: A unified model for spatial and temporal information. The Computer Journal 37(1), 26–34 (1994)
9. Zhang, D., Tsotras, V.: Improving min/max aggregation over spatial objects. In: Proceedings of ACM GIS (2001)

Preface to WISM 2014

The invited paper by Suarez and Jimenez-Guarin presents SPEAk, a high-level architecture and its implementation as a Semantic Web application that integrates government information with online news. SPEAk aims to better assist citizens in making informed political decisions based on both government and non-government sources. The core of the architecture is a named entity recognition component that associated entities recognized in news text to entities from a knowledge base. The proposed approach is positively evaluated using news articles, and a knowledge base using open government data and freebase data.

The first paper by Pinto and Parreiras presents a literature survey on the use of Semantic Web technologies in enterprises, i.e., on Linked Enterprise Data. The authors observe that these technologies are mainly used for integrating internal data sources only. The survey concludes on the need to investigate the benefits of interlinking internal and external enterprise data in the future.

The second paper by Vandic et al. proposes a framework for populating a product ontology with tabular product data from Web shops. Having the product information formalized in this manner allows one to produce better comparison and recommendation applications. Several lexical and syntactic matching techniques are used for mapping properties and instantiating values. The proposed framework is positively evaluated using consumer electronics products from three Web shops.

The third paper by Cao et al. formalizes service behavior as an ontology-annotated service flow net. Besides the ontological extensions the proposed approach adds implicit choice and loop constructs to regular flow nets, further increasing their expressivity. Using model transformations on previously specified service behavior one can automatically check the service adaptability (i.e., interface compatibility for two Web services).

The fourth and last paper by Becha and Sellami defines a consumer-centric non-functional properties-based Web service selection approach. The proposed solution has three steps: filtering for removing services that do not obey hard non-functional properties, matching for finding functionally-equivalent services, and ranking for sorting services based on matching soft non-functional properties. Due to the filtering step, the proposed approach is faster than a classical one for selecting Web services that satisfy user-defined functional and non-functional requirements.

We do hope that the exciting WIS modeling topics listed above invite the reader to have a closer look at the workshop proceedings. Last, we would also like to thank all the authors, reviewers, participants, and ER 2014 workshop chair for their input and support of the workshop.

October 2014

Flavius Frasincar
Geert-Jan Houben
Philippe Thiran
Workshop Co-Chairs
WISM 2014

Natural Language Processing for Linking Online News and Open Government Data

Daniel Sarmiento Suárez and Claudia Jiménez-Guarín

Systems and Computing Engineering Department
School of Engineering
Universidad de los Andes
Bogotá, Colombia
{d.sarmiento85,cjimenez}@uniandes.edu.co

Abstract. The value in the vast amount of linked data and open data produced during the last decade is widely recognized and being exploited by different initiatives. However, a remaining challenge is to integrate government information with semi-structured data in sources relevant to citizens, who have become skeptical of official versions and more interested in information associated with their own interests and values. We present a system that integrates and provides uniform access to government data linked to news portals, via an automated named entity linking process, and information provided by a parliament monitoring organization. We develop a prototype to show how this system can be used to develop semantic web applications that assist citizens in making informed political decisions using data linked to their interests and sources not affiliated with the government. This enables them to contrast the official information and find political figures associated to their own personal interests.

1 Introduction

The value in the vast amount of linked data and open government data produced during the last decade is being exploited by different initiatives [1]. One of the remaining challenges is to provide integrated information to citizens that, as a consequence of the network society we live today, are more responsible for the production and management of their own political identities [2]. This makes it important for governments to provide information linked to the topics the citizens care about as new generations are not satisfied with only the official version of events and are interested in information that is attached to their interests and values [2].

This work aims to use linked data technology as a means to integrate and provide uniform access [3]to Open Government Data (OGD) that reside in different data sets and other information sources like news portals and information provided by a Parliament Monitoring Organization (PMO). Its main objective is to propose a system to deliver relevant, accessible, and linked information to citizens about high-profile public figures, and to collect and integrate information from OGD and public data sources to create a Knowledge Base to assist researchers, and electors in general, in making informed political decisions.

M. Indulska and S. Purao (Eds.): ER Workshops 2014, LNCS 8823, pp. 243–252, 2014.

The main contribution of this paper is the high level architecture and implementation of a semantic web application to integrate and infer new information from the extracted semantic data collected from live online news portals, a PMO organization, and the Freebase data dump[1]. The online news data sources selected provide unstructured documents containing natural language that are automatically processed to extract semantic information and detect and link named entities considering their relationship to the Colombian congress.

The high level architecture and description of the proposed solution, named SPEAk for Linking State Public Data for Enlightenment about Political Actors, are presented in the next section. Section 3 presents a more detailed description of the individual components and the design decisions guiding the implementation presented in section 4. The results are analyzed in section 5. The two remain sections present related work (section 6) and the final section shows the conclusions and presents ideas for future work.

2   Proposed Solution: SPEAk

SPEAk automatically collects and links information from different sources such as online news portals, data stored in relational databases, and linked data repositories.

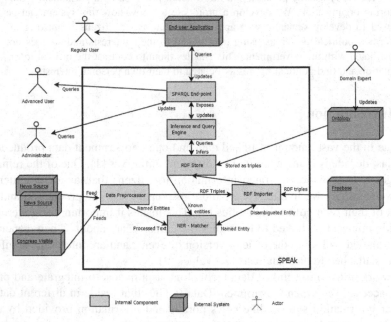

Fig. 1. SPEAk context diagram

---

[1] https://developers.google.com/freebase/data

The main processes SPEAk must perform are: discovering and gathering the data, pre-processing the collected data to extract relevant information and to detect references to named entities, which are ultimately linked to other entities in the SPEAk knowledge base, and finally storing the data using RDF standards in such a way that it can be linked to other semantic data sources and consumed by third-party applications.

The proposed system follows the semantic web application architecture and components proposed by Allemang and Hendler [4].

SPEAk main components, illustrated in **Fig. 1**, are the data preprocessor that interacts with the components needed to gather data from the different information sources, the RDF store, along with the query engine and inference model, the RDF importer, which provides the parser and serializer components used to import data to the RDF store. The SPARQL endpoint interacts with end user applications and also provides an interface for an advanced user to query the RDF store using the SPARQL Query Language [5]. The NER component is not part of the general architecture in [4], and is added to the proposed solution to recognize named entities in natural language text sources and link them to information stored in the RDF store.

3   Design

This section presents the proposed solution design guided by the processes and architecture described in the previous section. The design tries to keep the number of interfaces provided by each component low and use standard protocols and file formats to communicate and exchange information between two components.

We introduce the RDF Store, RDF importer, and SPARQL components first since all other components, directly or indirectly, interact with them. The components used in the process of recollecting and processing the news and PMO data sources are introduced afterwards.

The **RDF store component** stores RDF triples and provides the Update and Query interfaces used by the SPARQL component to expose two services with the same name to external applications using the SPARQL protocol. The **RDF importer** is designed to load triples stored in RDF files to the data store. The **Freebase component** is responsible for preprocessing and loading the Freebase Data Dump. It is designed as a separate component because it is tightly coupled to the Freebase data format and data dump contents. The sole responsibility of this component is to extract the triples of interest in the Freebase RDF dump and import them to the RDF store.

Like the Freebase component, the **PMO component** imports data from an external source, a parliamentary monitoring organization (PMO). The data provided by the PMO Congreso Visible[2], is stored in a relational database. This component is responsible for extracting the information from the relational database and converting it into an RDF graph.   Notice that this component is not responsible for linking the information to the information stored in SPEAk's knowledge base. The integration process is

---

[2] http://www.congresovisible.org/

performed using the relationship between the different information sources expressed in the ontology.

The **News module** corresponds to the main contribution of this work. The news sources come from independent publishers of news available in the Web. The news articles are represented as HTML documents, which must be transformed to RDF representation in order to be semantically processed and linked.

It includes the components to gather news from online news sources. It also parses the collected web documents to extract semantic data, such as RDFa[3] tags and construct a structured object, links the named entities in the news text, and stores the news article and contained entities in the Knowledge Base. The data flow diagram in **Fig. 2** shows the different intermediate data representation and process that transform a news article from a semi-structured Web document into an RDF graph.

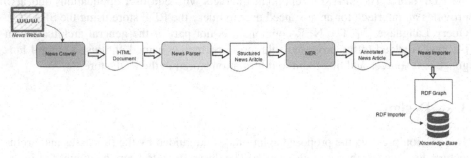

Fig. 2. Data flow diagram for a news article

— The **news crawler component** is responsible for the discovery and collection of web documents in the news sources. After the news articles are crawled, this component provides a structured representation of the collected web document using a parser class for each news source that includes any semantic information in the form of RDFa tags.

— The **NER component** returns the entities recognized in the text. The detected entities are then linked to the entities in the knowledge base. If a named entity cannot be linked to an entity, it is assigned a new URI and its appearance in the news source and entity name are stored as RDF triples in the RDF Store. After the news articles crawled are available as structured objects and the entities contained in the news article are linked to the KB, the News Importer component represents this information as RDF triples and uses the RDF Importer component to insert the triples in the RDF store.

3.1   Ontology

The SPEAk ontology is used to fulfill the objective of integrating and inferring new information from the data inside the knowledge base. The knowledge-engineering methodology proposed in [6]is used to create the ontology. Some well-known ontologies were used. For instance, properties from the Dublin Core vocabulary were used

---

3   http://www.w3.org/TR/rdfa-core/

to describe parliamentary documents and news articles, Friend of a Friend (FOAF) to describe members of the parliament and named entities, Facebook's Open Graph Protocol to describe news articles, and GeoNames to describe the cities and regions related to the parliament and its members. The ontology also contains classes related to the congress domain such as members of the congress and bills of law.

4   Implementation

To implement the design presented in the previous section, the components of the prosed architecture and the ontology are implemented. We present the implementation of the different modules and components of the architecture. The ontology is implemented using version 4.3 of the desktop edition of the Protégé ontology editor[4] and exported as an RDF/XML file.

- **RDF Module**: The RDF store and SPARQL components are implemented using the Jena Fuseki server. The RDF importer is implemented as a Python[5] module using the rdflib library[6] to access the SPARQL end-point.
- **Freebase component**: The functionality provided by this component could have been assigned to the RDF importer module responsibilities, but in order to keep the RDF component loosely coupled to the data sources, it is assigned to a component for this data source. The Freebase component extracts a subset of the Freebase RDF data dump, containing all the triples in the government domain and triples that reference subjects in the government domain, and imports it to the RDF store.
- **News Module**: This news module includes a crawler to collect news articles, the NER module to detect and link named entities and a News Importer that converts the news article to a RDF graph.
  - **News Crawler**. This component uses the Scrapy crawling framework[7]. For each news source (i.e. semana.com and elespectador.com) a subclass of the Scrapy's Crawl Spider class is implemented. This spider class inherits most of its functionality and only has to define some attributes to define a starting page for the crawling process and the rules to follow links and parse pages.
  - **NER and Linking Module**. The NER task is performed using the Open Calais[8] service. The Entity Extractor interacts with Open Calais through an HTTP API and returns the named entities deteted in the news article text. The named entity linking is performed using a separate class implemented in Python. This class relies on the FuzzyWuzzy library for fuzzy string matching[9].

---

[4] http://protege.stanford.edu/
[5] http://python.org
[6] http://www.rdflib.net/
[7] http:// scrapy.org
[8] http://www.opencalais.com/
[9] http://chairnerd.seatgeek.com/fuzzywuzzy-fuzzy-string-matching-in-python/

— **News Importer**. This component is implemented using a Python module and is run in parallel as a MapReduce job.

- **PMO Component**: The PMO component is implemented as a Python module that connects to a relational database containing a SQL dump of the Congreso Visible database. It uses a database connection library[10] that provides access to the RDBMS database, and the rdflib library that provides the functionality to generate the graph representation passed to the RDF importer.

5   Results and Discussion

The news and named entity recognition and linking components were evaluated using information retrieval metrics, while the complete solution is evaluated using open data standards and the results of the end-user prototype application. We conclude this section with a discussion of the obtained results.

5.1   Evaluation

Named Entity Recognition and Linking.
To evaluate the results of the named entity recognition and linking tasks a random sample of 370 news articles, out of the total number of 9,420 articles referred to in the KB for the news portal El Espectador, was manually annotated in order to calculate recall and precision figures for the named entity linking task.

For each news article, the results for each of the identified and linked entities was summarized in a spreadsheet and given to an expert evaluator. The spreadsheet contains a total of 3,907 rows, for an average of 10.5 named entities recognized per individual article. The expert determined there were 180 references to entities in the Knowledge Base (i.e. references to current and former members of the parliament present in the PMO database as of February, 2014).

Table 1. Summary the results of the manually evaluated articles sample

	Relevant Entities	Correctly Linked	Incorrently Linked	Not Linked
Evaluator	180			
SPEAk	148	127	21	53

This number is shown in the Relevant Entities column in **Table 1**, along with the number of entities that were correctly linked to an entity in the KB, and the number of entities that were incorrectly linked. Using the previously mentioned figures, the obtained recall and precision scores are 71% for the former and 86% for the latter.

---

[10] http://initd.org/psycopg/

Open Government Data Rating Models.
According to Berners-Lee five-star maturity model for publishing open data [6], the proposed solution follows linked data principles and links the available data, achieving a five stars rating. Kalampokis, Tambouris, and Tarabanis propose a more complete classification scheme [7]. This model takes two dimensions into account the technological dimension divided according to Tim Berners-Lee five-star technological maturity model just mentioned, and the organizational dimension corresponding to the way in which data is published by the different government agencies.

SPEAk is designed to provision the data indirectly from the different sources used, and, as mentioned earlier, link the available data. Thus, SPEAk is located in the Indirect Provision of Linked Data quadrant of Kalampokis et al. classification scheme.

End-User Prototype Application.
This application is implemented to test the use of SPEAk to meet the objective of delivering relevant, accessible and linked information to citizens about high-profile Colombian public figures. It presents a profile of every member of the congress in the KB and their related properties and appearances in the news and visualization designed for an exploratory data analysis. **Fig. 3** provides a screenshot of this application. The application presents a visual representation of the topics associated with the news were a particular member of the congress appears, along with news to the original news article. The information used to generate the news article visualization is extracted form RDFa tags present in the original news source.

Fig. 3. Screenshot of the SPEAk end-user application prototype

An important finding when interacting with SPEAk from an end-user application is that the RDF store response time is too high to provide the expected performance of a standard web application. A simple way to handle this problem while the RDF store is optimized is to use a caching mechanism wherever possible.

5.2   Discussion

The obtained results provide supporting arguments to conclude that the presented solution meets the expected requirements. In terms of linking members and former members of the parliament to news sources, the obtained recall and precision figures are widely accepted in the Information Retrieval context. The design decisions proved to be correct as the data sources could be integrated into the RDF store using existing solutions and using open source components wherever possible. This was possible because the designed components are loosely coupled since they use standard protocols and file representations to exchange information. Adding another data source is a simple process since an interface that news data sources can implement and reuse all other SPEAk components is included in the solution design.

Presenting a fully implemented solution shows that semantic technologies have reached a status were they can be used to build useful systems that can interoperate with existing technologies and use information such as open government data that has historically been confined inside databases not designed with data distribution and linking from the beginning.

6   Related Work

The work in the areas of building information systems to give insight about parliamentary work, recognizing and linking named entities, populating ontologies with named entities, and applications built to provide value added services to citizens are considered.

Roncacio [8] used a data-warehouse approach to build a system aimed at analyzing parliamentary work guided by the needs of academic experts in political science. SPEAk uses Roncancio's in depth dimensional analysis of the parliament as valuable input to model the ontology used for inference and data integration.

A similar solution that uses OGD to provide insights into government affairs is presented in [10]. Vafopoulos et al. preprocess, convert to RDF triples, and interlink with external sources spending data from seven countries to build a web application to make the data easily consumable by citizens. Their work uses a previously developed ontology for public spending [11]   and, unlike SPEAk, does not consider its design in terms of data integration with PMO and news sources.

The Tetherless World Constellation (TWC) independently proposed a similar architecture for their Linking Open Government Data (LOGD) [12]. They present a very valuable overview of their infrastructure and architecture. The main difference with SPEAk is the extraction of semantic content from news sources and the automatic named entity recognition and linking process.

7   Conclusions

This work proposes the use of Semantic Web technologies as a means to integrate and provide uniform access to open government data, linked to information from other non-government data sources, such as news websites and Wikipedia. The solution provides an interface that can be used by third party applications to provide value added services using the data and inference capabilities of the knowledge base.

The results obtained in the SPEAk end-user application prototype presented in section 5.1 validated this objective showing that the semantic web standards are a feasible alternative that can be used as a replacement or complement for more mature data storage technologies.

Information from RDF data sources was integrated with external sources using an initial ontology that although conceptually simple, provided enough metadata to allow inference and data reconciliation. The proposed system can also be used to develop semantic web applications that assist citizens in making informed political decisions using integrated data linked to their interests and sources not affiliated with the government that will enable them to contrast the official government information and find data that is linked to their own personal interests. However, in spite of the promising results, the current status of the Colombian Government Data initiatives did not allow a direct consumption of OGD and a PMO had to be used as an indirect source for this type of data. This is the biggest challenge that must be overcome in order to provide government information linked to the topics the citizens care about and that allows them to access external sources of information to form their own opinion.

7.1 Future Work

From the previous conclusions and delivered results a set of improvements and extensions can be identified:

- The named entity disambiguation component could be easily extended or replaced to exploit the semantic information stored in the data sources and SPEAk Knowledge Base using techniques like Wikification [12].
- Additional end user applications could be developed to use the information already stored in the KB. For example, applications were a citizen can ask questions in a domain specific language about political figures, and current news topics.

References

1. Wood, D. (ed.): Linking Government Data (2011)
2. Lance Bennett, W.: Changing citizenship in the digital age. Civic Life Online: Learning how Digital Media Can Engage Youth 1, 1–24 (2008)
3. Kalampokis, E., Tambouris, E., Tarabanis, K.: A classification scheme for open government data: towards linking decentralised data. International Journal of Web Engineering and Technology 6(3), 266–285 (2011)
4. Allemang, D., Hendler, J.: Semantic Web for the Working Ontologist, 2nd edn. Elsevier (2011)
5. W.W.W.W.C. Recommendation (March 2013), http://www.w3.org/TR/2013/REC-sparql11-query-20130321/
6. Noy, F.N., Mcguinness, L.D.: Ontology Development 101: A Guide to Creating Your First Ontology. Stanford Knowledge Systems Laboratory Technical Report KSL-01-05, 3 (2001)

7. Berners-Lee, T.: Design issues: linked data (June 18, 2009), http://www.w3.org/DesignIssues/LinkedData.html (accessed November 1, 2013)
8. Kalampokis, E., Tambouris, E., Tarabanis, K.: On publishing linked open government data. In: Proceedings of the 17th Panhellenic Conference on Informatics, pp. 25–32 (2013)
9. Roncancio, G.: Parliamentary Informatics: Building the Foundations for an Analytical Information System about Parliamentary Work using a Data-Warehousing approach (2012)
10. Vafopoulos, M., Meimaris, M., Álvarez, J.M., Xidias, I., Klonaras, M., Vafeiadis, G.: Insights in global public spending. In: I-SEMANTICS 2013 Proceedings of the 9th International Conference on Semantic Systems, Messe Graz (2013)
11. Vafopoulos, M., Meimaris, M., Anagnostopoulos, I., Papantoniou, A., Xidias, I., Alexiou, G., Vafeiadis, G., Klonaras, M., Loumos, V.: (March 2013), http://dx.doi.org/10.2139/ssrn.2233998
12. Ding, L., Lebo, T., Erickson, J.S., DiFranzo, D., Todd Williams, G., Li, X., Michaelis, J., Graves, A., Guang Zheng, J., Shangguan, Z., Flores, J., McGuinness, D.L., Hendler, J.A.: TWC LOGD: A portal for linked open government data ecosystems. Web Semantics: Science, Services and Agents on the World Wide Web 9(3), 325–333 (2011)
13. Mihalcea, R., Andras, C.: Wikify! Linking Documents to Encyclopedic Knowledge. In: CIKM 2007, Lisboa (2007)
14. Bunescu, R., Pasca, M.: Using encyclopedic knowledge for named entity disambiguation. In: EACL 2006 (2006)

Enterprise Linked Data: A Systematic Mapping Study

Vitor Afonso Pinto and Fernando Silva Parreiras

LAIS – Laboratory of Advanced Information Systems, FUMEC University
Av. Afonso Pena, 3880, Belo Horizonte 30130-009, Brazil
vitor.afonso.pinto@gmail.com, fernando.parreiras@fumec.br

Abstract. Over the past years we have witnessed the Web becoming an established channel for learning. Nowadays, hundreds of repositories are freely available on the Web aiming at sharing and reusing learning objects, but lacking in interoperability. In this paper, we present a comprehensive literature review on the state-of-the-art in the research field of Linked Enterprise Data. More precisely, this Systematic Literature Review intends to answer the following research question: What are the applications of Linked Data for Corporate Environments? Studies point out that there is a pattern regarding the frameworks used for implementing Semantic Web in enterprises. This pattern enables interlinking of both internal and external data sources.

1 Introduction

According to [1], Over the past years we have witnessed the Web becoming an established channel for learning. Nowadays, hundreds of repositories are freely available on the Web aiming at sharing and reusing learning objects, but lacking in interoperability. The explosion in the number of resources available on the global computer network is a challenge for indexing and searching through a continuously changing and growing "database".[2]. The existence of huge amounts of data on the Web has raised an increasing challenge to locate right information at right time, as well as to integrating information effectively to provide a comprehensive source of useful information.[3].

For [4], the Semantic Web is an evolving extension of the World Wide Web in which contents can be expressed not only in natural language, but also in a format that can be read and used by software agents, thus permitting them to find, share and integrate information more easily. The goal of the semantic Web initiative is to provide an open infrastructure for intelligent agents and Web services. This infrastructure is based on formal domains that are linked to each other on the Web. [5].

For [6], data has become a critical resource in many organizations, and therefore, efficient access to data, sharing the data, extracting information from the data, and making use of the information has become an urgent need. As a result, there have been many efforts on not only integrating the various data sources scattered across several sites, but extracting information from these databases

M. Indulska and S. Purao (Eds.): ER Workshops 2014, LNCS 8823, pp. 253–262, 2014.

in the form of patterns and trends. The same technologies aimed for organizing the World Wide Web can deliver value to closed environments of large enterprises that suffer similar problems of information overflow and disorganization, creating the Linked Enterprise Data. [7].

In this paper, it is presented a comprehensive literature review on the state-of-the-art in the research field of Linked Enterprise Data. More precisely, this Systematic Literature Review intends to answer the following research question: What are the applications of Linked Data for Corporate Environments? This paper is organized as follows. Section 2 describes the research methodology underlying this systematic review. Section 3 presents the results obtained. Section 4 presents the threats to validity of this SLR. Finally, section 5 Concludes the paper.

2   Design

This Systematic Literature Review intends to analyze publications related to the applications of Linked Data for Corporate Environments, by executing a systematic literature review. According to [8], a SLR is a means of evaluating and interpreting available research relevant to a particular research question, topic area, or phenomenon of interest. This kind of study comprises three consecutive phases: planning, execution and results. This Systematic Literature Review is based on guidelines proposed by [8] in order to ensure its validity.

2.1   Planning

The main purpose of this phase is to deliver a protocol which drives the research efforts. There are four stages associated with planning phase: (1) Research Background, (2) Research Questions, (3) Research Strategy and (4) Data Extraction Strategy.

Research Background. In this stage the existing literature related to Semantic Web its application on corporate environments was analyzed. Table 1 shows the theoretical foundations upon which we based this study on.

Table 1. SLR - Theoretical Foundations

Topic	Authors
Semantic Web	[9] [10] [11]
Linked Data	[12] [13] [14]
Linked Enterprise Data	[15] [16]

Research Questions. In this stage, the research questions addressed by this study were defined. The main research question addressed by this study is: RQ1. What are the applications of Semantic Web for Corporate Environments? With respect to linked enterprise data, the following issues were considered: RQ1.1

Which kind of data source enterprises who adopted Semantic Web often interlink? RQ1.2 What are the enterprises's concerns regarding Semantic Web adoption? RQ1.3 What are the similarities between the frameworks used to implement Semantic Web on Enterprises?

Research Strategy. Following guidelines proposed by [8], in this stage, it was defined the strategy used to search for primary studies, including search terms and resources to be searched. Searches for primary studies were conducted only in the following electronic databases: Association for Computing Machinery (ACM), Elsevier peer-reviewed full-text articles (ScienceDirect), Institute of Electrical and Electronics Engineers (IEEE), Web of Science (ISIWeb) and SpringerLink. Considering the research questions, three kinds of conceptual search strings were defined. In order to improve this initial structure, some synonyms, related terms and alternative spellings were determined. The final conceptual strings were used as basis to construct the search strings which were converted to each electronic database syntax. Table 2 presents the conceptual strings.

Table 2. SLR - Conceptual Search Strings

Conceptual Search Strings
("Linked Data" OR "Semantic Web") AND ("Enterprise")
("Linked Data" OR "Semantic Web") AND (("Portfolio" OR "Strategic") AND "Management")
("Linked Data" OR "Semantic Web") AND ("Enterprise Application Integration" OR "EAI")

The advanced search tool of each electronic database was used to convert the conceptual string to the database syntax. Because of the characteristics of each electronic database, it was required to search the terms in different fields. Table 3 presents the specific fields where those terms were searched at each electronic database.

Table 3. SLR - Searched Fields at Databases

Electronic Database	Searched Fields
ACM	Title and Abstract
Science Direct	Title and Abstract
IEEE	Title and Abstract
ISIWeb	Title
Springer Link	Title

Data Extraction Strategy. In this stage the exclusion criteria and the strategy to extract data from selected papers were defined. It was decided to include all studies returned by electronic databases, except those classified in the exclusion criteria presented in table 4.

Table 4. SLR - Exclusion Criteria

Exclusion Criteria #1	The study is written in other language than English
Exclusion Criteria #2	The study is not applying Semantic Web
Exclusion Criteria #3	The study has already been selected
Exclusion Criteria #4	The study is not an article or paper
Exclusion Criteria #5	The study is out of the scope

2.2   Execution

The main purpose of this phase is to perform activities which extract and synthesize data from papers. There are three stages associated with execution phase: 1) Select Primary Studies, 2) Execute Data Extraction and 3) Synthesize Extracted Data.

Select Primary Studies. The automatic search resulted 479 studies potentially being relevant for this research. SpringerLink delivered 58% of the results, followed by IEEE (27%), ISIWeb (7%), ScienceDirect (6%) and the ACM (2%). An initial manual filtering was then executed as a first step to refine the results, according to the defined data extraction strategy. The exclusion criteria were applied based on the abstract, introduction and conclusion of each study. From the 479 studies, 214 (about 45% from total) were retained for further detailed analysis. In this second step the exclusion criteria were applied based on the full text. After this detailed analysis, 167 primary studies were included in this review (about 35% from total). Figure 1 presents the reasons for the exclusion of studies from this Review intending to clearly describe how initial filtering and detailed analysis were done.

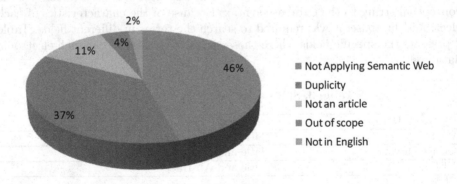

Fig. 1. SLR - Reasons for Exclusion of Studies
Source: Author

Execute Data Extraction. In this stage, the information needed to address the questions of this review were collected. After the search and selection procedures, the primary studies were examined. The papers were analysed considering the information required by each research question.

Synthesize Extracted Data. In this stage, the results of the included primary studies were collated and summarized. The data extracted and synthesized in this stage is presented in the results section, which can be read next.

3   Results

3.1   Studies Overview

Figure 2 shows studies included in this Systematic Literature Review grouped by publication year.

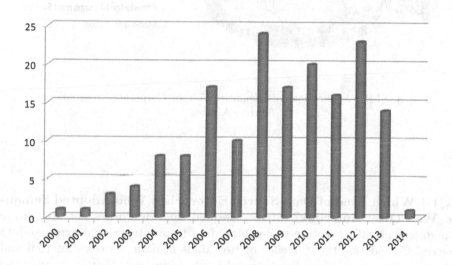

Fig. 2. SLR - Studies Grouped by Year of Publication
Source: Author

3.2   Research Questions Evaluation

RQ1 What Are the Applications of Semantic Web for Corporate Environments? A large majority of studies (65%) intended to use Semantic Web technologies to solve systems interoperability issues, such as: Web Services, Systems Integration, B2B Collaboration, etc. Part of studies (12%) intended to explain Semantic Web concepts or suggest any kind of optimization on existing concepts. A portion of studies (10%) focused on integration of things, such as: mobiles, tablets, RFID devices, automation devices, among others. Another portion of studies (12%) intended to create or optimize Knowledge Management Systems through Semantic Web. A small portion (5%) of studies intended to support corporate media integration, such as: streaming, music, among others. Figure 3 summarizes the applications of Semantic Web for Corporate Environments.

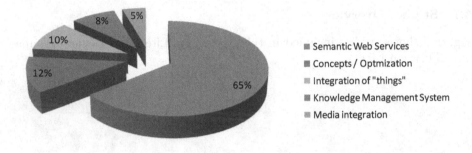

Fig. 3. SLR - Applications of Semantic Web for Corporate Environments
Source: Author

RQ1.1 Which Kind of Data Source Enterprises Who Adopted Semantic Web Often Interlink? Studies showed that enterprises not always use Semantic Web infrastructure to combine data from internal and external data sources. Considering the existence of two kinds of data sources - internal and external - most part of studies (about 51 %) pointed out that enterprises use Semantic Web technologies to interlink data generated both internal and external to their boundaries. However, some enterprises (about 31%) use technologies to interlink internal data sources only. Another part of the studies (about 18%) mentioned the use of Semantic Web technologies to interlink external data only.

RQ1.2 What Are the Enterprises's Concerns Regarding Semantic Web Adoption? Studies showed that enterprises have concerns regarding Semantic Web adoption in corporate environments. According to studies, the major concern (about 34%) is related to the complexity of technologies. In second place (about 23%), the requirement of rigid terminology seems to inhibit the adoption of Semantic Web. The enterprises are also concerned regarding the value added by Semantic Web (about 11%). Figure 4 shows the enterprises's concerns regarding Semantic Web adoption. All the concerns were categorized based on works of [17] and [14]. Table 5 explains these categories.

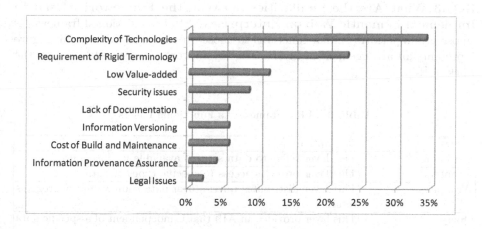

Fig. 4. SLR - Concerns Regarding Semantic Web Adoption
Source: Author

Table 5. SLR - Category of Concerns Regarding Semantic Web Adoption

Category	Description
Requirement of Rigid Terminology	Enterprises are concerned if Semantic Web adoption will require high standardization on existing terminologies to enable data and information sharing
Complexity of Technologies	Enterprises are concerned if Semantic Web adoption will demand highly specialized teams to handle technologies
Cost of Build and Maintenance	Enterprises are concerned if Semantic Web adoption will demand extra costs of build and maintenance
Low Value-added	Enterprises are concerned if Semantic Web adoption will benefit consumers and competitors but offer no quick wins for themselves, as data providers
Security issues	Enterprises are concerned if Semantic Web adoption will bring security issues, as unauthorized access, privacy, among others
Information Provenance Assurance	Enterprises are concerned if Semantic Web adoption will bring novel security issues, such as unauthorized access, privacy, among others
Information Versioning	Enterprises are concerned if Semantic Web adoption will bring issues related to information versioning and life cycle
Lack of Documentation	Enterprises are concerned if the existing documentation (ex.: schema mappings between datasets, technologies, etc) is sufficient to support Semantic Web adoption
Legal Issues	Enterprises are concerned if Semantic Web adoption will bring novel legal issues

RQ1.3 What Are the Similarities between the Frameworks Used to Implement Semantic Web on Enterprises? Studies mentioned frameworks whose layers perform similar functions to those presented in the table 6. Figure 5 presents an arrangement of layers. The layers were categorized based on the work of [18].

Table 6. SLR - Frameworks Functional Layers

Layer	Description
Data Sources	This layer refers to data sources available for integration
Adapters	This layer provides access to specific types of data
Wrapper	This layer distributes queries over data sources and aggregates results
Query	This layer provides an API that is independent of a specific data source and query language
Integration	This layer provides all the mapping functionality (semantics)
Presentation	This layer enables an interface to access data

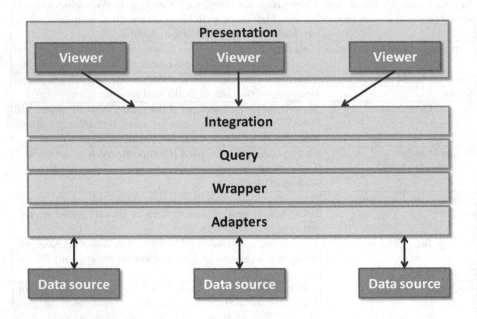

Fig. 5. SLR - Similar Functional Layers of Frameworks
Source: Adapted from [18]

4   Threats to Validity

In this Section, the limitations of this Systematic Literature Review are addressed. First, only papers written in English had been considered. Additionally, during data extraction stage, it was necessary to interpret the subjective information provided by studies. This happened because many studies did not present objective details regarding the topics investigated. Another potential threat to validity is the natural limitation of search engines, which may have caused the loss of relevant papers.

5   Conclusion

A state of the art survey on the applications of Semantic Web for Corporate Environments has been given in this section. The presented analysis shows that enterprises are using Semantic Web technologies for support their operations.

The major contribution of this study was to identify that there is a pattern regarding the frameworks used for implementing Semantic Web in enterprises. This pattern enables interlinking of both internal and external data sources. However, most part of the studies describes the use of Semantic Web technologies to facilitate Enterprise Application Integration (EAI), handling internal data sources only. We believe that studies focusing on benefits brought by interlinking both internal and external data are interesting in this context.

According to studies, enterprises still believe that Semantic Web technologies are complex and require high specialized teams. Enterprises are also concerned if Semantic Web adoption requires changes in existing systems. Thus, we believe that studies focusing on clarify concepts and demystify some of the concerns regarding Semantic Web for corporate environments are interesting in this context.

References

[1] Kawase, R., Fisichella, M., Niemann, K., Pitsilis, V., Vidalis, A., Holtkamp, P., Nunes, B.P.: Openscout: harvesting business and management learning objects from the web of data. In: Carr, L., Laender, A.H.F., Lóscio, B.F., King, I., Fontoura, M., Vrandecic, D., Aroyo, L., de Oliveira, J.P.M., Lima, F., Wilde, E. (eds.) WWW (Companion Volume), International World Wide Web Conferences Steering Committee / ACM, pp. 445–450 (2013)

[2] Li, W.: Intelligent information agent with ontology on the semantic web. In: Proceedings of the 4th World Congress on Intelligent Control and Automation, vol. 2, pp. 1501–1504 (2002)

[3] Costilla, C., Palacios, J.P., Rodríguez, M.J., Cremades, J., Calleja, A., Fernández, R., Vila, J.: Semantic web digital archive integration. In: DEXA Workshops, pp. 179–185. IEEE Computer Society (2004)

[4] Li, J.: Building distributed index for semantic web data. In: Awan, I., Younas, M., Hara, T., Durresi, A. (eds.) AINA, pp. 660–667. IEEE Computer Society (2009)

[5] Ha, Y., Lee, R.Y.: Integration of semantic web service and component-based development for e-business environment. In: SERA, pp. 315–323. IEEE Computer Society (2006)

[6] Thuraisingham, B.M.: Security issues for the semantic web. In: COMPSAC, pp. 632–637. IEEE Computer Society Press (2003)

[7] Westerski, A., Iglesias, C.A.: Exploiting structured linked data in enterprise knowledge management systems: An idea management case study. In: EDOCW, pp. 395–403. IEEE Computer Society Press (2011)

[8] Kitchenham, B.A.: Procedures for undertaking systematic reviews. Technical report, Computer Science Department, Keele University (2004)

[9] Willer, M., Dunsire, G.: Bibliographic Information Organization in the Semantic Web. Elsevier (2013)

[10] Parreiras, F.S.: Semantic Web and Model-Driven Engineering. Wiley-IEEE Press, Hoboken (2012)

[11] Berners-Lee, T., Hendler, J., Lassila, O.: The semantic web. Scientific American 284(5), 34–43 (2001)

[12] Galiotou, E., Fragkou, P.: Applying linked data technologies to greek open government data: A case study. Procedia - Social and Behavioral Sciences 73, 479–486 (2013); Proceedings of the 2nd International Conference on Integrated Information (IC-ININFO 2012), Budapest, Hungary, August 30-September 3 (2012)

[13] Heath, T., Bizer, C.: Linked Data: Evolving the Web into a Global Data Space, 1st edn. Morgan & Claypool (2011)

[14] Bechhofer, S., Buchan, I., De Roure, D., Missier, P., Ainsworth, J., Bhagat, J., Couch, P., Cruickshank, D., Delderfield, M., Dunlop, I., Gamble, M., Michaelides, D., Owen, S., Newman, D., Sufi, S., Goble, C.: Why linked data is not enough for scientists. Future Generation Computer Systems 29(2), 599 (2013); Special section: Recent advances in e-Science

[15] Allemang, D.: Semantic web and the linked data enterprise. In: Wood, D. (ed.) Linking Enterprise Data, pp. 3–23. Springer, US (2010)

[16] Hu, B., Svensson, G.: A case study of linked enterprise data. In: Patel-Schneider, P.F., Pan, Y., Hitzler, P., Mika, P., Zhang, L., Pan, J.Z., Horrocks, I., Glimm, B. (eds.) ISWC 2010, Part II. LNCS, vol. 6497, pp. 129–144. Springer, Heidelberg (2010)

[17] Alani, H., Chandler, P., Hall, W., O'Hara, K., Shadbolt, N., Szomszor, M.: Building a pragmatic semantic web. IEEE Intelligent Systems 23(3), 61–68 (2008)

[18] Oren, E., Haller, A., Hauswirth, M., Heitmann, B., Decker, S., Mesnage, C.: A flexible integration framework for semantic web 2.0 applications 24, 64–71 (2007)

Ontology Population from Web Product Information

Damir Vandic, Lennart J. Nederstigt, and Steven S. Aanen

Erasmus University Rotterdam,
PO Box 1738, NL-3000 DR, Rotterdam, The Netherlands
vandic@ese.eur.nl, {nederstigt,aanen}@appophetweb.nl

Abstract. Due to the explosion of information on the Web, there is a need to structure Web data in order to make it accessible to both users and machines. E-commerce is one of the areas in which increasing data volume on the Web has serious consequences. This paper proposes a framework that populates tabular product information from Web shops in a product ontology. By formalizing product information in this way, one can make better product comparison or recommender applications on the Web. Our approach makes use of lexical and syntactic matching techniques for mapping properties and instantiating values. The performed evaluation shows that instantiating TVs and MP3 players from two popular Web shops, Best Buy and Newegg.com, results in an F_1 score of 95.07% for property mapping and 76.60% for value instantiation.

1 Introduction

E-commerce has become nowadays very popular among consumers. According to a recent report from Forrester Research, e-commerce spending in the United States will hit approximately \$294 billion this year [14]. Furthermore, online spending is estimated to reach \$414 billion in 2018 [14], which is approximately a 11% compound annual growth rate compared to 2011. One of the reasons behind this growth is the increase in product specificity and consumer preference variation.

At the same time, we see the Web doubling in size roughly every five years. To keep up with this growth, in the past few years, some developments based on the ideas of the Semantic Web have been adopted for large-scale use. One of these developments is the Semantic Web vocabulary schema.org [5]. This vocabulary is proposed and supported by the four major Web search engines, i.e., Bing, Google, Yahoo!, and Yandex. It can be used by Web developers to annotate Web pages with semantic meta-data, serialized in either Microdata or RDFa. Furthermore, along this line of developments, Google introduced in 2012 the Knowledge Graph [8], for the purpose of augmenting search results with linked data.

The growth of the Web can have a negative impact on the accessibility of the available information. The field of e-commerce is one of the areas in which the data congestion on the Web can seriously limit its progress [16]. Today's

M. Indulska and S. Purao (Eds.): ER Workshops 2014, LNCS 8823, pp. 263–272, 2014.

search engines are still primarily using keywords for queries and are dependent on the language of the product offerings. Web-wide parametric product search is unavailable, making it difficult for users to find the optimal purchase for their needs. The ideas of the Semantic Web could be the key of the solutions to many of the previously mentioned problems. A prototype platform that utilizes Semantic Web technology to aggregate product information from multiple sources, as a means to achieve improved product comparison, has been implemented in an earlier study [15].

In this paper, we propose a framework that accommodates the recent Semantic Web developments in the e-commerce domain. More specifically, we focus on knowledge extraction from product pages on the Web. The framework that we propose is capable of large-scale ontology population of product information in the e-commerce domain. Using the tabular product data that is often available on Web shop product pages, the ontology-driven framework creates a structured knowledge base of product information. In order to achieve this goal, user-defined annotations for lexical and syntactic matching are employed, which facilitate the two main tasks of our framework, i.e., property mapping and value instantiation. For our knowledge base, we propose the OntoProduct ontology, which defines detailed properties of 24 consumer electronic product classes and is compatible with the well-known GoodRelations ontology for e-commerce [10].

In the literature, we can find related ontology population approaches. The authors of [11] propose a fully autonomous algorithm, using only initial seed domain knowledge. The OntoGenie approach, proposed in [13], makes use of the semantic lexicon WordNet. Ontosophie [6] is a semi-automatic system for ontology population, requiring user input for each information extraction cycle. With the exception of the approach presented in [11], the aforementioned methods are not specifically targeted at populating an ontology with (tabular) product information, gathered from the Web. Our approach also distinguishes itself from the others by utilizing an ontology that extends the well-known GoodRelations ontology, making it compatible with major search engines.

This paper is organized as follows. First, we discuss in Sect. 2 the proposed framework in detail. In Sect. 3, we evaluate our solution and compare it to a baseline approach. Last, in Sect. 4, we present conclusions and possible future work.

2   Ontology Population Architecture

Although significant effort has been put into establishing ontologies on the Web, an ontology for the domain of our interest (i.e., consumer electronic products), with the required amount of specificity, does not yet exist. Therefore, building on the foundations of existing work, we propose the *OntoProduct* ontology. The approach we took in devising the ontology is based on aspects covered by the OntoClean methodology [9]. OntoProduct is fully compatible with the Good-Relations ontology, even though GoodRelations is relatively high-level and does not describe actual product classes and their features. Although the CEO ontology provides a fruitful extension to GoodRelations, it only defines basic product properties and a taxonomy of product classes, but not the links between these. OntoProduct, nevertheless, uses CEO also as a base, extending it with new properties, product classes, and relations.

In e-commerce, many product features are quantitative and use a unit of measurement. For this purpose, OntoProduct requires a unit of measurement to be linked to quantitative values. Although GoodRelations does not provide a formal treatment of units of measurement, we were able to extend it with another ontology that does support this: the Units of Measurement Ontology (MUO) [4]. MUO provides the ontology structure for working with units of measurement, but does not contain the instances (e.g., centimeter). Another aspect of our proposed framework is that it is semi-automatic, which means that there is some manual work involved in the instantiation process. In this case, the manual work is the creation of the ontology annotations that are used for mapping raw product keys to ontology product properties and parsing values from the raw product data. In practice, this means that for new data sources (i.e., a new Web shop), the ontology needs to be updated with appropriate meta-data.

Besides lexical representations, the ontology annotations can be used for annotating quantitative object properties and data properties in the form of regular expressions. In this case, regular expressions provide a syntactic pattern to which the raw product values should match for a certain property to be instantiated. In addition, regular expressions are used to parse numeric data from the raw product values (using parenthesis). For instance, consider the key-value pair ['Refresh Rate','60Hz'], which can be mapped to the ontology property op:hasScreenRofreshRate. A screen refresh rate needs to have a unit of measurement for the frequency, commonly measured in Hertz (Hz), therefore we annotate the property with the following regular expression: (\d+)\s?(?:Hz|Hertz). Another example of the flexibility offered by regular expressions is demonstrated for the key-value pair ['Dimensions','55.3" x 33.2" x 1.3"']. Since there is no property to specify 'dimensions' in our domain ontology, it is required to break up the raw product value into multiple properties. Using lexical representations, the user could label the property ceo:hasWidth with 'Dimensions' for property matching in such cases.

In order to construct a semantic repository of product information and offerings, several steps are required: extracting of key-value pairs from (tabular) Web data; instantiating the product data into an ontology; product entity resolution for detecting and aggregating duplicate products from different Web sources; and an application that uses the instantiated ontology data for product search or recommendation. A lot of research effort has already been invested in the extraction of (tabular) Web site data [7], and in the detection of duplicate (product) records [2,3]. Therefore, these steps are left outside the scope of this research. Furthermore, in this research, we assume that we know the product class of a retrieved product description. One approach to obtain these classifications automatically is to make use of taxonomy mapping solutions [1,12], enabling the mapping of the Web shop product class taxonomy to the domain ontology (e.g., in our case OntoProduct). We could then directly use the product category from the description, which is usually present in Web shop pages.

Because we do not focus on HTML table extraction, the framework expects that product information on the collected Web pages is present in the form of key-value pairs. Our framework uses this *raw product data*, as we refer to it, for instantiating the individual products and their features into the OntoProduct ontology. The final output of the framework is an OntoProduct instance, representing the product and its features. In order to explain how this is done, we need to look at the two processes of our proposed framework: Property Matching and Value Instantiation.

2.1 Property Matching

The goal of Property Matching is to map each raw product key to one or more ontology properties, as a preparation for the Value Instantiation. An example of a raw product key that can be mapped to multiple ontology properties is 'maximum resolution', as 'resolution' can be represented by two properties (horizontal and vertical resolution). This feature is needed as there are many raw product key-value pairs that combine multiple characteristics of a product, while each of them is stored separately in the ontology.

In order to map a raw product key to an ontology property, the Property Match Score is computed. This score represents a similarity between each key-value pair from the raw product data and each property from the ontology. The Property Match Score consists of two components: a lexical comparison between the raw product key and the ontology property, and a regular expression match score. The regular expression match score is optional, and depends on whether the ontology property is annotated with a regular expression. The regular expressions work as a filter for finding the right ontology properties to match, based on the raw product values. For instance, key-value pair ['Product Height (without stand)','27-7/8"'] would not be mapped to property 'hasHeight' if the regular expression of this property would not match to values with fractions such as '27-7/8'.

The second component of the Property Match Score, i.e., the lexical comparison, uses a similarity score to compare the raw product key to each lexical representation of the ontology property. Property Match Score uses the normalized Levenshtein similarity, which inverts the distance to transform it to a similarity, and normalizes it by dividing it by the maximum sequence length in order to have range $[0, 1]$, where 1 would indicate that the sequences are equal. Of all lexical representations attached to the ontology property, the maximum similarity between a lexical representation and the raw product key is used.

For each key-value pair from the raw product, the ontology property with the highest Property Match Score is chose if its score exceeds the Similarity Threshold. This is a parameter of the framework that indicates how strict the Property Matching process should be. When the threshold is low, many raw product keys will be mapped, with the chance of having an increased error rate.

When the threshold is high, less raw product keys will be associated with a property, but the accuracy is likely to be higher.

One special situation that can occur is when multiple properties match to a key-value pair with the same Property Match Score. In this case, we choose all the properties with the highest score (assuming that the highest score is higher than the Similarity Threshold). This characteristic enables, for example, display resolution properties (width and height) of a TV to be linked correctly with the key-value pair for resolution. In this case, both properties share the same lexical representation of 'Maximum Resolution'. For this reason, the lexical score is equal.

2.2   Value Instantiation

After raw product properties have been mapped to ontology properties, the values can be instantiated. This part of the framework is mostly concerned with content spotting, parsing, and creating property assertions in the ontology. After the Value Instantiation, the raw product information from the Web pages has been structured and semantically annotated using a domain ontology.

In the Value Instantiation process, we make a clear distinction between quantitative and qualitative object properties, and data properties. Data properties are different from quantitative properties in the sense that a unit of measurement is not required. When the Property Matching process has linked a key-value pair to a qualitative object property, all qualitative values from the ontology that are in the range of the property are gathered. The goal is to find one or multiple of these qualitative values in the raw product value. Often, Web shops combine multiple qualitative values in one key-value pair, as is the case with a TV property 'Other Connectors', where the quantity of several types of connectors is stored. First, the lexical representations of all qualitative individuals are sorted descending on length. Then, the algorithm tries to find a matching lexical representation in the raw product value. If the search succeeds, the corresponding qualitative individual is attached to the product individual by means of the property found in the Property Matching process, and the matching part is removed from the raw product value string. This continues until no matches can be found anymore. The reason for sorting descending on length is that shorter labels might be contained in longer ones, leading to errors in parsing.

Qualitative individuals are usually instantiated through the control path just described. Property Matching maps the key-value pair to a qualitative object property, after which qualitative individuals are extracted from the raw product value. Two special situations arise, however, in which qualitative values are parsed differently. This special situation occurs when a qualitative property is found, but the Value Instantiation process is incapable of extracting qualitative values, or, when the Property Matching process for the key-value pair has failed. In these cases, the Value Instantiation process does not examine the raw product value for qualitative individuals, but the raw product key. Although this might seem counterintuitive, it is actually an important aspect of the Value Instantiation process.

For example, a common situation in which it is needed to examine the raw product key instead of the value, is for qualitative properties such as 'Features'. Many features, such as 'Sleep Timer', are structured using binary values, e.g., ['Sleep Timer', 'Yes'] instead of ['Feature', 'Sleep Timer']. In this case, Property Matching will be unsuccessful, as Sleep Timer is a qualitative individual, and not a property in the ontology. In this situation, the raw product key will be examined for matches with any qualitative individuals from the ontology, in a similar fashion as with 'normal' qualitative value instantiations, in which the Property Matching result is used. When a qualitative individual is found in the raw product key, the ontology is checked for properties that both have a range that includes the found individual and a domain that entails the product class of the current product individual. Such a property is needed to be able to map the qualitative individual to the product individual in case that the property was not previously discovered with the Property Matching process. Finding a qualitative individual in the raw product key does not provide sufficient information on itself to be able to assert ontology knowledge axioms. Whether the assertion can be made, also depends on the raw product value. Using what we call the *Boolean Value Converter*, the raw product value is checked on terms such as 'false', 'no', 'none', '0', '-', 'optional', 'null', 'N/A', 'not available', and 'not applicable', and aborts the instantiation when such a term is encountered. If the raw product value passes this test, the ontology is instantiated with property assertions, each containing one found qualitative individual.

The extraction of qualitative individuals from the raw product key enables the Value Instantiation process to handle key-value pairs like ['Sleep Timer',- 'Yes']. As mentioned before, this procedure is also followed when 'normal' qualitative value instantiation is unsuccessful, that is, when there is a result from Property Matching, but no qualitative individuals can be found in the raw product value. This problem arises for example with ['AM/FM Tuner','Yes'], which does have a match with ontology property 'hasRadioTuner' based on one of its lexical representations, but does not contain qualitative individuals in the raw product value. In this case, analyzing at the raw product key solves the problem and successfully instantiates hasRadioTuner to AM and hasRadioTuner to FM.

Quantitative values are processed differently from qualitative values, i.e., they are all parsed using regular expressions. By means of regular expression grouping, patterns can select the numeric data from the raw product value, disregarding additional content such as the unit of measurement. Because some key-value pairs need multiple instantiations, multiple groups may exist in the regular expression, or the complete expression can match multiple times in one raw product value. When Property Matching has mapped the key-value pair to a quantitative property, and no regular expression is attached, then a default regular expression for parsing values is used. The default regular expression is a generic extractor that is capable of gathering numerical values.

Usually, a quantitative value contains a *unit of measurement*. This unit of measurement is parsed in a similar fashion as parsing qualitative raw product values.

The quantitative properties refer to a fixed set of possible units of measurement. For every parsed numeric value from the raw product value, an associated unit of measurement is searched, and if possible, the new quantitative value individual is mapped to this unit individual by means of the 'hasUnitOfMeasurement' property. When no unit of measurement is found, the unit of measurement is omitted from the instantiation.

Data property values are the third and last type of instantiation. Data properties are less commonly used than object properties in the OntoProduct ontology. They are usually used for Boolean assertions (e.g., 'hasTouchscreen'), numeric data without unit of measurement (e.g., 'region code'), and strings (e.g., 'product name'). The values can be parsed in two ways: using a regular expression that is attached to the property, or, using a specific parsing method based on the data type range of the data property. When a key-value pair mapped to a data property needs to be instantiated, and the property, e.g., 'hasTouchscreen', appears to have a data range of xsd:boolean, a boolean parser is used. This parser aims to find, using exact lexical matching, terms in the raw product value that could indicate whether the data value should be true or false. Similar parsers are used for integers, floats, and strings (or literals).

3   Evaluation

In this section, we elaborate on the experimental design and discuss the performance of the framework by comparing it with the performance of a baseline approach. Before diving into the results, we need to discuss the evaluation design. The raw product data was obtained from two different Web sources (Best Buy and Newegg.com) and across 8 product categories. We used 60% of the data (1046 products) to create the ontology meta-data, i.e., lexical representations and regular expressions. The other 40% was used as the test set (672 products), on which the performance measures of the Property Matching and Value Instantiation processes are reported. Each process in the framework is evaluated separately using a golden standard, assuming that the product class of a product description is known.

Because generating the golden standard for the Property Matching process automatically is too difficult, and doing it manually is too time consuming, we chose to prompt the user for input whenever the algorithm comes across a mapping that it has not encountered before. The user can then select whether the mapping is correct, after which the answer is stored in a knowledge base for future access. For evaluating the Value Instantiation process, we manually instantiated products in the OntoProduct ontology and compared the generated triples with the manually generated triples. As manually instantiating products is a very time-consuming process, we decided to instantiate a subset of the data, namely TVs and MP3 players, consisting of 48 complete products from both considered Web shops. Because the evaluation of the Value Instantiation process is dependent on the evaluation of the Property Matching process, and no golden standard for Property Matching is available, the reported Value Instantiation performance is dependent on this other step.

As there is no freely available implementation of any relevant ontology population framework, and there is not enough information to precisely recreate such a framework, we decided to devise a baseline approach for the Property Matching process. This approach aims to find the highest normalized Levenshtein similarity score between a key-value pair from the raw product data and the lexical representations of a property from the ontology. In the evaluation we use a slightly modified binary classification scheme, as it is not a pure binary problem. For the Property Matching process, a *true positive* (TP) indicates that the framework has mapped a key-value pair to the correct ontology property. Unlike regular binary classification, a *false positive* (FP) here means that the algorithm mapped the key-value pair to an incorrect property instead. A *true negative* (TN) is a key-value pair that has correctly not been mapped, whereas a *false negative* (FN) represents the case when a key-value pair that should have been mapped to a property, is not mapped. For the evaluation of the Value Instantiation process, we adopt a similar scheme, where we compare the complete set of triples of a product from the golden standard with the generated triples from the instantiation process using these definitions.

3.1   Results

We applied a hill-climbing procedure in order to find the optimal value for the Similarity Threshold parameter, with a range from 0 to 1 in steps of 0.05. The optimal Similarity Threshold level was found to be 0.80. Table 1 shows the results of the Property Matching process for the considered approaches using this optimal Similarity Threshold value. We can see that our approach outperforms the baseline on all criteria except recall, where the baseline approach achieved 100% recall. If we consider the F_1 score, we observe that our approach achieves a score that is approximately 45% higher than the baseline approach. This difference is caused mostly because of the large difference in precision.

The test data set contained raw product keys that were not present in the training set. Despite this, the Property Matching was able to match many key-value pairs with ontology properties, due to the performed lexical variation matching. For example, the key 'Product Dimensions' is correctly mapped to ceo:hasWidth, ceo:hasHeight, and ceo:hasDepth.

The results on the test data for the Value Instantiation process, which uses the Property Matching process, are shown in Table 2. We can observe that our algorithm was able to instantiate all the products in the experiment, achieving a similar precision and recall that resulted in an F_1 score of 76.60%. Er-

Table 1. Results for Property Matching and baseline using the optimal Similarity Threshold value of 0.80

Process	Precision	Recall	Accuracy	Specificity	F_1 score
Baseline	48.30%	100.00%	48.30%	0.00%	65.14%
Our approach	96.95%	93.27%	94.80%	96.58%	95.07%

Table 2. Results for Value instantiation using the optimal Similarity Threshold value of 0.80

Precision	Recall	Accuracy	F_1	Instantiation rate
77.12%	76.09%	62.07%	76.60%	100.00%

ror analysis on the instantiated products reveals that the framework is occasionally not capable of instantiating all individuals from a list of qualitative values. For example, the key-value pair ['System Requirements','Windows: 2000 or later; Mac: OS X 10.4 or later'] is instantiated with the property ceo:hasCompatibleOperatingSystem. A user who would instantiate this key-value pair, would also instantiate property assertions for the versions of Windows and Mac OS X that were released after Windows 2000 and Mac OS X 10.4, respectively. However, for our Value Instantiation process it is difficult to determine for which individuals it should instantiate property assertions, as it is trying to match the value with the lexical representations of individuals from the ontology. Therefore, it is able to instantiate property assertions for the individuals 'ceo:Windows2000' and 'ceo:MacOSXTiger', as their lexical representations are also present in the value of the key-value pair, but 'later versions' is not recognized. Fortunately, because the Value Instantiation process is using a set of value extraction rules, we could easily add a new rule to replace 'or later' in the value with the lexical representations of the referred individuals.

4 Conclusion

This paper proposes a framework that is capable of (semi-)automatic ontology population of product information from Web shops. It employs a pre-defined ontology, compatible with the GoodRelations ontology for e-commerce, in order to formalize the raw product information contained in tabular format on product pages in Web shops. The performance of the framework is compared to the performance of a baseline approach, which merely uses lexical matching for the Property Matching processes. Product information from 1718 products, spread across eight different consumer electronic product categories, was gathered from Best Buy and Newegg.com. Due to the use of both lexical and syntactic pattern matching, the Property Matching process scores better than the baseline approach, with an F_1 score of 95.07% versus 65.14%. The evaluation of the Value Instantiation process was performed using an idiosyncratic approach, where comparing it to a manually instantiated ontology with 48 products resulted in a F_1 score of 76.60%.

Acknowledgment. Damir Vandic is supported by an NWO Mosaic scholarship for project *Semantic Web Enhanced Product Search (SWEPS)*, project 017.007.142.

References

1. Aanen, S.S., Nederstigt, L.J., Vandić, D., Frăsincar, F.: SCHEMA - an algorithm for automated product taxonomy mapping in E-commerce. In: Simperl, E., Cimiano, P., Polleres, A., Corcho, O., Presutti, V. (eds.) ESWC 2012. LNCS, vol. 7295, pp. 300–314. Springer, Heidelberg (2012)
2. de Bakker, M., Frasincar, F., Vandic, D.: A Hybrid Model Words-Driven Approach for Web Product Duplicate Detection. In: Salinesi, C., Norrie, M.C., Pastor, Ó. (eds.) CAiSE 2013. LNCS, vol. 7908, pp. 149–161. Springer, Heidelberg (2013)
3. de Bakker, M., Frasincar, F., Vandic, D., Kaymak, U.: Model Words-Driven Approaches for Duplicate Detection on the Web. In: 28th Symposium On Applied Computing (SAC 2013), pp. 717–723. ACM (2013)
4. Berrueta, D., Polo, L.: MUO — An Ontology to Represent Units of Measurement in RDF (2009), http://goo.gl/Gzyz2a
5. Bing, Google, Yahoo! and Yandex: schema.org (2014), http://schema.org
6. Celjuska, D., Vargas-Vera, M.: Ontosophie: A Semi-automatic System for Ontology Population from Text. In: 3rd International Conference on Natural Language Processing, ICON 2004 (2004)
7. Chang, C., Kayed, M., Girgis, R., Shaalan, K.: A Survey of Web Information Extraction Systems. IEEE Transactions on Knowledge and Data Engineering 18(10), 1411–1428 (2006)
8. Google: Knowledge Graph (2014), http://goo.gl/wgswGe
9. Guarino, N., Welty, C.: Evaluating ontological decisions with OntoClean. Communications of the ACM 45(2), 61–65 (2002)
10. Hepp, M.: GoodRelations: An Ontology for Describing Products and Services Offers on the Web. In: Gangemi, A., Euzenat, J. (eds.) EKAW 2008. LNCS (LNAI), vol. 5268, pp. 329–346. Springer, Heidelberg (2008)
11. Holzinger, W., Krüpl, B., Herzog, M.: Using Ontologies for Extracting Product Features from Web Pages. In: Cruz, I., Decker, S., Allemang, D., Preist, C., Schwabe, D., Mika, P., Uschold, M., Aroyo, L.M. (eds.) ISWC 2006. LNCS, vol. 4273, pp. 286–299. Springer, Heidelberg (2006)
12. Nederstigt, L.J., Aanen, S.S., Vandić, D., Frăsincar, F.: An automatic approach for mapping product taxonomies in E-commerce systems. In: Ralyté, J., Franch, X., Brinkkemper, S., Wrycza, S. (eds.) CAiSE 2012. LNCS, vol. 7328, pp. 334–349. Springer, Heidelberg (2012)
13. Patel, C., Supekar, K., Lee, Y.: Ontogenie: Extracting Ontology Instances from WWW. In: Workshop on Human Language Technology for the Semantic Web and Web Services, Springer (2003)
14. Sucharita Mulpuru: US eCommerce Grows, Reaching $414B by 2018, but Physical Stores Will Live On (2014), http://goo.gl/Y3gyVI
15. Vandic, D., van Dam, J.W., Frasincar, F.: Faceted Product Search Powered by the Semantic Web. Decision Support Systems 53(3), 425–437 (2012)
16. VijayaLakshmi, B., GauthamiLatha, A., Srinivas, D.Y., Rajesh, K.: Perspectives of Semantic Web in E- Commerce. International Journal of Computer Applications 25(10), 52–56 (2011)

Service Adaptability Analysis across Semantics and Behavior Levels Based on Model Transformation

Guorong Cao[1,2], Qingping Tan[1], Xiaoyan Xue[2], Wei Zhou[2], and Yongyong Dai[2]

[1] School of Computer, National University of Defense Technology, Changsha 410073, China
[2] Jiangnan Institute of Computing Technology, Wuxi 214083, China
{guorong.cao,qingping.tan,xiaoyan.xue,
wei.zhou,yongyong.dai}@gmail.com

Abstract. Web service adaptability analysis is a prominent aspect of service adaptation. Current Petri net-based approaches focus on behavior-level service adaptability analysis, lacking of cross-level analysis; Besides, they mainly rely on state exploration of the services which may result in state explosion. This paper firstly formalizes service behavior as an ontology-annotated service flow net which is an extended version of service flow net augmented with ontology concepts, thus we are able to discuss the notion of service adaptability across semantics and behavior levels. This paper secondly extends regular flow net with implicit choice and loop constructs, thus we are able to represent more service behaviors with ontology-annotated regular service flow nets. Last but not least, this paper efficiently achieves service adaptability checking by exploiting the regular characteristic of ontology-annotated regular service flow nets at behavior level, and completely avoids state explosion problems.

1 Introduction

Practically, not all incompatible services can be coordinated to achieve the desired targets, therefore, there are always risks that service adaptation would fail when mediating incompatible services without prior service adaptability analysis, especially in dynamic environments. Service adaptability analysis checks whether there exist adapters capable of mediating incompatible services in order to achieve the desired targets, which is an important step just before service adaptation. The research on service adaptability analysis would greatly contribute to the advancement of service adaptation technology, especially dynamic service adaptation technology.

So far, to the best of our knowledge, the research on service adaptability analysis has not been studied systematically, just partial notions and approaches along the research of service composition, adaptation and verification, where they formalize the problem as service adapter existence checking or adapter verification [1-3]. Besides, current approaches to service adaptability analysis focus on behavior-level adaptability analysis and generally model communications between pairs of services based on asynchronous communication [4]. Yellin et al. propose an approach to service adapter generation based on interface mappings [1]. It either produces a well-formed adapter consistent with the mappings or decides that no such adapter exists, where the

M. Indulska and S. Purao (Eds.): ER Workshops 2014, LNCS 8823, pp. 273–282, 2014.
© Springer International Publishing Switzerland 2014

analysis process on service adapter existence is subsumed by the adapter generation process. The approaches offered by Bracciali [5], Gierds [6] also have such kinds of characteristics regardless of their concrete details. These approaches may possibly generate none adapter due to their nondeterminacy, that is, the determination of the existence of the adapter is just within the adapter generation process. Li et al. propose an approach to service adaptation based on mediator patterns, suggesting adapter verification after generating the adapter [2]. Adapter verification is based on reachability analysis of the composition of the adapter and the pairs of services, verifying the correctness of the adapter. The approaches offered by Benatallah [7], Brogi [8] also have such features. These approaches are able to generate adapters regardless of whether they are correct or not. Tan et al. first propose service adapter existence checking before adapter generation [3]. The authors verify that Communicating Reachability Graph (CRG) contains all needed properties in adapter existence checking. By using stubborn sets, state-space exploration is sped up. However, it still depends on CRG, which may result in state explosion issues. This approach has characteristics of pessimism of the first mentioned kind of approaches and of determinacy of the second mentioned kind of approaches. The emergence of the third kind of approaches may pave the way for dynamic service adaptation as it does service adaptability analysis before service adaptation, and the service adaptation starts just when the result of the adaptability analysis is positive.

In conclusion, all the above works have three common deficiencies. Firstly, they are restricted to behavior-level service adaptability analysis. Secondly, the design of interface mappings or data mappings is a manual error-prone task which obliges the designer to have a full understanding of all service details. Thirdly, they almost rely on state exploration of services which may result in state explosion.

It is necessary to develop a special kind of formalism, as large as possible, having strong abilities for describing semantics as well as behavior information of services, and an efficient approach to service adaptability analysis across semantics and protocol behavior levels.

The rest of the paper is organized as follows. In section 2, we introduce the formalism of ontology-annotated service flow net and related concepts. In section 3, we present the two-phase service adaptability analysis approach. Finally, some concluding remarks are drawn in section 4.

2   Formalism of Service Behavior

2.1   Regular Flow Nets

This section reviews some basic notions and properties as required in the paper, readers can refer [9] for more details.

Definition 1 (flow net, FN [9]). *A flow net N is a tuple (C, T, F, i, o, split, join) such that:*

- *C is a finite set of control places,*
- *T is a finite set of transitions,*

- $F \subseteq (C \setminus \{o\} \times T) \cup (T \times C \setminus \{i\})$ *is a set of control flow relation where each node in the graph* $(C \cup T, F)$ *is in a directed path from i to o,*
- *i is the input place such that* $\bullet i = \Phi$ *representing that i does not have incoming flows,*
- *o is the output place such that* $o\bullet = \Phi$ *representing that o does not have outgoing flows,*
- *split:* $T \to \{AND, XOR, EMPTY\}$ *specifies the split behavior of each transition, and*
- *join:* $T \to \{AND, XOR, EMPTY\}$ *specifies the join behavior of each transition.*

We denote the elements of a FN N by C_N, T_N, F_N, i_N, o_N, $split_N$, $join_N$. We denote the pre-set of a node y by $\{x \mid <x, y> \in F_N\}$, and denote the post-set of x by $\{y \mid <x, y> \in F_N\}$.

Definition 2 (linear net [9]). *A FN N is a linear net iff* $\forall u \in (C_N \cup T_N): (u \neq i_N \to |\bullet u| = 1) \wedge (u \neq o_N \to |u\bullet| = 1)$.

Definition 3 (simple split-join net [9]). *A FN N is a simple split-join net iff*
- *there is a unique split node* $t_s \in T_N$ *such that* $<i_N, t_s> \in F_N$,
- *there is a unique join node* $t_j \in T_N$ *such that* $<t_j, o_N> \in F_N$,
- $split_N(t_s) = join_N(t_j)$, *and*
- $\forall u \in (C_N \cup T_N): (u \neq i_N \wedge u \neq t_j \to |\bullet u| = 1) \wedge (u \neq o_N \wedge u \neq t_s \to |u\bullet| = 1)$.

Definition 4 (simple implicit choice net). *A FN N is a simple implicit choice net iff* $\forall u \in (C_N \cup T_N) \setminus \{i_N, o_N\}: (|u\bullet| = |\bullet u| = 1) \wedge (|i_N\bullet| = |\bullet o_N|)$.

Definition 5 (simple cyclic path [9]). *Given a FN N, a cyclic path p in N is called simple if there is no cyclic path p' in N such that* $|p'| < |p|$ *and* $Nodes(p') \subset Nodes(p)$, *where Nodes(p) denotes the set of all nodes in p.*

Definition 6 (simple loop net [9]). *A simple loop net is a FN N such that:*
- *there is a unique simple cyclic path p in N,*
- *there is a unique node* t_{entry} *in* T_N *such that* $<i_N, t_{entry}> \in F_N$, *and* $join_N(t_{entry}) = XOR$, *and*
- *there is a unique node* t_{exit} *in* T_N *such that* $<t_{exit}, o_N> \in F_N$, *and* $split_N(t_{exit}) = XOR$.

Formally, the simple loop net with respect to its loop body is called a simple repeat-until net if the loop body is in an acyclic directed path from t_{entry} to t_{exit}. The simple loop net with respect to its loop body is called a simple while-do net if the loop body is in an acyclic directed path from t_{exit} to t_{entry}.

Definition 7 (simple implicit loop net). *A simple implicit loop net is a FN N such that:*
- *there is a unique simple cyclic path p in N,*
- *there is a unique node* c_{entry} *in* C_N *such that* $|\bullet c_{entry}| = 2$, *and*
- *there is a unique node* c_{exit} *in* C_N *such that* $|c_{exit}\bullet| = 2$.

Formally, the simple implicit loop net with respect to its loop body is called a simple implicit repeat-until net if the loop body is in an acyclic directed path from c_{entry} to c_{exit}. The simple implicit loop net with respect to its loop body is called a simple implicit while-do net if the loop body is in an acyclic directed path from c_{exit} to c_{entry}.

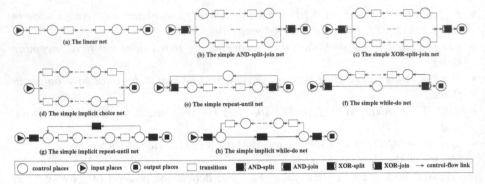

Fig. 1. Simple FNs

The linear, simple split-join, simple implicit choice, simple loop and simple implicit loop nets are called simple nets; their graphical representation is shown in Fig. 1. The dark gray rectangles identify tau transitions, furthermore, we suppose that each split or join transition except EMPTY transition is a tau transition, where such transitions may represent internal service behavior or only be responsible for managing the control flow.

Definition 8 (concatenation of FNs [9]). *Given two disjoint FNs N1 and N2, that is* $(C_{N1} \cup T_{N1}) \cap (C_{N2} \cup T_{N2}) = \Phi$, *the concatenation of N1 and N2, denoted by N1 $\oplus$ N2, is a new FN N such that:*

- $i_N = i_{N1}$ *and* $o_N = o_{N2}$,
- $C_N = C_{N1} \cup C_{N2} \backslash \{i_{N2}\}$, *and* $T_N = T_{N1} \cup T_{N2}$,
- $F_N = F_{N1} \cup (F_{N2} \backslash \{<i_{N2}, t> / <i_{N2}, t> \in F_{N2}\}) \cup \{<o_{N1}, t> / <i_{N2}, t> \in F_{N2}\}$, *and*
- $split_N = split_{N1} \cup split_{N2}$, *and* $join_N = join_{N1} \cup join_{N2}$.

The concatenation of two FNs is a sequential composition of the two nets. Formally, it reduces to collapse the input place of the second net into the output place of the first net.

Definition 9 (embedding of FNs [9]). *Given two disjoint FNs N1 and N2, and a transition t of N1 such that* $|\bullet t| = |t\bullet| = 1$. *The embedding of N2 into N1 on t, denoted by N1 Θ_t N2, is a new FN N such that:*

- $i_N = i_{N1}$ *and* $o_N = o_{N1}$,
- $C_N = C_{N1} \cup C_{N2} \backslash \{i_{N2}, o_{N2}\}$, *and* $T_N = (T_{N1} \backslash \{t\}) \cup T_{N2}$,
- $F_N = (F_{N1} \backslash (\{<c, t> / <c, t> \in F_{N1}\} \cup \{<t, c> / <t, c> \in F_{N1}\})) \cup (F_{N2} \backslash (\{<i_{N2}, u> / <i_{N2}, u> \in F_{N2}\} \cup \{<u, o_{N2}> / <u, o_{N2}> \in F_{N2}\})) \cup \{<c, u> / <c, t> \in F_{N1} \text{ and } <i_{N2}, u> \in F_{N2}\} \cup \{<u, c> / <t, c> \in F_{N1} \text{ and } <u, o_{N2}> \in F_{N2}\}$, *and*
- $split_N = split_{N1} \cup split_{N2}$, *and* $join_N = join_{N1} \cup join_{N2}$.

The embedding of a FN N2 into a FN N1 on a transition t consists of replacing transition t of N1 with N2.

Definition 10 (regular flow net, RFN). *A regular flow net is defined recursively*

- *each simple net N is a RFN,*
- *if N1, N2 are RFNs, then N1 $\oplus$ N2 is a RFN, and*
- *if N1 and N2 are RFNs and t is a transition of N1 such that* $|\bullet t| = |t\bullet| = 1$, *then N1 Θ_t N2 is a RFN.*

Compared to the definition of RFNs [9], we have extended the definition by considering implicit choice nets and implicit loop nets as RFNs, thus we can model more Web service behaviors as RFNs. The regular characteristic of RFNs is a control causal relation emphasizing that the service with a well-formed static structure must have a well-formed and consistent behavior structure, like programs just with sequence, branch and loop process controls.

2.2   Representation of Service Behavior Augmented with Ontology Concepts

Definition 11 (service flow net, SFN [9]). *A service flow net S is a tuple (N, D, H, guard) such that:*

- *N is a FN, which is called the base net of S,*
- *D is a finite set of data places, which contains two subsets ID and OD, representing the input data places and the output data places respectively,*
- $H \subseteq (D \setminus OD \times T) \cup (T \times D \setminus ID)$ *is a set of data flow relation representing data exchanges between transitions,*
- *guard:* $F_N \rightarrow EXP^{BOOL}$ *specifies the routing condition for each XOR-split edge in N. Namely for* $\forall <t, c> \in F_N$: *guard*$(<t, c>) \in EXP^{BOOL} \wedge vars(guard(<t, c>)) \subseteq D$, *if split(t)=XOR; otherwise, guard(<t, c>) is not defined, where* EXP^{BOOL} *is the set of Boolean expressions with variables ranging over D, and for each* $exp \in EXP^{BOOL}$, *vars(exp) is the set of variables contained in Boolean expression exp.*

A SFN *S* is called regular service flow net (RSFN) if its base set *N* is a RFN.

We denote the elements of a SFN *S* by C_S, T_S, F_S, i_S, o_S, D_S, H_S, $split_S$, $join_S$, $guard_S$. We denote the read-set of a transition *t* by $\{d \mid <d, t> \in H_S\}$, and the write-set of *t* by $\{d \mid <t, d> \in H_S\}$.

As our approach to service adaptability analysis takes into account both the semantics and behavior information, how to feature the semantics by SFNs and exploit the semantic relationships existing among service descriptions should be solved at first. As we know, for OWL-S specifications [10], two processes are type compatible if for each output of one that flows to the input of the other, the type of the output is a subtype of the type of the input, that is, the output is a sub-concept of the input. We now give the notion of sub-concept over different ontologies stored by dependency graph.

Definition 12 (sub-concept [11]). *Given a hypergraph HG=(V, E), two concepts c, d∈V, c is a sub-concept of d, denoted by* $c \prec d$, *iff* $\exists e_1, e_2, ..., e_n \in (E_\subset \cup E_\equiv)$ *such that* $c \in T(e_1) \wedge \{d\} = H(e_n) \wedge H(e_i) \subset T(e_{i+1})$, *for i=1,2,...,n-1.*

In Definition 12, $E_\subset$ and $E_\equiv$ are two disjoint subsets of hyperedges *E*, representing sub-concept relationships in an ontology and equivalent-concept relationships in two separate ontologies, respectively; and for each $(c, d) \in E_\subset$, we denote that *c* is a sub-concept of *d* by $c \subset d$; for each $(c, c') \in E_\equiv$, we denote that *c* is equivalent with *c'* by $c \equiv c'$ although they belong to different ontologies; and for each $e \in E$, we denote the tail of *E* by $T(e)$, and denote the head of *E* by $H(e)$. Readers can refer [11] for more details.

Definition 13 (service flow net augmented with ontology concepts, SFN-O). *Let HG=(V, E) be a dependency hypergraph. A service flow net augmented with ontology concepts S is a tuple (N, D, H, guard, concept) such that:*

- *(N, D, H, guard) is a SFN, and*
- *concept: D → V specifies the concept of each data place which maps each data place of D to a unique concept in V.*

Apparently, SFN-O has the same definition of marking, enabled transition and firing as well as the initial and final marking with SFN [9]. Accordingly, A SFN-O S is called ontology-annotated regular service flow net (RSFN-O) if its base set N_S is a RFN.

3   The Approach to Service Adaptability Analysis

Semantics adaptability analysis checks whether two given services are semantically adaptable or not. Intuitively, given two services, they are semantically adaptable if and only if for each input data place d of one service, there exists an output data place d' of its mate service such that d' is a sub-concept of d or they have the same concept, and vice versa. We now give below the notion for semantics adaptability analysis.

Definition 14 (semantic adaptability). *Given two SFN-Os S1 and S2, they are semantically adaptable iff $\forall d_2 \in ID_{S2}$: $(\exists d_1 \in OD_{S1}$: $(d_1 \approx d_2 \vee d_1 \prec d_2)) \wedge \forall d_1 \in ID_{S1}$: $(\exists d_2 \in OD_{S2}$: $(d_2 \approx d_1 \vee d_2 \prec d_1))$, where for any two data places d_1 and d_2, we by $d_1 \approx d_2$ denote that they have the same concept such that $concept_{S1}(d_1) = concept_{S2}(d_2)$.*

When for semantic adaptability analysis, we use a set f storing the result of data mappings. Each data mapping is an input onto a unique output such that the output is a sub-concept of the input or they have the same concept within an ontology.

In the following we proceed to describe our approach to behavior adaptability analysis by exploiting the regular characteristic of RSFN-O. The key idea behind the approach we propose consists of three main phases: (1) Transformation RSFN-O into abstract transition process; (2) Necessary simplification of transformed abstract transition process; and (3) Computing behavior adaptability based on abstract transition process.

The preliminary phase deals with transforming SFN-O into abstract transition process. This is the most important phase for behavior adaptability analysis as it takes full advantages of the regularity of service behavior representation based on RSFN-O, rather than exploring the reachability graph of RSFN-O. Now, we focus on the representation of service behavior in abstract transition process. An abstract transition process can be defined by the following grammar.

Definition 15 (abstract transition process, ATP). *An abstract transition process P is defined using the following constructs:*

$$P ::= 0 \mid \tau \mid ?d \mid !d \mid [g].P \mid P_1.P_2 \mid P_1 + P_2 \mid P_1 /\!/ P_2$$

Where 0 stands for termination. τ stands for non-observable actions (also called silent actions). d stands for data channel used for storing data value. ?d represents an input action. !d represents an output action. [g].P is used for specifying conditional behavior: [g].P behaves as P if g is evaluated to true, otherwise as 0. '.' is a sequence operator, e.g., a.P represents that a.P behaves as P after executing a, '+' is an exclusive choice operator, '//' is a parallel operator. The operators '+' and '//' are commutative, and '.', '+' and '//' are associative.

Next, we present the operational semantics of one ATP with the following three rules including sequence (Rule 1), choice (Rule 2) and parallel (Rule 3), that formalize the meaning of ATPs as Labeled Transition Systems.

$$\alpha.P \xrightarrow{\ \alpha\ } P \tag{1}$$

$$\frac{P \xrightarrow{\ \alpha\ } P'}{P + Q \xrightarrow{\ \alpha\ } P'} \tag{2}$$

$$\frac{P \xrightarrow{\ \alpha\ } P'}{P \,//\, Q \xrightarrow{\ \alpha\ } P' \,//\, Q} \tag{3}$$

Note that with respect to Definition 15, α is a label representing an input action, an output action, a silent action or a guard condition.

Behavior adaptability analysis checks whether two services are behaviorally adaptable. Intuitively, given pairs of services, they are behaviorally adaptable if and only if each input action of one service can eventually occur after some communications with its mate service, and vice versa.

Definition 16 (behavior adaptability). *Let S_1 and S_2 be two SFN-Os, f be the data mappings generated after semantic adaptability analysis. Suppose that P_1 and P_2 are their transformed ATPs respectively. S_1 and S_2 are behaviorally adaptable iff for each data place $d \in ID_{S1} \cup ID_{S2}$, the receive (or input) action ?d in P_1/P_2 eventually occurs after the execution of a send (or output) action !f(d) in P_2/P_1.*

From Definition 16, we know that we should adopt some mechanism to efficiently determine that each input action in both two ATPs can eventually occur. This is the job of the third phase.

The transformation from a RSFN-O S (with N as its base net) into its corresponding ATP is as follows:

- For a transition of S. All data places are transformed into data channels in ATP. A transition t with inputs $I_1, I_2, ..., I_n$ and outputs $O_1, O_2, ..., O_m$ is transformed into such an ATP $?I_1.?I_2....?I_n.!O_1.!O_2....!O_m$, a transition t with inputs $I_1, I_2, ..., I_n$ is transformed into such an ATP $?I_1.?I_2....?I_n$, a transition t with outputs $O_1, O_2, ..., O_m$ is transformed into such an ATP $!O_1.!O_2....!O_m$, and a tau transition t is transformed into τ.

- N is a linear net. Intuitively, a linear net is constructed by some transitions in sequential order, therefore, suppose that S has all transitions $t_1, t_2, ..., t_n$ in sequence, the ATP P of S is the sequential composition of some ATPs of transitions such that $P = P_1.P_2....P_n$ where $P_1, P_2, ..., P_n$ are respectively the transformed ATPs of the above transitions.

- N is a split-join net. Suppose that S has all branches $B_1, B_2, ..., B_n$, the ATP P of S is the parallel composition of $P_1, P_2, ...P_n$ such that $P = P_1 // P_2 // ... // P_n$ if N is an AND-split-join net, or the alternative composition of $P_1, P_2, ...P_n$ such that $P = [g_1].P_1 + [g_2].P_2 + ... + [g_n].P_n$ if N is a XOR-split-join net, where $P_1, P_2, ...P_n$ are respectively the transformed ATPs of the above branches, and $g_1,g_2,...,g_n$ are respectively the branch condition of $B_1,B_2,...,B_n$.

- N is an implicit choice net. Similar to the translation rule of split-join nets, suppose that S has all branches $B_1,B_2,...,B_n$, the ATP P of S is the alternative composition of $P_1,P_2,...P_n$ such that $P=P_1+P_2+...+P_n$, where $P_1,P_2,...P_n$ are respectively the transformed ATPs of the above branches $B_1,B_2,...,B_n$.

- N is a loop net. Suppose that N has a loop body B, the ATP P of S is the alternative composition of P_B and τ such that $P=P_B.([g].P+[\neg g].\tau)$ if N is a repeat-until net, or such that $P=[g].P_B.P+[\neg g].\tau$ if N is a while-do net, where g is the guard for the loop body B.

- N is an implicit loop net. Similar to the translation rule of loop nets, suppose that S has a loop body B, the ATP P of S is the alternative composition of P_B and τ such that $P=P_B.(P+\tau)$ if N is an implicit repeat-until net, or such that $P=P_B.P+\tau$ if N is an implicit while-do net.

- N is a RFN except all the above types. Thus let $N=N_1 \oplus N_2$ such that N_1 is a net of the above types, if N_2 is not a net of the above types, we let $N_2=N_3 \oplus N_4$ such that N_3 is a net of the above types, this process continues until a situation such that $N_p=N_q \oplus N_r$ and N_q and N_r are all nets of the above types. We assume that $P_1,P_3,...,P_q,P_r$ are respectively the ATPs of $S_1,S_3,...,S_q,S_r$, thus the ATP P of S is $P=P_1.P_3.....P_q.P_r$, where $S_1,S_3,...,S_q,S_r$ are SFN-Os respectively corresponding to $N_1,N_3,...,N_q,N_r$ augmented with data flow of S.

As for behavior adaptability analysis, we take into account actions executed just one time although we consider cycles, that is, the loop behaviors can be further transformed into two branch choices. Therefore, $P=[g].P_B.P+[\neg g].\tau$ can be further transformed into $P=[g].P_B +[\neg g].\tau$, $P=P_B.([g].P+[\neg g].\tau)$ can be further transformed into $P=P_B$; $P=P_B.P+\tau$ can be further transformed into $P=P_B +\tau$, $P=P_B.(P+\tau)$ can be further transformed $P=P_B$.

The second phase involves some necessary simplification rules on ATP which can simply ATP in the simplest form. These simplification rules are:

- τ rules: $P.\tau \Rightarrow P$; $\tau.P \Rightarrow P$; $P//\tau \Rightarrow P$.
- common-branch rules: $[g_1].P + [g_2].P \Rightarrow P$ where g_1 and g_2 are mutually exclusive; $P + P \Rightarrow P$.
- pre-common rules: $[g_1].(P.P_1) + [g_2].(P.P_2) \Rightarrow P.([g_1].P_1 + [g_2].P_2)$ where g_1 and g_2 are mutually exclusive; $(P.P_1) + (P.P_2) \Rightarrow P.(P_1 + P_2)$.
- post-common rules: $[g_1].(P_1.P) + [g_2].(P_2.P) \Rightarrow ([g_1].P_1 + [g_2].P_2).P$ where g_1 and g_2 are mutually exclusive; $(P_1.P) + (P_2.P) \Rightarrow (P_1 + P_2).P$.
- pre-output rules: $(!d_1.P_1) // (?d_2.P_2) \Rightarrow !d_1. (P_1 // ?d_2.P_2)$.
- post-input rules: $(P_1.!d_1) // (P_2.?d_2) \Rightarrow (P_1.!d_1) // (P_2).?d_2$.

One may note that the first two phases may be done off-line as we can save the simplest ATP of each service instead of its RSFN-O. Hence these two phases are not a burden for the behavior adaptability analysis.

In the following, we suppose that P_1 and P_2 are two ATPs used for behavior adaptability analysis, f is the data mappings generated after the semantics adaptability analysis. Therefore, we have two new ATPs $P_1[f]$ and $P_2[f]$. $[f]$ is the substitution which replace each data channel d in P_1 and P_2 used for input action with $f(d)$. Thus for each input action in $P_1[f]$ and $P_2[f]$, there must be a corresponding output action that they share the same data channel. We apply the following four rules to ATPs $P_1[f]$ and $P_2[f]$ for behavior adaptability analysis:

$$\frac{P \xrightarrow{!d} P'}{D, \Gamma \rhd P \sim Q \xrightarrow{!d} D \cup \{d\}, \Gamma \rhd P' \sim Q} \tag{4}$$

$$\frac{P \xrightarrow{?d} P', d \in D}{D, \Gamma \rhd P \sim Q \xrightarrow{?d} D, \Gamma \rhd P' \sim Q} \tag{5}$$

$$\frac{P \xrightarrow{[g]} P', (\Lambda_{b \in \Gamma \cup \{g\}} b) \text{ is not a contradiction}}{D, \Gamma \rhd P \sim Q \xrightarrow{[g]} D, \Gamma \cup \{g\} \rhd P' \sim Q} \tag{6}$$

$$\frac{P \xrightarrow{\tau} P'}{D, \Gamma \rhd P \sim Q \xrightarrow{\tau} D, \Gamma \rhd P' \sim Q} \tag{7}$$

Note that, P, P', Q are ATPs; d is a data channel; D is used to store available data channels shared by both ATPs P and Q. Γ is used to store available Boolean expressions in both ATPs P and Q. The predicate $D, \Gamma \rhd P \sim Q$ ($D, \Gamma \rhd Q \sim P$) is introduced to assert that P and Q can be behaviorally adaptable with respect to D and Γ, and '$\sim$' is commutative, therefore the symmetrical expressions or rules are omitted in the above.

To check the behavior adaptability between ATPs $P_1[f]$ and $P_2[f]$, we should initially construct the predicate $D, \Gamma \rhd P_1[f] \sim P_2[f]$ with $D=\Gamma=\varnothing$; and then based on the above rules, it is easy to derive our behavior adaptability result. If $P_1[f]=!d.P_1'$ and $P_2[f]=?d.P_2'$, then Rule 4 is applied, and we have $\{d\}, \Gamma \rhd P_1' \sim ?d.P_2'$; if $P_1'=?d'.P_1''$, then Rule 5 is applied, and we have $\{d\}, \Gamma \rhd ?d'.P_1'' \sim P_2'$; if $P_2'=[g].P_2''$, then Rule 6 is applied, and we have $\{d\}, \{g\} \rhd ?d'.P_1'' \sim P_2''$; if $P_2''=(!d''+\tau).P_2'''$, then Rules 4 and 7 are applied, and we have two results: $\{d, d''\}$, $\{g\} \rhd ?d'.P_1'' \sim P_2'''$ and $\{d\}, \{g\} \rhd ?d'.P_1'' \sim P_2'''$; Next we should apply the above rules to the two results. The process is finished when no rules can be applied to the generated predicates. If all the final predicates are in such a pattern $D^*, \Gamma^* \rhd P_1^* \sim P_2^*$ that $P_1^* =P_2^* =0$, then we determine that $P_1[f]$ and $P_2[f]$ are behaviorally adaptable, otherwise not.

The algorithm used for behavior adaptability analysis consists of two functions: *behaviorCheck* and *check*. The function *check* contains a two-level nested loop: the surrounding loop is used to determine the number of choice branches, we suppose the total number is k; the inner loop is used to extract one evolvable label and make the ATP continue to evolve, and we suppose after l times, the evolvable label can be found. Besides, the function *check* is recursively employed, however, the times for recursive call depends on the total number of labels and the total number of choice braches. From the illustration of the transformation from RSFN-O into ATP, we can easily obtain the total number of labels: it is the sum of the number of input, output data places and choice branches, that is, $|ID_{S1}|+|OD_{S1}|+|ID_{S2}|./OD_{S2}|+k$. Therefore, the total complexity of the algorithm is $O(l.(/ID_{S1}|+|OD_{S1}|+|ID_{S2}|+/OD_{S2}|+k))$, which is proportional to the complexity of the two services themselves.

4   Conclusion

Compared to the previous work [3], the proposed formalism of Web service – ontology-annotated service flow net is very expressive of representing service behavior as well as semantics information. The proposed approach based on model transformation is able to check both semantics and behavior adaptability of two services automatically; moreover, it can efficiently achieve behavior adaptability analysis by exploiting the regular structure of RSFN-Os including implicit choice and loop constructs, and completely avoid state explosion issues, thus it may significantly contribute to the improvement of the efficiency of dynamic service adaptation. Besides, RSFN-Os have strong similarities with popularly used concrete service description languages such as OWL-S [10], thus we are able to abstract almost all services in OWL-S descriptions.

References

1. Yellin, D.M., Strom, R.E.: Protocol Specifications and Component Adaptors. ACM Transactions on Programming Languages and Systems 19(2), 292–333 (1997)
2. Li, X.T., Fan, Y.S., Madnick, S., Sheng, Q.Z.: A Pattern-based Approach to Protocol Mediation for Web Services Composition. Inform. Softw. Technol. 52(3), 304–323 (2010)
3. Tan, W., Fan, Y.S., Zhou, M.C.: A Petri Net-Based Method for Compatibility Analysis and Composition of Web Services in Business Process Execution Language. IEEE Transactions on Automation Science and Engineering 6(1), 94–106 (2009)
4. Dijkman, R.: Notions of Behavioural Compatibility and Their Implications for BPEL Processes. Centre for Telemetrics and Information Technology, University of Twente, Enschede. Technical Report TR-CTIT-06-41 (2006)
5. Bracciali, A., Brogi, A., Canal, C.: A Formal Approach to Component Adaptation. Journal of System and Software 74(1), 45–54 (2005)
6. Gierds, C., Mooij, A., Wolf, K.: Specifying and Generating Behavioral Service Adapters based on Transformation Rules. Preprints CS-02-08 (2008)
7. Benatallah, B., Casati, F., Grigori, D., Nezhad, H.R.M., Toumani, F.: Developing Adapters for Web Services Integration. In: Pastor, Ó., Falcão e Cunha, J. (eds.) CAiSE 2005. LNCS, vol. 3520, pp. 415–429. Springer, Heidelberg (2005)
8. Brogi, A., Popescu, R.: Automated Generation of BPEL Adapters. In: Dan, A., Lamersdorf, W. (eds.) ICSOC 2006. LNCS, vol. 4294, pp. 27–39. Springer, Heidelberg (2006)
9. Xie, J., Tan, Q., Cao, G.: Modeling and Analyzing Web Service Behavior with Regular Flow Nets. In: Liu, W., Luo, X., Wang, F.L., Lei, J. (eds.) WISM 2009. LNCS, vol. 5854, pp. 309–319. Springer, Heidelberg (2009)
10. OWL-S Coalition, http://www.daml.org/services/owl-s/1.2/overview/
11. Brogi, A., Corfini, S., Popescu, R.: Semantic-based Composition-oriented Discovery of Web Services. ACM Transactions on Internet Technology 8(4), 1–39 (2008)

Prioritizing Consumer-Centric NFPs in Service Selection

Hanane Becha[1] and Sana Sellami[2]

[1] Aix Marseille University, CNRS, LIF UMR 7279, 13288 Marseille, France
[2]Aix Marseille University, CNRS, LSIS UMR 7296, 13397 Marseille, France
hanane.becha@univ-amu.fr, sana.sellami@lsis.org

Abstract. Service Selection continues to be a challenge in Service Oriented Architecture (SOA). In this paper, we propose a consumer-centric Non-Functional Properties (NFP) based services selection approach that relies on an externally-validated set of NFP descriptions integrated with the Web Service Description Language (WSDL). Our approach is based on three steps: (1) a Filtering step based on Hard NFPs defined in the consumer's request, (2) a Matchmaking step to discover the functionally-equivalent services, and (3) a Ranking step that sorts the resulting set of services based on the Soft NFPs defined by the consumer. The evaluation of our proposed service selection approach shows that the prioritization of NFP usage enhances the performance time of the service selection process while satisfying the functional and the non-functional requirements of the consumer.

Keywords: Service Oriented Architecture (SOA), Web Services, Non-Functional Properties (NFPs), Service Selection.

1 Introduction

The proliferation of Web Services raises some challenges with respect to the ability of the service consumers to select the service most appropriate to their needs. This problem is referred to as the service selection problem and can be divided as the *Matchmaking* problem of discovering the Web services that deliver a given functionality and the *Non-Functional Properties (NFP)-based Ranking* problem of evaluating these services.

The Matchmaking is a tedious, very time consuming step [19]. The NFP-based Ranking is very often treated as an extra burden once the Matchmaking is performed or even simply scarified [18]. In fact, the current service description languages such as Web Services Description Languages (WSDL) do not contain all the elements required to handle NFPs service descriptions [6] impeding the automation of the latter process. However, Non-Functional Properties (NFPs) play an important role in each stage of the SOA process lifecycle since they can impact the functional aspect of composed services as conflicting NFPs might cause redesign [1]. Indeed, NFPs are of critical importance and, at times, functional requirements might be sacrificed to meet them. There is a considerable amount of research effort that has placed emphasis on the importance of non-functional properties in service descriptions [1][2][3][8]. Hence, it seems worthwhile to get into account the consumer-centric NFPs even before performing the Matchmaking process. By consumer-centric (as opposed to

M. Indulska and S. Purao (Eds.): ER Workshops 2014, LNCS 8823, pp. 283–292, 2014.

provider centric), we mean the NFPs, once included in the service description, that can help the service consumer decide whether a given service suits best his needs. Exploring the NFP precedence in the service selection is the aim of this research effort that relies on a consumer-centric domain-independent, and externally validated NFP catalogue that was integrated into WSDL [8]. Our research hypothesize is that the prioritization of NFP usage will not only allow the selection of services that meet the user's non-functional requirements but can also improve the execution time of service discovery process. This paper is organized as follows. In Section 2, the related work is presented. Section 3 formalizes the proposed service selection approach. Section 4 details the validation method. Section 5 concludes and presents possible future work.

2   Related Work

NFP-aware service selection approaches in SOA can be classified into two categories. In the first category of service selection approaches, the available set of services is functionally heterogeneous. A Matchmaking procedure [16][17][18] is performed first to find the services that meet the required functionality. Then, an NFP-based Ranking step is performed to select the best services. The second category regroups most of the existing NFP-aware service selection solutions [1][5][12][13] [14][15]. These solutions are based on the hypothesis of the availability of a collection of functionally-equivalent services, and do not address the Matchmaking. The essence of these service selection solutions is concerned with *ranking* the already discovered set of services, including eliminating those that do not meet a given NFP threshold defined by the consumer. These two service selection categories are illustrated in Fig. 1.

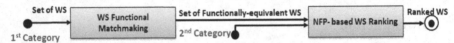

Fig. 1. Traditional approaches

In both categories, the service Ranking can be performed according to different methods [17] using either a unique NFP or a combination of a few NFP values having different weights. The combination of NFPs defines one representative NFP value usually using a Multiple Attribute Decision Making method [4]. However, these approaches have common shortcomings. The Ranking step is based either on NFPs that are defined only at the conceptual level (a.k.a. constraints) or defined based on a very limited set of non-validated NFPs with very simplistic data structures in an ad-hoc ways [7]. These solutions do not either have a clear focus on the service consumer's perspective or identify the publishing role of the service providers that should advertise the consumer-centric NFPs in their service descriptions. The service provider's publishing perspective is required, since the service consumers cannot just define on their own the NFPs that they are looking for at the service selection stage.

Many literature review studies such as [2] and [3] reveal that NFP-based consumer-centric service selection approaches are still needed. To the best of our knowledge, in all the reviewed papers, either the solutions rely on a pre-existing set of functionally-equivalent services or a Matchmaking is always performed before getting the NFPs into account. The NFP-based service Ranking is represented as an extra, separate, luxurious process after having gone (separately) through the tedious process of discovering functionally equivalent services [2] [19]. In opposition to the approach that prioritizes the NFPs, all these service selection approaches that prioritize the functional aspects are referred to in this paper as the traditional approaches, regardless the methods used in their Matchmaking and Web service Ranking processes.

3   NFP-Based WS Selection Approach

```
- <NFPdescription>
  - <price>
      <unit>EUR</unit>
    - <priceElements>
        <type>Invocation</type>
        <value>2</value>
      </priceElements>
    + <priceElements>
    </price>
  - <responseTime>
      <average>4.0</average>
      <best>2.0</best>
      <confidence>95</confidence>
      <unit>microseconds</unit>
      <worst>7.0</worst>
    </responseTime>
  - <serverLocation>
    - <countries>
        <code>CN</code>
      </countries>
    - <countries>
        <code>FR</code>
      </countries>
    </serverLocation>
  </NFPdescription>
```

Fig. 2. Example of WSDL Instance Document with NFP Description [6]

Fig. 3. The proposed Service Selection Approach

Our approach utilizes an externally-validated set of formal domain-independent catalogue of NFPs [6]. This catalogue defines a list of consumer-centric NFPs and their data structures to be published by service providers to better characterize services and enable consumers to perform NFP-aware service selection. The external validation details of this catalogue of NFPs (involving two surveys) can be found in[6]. This catalogue includes the following seventeen NFPs: (1) price, (2) response time, (3) reputation, (4) certification, (5) availability, (6) reliability, (7) usability, (8) accuracy, (9) standards compliance, (10) failure modes, (11) transactional service, (12) security, (13) jurisdiction, (14) service versioning, (15) resource requirements, (16) scalability, and (17) server location. The NFP catalogue description is integrated with the Web service description documents (e.g., WSDL documents) as shown by Fig. 2 and will be used as an additional input in our service selection process. The NFP description of the consumer's request respects a NFP schema provided in [6] and classifies the NFPs as Hard and Soft NFPs. Hard NFPs are the properties that must be absolutely satisfied. Soft NFPs are the nice to have properties [4]. This framework is extensible to support other NFPs (i.e., domain-specific NFPs) without changing the algorithms and tools for NFP-based service selection.

3.1   Use Case

Fig. 4 illustrates a use case of our approach. The box at the top is an example of consumer request that details the required functionality, Hard and Soft NFPs. The values of the NFPs in the request are thresholds of the required values. The request contains the maximum acceptable value for Price and the minimum values for Reputation and Usability. The box below contains the description offered services. WS1 is representative of services that meet the consumer request in terms of functionality as well as Hard NFPs. However, WS2 fails to meet the request since it charges the consumer *per subscription* and in *USD*. WS3 is representative of services that do not match the functionality looked for by the consumer. In this use case, only the subset of services represented by WS1 and WS3 satisfy the user's request in terms of Hard NFPs. The consumer will perform the Matchmaking process on these two subsets of services and will only retain the subset represented by WS1.

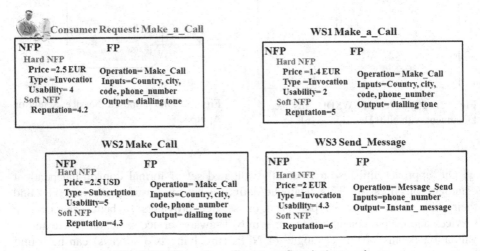

Fig. 4. Use Case of our Consumer-Centric Approach

Our proposed framework, illustrated by Fig. 3, is based on three different steps detailed below: *NFP Filtering*, *Matchmaking*, and *Service Ranking*. The initial set of the available services (*ServiceOffer*) in the registry are heterogeneous. Their descriptions address the functional as well as the NFPs. The request (*Request*) of the user defines the Hard NFPs, the Soft NFPs and the desired functionality. The NFPs description of the services and the NFPs in the consumer's request respect the NFP schema of the used consumer-centric NFP catalogue. The service selection algorithm is detailed in Fig. 5.

```
Algorithm   Selection (ServiceOffer, Request)

Input:  ServiceOffer: Set of available services
        Request: the consumer's Request
        σ: Matchmaking threshold
        tab[w]: Weights associated to the Soft NFPs
Output: RS: Ranked set of services
var:
    - SF: Set of services that correspond to the hard
          NFP per the consumer's request
    - SM:   Set   of   services   with   functionality
      corresponding to the consumer request
Begin{
  SF=∅;
  For each Service in  ServiceOffer
      SF= Filtering (Service, Request);
  SM =∅;
  For each ServiceSF in SF
      SM= Matchmaking (ServiceSF, Request,σ);
  RS =∅;
  For each ServiceSM in SM
      RS= Ranking (ServiceSM, Request,tab[w]);
  return RS;}
End
```

Fig. 5. Algorithm for Consumer-centric NFP-based Service Selection

3.2   Step 1: Services Filtering

The first step of our approach is to compare the NFPs of the available heterogeneous Web services (*ServiceOffer*) in the registry against the absolutely required NFPs defined in the consumer's service request. It filters out those that do not meet the NFP threshold values and return the filtered services *SF* (Fig. 6). When the service consumer denotes the Hard NFPs, this means that these NFPs shall be explicitly exposed as part of the service description, in a formal format and meet certain values expressed by the request as well. For example, in terms of pricing, the service consumer may only be interested in pay-per-invocation services and may not be willing to pay for monthly subscription services. To avoid repetition, the Filtering algorithm, defined by Fig. 6, considers five representative NFPs including Price, ResponseTime, Reputation, Availability and Scalability (eliminating the NFPs that have similar data structures and consequently same Filtering rules). Price and Response Time NFPs have complex data structures and call external comparison functions ComparePrice and CompareResponseTime that are not further explained here due to the space limitations.

```
Algorithm Filtering (ServiceOffer, Request)
Input: ServiceOffer: Set of available services
       Request: The consumer's Request
Output: SF: Set of services that correspond to the hard NFP
        per the consumer's request
Var: -HardNFP: hard NFPs defined in the request out of the
     used NFP catalogue that contains 17 NFPs
-   ComparePrice(Service.Price, Request.Price): function to
    compare the Price NFP of the offered service versus the
    Request. Price has a complex data structure
-   CompareResponseTime(Service.ResponseTime,
    Request.ResponseTime): function to compare the ReponseTime
    NFP of the offered service versus the Request. ReponseTime
    has a complex data structure
Begin{
 Boolean Valid = TRUE;
 For each (Service in ServiceOffer){
  For each (HardNFP in Request){
// For the following NFPs, exact values or less are //better
for consumer's satisfaction
//Comparison of Price by invoking the ComparePrice //function.
It returns TRUE if the Service is "too //expensive" compared
to the Request.
    If (HardNFP==Price)
      If (ComparePrice (Service.Price, Request.Price))
      Valid = FALSE;
// CompareResponseTime returns TRUE if the Service is
too //slow compared to the Request
      If (HardNFP == ResponseTime)
         If(CompareResponseTime(Service.ResponseTime,
Request.ResponseTime))
            Valid = FALSE;
//For the following NFPs, exact values or higher are //better
for consumer's satisfaction
  //Reputation is very similar to Usability NFP
      If (HardNFP == Reputation)
        If (Service. Reputation < Request.Reputation)
           Valid = FALSE;
      // Reliability is very similar to Availability
         If (HardNFP == Availability)
           If(Service.Availability<
Request.Availability)
             Valid = FALSE;
          If (HardNFP == Scalability)
             If(Service.Scalability                    <
Request.Scalability)
             Valid = FALSE;}
         If (Valid==TRUE) ADD(Service, SF); }
     return SF;}End
```

Fig. 6. Algorithm for Web Services Filtering based on the Consumer's Hard NFPs

3.3   Step 2: Web Services Matchmaking

The input of this process is the set of filtered services (*SF*) that meet the Hard NFPs per step 1. In this step, service Matchmaking process is performed to discover the services that offer similar functionality (*SM*) defined in the consumer's request. The Matchmaking can be based on different techniques [9][10]. The matchmaker [9] is used in our proposed approach. The Matchmaking techniques support partial matches and associate correspondence degrees that have to exceed a given threshold σ defined in the consumer's request. Partial matches enable the consumer to trade the functional aspect in favor of the prioritized NFPs.

3.4   Step 3: Web Services Ranking

The input of this step is a set of services that deliver the required functionality and meet the Hard NFPs (*SM*) defined in the consumer's request. This set is inherently sorted based on the correspondence degree of the Matchmaking. The essence of this step is to select the service that suits best the needs of the service consumer. To do so, the services are ranked (*RS*) based on the Soft NFPs that have different weights defined by the consumers to reflect its preferences over these properties. The Ranking can be performed as described in Preference based Universal Ranking Integration framework (PURI) [11].

4   Experiment Design and Evaluation

The aim of this experiment is to assess the impact of the prioritization of NFP usage on the execution time of service selection process.

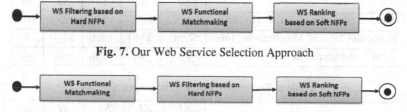

Fig. 7. Our Web Service Selection Approach

Fig. 8. Traditional Web Service Selection Approach

The experiments measure the total execution time of the Filtering and Matchmaking steps of our approach (Fig. 7) versus the approach that prioritizes the functional aspects (Fig. 8). The same Matchmaking and Filtering processes are invoked but in different order. Both approaches will select the services having the same quality. The Ranking process is not taken into account as it is the same in both approaches.

Experiments are performed on a test collection of 100 Web services[1] from the communication domain described using the language SAWSDL[2] (Semantic Annotations for WSDL). The Web services descriptions are extended using the NFPs catalogue [6] which defines a library of complex types as an XML schema that can be fully or partially populated and that apply to the whole service as one unit.

---

[1] http://www.semwebcentral.org/projects/sawsdl-tc/
[2] http://www.w3.org/TR/sawsdl/

The Filtering process (Fig. 6) is implemented using the Xquery language and executed over the BaseX[3] database. The consumer's request contains 5 NFPs out of the 17 proposed in the catalogue. Reputation and Reliability are the Soft NFPs. Price, Response Time and Availability are the Hard NFPs. We performed the Matchmaking procedure using the SAWSDL-MX1 matchmaker [9]. We considered five different scenarios that differ in terms of the number of eliminated services after having performing the NFP-based Filtering step.

Table 1 and Table 2 summarize the scenarios of our experiments. Table 1 represents our approach where the first performed process is the Hard NFP-based Filtering. Table 2 represents the approach where the first performed process is the semantic Matchmaking. The initial set of heterogeneous services in the WS registry contains 100 Web services. The first rows of both tables detail the number of the eliminated services after having performed the first process of each approach. Then, the execution time of the second process is measured for each scenario for both approaches. In the first scenario S1, the Filtering step does not eliminate any service (e.g., the entire set of services meet the consumer's Hard NFPs). The execution time of the Filtering process performed against the initial set of 100 WS is 256 ms. The execution time of Matchmaking performed against the initial set of WS is 2790 ms. Respectively, in the four following scenarios, the Filtering step eliminates 25%, 50%, 75%, and 100% of the available services. In last scenario, no service corresponds to the Hard NFPs of the consumer's request. The Hard NFPs have to be met even in the detriment of the functional requirements. As shown by the tables, the execution time of both processes varies as a function of the number of the services against which are performed.

Table 1. Our WS Selection Approach

	S1	*S2*	*S3*	*S4*	*S5*
Number of eliminated (filtered) WS	0	25	50	75	100
Execution Time of Matchmaking (ms)	2790	2340	1880	1760	0
Total Execution Time (ms)	3046	2596	2136	2016	256

Table 2. Traditional WS Selection Approach

	S1	*S2*	*S3*	*S4*	*S5*
Number of eliminated (unmatched) WS	0	25	50	75	100
Execution Time of Filtering (ms)	256	200	162	112	0
Total Execution Time (ms)	3046	2990	2952	2902	2790

Fig. 9 illustrates the results of our empirical experiment. In the scenarios described above, our selection approach is shown to be more efficient than the solution that prioritizes the functional aspects over the NFPs. Prioritizing the NFPs in the service selection enhances the performance time while satisfying the functional and the non-functional requirements of the consumer. In fact the Matchmaking process is very costly when compared to the Filtering process. The cost of Matchmaking performed against a single service is as costly as the Filtering step performed against the initial set of available services. The more irrelevant services that can be eliminated during the Filtering process, the faster the Matchmaking. Even when the Filtering step

---

[3] http://basex.org/

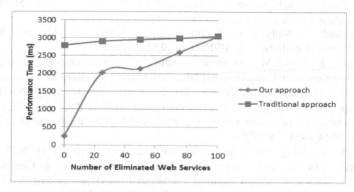

Fig. 9. Performance Comparison of WS Selection Approaches

eliminates just a very few services before getting to the Matchmaking step, it is still worth to use our proposed approach.

However, we recognize the limits of our empirical experiment. In order to generalize our findings, further experimentations and/or statistic study are required to access the impact of the complexity of the consumer's request and the NFP descriptions over the time performance of each process. Part of the threats to our validation is the definition of 'extreme' scenarios where the number of Hard NFPs is higher, the data structures of NFPs are more complex (Security can have multiple sub parts), the NFP descriptions of the offered WS is larger, and the functionality looked for is simpler than the scenarios considered in our experimentation.

5   Conclusion and Future Work

In this paper, we presented a consumer-centric NFP-based approach for Web service selection that relies on an externally-validated set of NFPs. The proposed approach filters out of the services that do not meet the Hard NFPs defined by the consumer before even performing the Matchmaking. The evaluation of this service selection approach shows that the prioritization of NFPs usage can enhance the performance time of the service selection process while satisfying the functional and the non-functional requirements of the consumer.

In future work, we will plan to perform statistical study and test in different scenarios to further measure the performance of our approach versus the traditional one. In addition, the required extensions to enable BPEL to support the NFPs should be identified to encourage NFPs usages in service selection and composition. As SOA is technology agnostic, it is interesting to test our approach in the context of REST services.

Acknowledgments. Special thanks to Prof. Daniel Amyot for his collaboration.

References

1. Klose, K., Knackstedt, R., Beverungen, D.: Identification of services - a stakeholderbased approach to SOA development and its application in the area of production planning. In: ECIS, pp. 1802–1814. University of St. Gallen (2007)

2. Hai, D., Farookh, K., Elizabeth, C.: Semantic Web Service matchmakers: State of the art and challenges. Concurrency Computation Practice and Experience (2012)
3. Teka Abelneh, Y., Nelly, C.-F., Brahmananda, S.: A Systematic Literature Review on Service Description Methods. In: REFSQ, pp. 239–255 (2012)
4. Bartalos, P., Bielikova, M.: Automatic dynamic web service composition: A survey and problem formalization. Computing and Informatics 30(4), 793–827 (2011)
5. Becha, H., Mussbacher, G., Amyot, D.: Modeling and Analyzing Non-Functional Requirements in Service Oriented Architecture with the User Requirements Notation. In: Non-Functional Properties in Service Oriented Architecture: Requirements, Models and Methods, IGI Global, USA (2011)
6. Becha, H.: Exposing and Aggregating Non-functional Properties in SOA from the Perspective of the Service Consumer. Ph.D. thesis, University of Ottawa, Canada (2012)
7. Becha, H., Amyot, D.: Non-Functional Properties in Service Oriented Architecture: A Consumer's Perspective. Journal of Software 7(3), 575–587 (2012)
8. Becha, H., Amyot, D.: Consumer-Centric Non-functional Properties of SOA-Based Services. In: 6th International Workshop on Principles of Engineering Service-Oriented and Cloud Systems, PESOS (to appear, 2014)
9. Klusch, M., Kapahnke, P., Zinnikus, I.: Hybrid adaptive web service selection with SAWSDL-MX and WSDL-analyzer. In: Aroyo, L., Traverso, P., Ciravegna, F., Cimiano, P., Heath, T., Hyvönen, E., Mizoguchi, R., Oren, E., Sabou, M., Simperl, E. (eds.) ESWC 2009. LNCS, vol. 5554, pp. 550–564. Springer, Heidelberg (2009)
10. Sellami, S., Boucelma, O.: Towards a Flexible Schema Matching Approach for Semantic Web Service Discovery. In: Proceeding of the IEEE 20th International Conference on Web Services, pp. 611–612 (2013)
11. María, G.J., Martin, J., David, R., Sudhir, A., Antonio, R.C.: Integrating semantic Web services ranking mechanisms using a common preference model. Knowl.-Based Syst. 49, 22–36 (2013)
12. Askaroglu, E., Senkul, P.: Automatic QoS evaluation method for web services. In: IEEE Symposium on Computers and Communications, ISCC, pp. 367–369 (2012)
13. Kritikos, K., Plexousakis, D.: OWL-Q for Semantic QoS-based Web Service Description and Discovery. In: Proceedings of the SMRR 2007 Workshop on Service Matchmaking and Resource Retrieval in the Semantic Web (SMRR 2007) co-located with ISWC 2007 + ASWC (2007)
14. Shi, C., Lin, D., Ishida, T.: User-Centered QoS Computation for Web Service Selection. In: IEEE 19th International Conference on Web Services, ICWS, pp. 456–463 (2012)
15. Muñoz Frutos, H., Kotsiopoulos, I., Vaquero Gonzalez, L.M., Rodero Merino, L.: Enhancing service selection by semantic qoS. In: Aroyo, L., Traverso, P., Ciravegna, F., Cimiano, P., Heath, T., Hyvönen, E., Mizoguchi, R., Oren, E., Sabou, M., Simperl, E. (eds.) ESWC 2009. LNCS, vol. 5554, pp. 565–577. Springer, Heidelberg (2009)
16. Ajao, T.A., Deris, S.: Optimal Web Service Selection with Consideration for User's Preferences. IJCSI International Journal of Computer Science Issues 10(2(3)) (2013)
17. Lin, S.-Y., Lai, C.-H., Wu, C.-H., Lo, C.: A trustworthy QoS-based collaborative filtering approach for webservice discovery. The Journal of Systems and Software (2014)
18. Huang, A.F.M., Lan, C.-W., Yang, J.H.: An optimal QoS-based Web service selection scheme. Inf. Sci. 179(19), 3309–3322 (2009)
19. Mukpadhyay, D., Chougule, A.: A Survey on Web Service Discovery Approaches. CoRR abs/1206.5582 (2012)

Personal eHealth Knowledge Spaces though Models, Agents and Semantics

Haridimos Kondylakis[1], Dimitris Plexousakis[1], Vedran Hrgovcic[2], Robert Woitsch[2],
Marc Premm[3], and Michael Schuele[3]

[1] Institute of Computer Science, FORTH, N. Plastira 100, Heraklion, Greece
{kondylak,dp}@ics.forth.gr
[2] BOC Asset Management GmbH, Operngasse 20B, Vienna, 1040, Austria
{vedran.hrgovcic,robert.woitsch}@boc-eu.com
[3] Universität Hohenheim, Information Systems 2 (530 D), 70593 Stuttgart, Germany
{marc.premm,michael.schuele}@uni-hohenheim.de

Abstract. In this paper, we present a web-based platform that generates a Personal eHealth Knowledge Space as an aggregation of several knowledge sources relevant for the provision of individualized personal services. To this end, novel technologies are exploited and demonstrated, such as *knowledge on demand* to lower the information overload for the end-users, *agent-based communication and reasoning* to support cooperation and decision making, and *semantic integration* to provide uniform access to heterogeneous information. All three technologies are combined to create a novel web based platform allowing seamless user interaction through a portal that supports personalized, granular and secure access to relevant information. We demonstrate the portal and then the aforementioned technologies using real medical scenarios.

1 Introduction

Medicine is undergoing a revolution that is transforming the nature of healthcare from reactive to preventive. The changes are catalyzed by a new systems approach which focuses on integrated diagnosis, treatment and prevention of disease in individuals. This will replace the current practice of medicine over the coming years with a personalized predictive treatment. While the goal is clear, the path is fraught with challenges.

One of these challenges is that in order to decide on preventive or therapeutic actions, physicians, patients and caregivers are required to obtain all relevant user-specific knowledge. However, this knowledge is fragmented into relevant knowledge sources such as health records, databases on medical literature or environmental information, wearable or portable devices for health monitoring, and common ubiquitous internet services (including user generated information). Currently petabytes of data are produced every day, which generate the following problems: (1) inability to access correct data – e.g. by not being able to select the right knowledge source within an available timeframe; (2) inability to process the relevant data with available

M. Indulska and S. Purao (Eds.): ER Workshops 2014, LNCS 8823, pp. 293–297, 2014.

resources; and (3) inability to easily downsize and save the selected data so that they become portable – creating thus personal knowledge spaces [1].

The eHealthMonitor (http://www.ehealthmonitor.eu/) project aspires to create a platform that generates a Personal eHealth Knowledge Space (PeKS) as an aggregation of all relevant sources (e.g., EHRs, PHRs, medical sensors, weather services etc.) relevant for the provision of individualized personal eHealth Services.

The first step in providing such services is *the identification of the available knowledge and data sources* concerning a *particular domain* or part thereof in a specific *timeframe* for each specific *user* type, i.e. the knowledge space. To do that a set of modelling toolkits are used by doctors, assisted by technicians in the beginning, and knowledge engineers to define which information, data sources and apps will be presented in the portal to each user [2]. For example a doctor can configure the platform to switch from normal UI to single yes/no buttons for a dementia patient if the patient's dementia stage goes beyond a specific value. This configuration is enabled by graphically specifying such a rule using a graphical modelling toolkit.

Besides identifying the data sources relevant to the users we also need to *establish a seamless, transparent mechanism to access and query them*. For example, a weather service can be provided through a web service with an XML output, a medical device can provide a custom API whereas EHR/PHR systems might store data in a relational database. To aggregate all these diverse and heterogeneous data sources semantic integration techniques are used and extended. More specifically we use a *novel ontology* called *eHM Ontology suite*, as global schema in order to formulate SPARQL queries that are issued to our engine. This query is then rewritten to the subsequent sources to be answered. Moreover, since our platform will be used as a continuous companion of a citizen, it should allow knowledge to evolve. Novel mechanisms allow *data integration under evolving ontologies* that are used as global schema [3], [4].

However, even when we have uniform access to the information under consideration *different privacy requirements and conflicting interests might exist among the participating entities*. For example, an insurance company might have an interest in accessing the entire medical history of patients, whereas, for the patients themselves, it would be better if the insurance company had access only to specific data that their contract requires to share. Moreover, personal medical information that is known to a patient and a physician should not be shared with any other participant that is not explicitly authorized to access this information. In order to handle those complex relationships, traditional methods are not enough. Hence, software agents are used, one agent for each participating actor implementing his/her interests. Then, we map their mutual relationships to a multi-agent organisation. Adaptive coordination methods among several agents, are used to analyse the provision of personal guidance services for cooperative decision making in eHealth service networks [5].

Other projects with similar goals include the p-Medicine (www.p-medicine.eu), the INTEGRATE (www.fp7-integrate.eu), the EURECA (eurecaproject.eu) and the Commodity12 (www.commodity12.eu) projects. However, although the goals are similar, different strategies have been selected to resolve the problems in the domain. For example there are no adaptive coordination methods to enable collaborative decision making and no knowledge on demand mechanisms for generating personal knowledge spaces. Other projects in the area employee semantic integration method-ologies using ontologies, such as MyHealthAvatar (www.myhealthavatar.eu) and MD-Paedigree (www.md-paedigree.eu/) or dealing with concerned with the patient empowered knowledge spaces, such as PatientLikeMe (www.patientslikeme.com), Microsoft's HealthVaulth (www.healthvault.com). However, as opposed to the work presented here they do not proactively support the cooperative decision making process (e.g. by dynamically enlarging the decision set), but act as a static knowledge spaces – providing storage and role based access to the knowledge resources. To the best of our knowledge eHealthMonitor is the first project to combine knowledge on demand, semantic integration and agents with novel contributions in each one of the aforementioned fields.

2   Demonstration Content

To demonstrate the functionalities of the eHealthMonitor platform we will present the three components of the smart layer and their integration through the web portal as shown in Fig. 1 . The demonstration will proceed in the following four phases:

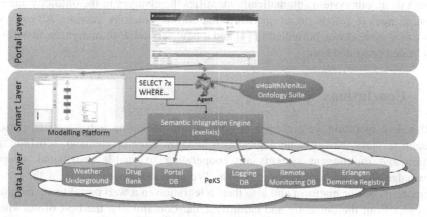

Fig. 1. eHealthMonitor Platform Architecture

(i) **Portal Demonstration**: The demonstration will start by presenting the web portal that the doctors and the patients are using. Real scenarios from cardiovascular and dementia domains will be presented. For example we will demonstrate a dementia patient whose stage is changing and a patient suffering from chronic obstructive pulmonary disease (COPD) who is travelling in a place with high pollution and should be notified automatically with an alert. The portal is already available (https://131.188.43.102/ username: george.smith@ehm.eu password: passEhm.) but it will be customized in real time when demonstrating the aforementioned scenarios.

(ii) **Modelling Component Demonstration**: Then the modelling component will be demonstrated to show how the specific resources are being selected for each patient and how the rules for the individual apps and resources are created. Then the automatic creation of configuration files for each agent will be presented. Finally, we will demonstrate updating the portal user interface according to the choices and the work-flows specified in the modelling environment.

(iii) **Multi-agent Component Demonstration**: In the next phase we will demonstrate the representation of the participating actors using intelligent software agents and how their mutual relationships formulate a multi-agent organization. We will demonstrate how the agents act proactively on behalf of the the users in order to notify them. For example in case of high pollution level in the atmosphere patients suffering from COPD should be notified to avoid going out. Moreover, we will show how the agents use semantic reasoning to resolve conflicting interests for sharing information among themselves.

(iv) **Semantic Integration Component**: Finally we will demonstrate *exelixis,* our novel system for integrating heterogeneous data sources. The system is online (http://139.91.183.29:8080/exelixis/) implementing novel algorithms for rewriting queries, formulated using one version of eHM Ontology Suite, to the underlying data sources. We have to note that due to the rapid development of research we expect that the eHM Ontology Suite will evolve. The problem that occurs is the following: when the ontology changes, the mappings to the sources become invalid and should some-how be updated. Instead of invalidating the mappings and then forcing the experts to correct them, our system automatically identifies the changes in the ontology and uses those changes to rewrite input queries to the correct ontology version. An early ver-sion of the system was presented in [4] and a new version with many new features [3] will be demonstrated here.

3   Conclusions

In this demonstration we present a novel platform providing individualized personal eHealth services. Novel technologies such as knowledge on demand, semantic inte-gration and multi-agent systems are cooperating to enable distributed, adaptive knowledge sharing coordination methods. We demonstrate each one of these novel components of our platform and also their integration in a web portal using pragmatic use-cases from the dementia and cardiovascular domains. To the best of our knowl-edge it is the first time that all these technologies are applied altogether.

Acknowledgement. This work has been supported by the eHealthMonitor (www.ehealthmonitor.eu) and the MyHealthAvatar (http://www.myhealthavatar.eu/) EU projects and has been partly funded by the European Commission under the con-tracts FP7-287509 and FP7-600929.

References

1. Hrgovcic, V., Woitsch, R.: Evolution of eHealth Knowledge Spaces: Meta Model Based Approach for Semantic Lifting. In: Echallenges e-2013 Conference (2013), Best Paper Award

2. Hrgovcic, V., Utz, W., Woitsch, R.: Knowledge engineering in future internet. In: Karagiannis, D., Jin, Z. (eds.) KSEM 2009. LNCS, vol. 5914, pp. 100–109. Springer, Heidelberg (2009)
3. Kondylakis, H., Plexousakis, D.: Ontology evolution without tears. Journal of Web Semantics: Science, Services and Agents on the World Wide Web 19, 42–58 (2013)
4. Kondylakis, H., Plexousakis, D.: Exelixis: Evolving Ontology-Based Data Integration System. In: SIGMOD Conference, pp. 1283–1286 (2011)
5. Widmer, T., Premm, M., Karaenke, P.: Sourcing Strategies for Energy-Efficient Virtual Organizations in Cloud Computing. In: Business Informatics(CBI) Conference, pp. 159–166 (2013)

Lightweight Semantic Prototyper for Conceptual Modeling

Gayane Sedrakyan and Monique Snoeck

Katholieke Universiteit Leuven,
Department of Decision Sciences and Information Management,
Naamsestraat 69, 3000 Leuven
{gayane.sedrakyan,monique.snoeck}@kuleuven.be

Abstract. While much research work was devoted to conceptual model quality validation techniques, most of the existing tools in this domain focus on syntactic quality. Tool support for checking semantic quality (correspondence between the conceptual model and requirements of a domain to be engineered) is largely lacking. This work introduces a lightweight model-driven semantic prototyper to test/validate conceptual models. The goal of the tool is twofold: (1) to assist business analysts in validating semantic quality of conceptual business specifications using a fast prototyper to communicate with domain experts; (2) to support the learning perspective of conceptual modeling for less experienced modelers (such as students or novice analysts in their early career) to facilitate their progression to advanced level of expertise. The learning perspective is supported by providing automated feedback that visually links the test results to their causes in the model's design. The effectiveness of the tool has been confirmed by means of empirical experimental studies.

Keywords: Conceptual modeling, semantic quality, prototyping, testing, validation, feedback.

1   Introduction

Recent research highlights the need of shifting testing of a system to the earliest phases of engineering in order to reduce the time and resources spent on building a software application by minimizing the number of errors resulting from miscommunicated and/or wrongly specified requirements. Conceptual modeling is described as the process of formally describing a problem domain for the purpose of understanding and communicating system requirements [1]. Formalization of requirements through models is known to enable quality control at a level that is impossible to reach with requirements articulated in natural language. Being a sub-discipline of requirements engineering (as a means of communicating requirements) and software engineering (by providing a foundation for building information systems) [2] makes conceptual models the earliest formally testable artefact. However, despite the amount of research devoted to conceptual model quality validation methods, most of the existing tools in this domain focus on syntactic quality. Tool support for checking semantic

M. Indulska and S. Purao (Eds.): ER Workshops 2014, LNCS 8823, pp. 298–302, 2014.

quality (the level to which the statements in a model reflect the real world in a valid and complete way) is largely lacking.

It is commonly accepted that prototyping is capable of achieving the most concrete form of a prospective system allowing early feedback from stakeholders thus contributing to improved semantic quality. Current methodologies for the fast prototyping of highly abstract specifications include Model Driven Engineering (MDE) of the OMG, which uses UML -the widely accepted modeling language standard [3]. However methodologies to make the MDE approach easily applicable to conceptual modeling are lacking or not (well-)defined, e.g. a way of combining structural and behavioral views into a single model. The absence of a methodology for an integrated approach combining conceptual modeling and MDE-based simulation, and prototyping in particular, also implies semantic compliance issues (is it the right prototype for a given design?). Moreover, many researchers point out the technical complexity of UML to identify a relevant subset for conceptual modelling as well as being not precise enough for rapid prototyping. Finally, a prototype's testing results are not easily interpretable since the link between a prototype and its design is not explicit. In this demo we introduce an integrated environment that allows fast prototyping of conceptual models the testing effectiveness of which is enhanced by automated feedback.

2   MERODE Prototype: Benefits of Integrated Approach

The prototyping tool introduced in this work is an integrated part of the MERODE [4] conceptual modeling environment[1]. MERODE is based on the framework that overcomes the shortcomings of UML (being technically too complex for conceptual modelling and not precise enough for rapid prototyping). The framework is based on three kinds of model views (restricted class diagrams, interaction model, state charts) and uses a "consistency by construction" approach that completes missing model elements automatically thus allowing simple transformations [5, 6]. A generated prototype supports the execution of business events by also providing textual and graphical feedback when and why the execution of a triggered business event is refused, thus making the links between a prototype and its design explicit. We opt for the MERODE approach for the following benefits:
- using a limited subset of UML relevant for conceptual modeling that allows removing or hiding details irrelevant for a conceptual modeling view
- framework combining structural and behavioral views into a single model
- providing integrated environment for modeling and simulation
- models designed are readily transformable for execution

The prototyping feature introduced in this work differs from similar approaches by introducing:
- easy and fast transformation using one-click approach
- intuitive graphical interface (both for a prototyping tool and generated prototypes)

---

[1] http://merode.econ.kuleuven.ac.be/mermaid.aspx

- an embedded data storage that can be queried via simple user interface invoked from inside a prototype application
- use of cognitive feedback in a prototype allowing for less experienced modelers to benefit from easy discovery of semantic compliance issues resulting from misinterpreted use of modeling language constructs

The lightweight prototyper will be of benefit to practitioners, researchers, educators and novice modelers (such as students and junior business analysts) in the domain of conceptual modeling.

3   Demonstration Highlights

We demonstrate how semantic validation of models can be facilitated by the use of a feedback-enabled prototyper. A short demo using a simple model can be viewed at http://merode.econ.kuleuven.ac.be/demo.aspx. A visitor to our demonstration will be invited to assume a role of a tester. S/he will be able to test the prototype of a pre made model and will be able to create and test an own model. The demo will focus on

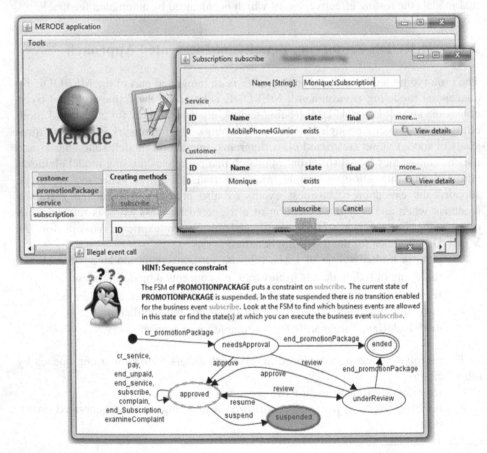

Fig. 1. An example of testing with a prototype: execution refusal due to a sequence constraint

the model-based feedback features and their effectiveness in model-understanding and validation. An example of testing an erroneous model is shown in **Fig. 1** by means of a model about (mobile phone) services which customers can subscribe to, and for which promotion packages are offered regularly. Testing the prototype reveals a semantic mismatch (design error): trying to subscribe to a service results in execution failure due to a sequence constraint violation (the state of the PromotionPackage object to which the chosen service is associated is "suspended"). The scenario fails because of a behavioral constraint, but it actually reveals a wrong hidden dependency from "Service" to "PromotionPackage": it seems a service depends on the availability of a promotion, which is incorrect. For a less experienced modeler the explanation can be extended with graphical visualization linking to a specific part of a model design that causes the error. Extensive experimental testing has demonstrated the positive effect of prototype-based simulation on junior modelers understanding of a model [7].

4   Conclusion

The MERODE semantic prototyper provides a fast and easy way of validating semantic quality of conceptual models thus enabling a shift of testing of a prospective system into earlier phases of its engineering, namely, conceptual specification level. Furthermore, for educational perspective the tool provides an innovative method of teaching conceptual modeling allowing novice modelers to test a working prototype of a conceptual design and learn by experiencing [8]. The integrated feedback facilitates fast progression to more advanced levels of expertise. Effectiveness of the method over traditional manual inspection and validation was confirmed by empirical experimental studies using an experimental sample of 120 users.

References

1. Siau, K.: Informational and Computational Equivalence in Comparing Information Modeling Methods. Journal of Database Management (JDM) 15(1), 73–86 (2004)
2. Moody, D.L.: Theoretical and practical issues in evaluating the quality of conceptual models: current state and future directions. Data & Knowledge Engineering 55(3), 243–276 (2005), ISSN 0169-023X
3. OMG, Model-Driven Architecture (2014), http://www.omg.org/mda/
4. Snoeck, M., Dedene, G., Verhelst, M., Depuydt, A.: Object-oriented enterprise modelling with MERODE. Leuvense Universitaire Pers, Leuven (1999)
5. Sedrakyan, G., Snoeck, M.: A PIM-to-Code requirements engineering framework. In: Proceedings of Modelsward 2013-1st International Conference on Model-driven Engineering and Software Development-Proceedings, pp. 163–169 (2013)
6. Sedrakyan, G., Snoeck, M.: Feedback-enabled MDA-prototyping effects on modeling knowledge. In: Nurcan, S., Proper, H.A., Soffer, P., Krogstie, J., Schmidt, R., Halpin, T., Bider, I. (eds.) BPMDS 2013 and EMMSAD 2013. Lecture Notes in Business Information Processing, vol. 147, pp. 411–425. Springer, Heidelberg (2013)

7. Sedrakyan, G., Snoeck, M., Poelmans, S.: Assessing the effectiveness of feedback enabled simulation in teaching conceptual modeling. Review at Computers & Education
8. EuropeanCommission, Opening up education: Innovative teaching and learning for all through new technologies and open educational resources (2013)

SQTime: Time-Enhanced Social Search Querying

Panagiotis Lionakis[1], Kostas Stefanidis[2], and Georgia Koloniari[3]

[1] Department of Computer Science, University of Crete, Heraklion, Greece
lionakis@csd.uoc.gr
[2] Institute of Computer Science, FORTH, Heraklion, Greece
kstef@ics.forth.gr
[3] Department of Applied Informatics, University of Macedonia, Thessaloniki, Greece
gkoloniari@uom.edu.gr

Abstract. In this paper, we present SQTime, a system for social search queries that exploit temporal information available in social networks. Specifically, SQTime introduces different types of queries aiming at satisfying information needs from different perspectives. SQTime is built upon a social graph and query model both augmented with time, and develops methods for query processing and time-dependent ranking.

1 Introduction

Due to the increasing popularity of social networks and the vast amount of information they contain, recently, there have been many efforts in enhancing Web search based on social data. An important dimension of social networks is their dynamic nature. New information is added through user activities and updates, representing changes in their interests. To deal with this temporal aspect, we use an annotated graph model that incorporates time, similarly to [2], for representing the social network, and propose a new time-enhanced query model.

Unlike previous approaches that focus on graph evolution [4,5], our query model deals with social search and introduces two query types: *user-centric* and *system-centric* queries. User-centric queries offer a personalized search feature by exploiting a user's social relationships. System-centric queries provide a global search feature with applications in online-shopping and target-advertising, so as to select the best target group for a new product or the best products to promote to a given user. We allow both the explicit and implicit use of time [3]. To allow queries to express time explicitly, we extend user- and system-centric queries to time-dependent queries that include temporal hard constraints. Furthermore, we enhance query results with an implicit use of time by providing a time-dependent ranking, so that more recent results are returned first.

SQTime incorporates a framework for processing queries based on the time-enhanced query model, we first introduced in [6], and offers the user the opportunity to explore both the explicit and implicit use of temporal information and its impact when querying the social graph.

M. Indulska and S. Purao (Eds.): ER Workshops 2014, LNCS 8823, pp. 303–307, 2014.

2   The SQTime Framework

We model a social network as an undirected graph, $G = (V, E)$. Nodes in V correspond to the entities that belong to the social network, while edges in E capture the relationships between the entities in V. We discern between two types of entities: (i) users U, that consist of the social network participants, and (ii) objects O, that include all other entities in the social network, e.g., applications, events and photos. Edges between users capture the friendships between them, while edges between users and objects declare that users consume the objects. We consider extending the typical graph model with temporal information towards making social search time-dependent. This way, an element, node or edge, of G is *valid* for the time period for which the corresponding element of the social network it represents is also valid. To incorporate times into the graph, each element is annotated with a label $l = (t_{start}, t_{end})$ that determines the time interval for which the element is valid.

Our goal is to support queries for the graph structure that also exploit the time dimension of the graph elements. In user-centric queries, a user is interested in retrieving information about other users or objects that satisfy specific predicates and are connected to the user directly or through their friends. We consider two general query categories. The first category gives priority to the friends of the user, while the second one to the objects to be consumed. This model is enhanced with time by including separate constraints for the validity in specific time intervals, for the elements that are included in a query. For example, "*get my friends, valid in 2013, that have been attended sports events*" retrieves my friends, valid in 2013, that have some connection to events that satisfy the given predicate, even if the events themselves are valid at another time period.

In general, given the graph $G = (V, E)$, for a user-centric query for friends $Q(u_i, P)$, where P is a set of query predicates, processing proceeds as follows:

Step 1: Retrieve the user nodes $u_j \in U$, say U', st. $\exists (u_i, u_j) \in E$.
Step 2: Retrieve the object nodes $o_l \in O$, say O', st. o_l satisfies all predicates in P.
Step 3: Remove all nodes u_j from U', st., for at least one node $o_l \in O'$, $\nexists (u_j, o_l) \in E$.
Step 4: The remaining nodes form the result $res(Q)$.

For the time-dependent query (Q, T), where $T = [s, d)$ is a time constraint, T concerns the nodes in Step 2, and is treated as another predicate in P, or the result nodes in Step 4, and therefore, introduces the following filtering steps:

Step 5: From the nodes in $res(Q)$ remove all nodes v_j, st. $l(v_j).t_{start} < s$ or $l(v_j).t_{end} \geq d$.
Step 6: The remaining nodes form the result $res(Q, T)$.

Similarly, for system-centric queries, the system requires locating: (i) users connected to particular objects, or (ii) objects connected with particular users, and augment them with time, to retrieve only valid information (details in [6]).

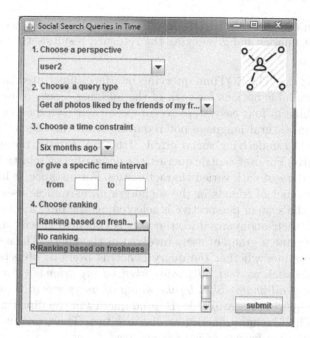

Fig. 1. SQTime querying interface

SQTime ranks results according to the freshness of the connections between users and objects. Freshness is recorded in our graph model on the edges' labels. In general, our motivation is based on the fact that recently added edges better reflect the current trends and thus, they could contribute in ranking the results. For example, assume a user-centric query for friends $Q(u_i, P)$. $ranked\_res(Q)$ of Q is a ranked list of the users in $res(Q)$; ranking is achieved with respect to the labels of the edges that connect the users in $res(Q)$ with the objects satisfying P and, in particular, with respect to the time the connections were established. Abstractly, for ranking, we first assign to each result element a score equal to the maximum t_{start} value among the values of the labels of its connections to the nodes that satisfy the predicates of the query, and then sort the resulting elements according to that score.

3   Demonstration

This demo of SQTime aims at allowing users to explore the different types of social search queries in our model, and the implications of enhancing queries with time both implicitly and explicitly. SQTime is built on top of a social graph we constructed with a data set from [1], that includes anonymized information about the evolution of the Flickr social network and in particular, user-to-user links, photos and favorite markings of photos by users. The photos shown in the demo are randomly assigned to given photo ids to preserve the relationships among them and the users. The demo offers a graphical interface for running time-dependent queries and visualizing the returned results sets.

Querying Interface. The SQTime querying interface, illustrated in Fig. 1, provides lists of available options for each of the building blocks of a query, which users can combine in four easy steps to compose their own queries. All options are expressed in natural language not requiring from the user to have an understanding of the underlying social graph structure. Firstly, the user selects a query perspective. For user-centric queries, the demo offers a selection of different users from our dataset with varied characteristics. For instance, it includes users with a large number of friends in the social graph, as well as users with fewer friends. When the system perspective is selected, as the only available attribute for the users is their anonymized id, the user is called to specify a selection on the ids to determine a group of users involved in the query. The second part of the query determines whether the query concerns users or objects, i.e., Flickr photos. Options such as *"get all photos liked by my friends"*, for user-centric queries, and *"get all photos liked by the group of users specified in step 1"*, for system-centric queries, are available. Beyond queries in the direct neighborhood of a user, SQTime includes queries at distance two. Thus, one may also select to *"get all photos the friends of my friends liked"*.

The first two steps guide the user to forming her basic social query. The next two steps guides the user to augment her query with time. Step 3 supports the explicit use of time allowing users to add a time constraint in their queries. One can either select a predefined constraint that concern the most recent past, as such queries are more popular, or specify her own time period for the constraint. For example, if we select the time constraint *"six months ago"*, *"get all my friends"* is transformed into *"get all my friends that were valid six months ago"*. The last parameter SQTime enables us to configure, is ranking. Two options are provided, *"no ranking"*, where all results are returned in random order, and *"ranking based on freshness"*. This option enables the user to see the implicit use of time, as the results are returned ranked based on their freshness.

Results Presentation. The result presentation interface visualizes query results in a way that is intuitive and clearly illustrates their temporal relationships. For a query for objects, the qualifying photos are displayed to the user and listed in a results' text box. For clarity, the demo limits the returned results to 10. If no ranking is used 10 random photos from the result set are returned. When ranking based on freshness is selected, the 10 fresher results are displayed. As shown in Fig. 2 (left), SQTime displays results as photos of different size, where photos of bigger size represent the higher ranked objects, i.e., the fresher ones. For queries for users, a graph is used to display the qualifying users and their relationships. For instance, Fig. 2 (right) illustrates the results for a user-centric query for friends. The user in the center of the displayed graph is the user whose perspective we have selected, while the user ids around him represented the returned friends. When ranking based on freshness is used, shades of green are

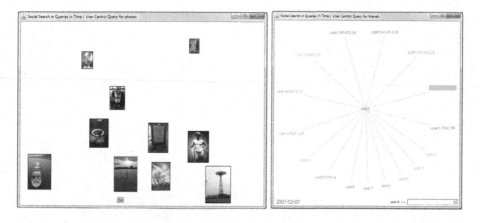

Fig. 2. SQTime results presentation

used to represented the ids of each user, with bolder colored ids reflecting the fresher results. Note that in this case all qualifying users are returned.

References

1. Cha, M., Mislove, A., Gummadi, K.P.: A Measurement-driven Analysis of Information Propagation in the Flickr Social Network. In: WWW (2009)
2. Gutierrez, C., Hurtado, C.A., Vaisman, A.A.: Introducing time into RDF. IEEE Trans. Knowl. Data. Eng., 207–218 (2007)
3. Joho, H., Jatowt, A., Blanco, R.: A survey of temporal web search experience. In: WWW (2013)
4. Khurana, U., Deshpande, A.: Efficient snapshot retrieval over historical graph data. In: ICDE (2013)
5. Koloniari, G., Souravlias, D., Pitoura, E.: On graph deltas for historical queries. In: WOSS (2012)
6. Koloniari, G., Stefanidis, K.: Social search queries in time. In: PersDB (2013)

Author Index